INDIANA

Mathematics

SCOTT FORESMAN · ADDISON WESLEY

Authors

Randall I. Charles

Janet H. Caldwell
Mary Cavanagh
Dinah Chancellor
Alma B. Ramirez

Warren Crown

Jeanne F. Ramos
Kay Sammons
Jane F. Schielack

Francis (Skip) Fennell

William Tate
Mary Thompson
John A. Van de Walle

Consulting Mathematicians

Edward J. Barbeau
Professor of Mathematics
University of Toronto
Toronto, Ontario, Canada

David M. Bressoud
DeWitt Wallace Professor
 of Mathematics
Macalester College
Saint Paul, Minnesota

Gary Lippman
Professor of Mathematics
 and Computer Science
California State University
 Hayward
Hayward, California

PEARSON
Scott
Foresman

Editorial Offices: Glenview, Illinois • Parsippany, New Jersey • New York, New York

Sales Offices: Parsippany, New Jersey • Duluth, Georgia • Glenview, Illinois
Coppell, Texas • Ontario, California • Mesa, Arizona

Reading Consultants

Peter Afflerbach
Professor and Director of
   The Reading Center
University of Maryland
College Park, Maryland

Donald J. Leu
John and Maria Neag
   Endowed Chair in Literacy and Technology
University of Connecticut
Storrs, Connecticut

Reviewers

Donna McCollum Derby
Teacher
Kernersville Elementary School
Kernersville, North Carolina

Terri Geaudreau
Title I Math Facilitator
Bemiss Elementary
Spokane, Washington

Sister Helen Lucille Habig, RSM
Assistant Superintendent of
   Catholic Schools
Archdiocese of Cincinnati
Cincinnati, Ohio

Kim Hill
Teacher
Hayes Grade Center
Ada, Oklahoma

Martha Knight
Teacher
Oak Mountain Elementary
Birmingham, Alabama

Catherine Kuhns
Teacher
Country Hills Elementary
Coral Springs, Florida

Susan Mayberger
Supervisor of English as a Second
   Language/Director of Migrant Education
Omaha Public Schools
Omaha, Nebraska

Judy Peede
Elementary Lead Math Teacher
Wake County Schools
Raleigh, North Carolina

Lynda M. Penry
Teacher
Wright Elementary
Ft. Walton Beach, Florida

Jolyn D. Raleigh
District Math Curriculum Specialist K–2
Granite School District
Salt Lake City, Utah

Vickie H. Smith
Assistant Principal
Phoenix Academic Magnet
   Elementary School
Alexandria, Louisiana

Ann Watts
Mathematics Specialist
East Baton Rouge Parish School System
Baton Rouge, Louisiana

ISBN: 0-328-07328-8

CHAPTER 1
Understanding Addition and Subtraction

 Instant Check System
- Check, daily
- Think About It, daily
- Diagnostic Checkpoint, 11, 21, 33

 Test Prep
- Test Talk, 37
- Cumulative Review and Test Prep, 12, 22, 34

 **Reading For Math Success**
- Math Story, 1A
- Reading for Math Success, 7

Writing in Math
- Writing in Math exercises, 8, 16, 20, 24, 32, 35

 Problem-Solving Applications, 31

 Discovery CHANNEL SCHOOL Discover Math in Your World, 38

Additional Resources
- Home-School Connection, 1
- Practice Game, 2
- Enrichment, 35
- Learning with Technology, 36
- Chapter 1 Test, 39

© Pearson Education, Inc.

Fact Strategies for Addition and Subtraction

Place Value to 100 and Money

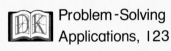

Mental Math: Addition and Subtraction

© Pearson Education, Inc.

Two-Digit Addition

CHAPTER 6
Two-Digit Subtraction

 Instant Check System
- Check, daily
- Think About It, daily
- Diagnostic Checkpoint, 223, 237

 Test Prep
- Test Talk, 241
- Cumulative Review and Test Prep, 224, 238

 Cumulative Review and Test Prep for Indiana!, 244A

 Reading For Math Success
- Math Story, 6A
- Reading for Math Success, 219

Writing in Math
- Writing in Math exercises, 224, 232, 236, 238, 239, 244B

 Problem-Solving Applications, 235

Discovery CHANNEL SCHOOL Discover Math in Your World, 242

Additional Resources
- Home-School Connection, 209
- Practice Game, 210
- Enrichment, 239
- Learning with Technology, 240
- Chapter 6 Test, 243

Geometry and Fractions

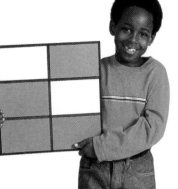

 Instant Check System
- Check, daily
- Think About It, daily
- Diagnostic Checkpoint, 307, 317, 331

 Test Prep
- Test Talk, 335
- Cumulative Review and Test Prep, 308, 318, 332

 Cumulative Review and Test Prep for Indiana!, 338A

 Reading For Math Success
- Math Story, 8A
- Reading for Math Success, 309

Writing in Math
- Writing in Math exercises, 296, 308, 316, 318, 322, 326, 330, 332, 333, 338B

Problem-Solving Applications, 329

DISCOVERY CHANNEL SCHOOL Discover Math in Your World, 336

Additional Resources
- Home-School Connection, 289
- Practice Game, 290
- Enrichment, 333
- Learning with Technology, 334
- Chapter 8 Test, 337

CHAPTER 9 Measurement and Probability

Numbers to 1,000

Instant Check System
- Check, daily
- Think About It, daily
- Diagnostic Checkpoint, 441, 457

 Test Prep
- Test Talk, 461
- Cumulative Review and Test Prep, 442, 458

 Reading For Math Success
- Math Story, 11A
- Reading for Math Success, 437

Writing in Math
- Writing in Math exercises, 440, 442, 454, 456, 458, 459

 Problem-Solving Applications, 455

Discovery CHANNEL SCHOOL Discover Math in Your World, 462

Additional Resources
- Home-School Connection, 425
- Practice Game, 426
- Enrichment, 459
- Learning with Technology, 460
- Chapter 11 Test, 463

© Pearson Education, Inc.

Instant Check System
- Check, daily
- Think About It, daily
- Diagnostic Checkpoint, 481, 491

Test Prep
- Test Talk, 495
- Cumulative Review and Test Prep, 482, 492, 498A

Reading For Math Success
- Math Story, 12A
- Reading for Math Success, 477

Writing in Math
- Writing in Math exercises, 468, 482, 486, 490, 492, 493, 498B

 Problem-Solving Applications, 489

 Discover Math in Your World, 496

Additional Resources
- Home-School Connection, 465
- Practice Game, 466
- Enrichment, 493
- Learning with Technology, 494
- Chapter 12 Test, 497

xiv

Read Together

Ten in the Bed

An Old Rhyme Retold by Anne Miranda
Illustrated by Bridget Starr Taylor

This Math Storybook belongs to

_____

There were **10** in the bed,
and the little one said,
"Roll over. Roll over!"
So they all rolled over,
and **I** fell out.

Then there were **9** in the bed,
and the little one said,
"Roll over. Roll over!"
So they all rolled over,
and **2** more fell out.

Then there were **7** in the bed,
and the little one said,
"Roll over. Roll over!"
So they all rolled over,
and **3** more fell out.

Then there were **4** in the bed,
and the little one said,
"Roll over. Roll over!"
So they all rolled over,
and all **4** fell out.

Then there were ZERO in the bed,
and the little one said,
"What happened?
What happened?"
So they all got up
and went back to bed.

There were **10** in the bed,
and the little one said,
"Roll over. Roll over!"

But the other **9** said,
"No! Go to sleep!"
And he did, without another peep!

Dear Family,

Today my class started Chapter 1, **Understanding Addition and Subtraction.** I will learn that adding means joining groups of things together, and that subtracting means taking things away from a group, or comparing two groups to see which one has more. Here are some of the math words I will be learning and some things we can do to help me with my math.

Love,

_____

Math Activity to Do at Home

Gather a collection of objects and help your child use them to make up and solve "joining" stories, "taking away" stories, and "comparing" stories. *A joining story:* "I have 8 books, and here are 4 more. So now how many books do I have? I have 12 books in all."

Books to Read Together

Reading math stories reinforces concepts. Look for these titles in your local library:

12 Ways to Get to 11
By Eve Merriam
(Simon & Schuster, 1993)

Rooster's Off to See the World
By Eric Carle
(Turtleback Books, 1999)

Take It to the NET
More Activities
www.scottforesman.com

My New Math Words

addend Each number that is being added to another number is called an addend.

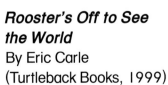

$$4 + 3 = 7 \longleftarrow \text{sum}$$

sum When numbers are added together, the answer is called the sum. (See above.)

difference When one number is subtracted from another number, the answer is called the difference.

$$8 - 3 = 5$$

$$\begin{array}{r} 8 \\ - 3 \\ \hline 5 \end{array}$$

fact family A fact family is a group of related facts. A fact family has either two members (e.g., $4 + 4 = 8$ and $8 - 4 = 4$) or four members (e.g., $4 + 8 = 12$, $8 + 4 = 12$, $12 - 4 = 8$, and $12 - 8 = 4$).

Name _____

Spin and Subtract

How to Play

1. Take turns spinning to find the number of pigs that have fallen out of bed.
2. Subtract that number from 10.
3. Place your marker on the answer. (Once an answer is covered, you may not use it again.)
4. Continue taking turns until you have covered all of the answers.

4

2

3

5

5   3
8   6
4   9
7   1
2   10

7

9

8   6   1   0

Name_____

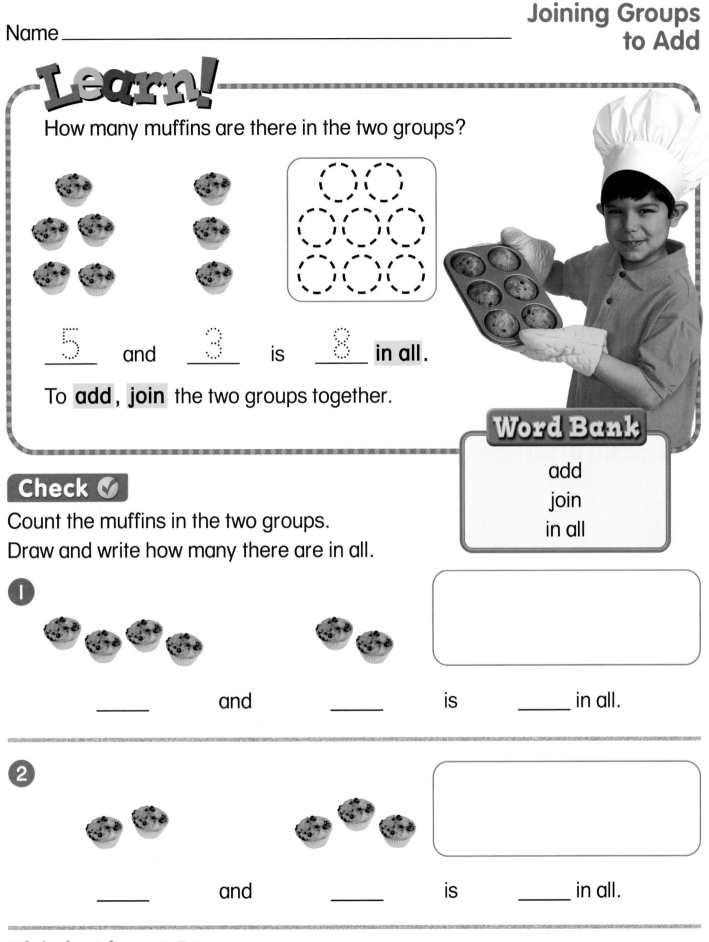

Learn!

How many muffins are there in the two groups?

___5___ and ___3___ is ___8___ **in all**.

To **add** , **join** the two groups together.

Word Bank

add
join
in all

Check ✓

Count the muffins in the two groups.
Draw and write how many there are in all.

1

_____ and _____ is _____ in all.

2

_____ and _____ is _____ in all.

Think About It   Reasoning

When you join two groups together, do
you get more or fewer objects? Explain.

Count the fruit in the two groups.
Draw and write how many there are in all.

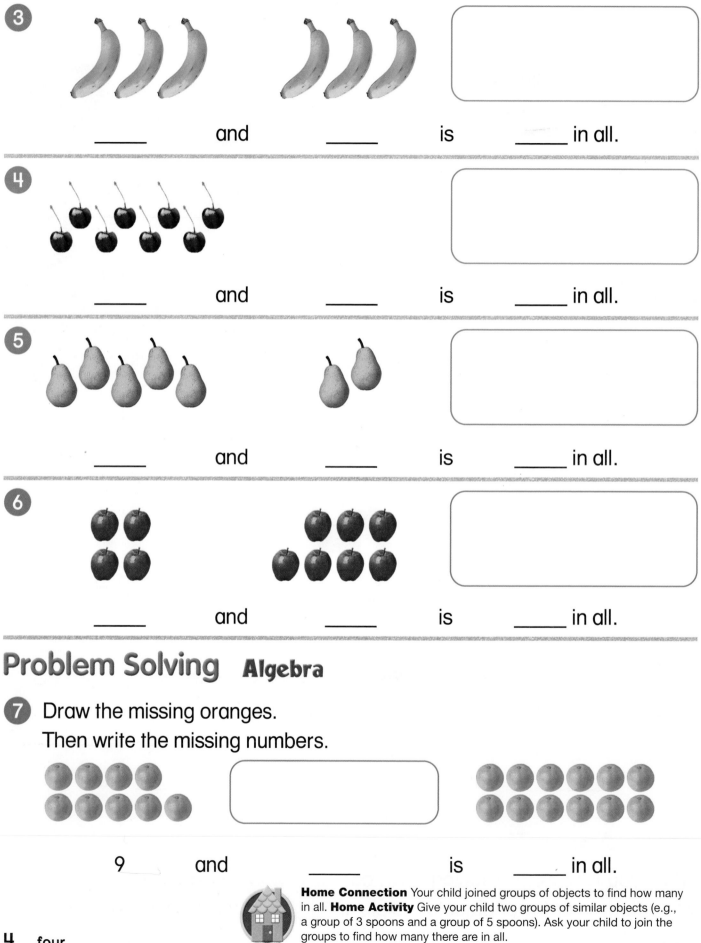

3

_____ and _____ is _____ in all.

4

_____ and _____ is _____ in all.

5

_____ and _____ is _____ in all.

6

_____ and _____ is _____ in all.

Problem Solving Algebra

7 Draw the missing oranges.
   Then write the missing numbers.

9 and _____ is _____ in all.

Home Connection Your child joined groups of objects to find how many in all. **Home Activity** Give your child two groups of similar objects (e.g., a group of 3 spoons and a group of 5 spoons). Ask your child to join the groups to find how many there are in all.

Name_____

Learn! Algebra

How many balloons are there in all?

__7__ and __2__ is __9__ .

__7__ **plus** __2__ **equals** __9__ .

__7__ + __2__ = __9__ balloons

addend   addend   sum

In an **addition sentence**, the number that tells how many in all is the sum.

Word Bank

plus (+)
equals (=)
addend
sum
addition sentence

Check ✓

Write the addition sentence.
Use counters if you need to.

1. There are 6 blue cups.
   There are 4 red cups.
   How many cups are
   there in all?   ____ + ____ = ____ cups

2. There are 9 large plates
   and 3 small plates.
   How many plates are there in all?   ____ + ____ = ____ plates

3. There are 2 gifts with ribbons.
   There are 2 gifts with bows.
   How many gifts are there in all?   ____ + ____ = ____ gifts

Think About It   Number Sense

Tell a number story to go with
the addition sentence 8 + 3 = 11.

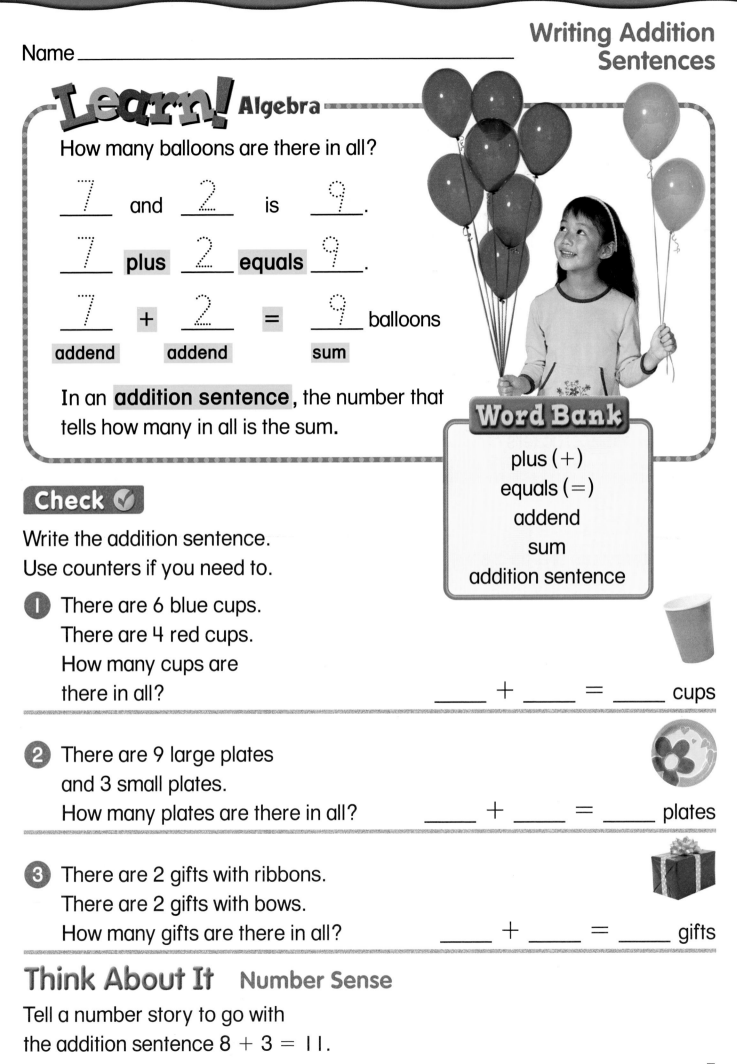

Write an addition sentence. Use counters if you need to.

4. 5 flags are on the long pole.
3 flags are on the short pole.
How many flags are there in all?

____ + ____ = ____ flags

5. There are 3 blue chairs.
There are 2 red chairs.
How many chairs are there in all?

____ + ____ = ____ chairs

6. 9 crackers are on a plate.
0 crackers are in a bowl.
How many crackers are there in all?

____ + ____ = ____ crackers

7. 4 party hats are in a box.
7 party hats are on a shelf.
How many party hats
are there in all?

____ + ____ = ____ hats

8. There is 1 red flower.
There are 5 yellow flowers.
How many flowers
are there in all?

____ + ____ = ____ flowers

Problem Solving   Visual Thinking

Complete the addition sentence.

9. There are 11 balls in all.
How many balls are in the bag?

____ + ____ = ____ balls

Home Connection Your child wrote addition sentences to tell how many in all. **Home Activity** Show your child two groups of objects. Have him or her add and write an addition sentence that tells how many objects there are in all.

Name _____

Identify the Main Idea

1 Read this number story:

Kevin and Kelsey need 4 puppets to tell a story.
Kevin has 2 puppets. Kelsey has 2 puppets.
Do they have enough puppets to tell the story?

2 What is the main idea in this number story?
  a. The little pigs are very cute.
  b. The wolf is kind of scary-looking.
  c. Kevin and Kelsey have enough puppets.

3 Write a number sentence about the puppets shown below.

____ + ____ = ____ puppets in all

4 Write another number sentence about the puppet show.

____ + ____ = ____ hands in all

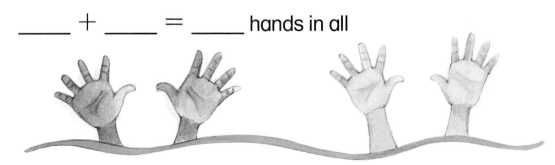

Think About It   Reasoning

In a number sentence, what does the word **equals** mean?

5 Read another number story:

Here are the three houses of the three little pigs.
The first house is made of straw.
The wolf can blow it down.
The second house is made of twigs.
The wolf can blow it down.
The third house is made of bricks.
The wolf cannot blow it down.

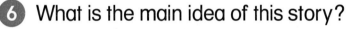

6 What is the main idea of this story?
   a. All three houses have pretty flower gardens.
   b. Brick is stronger than straw and twigs.
   c. The wolf has bad breath.

7 Write a number sentence about the houses.

_____ − _____ = _____ house

8 **Writing in Math**

 How many subtraction sentences can you write that have a difference of 1?

© Pearson Education, Inc.

 Home Connection Your child identified the main ideas in two stories and wrote number sentences about those stories. **Home Activity** Talk with your child about the main idea of a number sentence: the numbers before the equal sign and the number after the equal sign are different ways of naming the same amount.

Name _____

Learn! Algebra

How do we solve a story problem?

Read and Understand

Will has 3 gold fish.
He also has 4 red fish.
How many fish does he
have **altogether**?

Plan and Solve

You need to find out how many
fish Will has altogether.

This is a joining story, so you can
write an addition sentence.

_3_ ⊕ _4_ ⊜ _7_ fish

Look Back and Check

Did you answer the question?

Word Bank

altogether

Check ✓

Write a number sentence. Use counters if you need to.

1 2 turtles are in one tank.
5 turtles are in another tank.
How many turtles are
there altogether?

____ ◯ ____ ◯ ____ turtles

2 7 ducklings are sleeping.
1 other duckling begins to cheep.
How many ducklings are
there in all?

____ ◯ ____ ◯ ____ ducklings

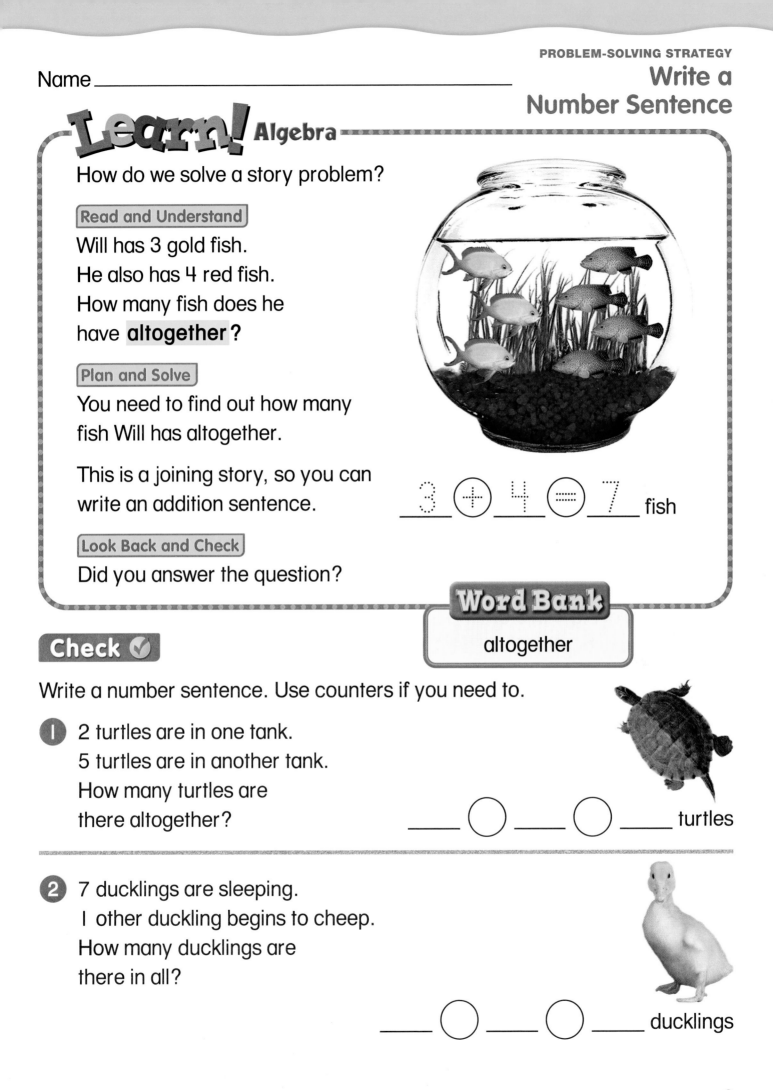

Write a number sentence. Use counters if you need to.

3 5 yellow birds are in one cage.
6 gray birds are in another cage.
How many birds are there in all?

____ ◯ ____ ◯ ____ birds

4 There are 4 kittens sleeping.
There are 8 kittens playing.
How many kittens are there?

____ ◯ ____ ◯ ____ kittens

5 3 hamsters are eating.
No hamsters join them.
How many hamsters are
there altogether?

____ ◯ ____ ◯ ____ hamsters

6 Max is playing with 5 puppies.
Zoe is playing with 5 other puppies.
How many puppies in all are there?

____ ◯ ____ ◯ ____ puppies

7 9 rabbits are following butterflies.
3 rabbits are following grasshoppers.
How many rabbits are there?

____ ◯ ____ ◯ ____ rabbits

8 8 pandas are playing in the
tree. 2 pandas are hiding under
the bush. How many pandas
are there altogether?

____ ◯ ____ ◯ ____ pandas

Home Connection Your child learned to write number sentences to solve problems. **Home Activity** Tell your child addition stories and have him or her write the addition sentences that solve the problems.

Name _____

Count the fruit in the two groups.
Draw and write how many there are in all.

1

_____ and _____ is _____ in all.

2

_____ + _____ = _____ in all.

Write the addition sentence. Use counters if you need to.

3 There are 5 books about dogs.
There are 7 books about cats.
How many books are there in all?

_____ + _____ = _____ books

4 There are 9 red pens.
There are 2 blue pens.
How many pens are there in all?

_____ + _____ = _____ pens

Write a number sentence. Use counters if you need to.

5 Hank has 3 games.
Mary has 6 games.
How many games are there in all?

_____ ◯ _____ ◯ _____ games

6 Jon has 8 car models
and no boat models.
How many models does Jon have?

_____ ◯ _____ ◯ _____ models

Name _____

1 Mark the coin with the value of five cents.

Ⓐ   Ⓑ   Ⓒ   Ⓓ

2 Which number comes next?

55, 56, _____

54   56   57   58
Ⓐ   Ⓑ   Ⓒ   Ⓓ

3 Which drawing shows equal parts?

Ⓐ   Ⓑ   Ⓒ   Ⓓ

4 Mark the statement that is true.

10 > 19   25 = 28   32 < 31   40 > 39
Ⓐ   Ⓑ   Ⓒ   Ⓓ

5 Add or subtract.

$$\begin{array}{r} 0 \\ + 7 \\ \hline \end{array}$$

0   7   9   10
Ⓐ   Ⓑ   Ⓒ   Ⓓ

6 Add or subtract.

$$\begin{array}{r} 11 \\ - 0 \\ \hline \end{array}$$

11   10   0   1
Ⓐ   Ⓑ   Ⓒ   Ⓓ

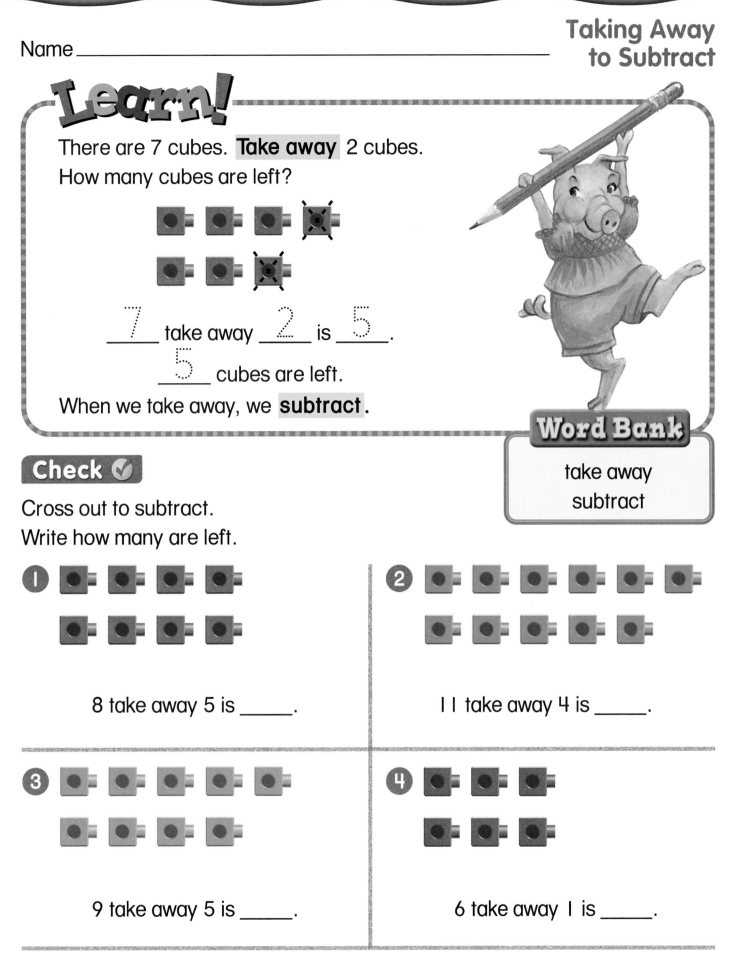

Learn!

There are 7 cubes. **Take away** 2 cubes.
How many cubes are left?

_7_ take away _2_ is _5_.
_5_ cubes are left.

When we take away, we **subtract**.

Word Bank

take away
subtract

Check ✓

Cross out to subtract.
Write how many are left.

1. 8 take away 5 is _____.

2. 11 take away 4 is _____.

3. 9 take away 5 is _____.

4. 6 take away 1 is _____.

Think About It   Reasoning

When you subtract, do you get more than or
less than the number of objects you started with? Explain.

Take away to subtract. Write the numbers.

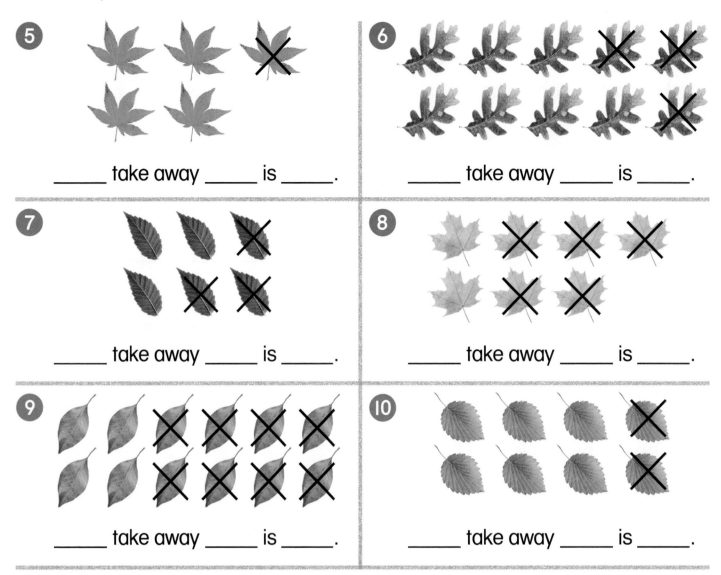

5 _____ take away _____ is _____.

6 _____ take away _____ is _____.

7 _____ take away _____ is _____.

8 _____ take away _____ is _____.

9 _____ take away _____ is _____.

10 _____ take away _____ is _____.

Problem Solving   Algebra

Circle the tray that answers the question.

11 Pam ate 1 strawberry.
She has 2 strawberries left.
How many strawberries did she start with?

Learn!

How many **more** green cubes than yellow cubes are there?
Compare the number of cubes in each color.

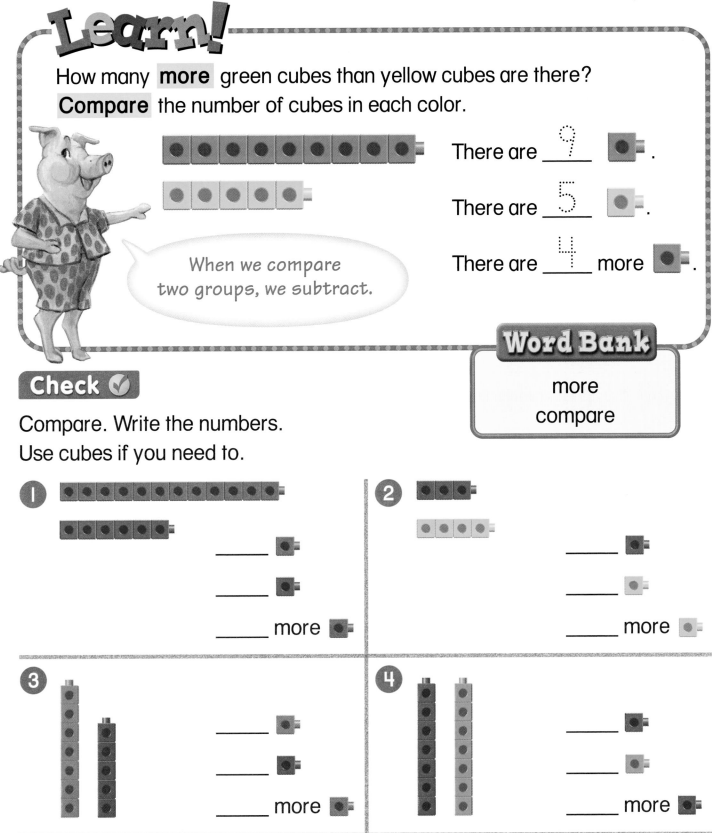

There are ___9___ 🟩.

There are ___5___ 🟨.

There are ___4___ more 🟩.

When we compare two groups, we subtract.

Word Bank
more
compare

Check ✓

Compare. Write the numbers.
Use cubes if you need to.

1
_____ 🟩
_____ 🟩
_____ more 🟩

2
_____ 🟪
_____ 🟨
_____ more 🟨

3
_____ 🟩
_____ 🟩
_____ more 🟩

4
_____ 🟩
_____ 🟨
_____ more 🟩

Think About It   Reasoning

Tell how the pictures help you decide
how many more there are.

Compare the number of objects in each group.
Write the numbers.

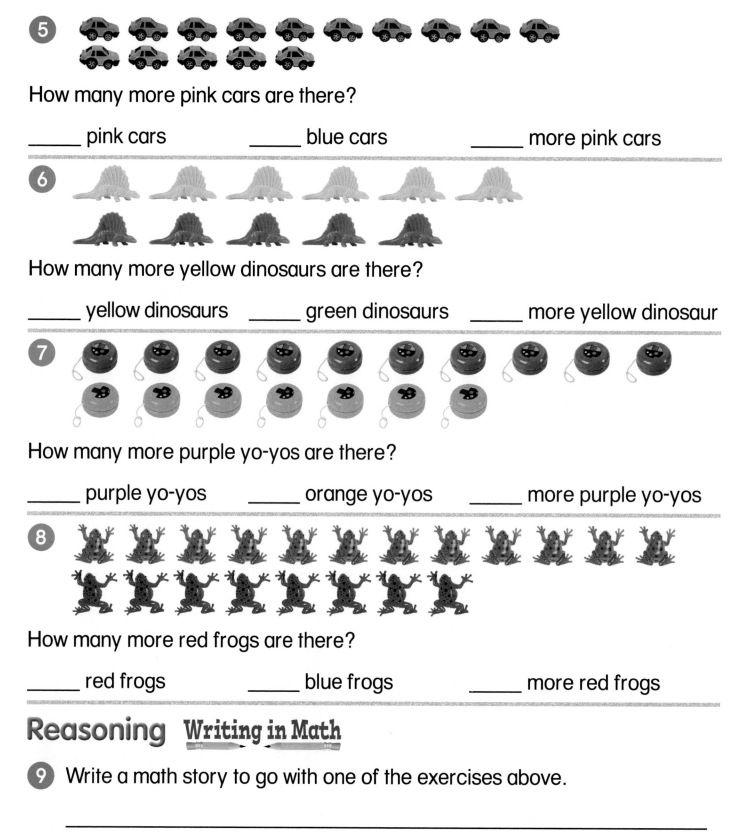

5

How many more pink cars are there?

_____ pink cars   _____ blue cars   _____ more pink cars

6

How many more yellow dinosaurs are there?

_____ yellow dinosaurs   _____ green dinosaurs   _____ more yellow dinosaur

7

How many more purple yo-yos are there?

_____ purple yo-yos   _____ orange yo-yos   _____ more purple yo-yos

8

How many more red frogs are there?

_____ red frogs   _____ blue frogs   _____ more red frogs

Reasoning   Writing in Math

9   Write a math story to go with one of the exercises above.

_____

_____

Home Connection Your child counted objects in two groups and
determined how many more objects one group had. **Home Activity** Show
your child two groups of objects and have him or her tell you how many
more objects are in the larger of the two groups.

Learn! Algebra

How many flowers are left in the pot?

__7__ take away __2__ is 5.

__7__ **minus** __2__ is 5.

__7__ − __2__ = __5__ flowers left

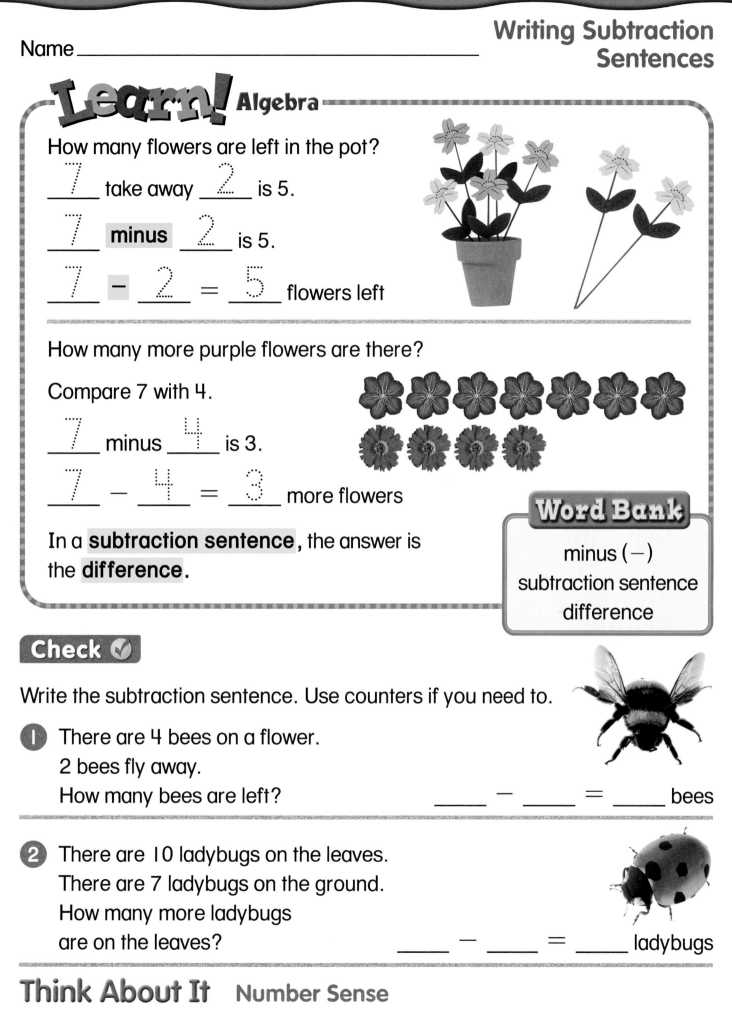

How many more purple flowers are there?

Compare 7 with 4.

__7__ minus __4__ is 3.

__7__ − __4__ = __3__ more flowers

In a **subtraction sentence**, the answer is the **difference**.

Word Bank

minus (−)
subtraction sentence
difference

Check ✓

Write the subtraction sentence. Use counters if you need to.

1. There are 4 bees on a flower.
   2 bees fly away.
   How many bees are left?   _____ − _____ = _____ bees

2. There are 10 ladybugs on the leaves.
   There are 7 ladybugs on the ground.
   How many more ladybugs
   are on the leaves?   _____ − _____ = _____ ladybugs

Think About It   Number Sense

Tell a subtraction story for $11 - 8 = 3$.

Write the subtraction sentence. Use counters if you need to.

3 There were 10 butterflies.
Then 2 butterflies flew away.
How many butterflies are left?

_____ − _____ = _____ butterflies

4 Meg found 5 grasshoppers.
Jack found 4 grasshoppers.
How many more grasshoppers
did Meg find?

_____ − _____ = _____ grasshopper

5 There were 12 flowers in the garden.
Juan picked 8 of them.
How many flowers are left?

_____ − _____ = _____ flowers

6 9 birds are eating.
7 birds are flying.
How many more birds are eating?

_____ − _____ = _____ birds

Problem Solving   Reasonableness

Circle the answer to the question.

7 Molly had 8 bug books.
She gave some to Ned.
Which answer tells how many books
she might have left? Explain.

8 books   10 books   4 books

Name _____

Learn! Algebra

Two groups of children join together. Add.

Some children **separate** from the group. Subtract.

6 children are dancing.
2 more children join them.
How many children in all
are dancing?

___6___ ⊕ ___2___ ⊖ ___8___ children

addition

5 children are riding bikes.
3 children stop riding.
How many children
are left riding bikes?

___5___ ⊖ ___3___ ⊖ ___2___ children

subtraction

Word Bank

separate
addition
subtraction

Check ✓

Circle **add** or **subtract**. Use counters if you need to.
Then write the number sentence.

1 There are 4 blue footballs
and 4 red footballs.
How many footballs
are there in all?

add   subtract

____ ◯ ____ ◯ ____ footballs

2 Mia had 7 golf balls.
She hit 6 of them away.
How many golf balls does
she have left?

add   subtract

____ ◯ ____ ◯ ____ golf ball

Think About It Reasoning

How do you know whether you should add or subtract?

Circle **add** or **subtract**.
Then write the number sentence. Use counters if you need to.

3 Jana has 12 markers.
Maddie has 9 markers.
How many more markers
does Jana have?

add   subtract

____ ◯ ____ ◯ ____ markers

4 Trevor has 7 erasers.
He buys 2 more.
How many erasers does
he have?

add   subtract

____ ◯ ____ ◯ ____ erasers

5 11 pencils are in a pencil case.
6 pencils are taken out.
How many pencils are left
in the case?

add   subtract

____ ◯ ____ ◯ ____ pencils

6 Jess read 3 books last week.
This week she read 4 books.
How many books did she read?

add   subtract

____ ◯ ____ ◯ ____ books

Reasoning Writing in Math

7 Write a math story. Have a friend write
a number sentence to solve it.

_____

_____

_____

Home Connection Your child chose whether to add or subtract to solve each problem. **Home Activity** Have your child tell two math stories: one that involves addition and one that involves subtraction.

Name _____

Write the numbers.

1

■ ■ ■ ■ ■ ■ ✕ ✕ ✕

_____ take away _____ is _____ .

2

■ ■ ■ ✕ ✕ ✕ ✕ ✕

_____ take away _____ is _____ .

Compare the number of objects in each group.
Write the numbers.

3

How many more blue clips are there?

_____ blue clips   _____ red clips   _____ more blue clips

Circle **add** or **subtract**.
Write the number sentence. Use counters if you need to.

4 There are 3 girls and
9 boys playing soccer.
How many children are
playing soccer in all?

add   subtract

____ ◯ ____ ◯ ____ children

Write the subtraction sentence. Use counters if you need to.

5 There were 6 crackers.
Tom ate 2 of them.
How many crackers were left?

____ − ____ = ____ crackers

6 Emma has 8 cows and 4 horses.
How many more cows than horses
does Emma have?

____ − ____ = ____ cows

Name_____

1 Count by twos.
Which number comes next?

$$10, 12, 14, \_\_\_\_$$

15	16	17	18
Ⓐ	Ⓑ	Ⓒ	Ⓓ

2 How much money is shown?

40¢	35¢	30¢	25¢
Ⓐ	Ⓑ	Ⓒ	Ⓓ

3 How many scissors are there in all?

Ⓐ 8 in all
Ⓑ 9 in all
Ⓒ 10 in all
Ⓓ 3 in all

4 Add. $4 + 4 = \_\_\_\_$

8	9	10	0
Ⓐ	Ⓑ	Ⓒ	Ⓓ

5 Add. $5 + 6 = \_\_\_\_$

9	10	11	1
Ⓐ	Ⓑ	Ⓒ	Ⓓ

Name _____

Learn! Algebra

What happens to the sum when we change the order of the addends?

The sums are the same when two numbers are added in a different order.

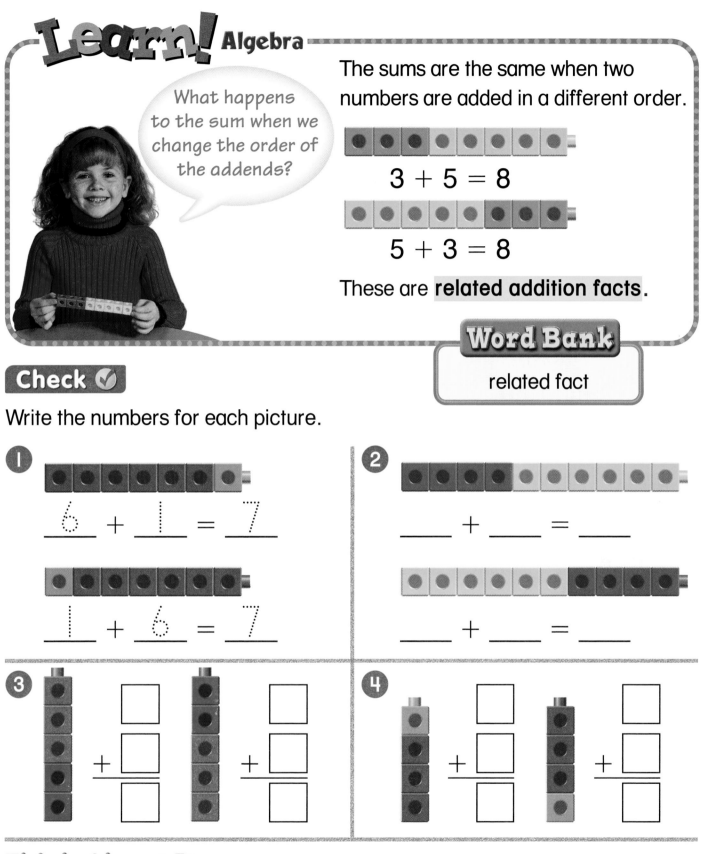

$3 + 5 = 8$

$5 + 3 = 8$

These are **related addition facts**.

Word Bank

related fact

Check ✓

Write the numbers for each picture.

1

$\underline{6} + \underline{1} = \underline{7}$

$\underline{1} + \underline{6} = \underline{7}$

2

$\underline{} + \underline{} = \underline{}$

$\underline{} + \underline{} = \underline{}$

3

$+$

$+$

4

$+$

$+$

Think About It   Reasoning

Does this picture have a related addition fact? Explain.

Write the sum.
Then write the related addition fact.

5 $5 + 6 = $ _____

_____

6 $4 + 2 = $ _____

_____

7 $4 + 5 = $ _____

_____

8 $8 + 3 = $ _____

_____

9

$$
\begin{array}{r}
4 \\
+ \ 3 \\
\hline
\square
\end{array}
\qquad
\begin{array}{r}
\square \\
+ \ \square \\
\hline
\square
\end{array}
$$

10

$$
\begin{array}{r}
2 \\
+ \ 6 \\
\hline
\square
\end{array}
\qquad
\begin{array}{r}
\square \\
+ \ \square \\
\hline
\square
\end{array}
$$

Problem Solving Writing in Math

Solve each problem.

11 Jill has 4 black and 8 brown toy horses.
How many toy horses does she have in all?
Write a number sentence to solve the problem.

_____ $\bigcirc$ _____ $\bigcirc$ _____ toy horses

12 Change the order of the addends in the
number sentence in Exercise 11. Write the
new number sentence. Then write a story
for this new number sentence.

Home Connection Your child learned that we can add numbers in any order
and the sum will be the same. **Home Activity** Write addition sentences such as
$6 + 1 = 7$, $4 + 8 = 12$, and $2 + 3 = 5$. Have your child switch the order of the
addends and write the related addition facts. *(1 + 6 = 7, 8 + 4 = 12, 3 + 2 = 5)*

© Pearson Education, Inc.

Name_____

Learn! Algebra

How can we make 10?

Remember ways to make 10 by thinking of a ten-frame.

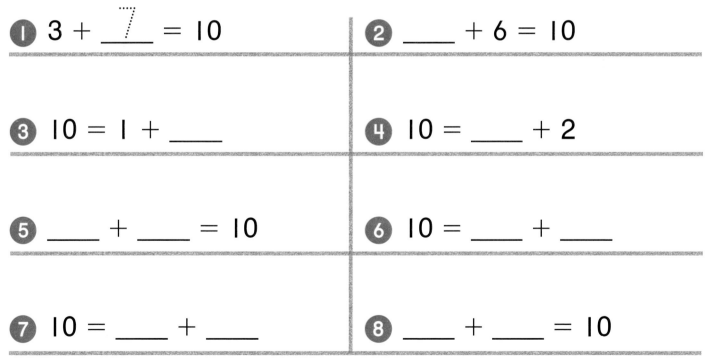

$8 + \underline{2} = 10$

Check ✓

Use counters and Workmat 2 to find
different ways to make 10.
Complete each number sentence.

1 $3 + \underline{7} = 10$

2 $\underline{} + 6 = 10$

3 $10 = 1 + \underline{}$

4 $10 = \underline{} + 2$

5 $\underline{} + \underline{} = 10$

6 $10 = \underline{} + \underline{}$

7 $10 = \underline{} + \underline{}$

8 $\underline{} + \underline{} = 10$

Think About It   Number Sense

Did you write all of the number sentences
with sums of 10? Explain.

Chapter 1 ★ Lesson 9   twenty-five   **25**

Find different ways to make 10. Use counters and Workmat 2
if you need to. Complete each number sentence.

⑨ $2 +$ ___ $= 10$

⑩ $10 = 6 +$ ___

⑪ $10 =$ ___ $+ 10$

⑫ ___ $+ 9 = 10$

⑬ $10 = 7 +$ ___

⑭ ___ $+ 5 = 10$

Write five more ways to make 10. Use different
number sentences from those in Exercises 9–11.

⑮ ___ $+$ ___ $= 10$

⑯ ___ $+$ ___ $= 10$

⑰ ___ $+$ ___ $= 10$

⑱ ___ $+$ ___ $= 10$

⑲ ___ $+$ ___ $= 10$

Problem Solving   Mental Math

Look at the pattern.
Find the missing numbers.

What patterns
can you find?

⑳

10	+	0	=	9	+	1
10	+	1	=	9	+	2
10	+	2	=		+	3
10	+		=		+	
	+		=		+	

Home Connection Your child learned different ways to make ten.
Home Activity Ask your child to write three ways to make ten using
addition.

Name_____

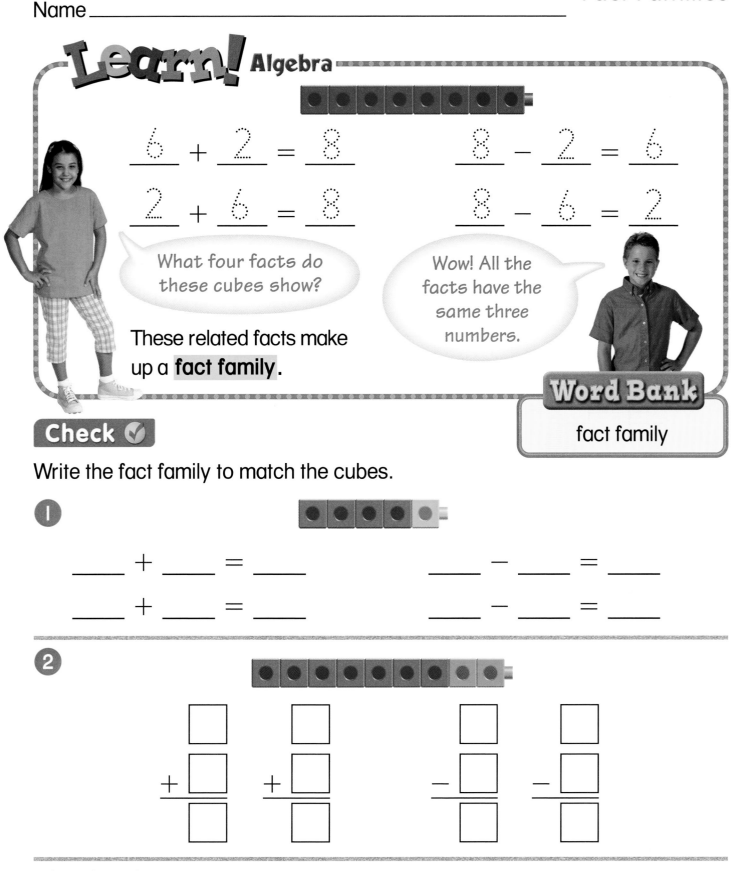

Learn! Algebra

$\underline{6} + \underline{2} = \underline{8}$ $\underline{8} - \underline{2} = \underline{6}$

$\underline{2} + \underline{6} = \underline{8}$ $\underline{8} - \underline{6} = \underline{2}$

What four facts do these cubes show?

Wow! All the facts have the same three numbers.

These related facts make up a **fact family**.

Word Bank

fact family

Check ✓

Write the fact family to match the cubes.

1

___ + ___ = ___   ___ − ___ = ___

___ + ___ = ___   ___ − ___ = ___

2

☐ + ☐ = ☐   ☐ + ☐ = ☐   ☐ − ☐ = ☐   ☐ − ☐ = ☐

Think About It   Reasoning

Give an example of a fact family that has only two facts. Explain why it does not have four facts.

Complete each fact family.

3 4 + 6 = ___

___ + ___ = ___

___ − ___ = ___

___ − ___ = ___

4 ___ + ___ = ___

___ + ___ = ___

9 − 3 = ___

___ − ___ = ___

5

□	2	□	□
+ □	+ 5	− □	− □
□	□	□	□

6

□	□	□	12
+ □	+ □	− □	− □
□	□	□	7

Write your own fact families.

7 ___ + ___ = 11

___ + ___ = ___

___ − ___ = ___

___ − ___ = ___

8

□	8
+ □	− □
□	□

Problem Solving   Number Sense

9 Elsa had 7 pencils. Robert gave her 4 more. How many pencils does Elsa have in all?

___ ◯ ___ ◯ ___ pencils

10 Robert took back his 4 pencils. Now how many pencils does Elsa have?

___ ◯ ___ ◯ ___ pencils

Home Connection Your child learned about related addition and subtraction equations called *fact families.* **Home Activity** Write an addition or subtraction fact and have your child write the other facts that belong to that fact family.

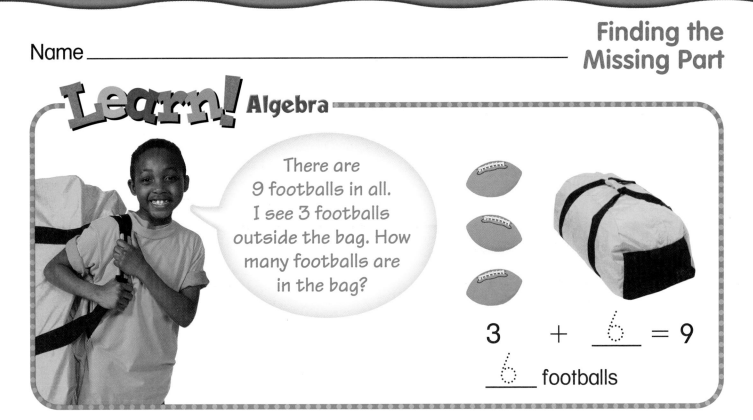

Learn! **Algebra**

There are 9 footballs in all. I see 3 footballs outside the bag. How many footballs are in the bag?

3 + 6 = 9

6 footballs

Check ✓

Use counters. Find out how many objects are in the bag.

1 There are 12 books in all.
   How many of them are in the bag?

8 + ___ = 12

___ books

2 There are 6 cans in all.
   How many of them are in the bag?

3 + ___ = 6

___ cans

Think About It Reasoning

What subtraction sentence could help you solve Exercise 1? Explain.

Find out how many objects are in the chest.
Use counters if you need to.

3 There are 5 trucks in all.
How many of them are
in the chest?

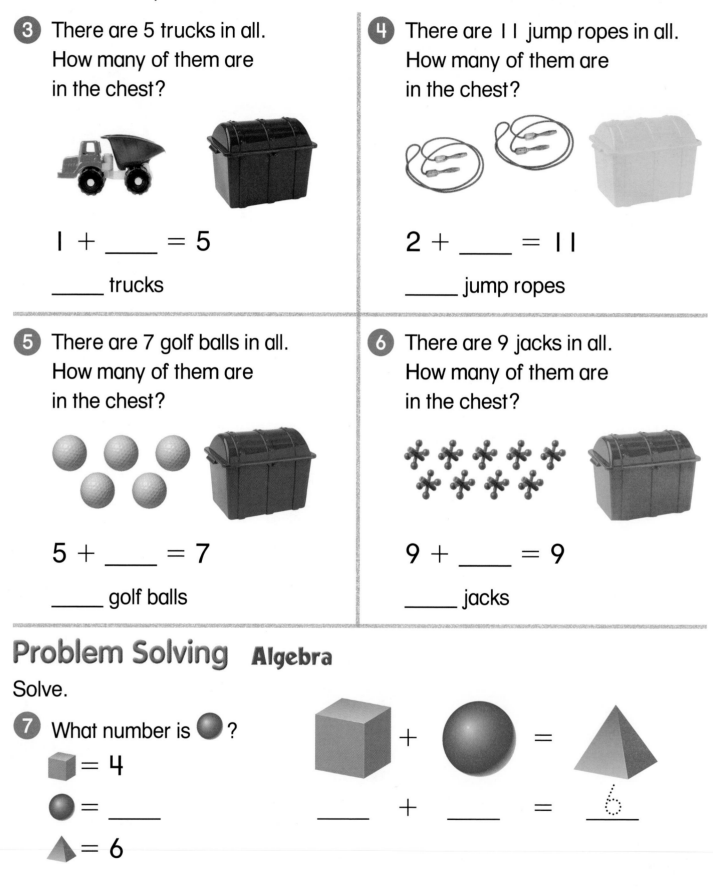

$1 + \_\_\_ = 5$

____ trucks

4 There are 11 jump ropes in all.
How many of them are
in the chest?

$2 + \_\_\_ = 11$

____ jump ropes

5 There are 7 golf balls in all.
How many of them are
in the chest?

$5 + \_\_\_ = 7$

____ golf balls

6 There are 9 jacks in all.
How many of them are
in the chest?

$9 + \_\_\_ = 9$

____ jacks

Problem Solving   Algebra

Solve.

7 What number is ⬤ ?

🔲 = 4

⬤ = ___

🔺 = 6

🔲 + ⬤ = 🔺

___ + ___ = 6

Home Connection Your child used counters to find the missing part, or addend, in each addition sentence. Home Activity Gather a group of small objects. Place some in a closed container and place the remaining objects outside the container. Tell your child how many objects there are in all. Ask him or her to figure out how many objects are in the container.

Frogs and Toads

Name _____

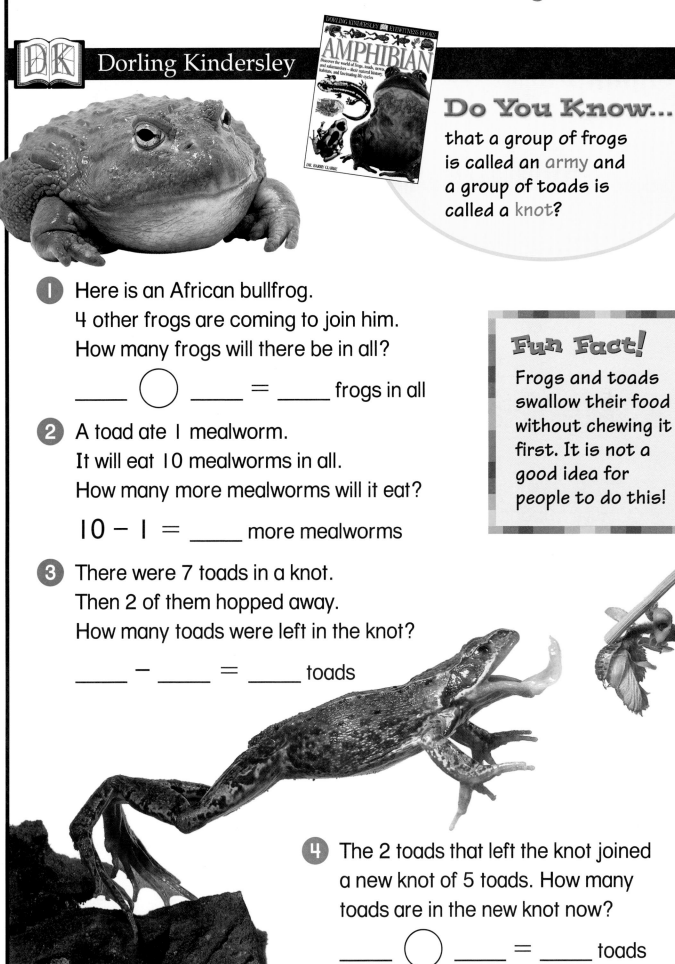

Dorling Kindersley

AMPHIBIAN

Do You Know...

that a group of frogs is called an army and a group of toads is called a knot?

1 Here is an African bullfrog.
4 other frogs are coming to join him.
How many frogs will there be in all?

_____ ◯ _____ = _____ frogs in all

2 A toad ate 1 mealworm.
It will eat 10 mealworms in all.
How many more mealworms will it eat?

$10 - 1 =$ _____ more mealworms

Fun Fact!

Frogs and toads swallow their food without chewing it first. It is not a good idea for people to do this!

3 There were 7 toads in a knot.
Then 2 of them hopped away.
How many toads were left in the knot?

_____ − _____ = _____ toads

4 The 2 toads that left the knot joined a new knot of 5 toads. How many toads are in the new knot now?

_____ ◯ _____ = _____ toads

These are poison-dart frogs. They have skin that is bright in color and poisonous!

Poison-dart frogs live in small groups, called armies.

5 A female toad might weigh 4 pounds. A male might weigh only 2 pounds. How many more pounds does the female weigh?

____ − ____ = ____ more pounds

6 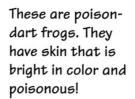 **Writing in Math**

 Write a number story about toads and mealworms.

Poison-dart frogs carry their tadpoles to small pools so that their skin can become colorful and they can grow.

7 There are 2 tree frogs up in the tree. 4 more tree frogs climb up to join them. How many tree frogs are up there now?

____ ◯ ____ = ____ tree frogs

 Home Connection Your child learned to solve problems by applying his or her math skills. **Home Activity** Talk to your child about how he or she solved the problems on these two pages.

Change the order of the addends and solve.

1 7 + 4 = ____

_____

2

```
      2          □
  +   6      + □
    ___          ___
    □          □
```

Complete each fact family.

3 3 + 6 = ____

____ + ____ = ____

____ − ____ = ____

____ − ____ = ____

4

```
  □    □        □    □
+ □  + □  − 8  − □
  ___    ___      ___    ___
  □    □    1    □
                 □    □
```

Complete each number sentence.
Use counters and Workmat 2 if you need to.

5 5 + ____ = 10

6 ____ + 7 = 10

7 10 = ____ + 10

8 10 = 4 + ____

Find out how many objects are in the bag.
Use counters if you need to.

9 There are 6 gifts in all.
How many of them are in the bag?

2 + ____ = 6

____ gifts

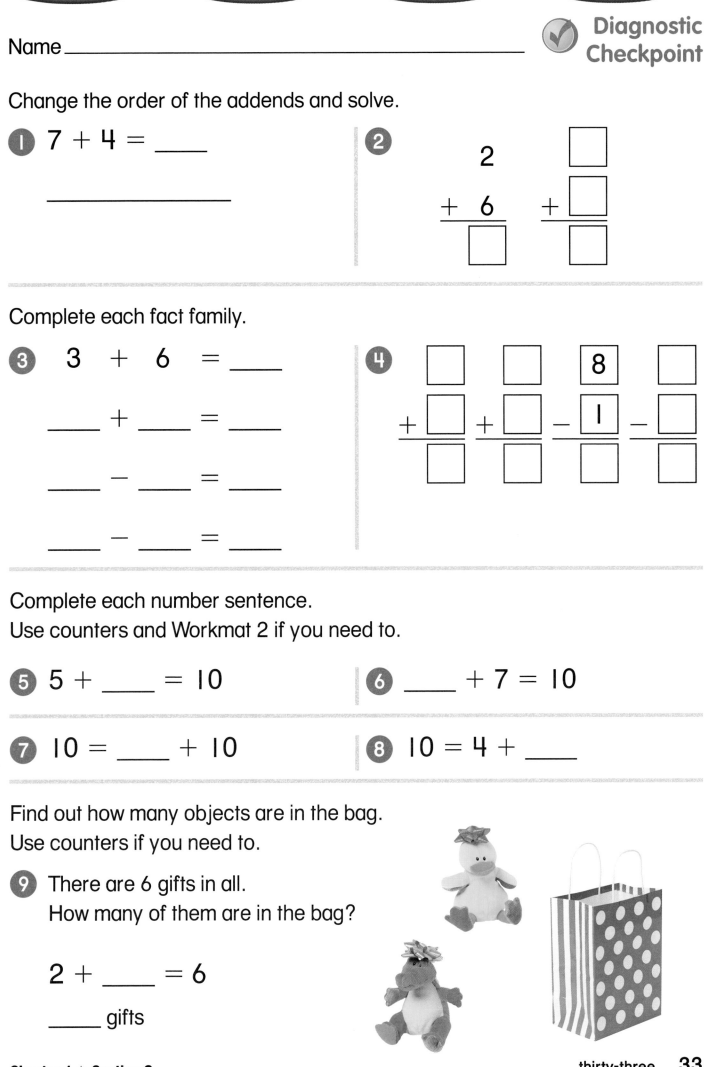

1 How many more blue marbles than yellow marbles are there?

Ⓐ 3 more blue marbles

Ⓑ 2 more blue marbles

Ⓒ 8 more blue marbles

Ⓓ 12 more blue marbles

2 Mark the fifth balloon.

first
Ⓐ   Ⓑ   Ⓒ   Ⓓ

3 Mark the clock that shows 3:00.

Ⓐ   Ⓑ   Ⓒ   Ⓓ

4 Add or subtract.

$$\begin{array}{r} 12 \\ -\ 3 \\ \hline \end{array}$$

9	3	8	15
Ⓐ	Ⓑ	Ⓒ	Ⓓ

5 Add or subtract.

$$\begin{array}{r} 9 \\ +\ 6 \\ \hline \end{array}$$

15	13	10	3
Ⓐ	Ⓑ	Ⓒ	Ⓓ

6 Add or subtract.

$$8 + 4 = \underline{\quad}$$

11	4	12	13
Ⓐ	Ⓑ	Ⓒ	Ⓓ

7 Add or subtract.

$$9 - 1 = \underline{\quad}$$

1	9	7	8
Ⓐ	Ⓑ	Ⓒ	Ⓓ

Equivalent Expressions Algebra

There are different names for the same number.

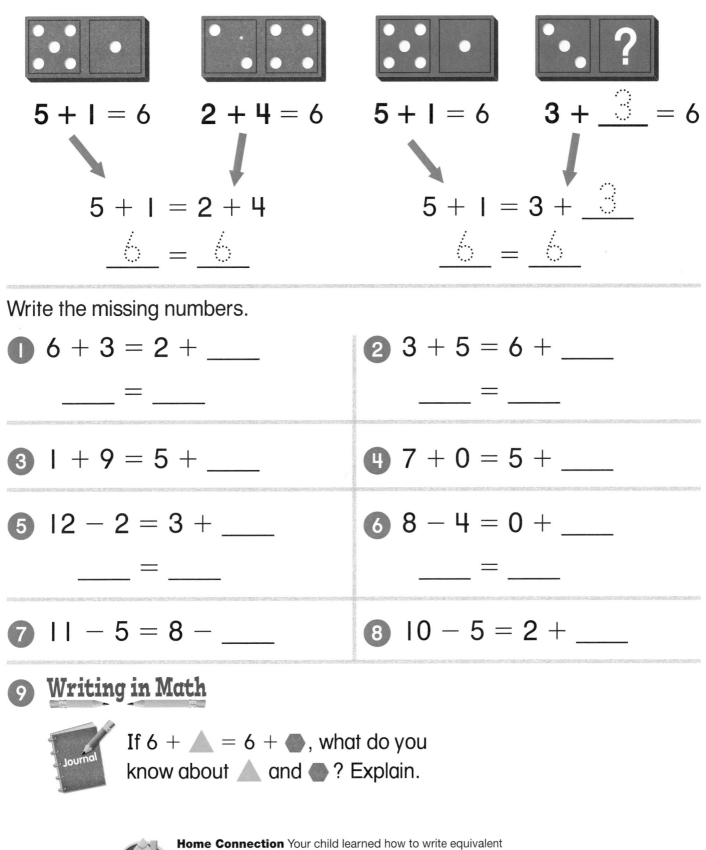

$5 + 1 = 6$ $2 + 4 = 6$ $5 + 1 = 6$ $3 + \underline{3} = 6$

$5 + 1 = 2 + 4$ $5 + 1 = 3 + \underline{3}$

$\underline{6} = \underline{6}$ $\underline{6} = \underline{6}$

Write the missing numbers.

1 $6 + 3 = 2 + \underline{}$

$\underline{} = \underline{}$

2 $3 + 5 = 6 + \underline{}$

$\underline{} = \underline{}$

3 $1 + 9 = 5 + \underline{}$

4 $7 + 0 = 5 + \underline{}$

5 $12 - 2 = 3 + \underline{}$

$\underline{} = \underline{}$

6 $8 - 4 = 0 + \underline{}$

$\underline{} = \underline{}$

7 $11 - 5 = 8 - \underline{}$

8 $10 - 5 = 2 + \underline{}$

9 **Writing in Math**

If $6 + \triangle = 6 + ⬡$, what do you know about $\triangle$ and $⬡$? Explain.

Home Connection Your child learned how to write equivalent expressions. **Home Activity** Ask your child to find the missing number for each of the following problems: $1 + 2 = 3 + \underline{}$; $5 + 2 = 3 + \underline{}$; $10 - 1 = 7 + \underline{}$; and $9 - 3 = 2 + \underline{}$.

Name_____

Make Fact Families Using a Calculator

Use a calculator to make fact families.
Write the numbers you press for each fact.
Write the number in the display for each fact.
Press ON/C each time you begin.

1 Make a fact family.

[ ] **+** [ ] **=** _7_

[ ] **+** 5 **=** ___

[ ] **−** [ ] **=** _2_

[ ] **−** [ ] **=** ___

2 Make another fact family.

[ ] **+** [ ] **=** _12_

4 **+** [ ] **=** ___

[ ] [ ] **−** 8 **=** ___

[ ] [ ] **−** [ ] **=** ___

3 Make a fact family using greater numbers.

8 **+** [ ] **=** ___

7 **+** [ ] **=** ___

1 5 **−** [ ] **=** ___

[ ] [ ] **−** 7 **=** ___

4 Make your own fact family.

[ ] **+** [ ] **=** ___

[ ] **+** [ ] **=** ___

[ ] **−** [ ] **=** ___

[ ] **−** [ ] **=** ___

Think About It   Number Sense

How could you use a calculator to find the missing number in this addition sentence? $4 + \boxed{} = 11$

Home Connection Your child used a calculator to make fact families.
Home Activity Ask your child to explain how he or she would make a fact family for 10 on a calculator. *(Sample response: I would press 6 + 4 =, 4 + 6 =, 10 − 4 =, and 10 − 6 =.)*

Name _____

 Read Together

Understand the Question

There are important words
in math problems.

These words help you understand
the problems.

1 A toy set has 6 cars and 2 trucks.
How many more cars
than trucks are there?

Ⓐ 4 more cars

Ⓑ 8 more cars

Ⓒ 6 more cars

Ⓓ 9 more cars

Test-Taking Strategies
Understand the Question
Get Information for the Answer
Plan How to Find the Answer
Make Smart Choices
Use Writing in Math

Read the problem again.
The most important words are **how many more**.
These words tell you to compare the number of cars
with the number of trucks. Compare 6 and 2.
Solve the problem and fill in the answer bubble.

Your Turn

Find the most important words in this math problem.
Then solve the problem and fill in the answer bubble.

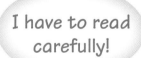

I have to read
carefully!

2 Nick had 5 puppets. He gave away 3 of them.
How many puppets does Nick have left?

Ⓐ 2 puppets

Ⓑ 5 puppets

Ⓒ 3 puppets

Ⓓ 8 puppets

 Home Connection Your child prepared for standardized tests by identifying the
most important words in a math problem. **Home Activity** Ask your child which
words he or she identified as being the most important words in Exercise 2.
(Gave away, have left)

Name _____

Discover Math in Your World

Using Your Eyes

We use our eyes to learn about the world around us.

Eyeing Your Classroom

Look around your classroom.

① How many colors can you see? _____

② Find some things in your classroom
that are **red** or **yellow** or **blue.**
These colors are called the primary colors.
They can be used to make all of the
other colors. Use a tally mark to record
each thing you find. Then count the things
in each group and record the totals.

Red Things	Yellow Things	Blue Things
Total: _____	Total: _____	Total: _____

③ Now write a number sentence that tells how many
things you found in all.

_____ + _____ + _____ = _____ things in all

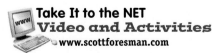
Take It to the NET
Video and Activities
www.scottforesman.com

Home Connection Your child counted objects of different colors in
the classroom and wrote a number sentence to tell how many objects
he or she found in all. **Home Activity** Ask your child to go on a similar
"color hunt," perhaps limiting the search area to one room.

Count the bagels in each group.
Draw and write how many there are in all.

1

_____ and _____ is _____ in all.

Compare to find how many more there are. Write the numbers.

2

_____ blue whistles   _____ green whistles   _____ more blue whistles

Write the addition sentence.

3 Nick has 2 toy sailboats
and 7 toy speedboats.
How many toy boats
in all does Nick have?

____ + ____ = ____ boats

Write a number sentence.

4 5 mice are sleeping.
3 mice are playing.
How many mice are there altogether?   ____ ◯ ____ ◯ ____ mice

Write the sum.
Then write the related addition fact.

5 $6 + 0 =$ ___

_____

6
$$\begin{array}{r} 3 \\ + 4 \\ \hline \end{array}$$

$$\begin{array}{r} \square \\ + \square \\ \hline \square \end{array}$$

7 Write the numbers.

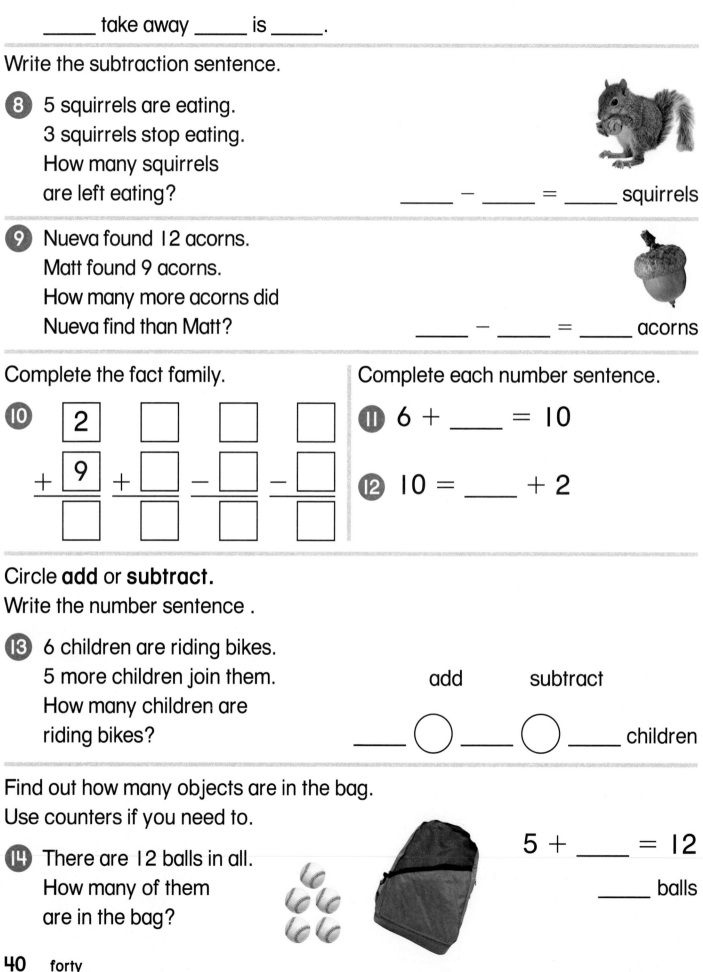

_____ take away _____ is _____.

Write the subtraction sentence.

8 5 squirrels are eating.
3 squirrels stop eating.
How many squirrels
are left eating?

_____ − _____ = _____ squirrels

9 Nueva found 12 acorns.
Matt found 9 acorns.
How many more acorns did
Nueva find than Matt?

_____ − _____ = _____ acorns

Complete the fact family.

10

$$2 \quad \square \quad \square \quad \square$$
$$+\,9 \quad +\,\square \quad -\,\square \quad -\,\square$$
$$\overline{\square} \quad \overline{\square} \quad \overline{\square} \quad \overline{\square}$$

Complete each number sentence.

11 $6 + \underline{\hphantom{00}} = 10$

12 $10 = \underline{\hphantom{00}} + 2$

Circle **add** or **subtract.**
Write the number sentence .

13 6 children are riding bikes.
5 more children join them.
How many children are
riding bikes?

add   subtract

____ ◯ ____ ◯ _____ children

Find out how many objects are in the bag.
Use counters if you need to.

14 There are 12 balls in all.
How many of them
are in the bag?

$5 + \underline{\hphantom{00}} = 12$

_____ balls

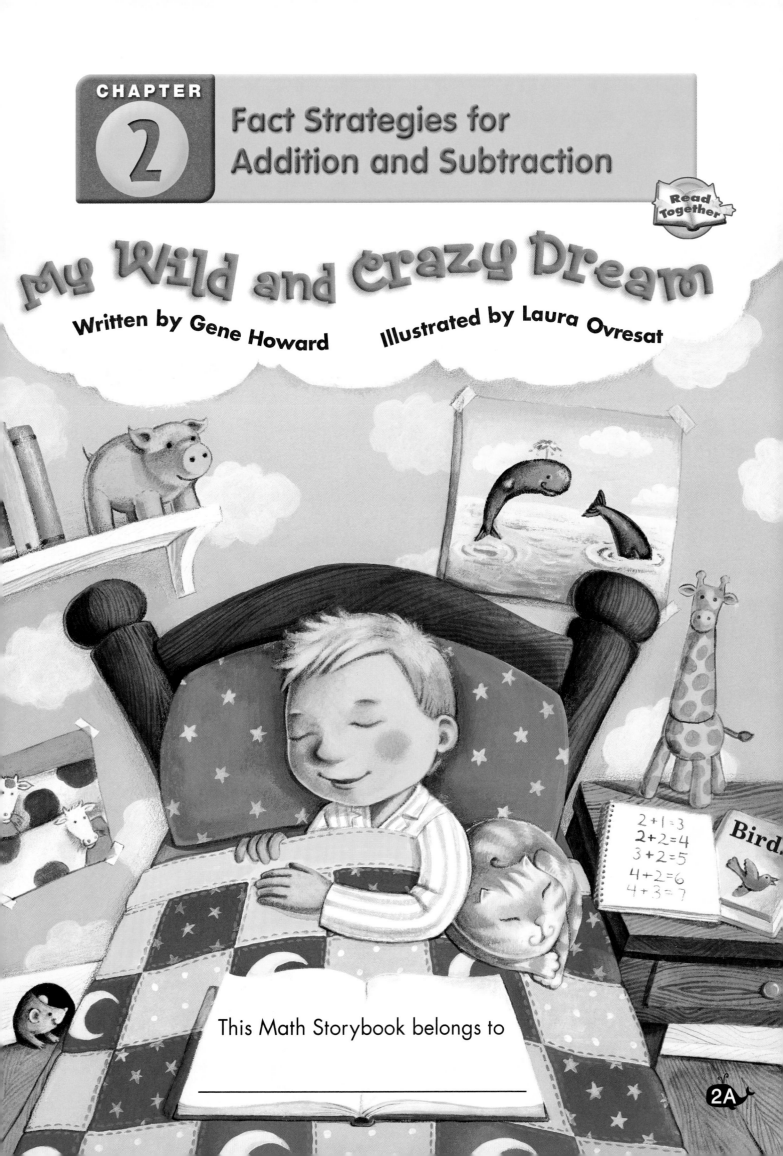

My Wild and Crazy Dream

Written by Gene Howard   Illustrated by Laura Ovresat

2 + 1 = 3
2 + 2 = 4
3 + 2 = 5
4 + 2 = 6
4 + 3 = 7

Bird.

This Math Storybook belongs to

_____

2A

In my dream I saw **2** flying pigs.
And then **1** more flying pig.
And all **3** were wearing wigs!

"**3** pigs? Wearing wigs?
What is going on?" I asked.

But they just smiled and flew away.

2B

In my dream I saw **2** flying cats.
And then **2** more flying cats.
And all **4** were wearing hats!

"**4** cats? Wearing hats?
What is going on?" I asked.

But they just smiled and flew away.

In my dream I saw **3** flying whales.
And then **2** more flying whales.
And all **5** were wearing tails!

"**5** whales? Wearing tails?
What is going on?" I asked.

But they just smiled and flew away.

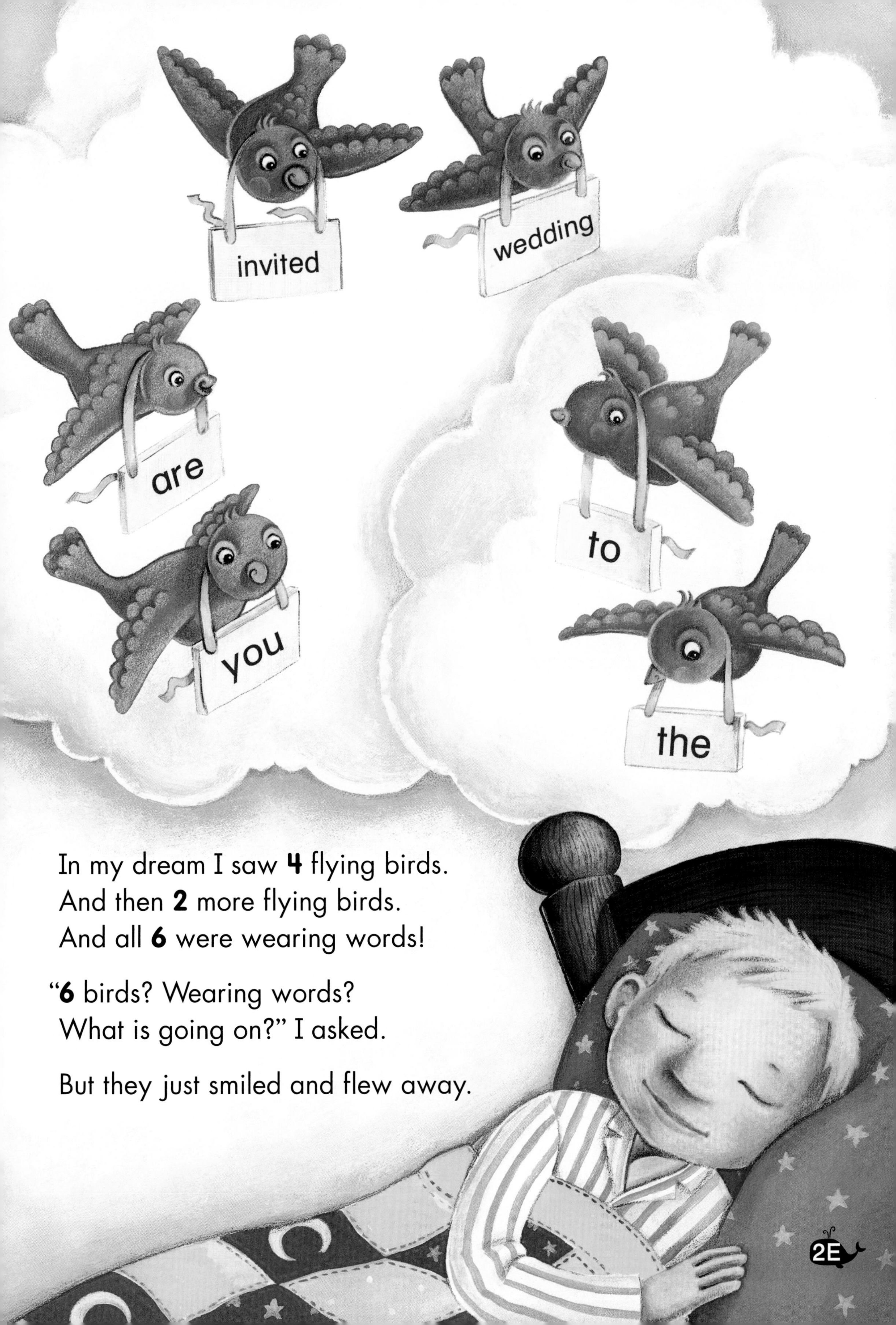

invited

wedding

are

you

to

the

In my dream I saw **4** flying birds.
And then **2** more flying birds.
And all **6** were wearing words!

"**6** birds? Wearing words?
What is going on?" I asked.

But they just smiled and flew away.

2E

In my dream I saw **4** flying mice.
And then **3** more flying mice.
And all **7** were throwing rice!

3 pigs wearing wigs.
4 cats wearing hats.
5 whales wearing tails.
6 birds wearing words.
7 mice throwing rice...

Now I know what's going on!

I do!

I do!

2F

Home-School Connection

Dear Family,

Today my class started Chapter 2, **Fact Strategies for Addition and Subtraction.** I will learn different ways to add numbers that have sums all the way up to 18, and I will learn different ways to subtract from numbers all the way up to 18. Here are some of the math words I will be learning and some things we can do to help me with my math.

Love,

_____

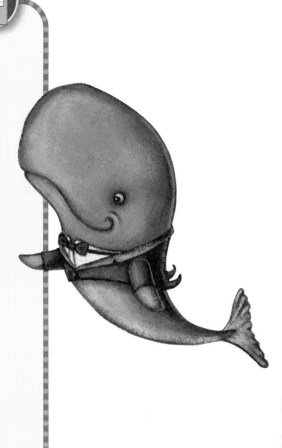

Math Activity to Do at Home

Play "Doubles" with 18 pennies. Count out 7 pennies and say, "Double it!" Your child then counts out an additional 7 pennies, and together you say, "7 plus 7 equals 14 in all. 7 cents plus 7 cents equals 14 cents." Take turns, using other numbers.

Books to Read Together

Reading math stories reinforces concepts. Look for these titles in your local library:

Seven Blind Mice
By Ed Young
(Penguin Putnam, 1992)

Animals on Board
By Stuart J. Murphy
(HarperCollins, 1998)

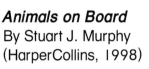

Take It to the NET
More Activities
www.scottforesman.com

My New Math Words

count on An addition strategy: children count on 1, 2, or 3 from the greater addend.

Start at 7 and then count on 8, 9, 10.

count back A subtraction strategy: children count back 1 or 2 from the greater number.

Start at 10 and then count back 9, 8.

doubles A doubles fact is one in which the two addends are the same (e.g., 4 + 4 = 8).

doubles plus 1 A doubles-plus-1 fact is one in which one addend is only one more than the other addend (e.g., 4 + 5 = 9).

Name _____

Race to the Wedding

How to Play

1. Place your markers on START.
2. Take turns tossing the cubes.
3. Add the 2 numbers together and move that number of spaces.
4. If you land on a space with a word, go back to START!
5. The first person to get to the wedding wins the game!

What You Need

2 dot cubes

2 game markers ○ ●

Wedding

17 18 19 20

to 16

15 13 12 11 10 9

14 invited

8 are

7

START 1 2 3 4 5 6

the

you

Name_____

Learn!

You can **count on** to **add** 1, 2, or 3 to the greater number.

Start at 7.
Count on 8, 9.
7 + 2 = 9

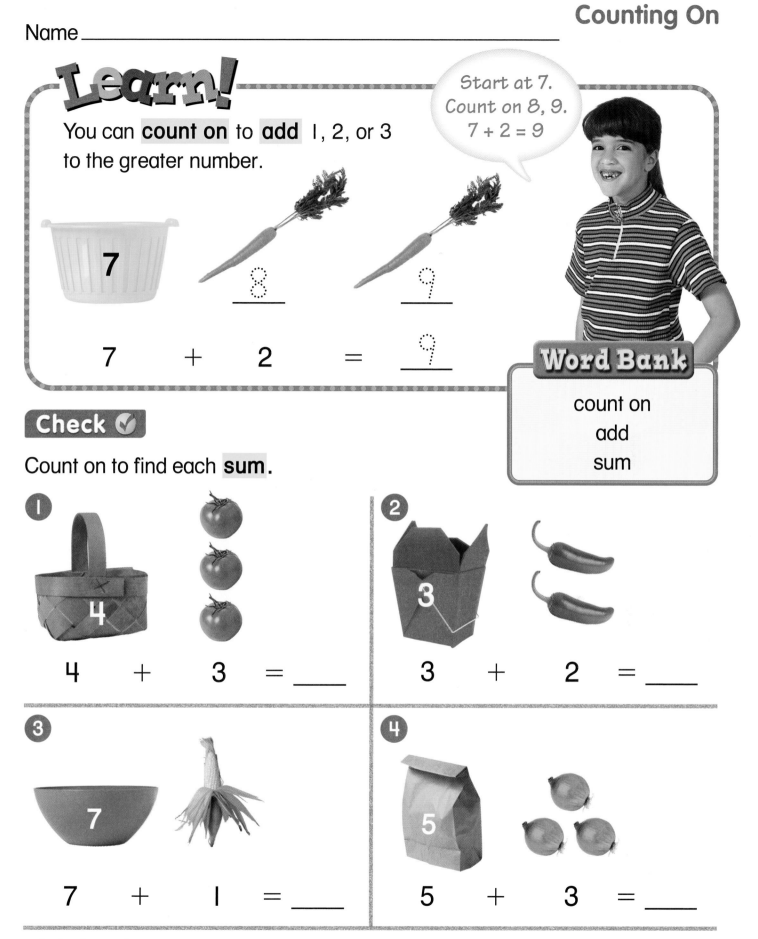

7   8   9

7   +   2   =   9

Word Bank

count on
add
sum

Check ✓

Count on to find each **sum**.

1

4   +   3   = ____

2

3   +   2   = ____

3

7   +   1   = ____

4

5   +   3   = ____

Think About It Reasoning

Do you need to count on to add zero to another number? Explain.

Count on to find each sum.

5 $9 + 1 = \underline{10}$ $3 + 5 = \underline{}$ $1 + 5 = \underline{}$

6 $8 + 1 = \underline{}$ $\underline{} = 2 + 6$ $1 + 7 = \underline{}$

7 $\underline{} = 4 + 2$ $3 + 3 = \underline{}$ $3 + 4 = \underline{}$

8 $2 + 9 = \underline{}$ $3 + 7 = \underline{}$ $\underline{} = 2 + 3$

9

8	7	3	1	9	1
+ 3	+ 2	+ 9	+ 3	+ 1	+ 8

10

3	4	7	2	2	3
+ 6	+ 1	+ 3	+ 9	+ 6	+ 8

Problem Solving   Number Sense

Complete each list of number pairs.

11

Number of Tricycles	Number of Wheels
1	3
2	___
___	___

12

Number of Dogs	Number of Legs
0	0
2	___
___	___

Home Connection Your child learned that *counting on* is a strategy for adding 1, 2, or 3 to a greater number. **Home Activity** Say a number less than 18 and have your child count on 1, 2, or 3 from that number.

Name_____

Learn!

Doubles facts are addition facts with two addends that are the same.

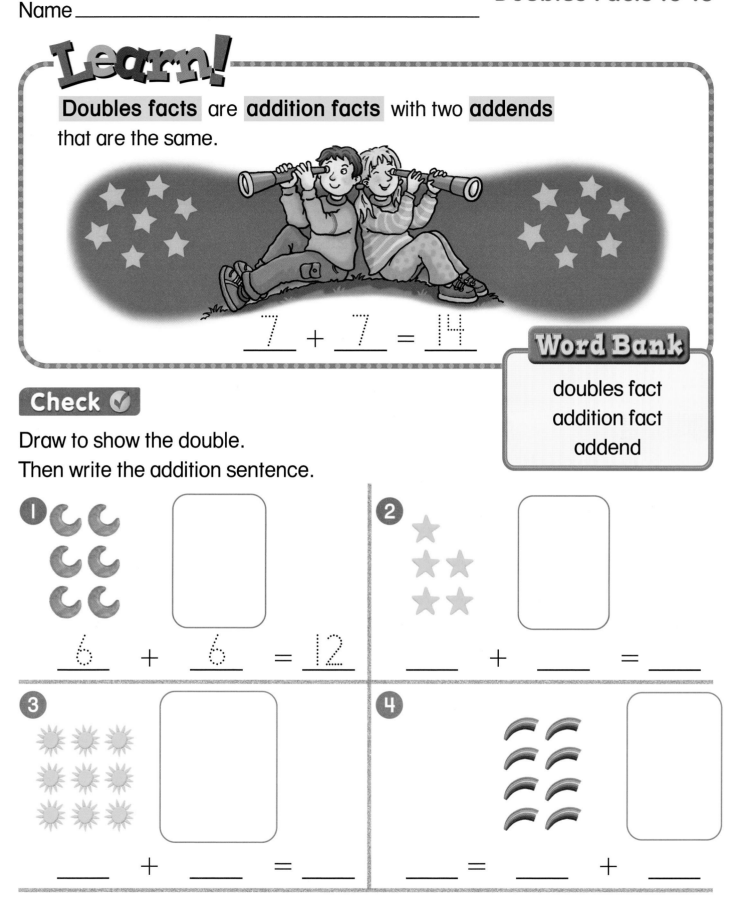

___7__ + ___7__ = ___14__

Word Bank
doubles fact
addition fact
addend

Check ✓

Draw to show the double.
Then write the addition sentence.

❶
___6__ + ___6__ = ___12__

❷
___ + ___ = ___

❸
___ + ___ = ___

❹
___ = ___ + ___

Think About It Reasoning

Write all 5 of the sums on this page in order from least to greatest.
What pattern do you see in the sums?

Solve. Circle the doubles facts.

5 (14 = 7 + 7)   1 + 7 = ___   ___ = 3 + 6

6 9 + 3 = ___   ___ = 4 + 4   1 + 8 = ___

7 1 + 1 = ___   ___ = 2 + 3   0 + 0 = ___

8
$$9 + 9$$ $$5 + 2$$ $$2 + 2$$ $$7 + 1$$ $$6 + 6$$ $$2 + 8$$

9
$$6 + 8$$ $$9 + 1$$ $$5 + 5$$ $$7 + 7$$ $$8 + 4$$ $$5 + 3$$

10
$$8 + 8$$ $$4 + 2$$ $$2 + 6$$ $$9 + 9$$ $$6 + 3$$ $$3 + 3$$

Problem Solving   Visual Thinking

Draw a picture to solve the problem.
Write the number sentence.

11 Dale bought 8 lemons.
Myra bought the same number
of limes. How many pieces
of fruit did they buy in all?

___ + ___ = ___

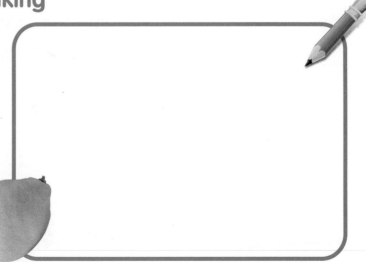

Home Connection Your child learned that facts such as 7 + 7 and 9 + 9 are called *doubles facts*. **Home Activity** Have your child use small objects to make doubles and write an addition sentence for each double that he or she makes.

© Pearson Education, Inc.

Name _____

Learn!

You can use doubles facts to find other sums.

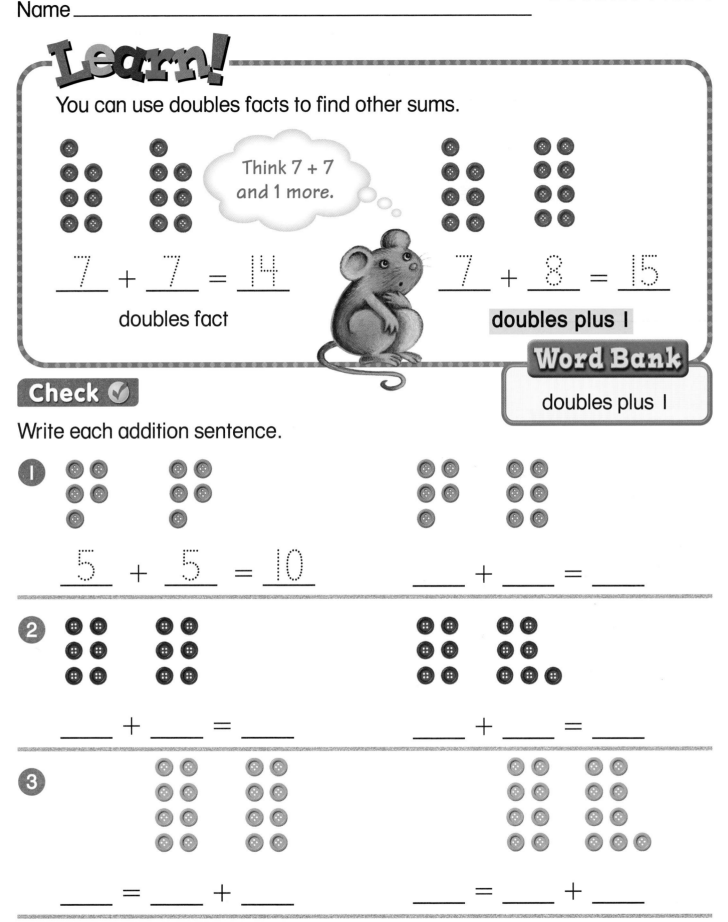

Think 7 + 7 and 1 more.

__7__ + __7__ = __14__

doubles fact

__7__ + __8__ = __15__

doubles plus 1

Word Bank

doubles plus 1

Check ✓

Write each addition sentence.

① __5__ + __5__ = __10__   ___ + ___ = ___

② ___ + ___ = ___   ___ + ___ = ___

③ ___ = ___ + ___   ___ = ___ + ___

Think About It   Reasoning

How does knowing 8 + 8 = 16 help you find 8 + 7?

Add. Use doubles facts to help you.

4
   5   6   4   6   3   2
+ 6   + 7   + 5   + 6   + 4   + 2

5
   9   2   8   7   8   5
+ 9   + 3   + 9   + 7   + 7   + 4

6
   3   8   1   6   9   4
+ 3   + 8   + 1   + 5   + 8   + 3

7 $1 + 2 =$ ___ $3 + 2 =$ ___   ___ $= 5 + 5$

8 $9 + 9 =$ ___   ___ $= 7 + 6$ $8 + 9 =$ ___

Problem Solving Writing in Math

9 Use pictures, numbers, or words to tell how
7 + 9 and 7 + 7 are related.

© Pearson Education, Inc.

Home Connection Your child learned that doubles-plus-1 facts
are one more than doubles facts. **Home Activity** Name a doubles
fact (e.g., 6 + 6 = 12) and ask your child to tell you its doubles-plus-1
fact (in this case, 6 + 7 = 13).

Name _____

Learn! Algebra

You can group numbers in any order and get the same sum.

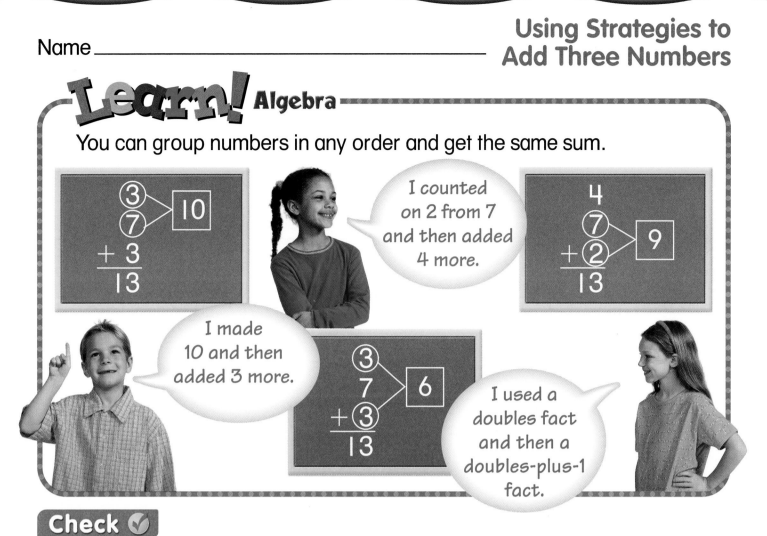

I counted on 2 from 7 and then added 4 more.

I made 10 and then added 3 more.

I used a doubles fact and then a doubles-plus-1 fact.

Check ✓

Find each sum in two different ways.
Circle the numbers you added first
and write their sum in the box.

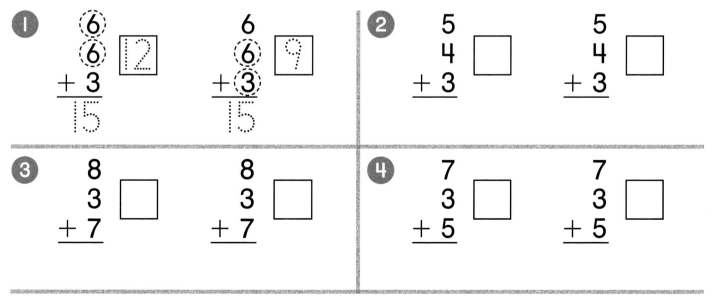

Think About It   Reasoning

Tell two different ways you could add 2 + 8 + 2.

Add. Try different ways.

5 $8 + 2 + 8 =$ _18_

6 ____ $= 4 + 1 + 6$

7 $8 + 3 + 0 =$ ____

8 ____ $= 9 + 3 + 2$

9

4	7	3	2	8	2
4	6	9	3	0	7
+ 4	+ 5	+ 3	+ 4	+ 9	+ 3

10

6	9	2	9	8	6
4	7	7	9	2	1
+ 6	+ 2	+ 7	+ 0	+ 7	+ 1

11

7	1	9	5	5	8
7	8	0	3	5	4
+ 4	+ 8	+ 3	+ 5	+ 5	+ 6

Problem Solving   Algebra

Find the missing numbers. The same shapes are
the same numbers. The numbers in ◯ are sums.
Add across and down.

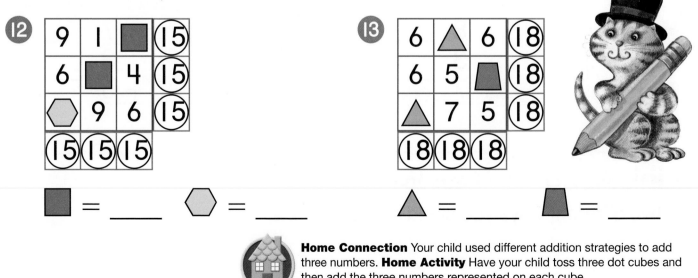

12

9	1	■	(15)
6	■	4	(15)
⬡	9	6	(15)
(15)	(15)	(15)	

■ = ____   ⬡ = ____

13

6	▲	6	(18)
6	5	▱	(18)
▲	7	5	(18)
(18)	(18)	(18)	

▲ = ____   ▱ = ____

Home Connection Your child used different addition strategies to add
three numbers. **Home Activity** Have your child toss three dot cubes and
then add the three numbers represented on each cube.

Name _____

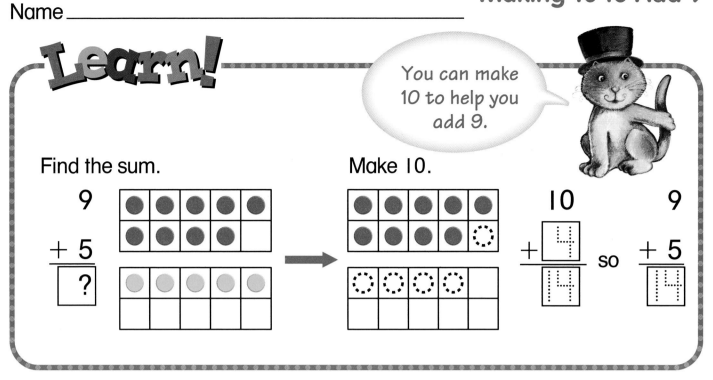

You can make 10 to help you add 9.

Find the sum.

$$9 + 5 = ?$$

Make 10.

$$10 + 4 = 14$$ so $$9 + 5 = 14$$

Check ✓

Make 10 to add 9.

Use counters and Workmat 3.

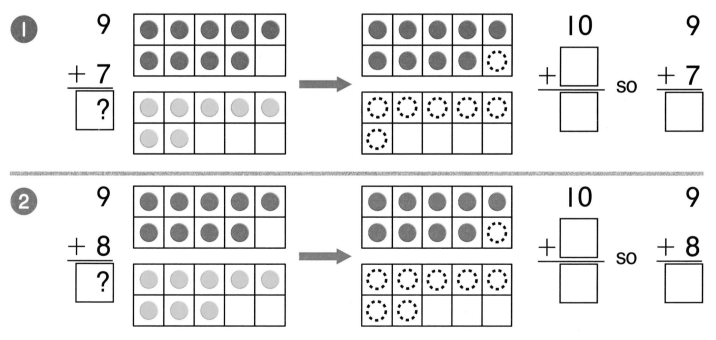

1. $$9 + 7 = ?$$

$$10 + \boxed{} = \boxed{}$$ so $$9 + 7 = \boxed{}$$

2. $$9 + 8 = ?$$

$$10 + \boxed{} = \boxed{}$$ so $$9 + 8 = \boxed{}$$

Think About It Number Sense

Compare adding 9 to any number and adding 10 to that same number. What is different?

Add. Use counters and Workmat 3 if you need to.

3

9	6	0	9	3	9
+ 2	+ 9	+ 9	+ 8	+ 9	+ 1

4

7	9	8	4	9	2
+ 9	+ 3	+ 9	+ 9	+ 9	+ 9

5

9	5	9	9	1	4
+ 0	+ 9	+ 4	+ 7	+ 9	+ 9

6 9 + 6 = ___   9 + 7 = ___   8 + 9 = ___

7 5 + 9 = ___   4 + 9 = ___   3 + 9 = ___

Problem Solving Reasoning

Solve by using pictures, numbers, or words.

8 Harriet had 7 trees in her yard. She planted some more.
Now she has 16 trees. How many new trees did Harriet plant?

Home Connection Your child learned that it is helpful to make 10 when adding 9. **Home Activity** Ask your child to explain how to add 9 + 7 by first making 10.

Name _____

Learn!

Make 10 to add 7 or 8.

$$\begin{array}{r} 7 \\ + 6 \\ \hline ? \end{array}$$

$$\begin{array}{r} 10 \\ + 3 \\ \hline 13 \end{array}$$ so $$\begin{array}{r} 7 \\ + 6 \\ \hline 13 \end{array}$$

$$\begin{array}{r} 8 \\ + 6 \\ \hline ? \end{array}$$

$$\begin{array}{r} 10 \\ + 4 \\ \hline 14 \end{array}$$ so $$\begin{array}{r} 8 \\ + 6 \\ \hline 14 \end{array}$$

Check ✓

Make 10 to add 7 or 8.

Use counters and Workmat 3.

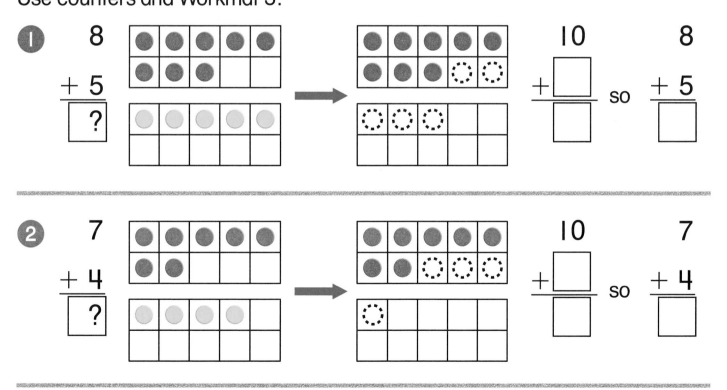

1. $$\begin{array}{r} 8 \\ + 5 \\ \hline ? \end{array}$$ $$\begin{array}{r} 10 \\ + \square \\ \hline \square \end{array}$$ so $$\begin{array}{r} 8 \\ + 5 \\ \hline \square \end{array}$$

2. $$\begin{array}{r} 7 \\ + 4 \\ \hline ? \end{array}$$ $$\begin{array}{r} 10 \\ + \square \\ \hline \square \end{array}$$ so $$\begin{array}{r} 7 \\ + 4 \\ \hline \square \end{array}$$

Think About It   Number Sense

How would you make 10 to find the sum of 7 + 8?

Add. Use counters and Workmat 3 if you need to.

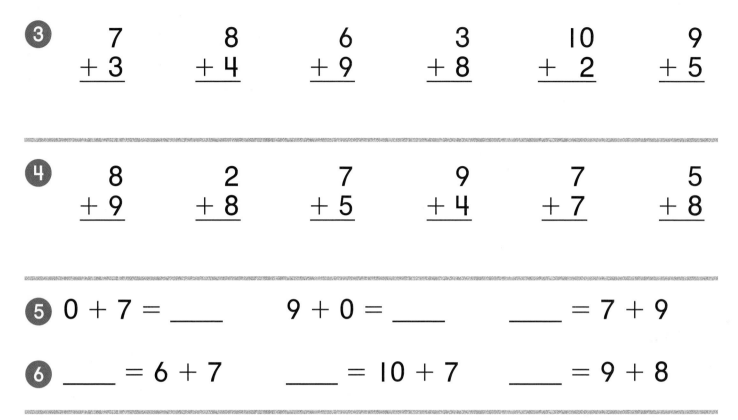

3
$$\begin{array}{r} 7 \\ +3 \\ \hline \end{array} \qquad \begin{array}{r} 8 \\ +4 \\ \hline \end{array} \qquad \begin{array}{r} 6 \\ +9 \\ \hline \end{array} \qquad \begin{array}{r} 3 \\ +8 \\ \hline \end{array} \qquad \begin{array}{r} 10 \\ +2 \\ \hline \end{array} \qquad \begin{array}{r} 9 \\ +5 \\ \hline \end{array}$$

4
$$\begin{array}{r} 8 \\ +9 \\ \hline \end{array} \qquad \begin{array}{r} 2 \\ +8 \\ \hline \end{array} \qquad \begin{array}{r} 7 \\ +5 \\ \hline \end{array} \qquad \begin{array}{r} 9 \\ +4 \\ \hline \end{array} \qquad \begin{array}{r} 7 \\ +7 \\ \hline \end{array} \qquad \begin{array}{r} 5 \\ +8 \\ \hline \end{array}$$

5 $0 + 7 =$ ___ $\qquad 9 + 0 =$ ___ $\qquad$ ___ $= 7 + 9$

6 ___ $= 6 + 7 \qquad$ ___ $= 10 + 7 \qquad$ ___ $= 9 + 8$

Problem Solving Algebra

Find the pattern. Write the missing numbers.

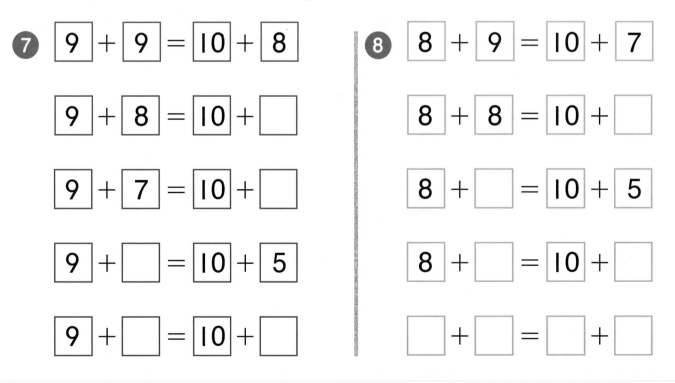

7
$$9 + 9 = 10 + 8$$
$$9 + 8 = 10 + \boxed{}$$
$$9 + 7 = 10 + \boxed{}$$
$$9 + \boxed{} = 10 + 5$$
$$9 + \boxed{} = 10 + \boxed{}$$

8
$$8 + 9 = 10 + 7$$
$$8 + 8 = 10 + \boxed{}$$
$$8 + \boxed{} = 10 + 5$$
$$8 + \boxed{} = 10 + \boxed{}$$
$$\boxed{} + \boxed{} = \boxed{} + \boxed{}$$

Home Connection Your child learned that it is helpful to make 10 when adding 7 or 8. **Home Activity** Have your child toss a dot cube and add that number to 7, 8, and then 9. Ask your child to tell you how he or she found each of the sums.

Identify the Main Idea

1 Read and solve this number riddle:

As I was going to Red Run,

I met a man with seven sons.

Every son had seven sacks.

Every sack had seven cats.

Every cat had seven kits.

Kits, cats, sacks, sons,

How many were going to Red Run?

2 Write your answer. _____

3 Explain your thinking.

_____

_____

_____

Think About It   Number Sense

Suppose you had seven cats.
Some are gray. Some are orange.
How many of each color might you have?

See if you can solve these three number riddles.

4 I am the number of hours in the day.
I am what you get if you add 12 + 12.
I am made of two tens and four ones.

What number am I? _____

5 I am the number of senses you have.
I am one more than four. I am one less than six.

What number am I? _____

6 I am the number of states in the United States of America.
I am half of 100.
I am ten more than 40.

What number am I? _____

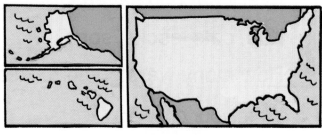

United States

7 Writing in Math

Write your own number riddle.

I am _____.

I am _____.

I am _____.

What number am I? _____

Home Connection Your child identified the main ideas in different number riddles and used logical thinking to solve them. **Home Activity** Help your child write additional number riddles. Also, second graders love riddles of all kinds, so consider looking for some riddle books at the library.

PROBLEM-SOLVING STRATEGY

Write a Number Sentence

Learn! Algebra

Read and Understand

Juan and Elisa played a bean bag tossing game. Here are their scores.

How many points did Juan score in all three games?

Bean Bag Toss			
	Game 1	Game 2	Game 3
Juan	5	6	4
Elisa	7	3	7

Plan and Solve

You need to find out how many points Juan scored in all. Write a **number sentence** using Juan's points from the chart.

$$5 + 6 + 4 = 15 \text{ points}$$

Look Back and Check

Which fact strategies did you use to solve this problem? Does your answer make sense?

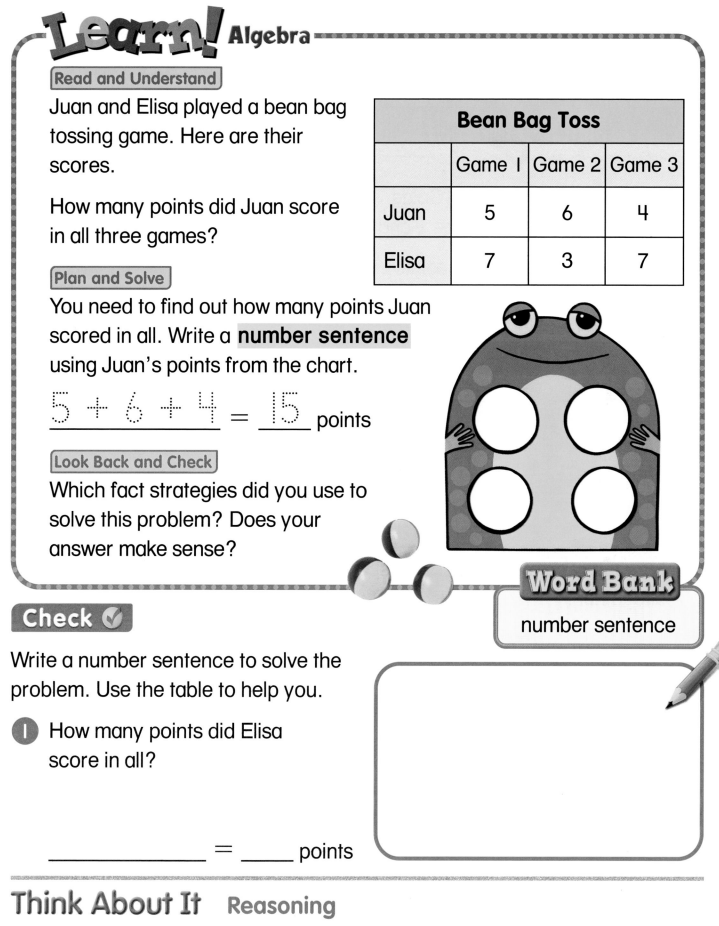

Word Bank

number sentence

Check ✓

Write a number sentence to solve the problem. Use the table to help you.

1. How many points did Elisa score in all?

_____ = _____ points

Think About It   Reasoning

In Exercise 1, explain two ways to add. Which way is easier? Tell why.

Write a number sentence
to solve the problem.
Use the table to help you.

Game Scores			
	Game 1	Game 2	Game 3
Golds	8	2	8
Blues	6	7	3

2 How many points did the Golds
score altogether in Games 1 and 2?

_____ = _____ points

3 How many points did the Blues score
altogether in Games 1 and 2?

_____ = _____ points

4 Which team had scored more points
after Game 2?

_____

5 How many points did the Blues score
altogether?

_____ = _____ points

6 How many points did the Golds
score altogether?

_____ = _____ points

7 Which team, the Golds or the Blues,
scored more points altogether?

_____

How many more? _____ more points

Home Connection Your child wrote number sentences, with two or three
addends, to solve problems. **Home Activity** Give your child three scores
using 1 to 9 points. Ask your child to find the total number of points.

Name _____

Count on to find each sum.

1 $3 + 2 =$ _____ $7 + 3 =$ _____ $2 + 9 =$ _____

2 _____ $= 1 + 5$ _____ $= 3 + 8$ _____ $= 6 + 3$

Add. Circle the doubles facts.

3
8	7	8	5	5	9
+ 9	+ 7	+ 8	+ 6	+ 5	+ 7

Add. Try different ways.

4 $5 + 6 + 4 =$ _____ $9 + 1 + 8 =$ _____

Add. Make 10 to help you.

5
9	4	6	7	8	9
+ 5	+ 7	+ 8	+ 9	+ 5	+ 4

Write the number sentence to solve the problem.
Use the table to help you.

6 How many points did
Adam score in all?

Game Points			
	Game 1	Game 2	Game 3
Emma	2	7	3
Adam	8	5	2

_____ points

Name_____

1 Count the pineapples in the two groups.
Draw and write how many there are in all.

4	and	2	is	_____ in all.
2	5	6	8
Ⓐ	Ⓑ	Ⓒ	Ⓓ

4   and   2   is   _____ in all.

2   5   6   8

Ⓐ   Ⓑ   Ⓒ   Ⓓ

2 There are 8 tulips. Amanda picks 5.
Which number sentence tells how many tulips are left?

8   5

$8 + 5 = 13$ $8 - 5 = 3$ $5 + 3 = 8$ $13 - 5 = 8$

Ⓐ   Ⓑ   Ⓒ   Ⓓ

3 Which number sentence does not tell about the picture?

$8 + 1 = 9$ $4 + 5 = 9$ $5 + 4 = 9$ $9 = 5 + 4$

Ⓐ   Ⓑ   Ⓒ   Ⓓ

4 Mark the number sentence that is true.

$3 + 3 + 4 = 12$ $8 + 8 = 17$ $7 + 3 + 7 = 17$ $5 + 4 = 12$

Ⓐ   Ⓑ   Ⓒ   Ⓓ

5 Which doubles fact helps you solve the problem?

$$\begin{array}{r} 7 \\ + 8 \\ \hline \end{array}$$

$$\begin{array}{r} 5 \\ + 5 \\ \hline 10 \end{array} \qquad \begin{array}{r} 9 \\ + 9 \\ \hline 18 \end{array} \qquad \begin{array}{r} 6 \\ + 5 \\ \hline 11 \end{array} \qquad \begin{array}{r} 7 \\ + 7 \\ \hline 14 \end{array}$$

Ⓐ   Ⓑ   Ⓒ   Ⓓ

Name _____

Learn!

You can **count back** to **subtract** 1 or 2.

Start at 8.
Then count back 2:
8, 7, 6.

$8 - 2 = \underline{6}$

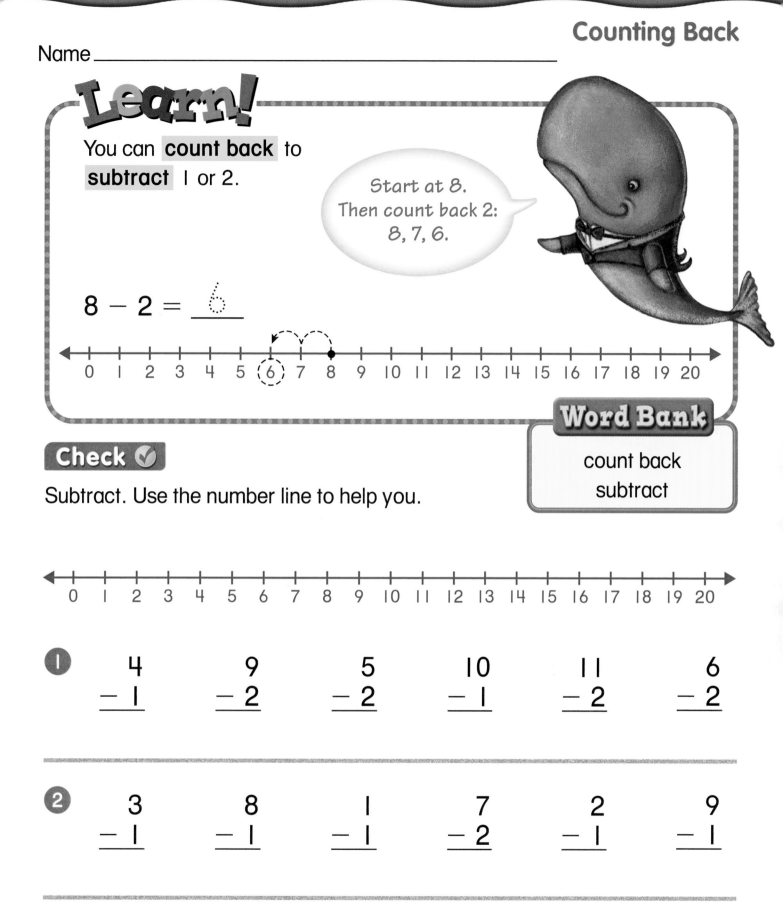

Check ✓

Subtract. Use the number line to help you.

1.

4	9	5	10	11	6
− 1	− 2	− 2	− 1	− 2	− 2

2.

3	8	1	7	2	9
− 1	− 1	− 1	− 2	− 1	− 1

Think About It   Number Sense

Should you count back to solve $7 - 0$? Explain.

Subtract. Use the number line if you need to.

0 1 2 3 4 5 6 7 8 9 10 11 12 13 14 15 16 17 18 19 20

3 6 − 2 = ___   12 − 6 = ___   ___ = 8 − 1

4 7 − 1 = ___   ___ = 17 − 9   13 − 5 = ___

5
9   10   15   1   4   12
− 2   − 2   − 8   − 1   − 2   − 3

6
6   14   10   7   5   13
− 5   − 7   − 1   − 1   − 2   − 6

7
11   9   4   3   11   16
− 6   − 1   − 0   − 1   − 2   − 8

Problem Solving   ## Writing in Math

Write a story or draw
a picture to go with
the problem. Then solve.

8 10 − 2 = ___

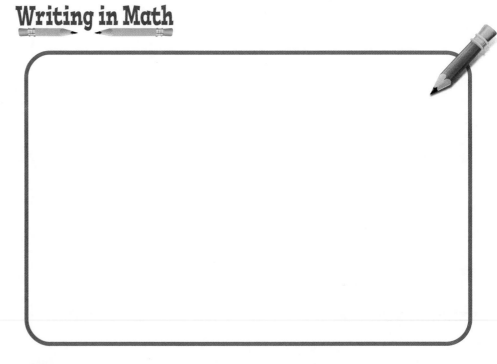

Home Connection Your child used the counting-back strategy for subtracting 1 or 2 from a greater number. **Home Activity** Say a number less than 18. Ask your child to count back 1 or 2 from that number.

Name_____

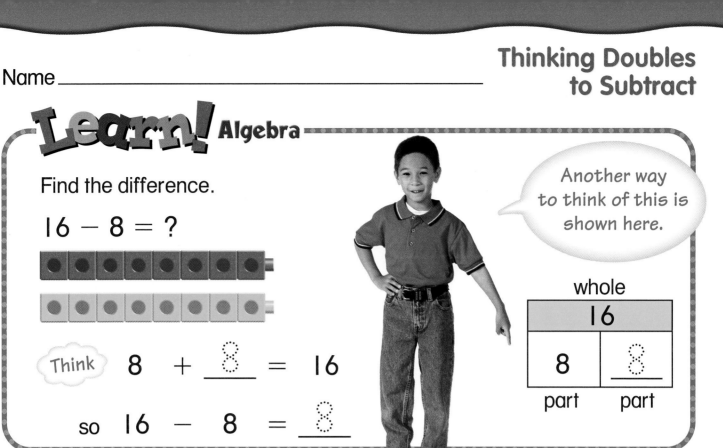

Learn! Algebra

Find the difference.

$16 - 8 = ?$

Think $8 + \underline{} = 16$

so $16 - 8 = \underline{}$

Another way to think of this is shown here.

whole

16	
8	$\underline{}$
part	part

Check ✓

Use doubles facts to help you subtract.

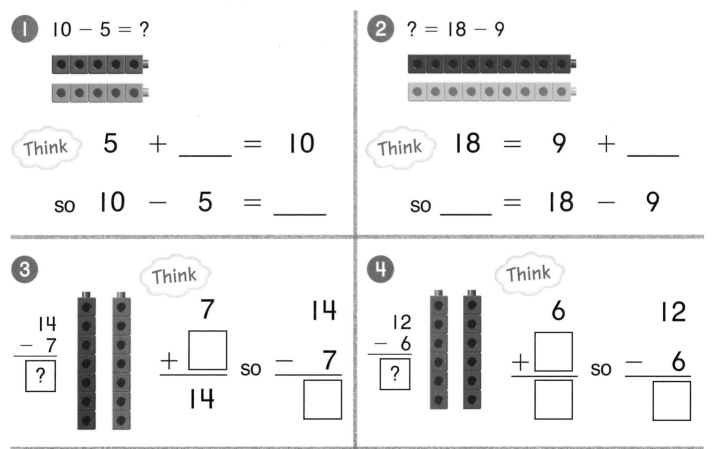

1 $10 - 5 = ?$

Think $5 + \underline{} = 10$

so $10 - 5 = \underline{}$

2 $? = 18 - 9$

Think $18 = 9 + \underline{}$

so $\underline{} = 18 - 9$

3
$\begin{array}{r} 14 \\ -\ 7 \\ \hline ? \end{array}$

Think

$\begin{array}{r} 7 \\ +\ \square \\ \hline 14 \end{array}$ so $\begin{array}{r} 14 \\ -\ 7 \\ \hline \square \end{array}$

4
$\begin{array}{r} 12 \\ -\ 6 \\ \hline ? \end{array}$

Think

$\begin{array}{r} 6 \\ +\ \square \\ \hline \square \end{array}$ so $\begin{array}{r} 12 \\ -\ 6 \\ \hline \square \end{array}$

Think About It   Reasoning

Can you use doubles to solve $17 - 8$? Explain.

Subtract. Write the doubles fact that helps you.

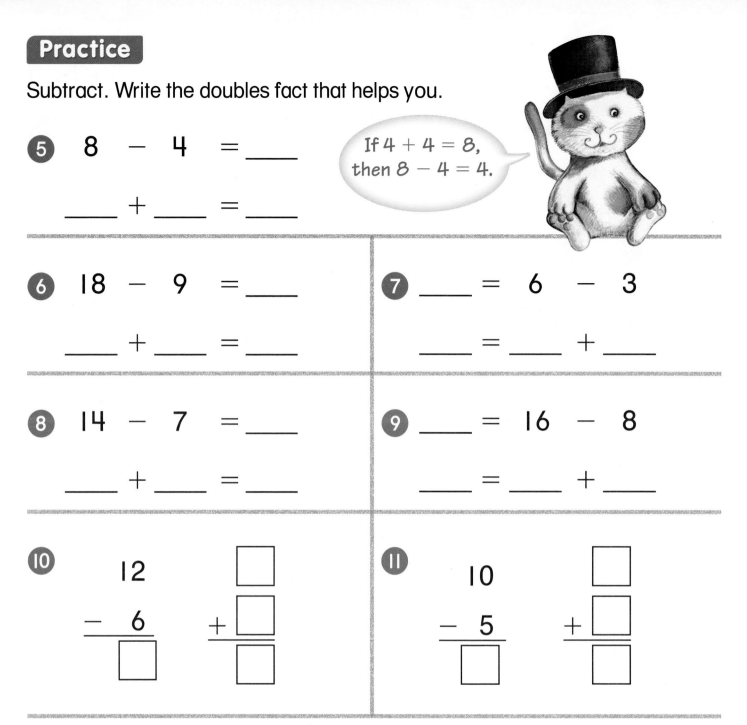

5   8 − 4 = ___

___ + ___ = ___

> If 4 + 4 = 8,
> then 8 − 4 = 4.

6   18 − 9 = ___

___ + ___ = ___

7   ___ = 6 − 3

___ = ___ + ___

8   14 − 7 = ___

___ + ___ = ___

9   ___ = 16 − 8

___ = ___ + ___

10
```
   12          ☐
 −  6      +  ☐
 ────         ──
   ☐          ☐
```

11
```
   10          ☐
 −  5      +  ☐
 ────         ──
   ☐          ☐
```

Problem Solving   Writing in Math

12 Lou's grandma gave him 18 sports cards to
share equally with his brother. If Lou gives his
brother 8 cards, is he being fair? Explain.

_____

_____

_____

Home Connection Your child used doubles facts to subtract.
Home Activity Ask your child to tell you which doubles fact he or
she would use to solve 14 − 7. (7 + 7 = 14)

Learn! Algebra

Find the difference.

13 − 6 = ?

I know that
6 + 7 = 13,
so 13 − 6 = 7.

Think 6 + _7_ = 13

so 13 − 6 = _7_

13	
6	7

Check ✓

Use addition facts to help you subtract.

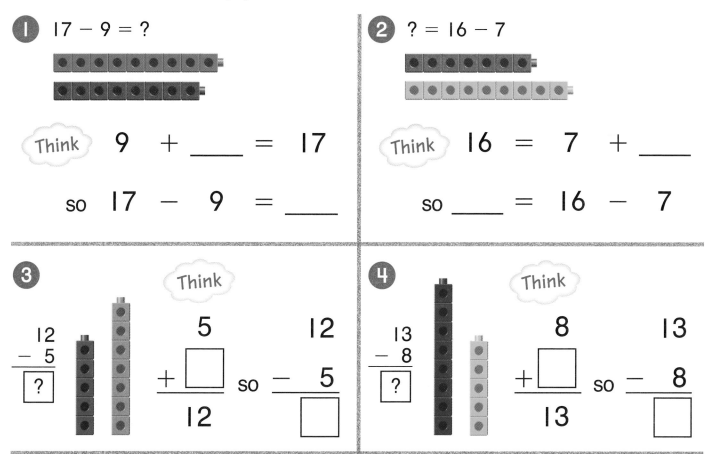

1 17 − 9 = ?

Think 9 + ___ = 17

so 17 − 9 = ___

2 ? = 16 − 7

Think 16 = 7 + ___

so ___ = 16 − 7

3

12
− 5
[?]

Think
5
+ □
12

so
12
− 5
□

4

13
− 8
[?]

Think
8
+ □
13

so
13
− 8
□

Think About It Number Sense

What pair of addition facts helps you solve 14 − 8?

Solve. Draw a line to match each subtraction fact with its related addition fact.

5 $15 - 8 = \underline{7}$ $7 + \underline{} = 12$

$12 - 7 = \underline{}$ $8 + \underline{} = 13$

$14 - 9 = \underline{}$ $8 + \underline{7} = 15$

$11 - 7 = \underline{}$ $9 + \underline{} = 14$

$13 - 8 = \underline{}$ $7 + \underline{} = 11$

6 $\underline{9} = 12 - 3$ $16 = 9 + \underline{}$

$\underline{} = 11 - 6$ $12 = 3 + \underline{9}$

$\underline{} = 18 - 9$ $11 = 6 + \underline{}$

$\underline{} = 16 - 9$ $18 = 9 + \underline{}$

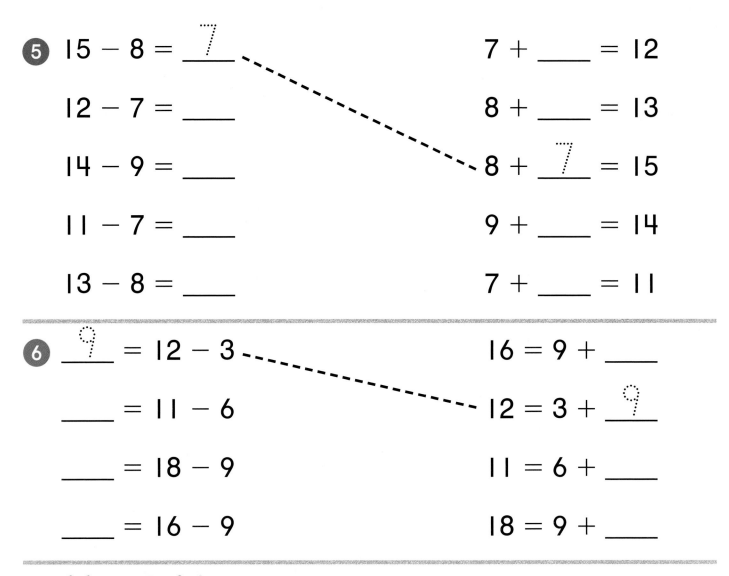

Problem Solving   Mental Math

7 Chen got 15¢. He bought a used book for 8¢. Circle the used toy that he has enough money left to buy.

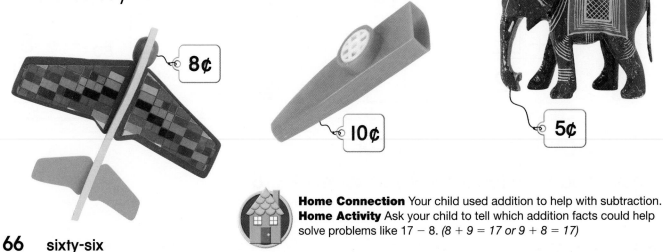

8¢

10¢

5¢

Home Connection Your child used addition to help with subtraction.
Home Activity Ask your child to tell which addition facts could help solve problems like $17 - 8$. *($8 + 9 = 17$ or $9 + 8 = 17$)*

Name_____

Learn! Algebra

What does  weigh?

7 ▮ 15

If 7 + _8_ = 15,

then 15 − 7 = _8_ .

▮ weighs _8_ pounds.

Complete the number sentence.

Check ✓

Find and write the missing numbers.

1 What does ▮ weigh?

9 ▮ 16

If 9 + ___ = 16,

then 16 − 9 = ___ .

▮ weighs ___ pounds.

2 What does ▮ weigh?

7 ▮ 13

If ___ + 7 = 13,

then 13 − ___ = 7.

▮ weighs ___ pounds.

Think About It Reasoning

If 16 + 2 = 18, then 16 + ____ = 20.
Explain.

Find and write the missing numbers.

3 What does 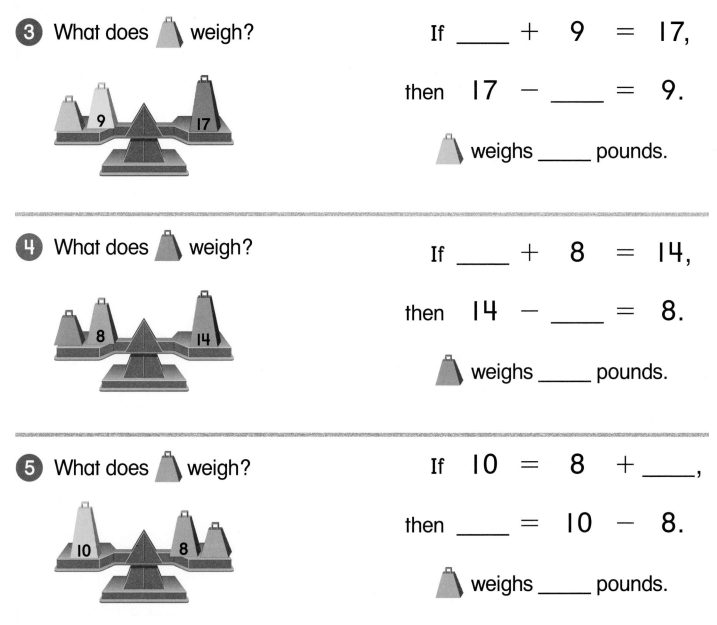 weigh?

If ____ + 9 = 17,

then 17 − ____ = 9.

weighs ____ pounds.

---

4 What does weigh?

If ____ + 8 = 14,

then 14 − ____ = 8.

weighs ____ pounds.

---

5 What does weigh?

If 10 = 8 + ____,

then ____ = 10 − 8.

weighs ____ pounds.

Reasoning

Write the missing number for each number sentence.

6 7 + ____ = 15

14 = 6 + ____

18 = ____ + 9

7 7 + 7 + ____ = 16

4 + ____ + 6 = 13

17 = 8 + ____ + 1

Home Connection Your child found the missing number in addition and subtraction sentences. **Home Activity** Write some addition and subtraction facts with missing numbers. Have your child write the missing numbers.

Name _____

DK Dorling Kindersley

BIRD
Discover the fascinating world of birds – their natural history, behavior, courtship, and secret life.

Do You Know...
that a baby bird hatched in a nest in a tree is called a *nestling*?

1 These 3 birds are old enough to be out of their nest. If 3 birds are on one branch and 3 birds are on another branch, how many birds are there in all?

_____ ◯ _____ = _____ birds in all

Fun Fact!
Here are three different kinds of outer wing feathers. They are called the flight feathers. Aren't they beautiful?

2 Many kinds of mother and father birds go hunting for food for their nestlings. They hunt hour after hour. A father bird made 20 hunting trips in 2 hours. He made 10 trips in the first hour. How many trips did he make in the second hour?

$10 +$ _____ $= 20$ trips

He made _____ trips in the second hour.

3 A group of nestlings is 13 days old. In 5 more days they will be ready to leave the nest. How old will they be then?

Carrying a nestling to safety

_____ ◯ _____ = _____ days old

4 Many kinds of nestlings are cared for by their parents. If there were 8 eggs, and 2 nestlings hatched, how many eggs would still be in the nest?

_____ − _____ = _____ eggs

5 Not all birds are hatched in nests in trees. Flamingos are hatched in nests on the ground. If there are 13 parrots and 20 flamingos at the zoo, how many parrots and flamingos are there in all?

_____ parrots and flamingos

6 **Writing in Math**

Write a story about flamingos at a zoo. Try to use both addition and subtraction in your story.

Home Connection Your child learned to solve problems by applying his or her math skills. **Home Activity** Talk to your child about how he or she solved the problems on these two pages.

© Pearson Education, Inc.

Subtract.

1

7	10	5	12	11	16
− 2	− 2	− 0	− 6	− 2	− 9

Subtract. Write the doubles fact that helps you.

2 14 − 7 = ____

____ + ____ = ____

3

18
− 9
□

□
+ □
□

Solve. Draw a line to match each subtraction fact
with its related addition fact.

4 16 − 8 = ____   9 + ____ = 14

14 − 9 = ____   7 + ____ = 13

13 − 7 = ____   8 + ____ = 16

Find and write the missing number.
Complete the number sentence.

5 What does ⬛ weigh?

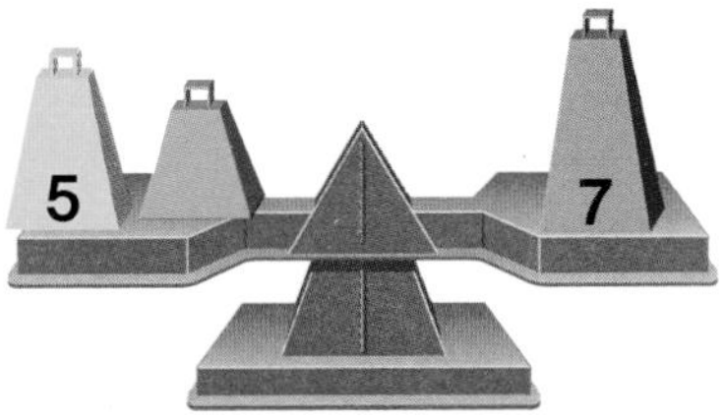

5   7

If 5 + ____ = 7,

then 7 − 5 = ____.

⬛ weighs ____ pounds.

1 There are 6 purple forks. 2 yellow forks are added. Mark the number sentence that tells how many forks there are in all.

6   2

6 + 2 = 8 forks   8 + 6 = 14 forks   8 + 2 = 10 forks   6 − 2 = 4 forks
   Ⓐ   Ⓑ   Ⓒ   Ⓓ

2 How many more blue bowls than orange bowls are there?

Ⓐ   1 more blue bowl
Ⓑ   2 more orange bowls
Ⓒ   2 more blue bowls
Ⓓ   3 more blue bowls

3 There are 9 cups in all. How many cups are inside the basket?

6   +   ___   = 9

Ⓐ 7
Ⓑ 3
Ⓒ 11
Ⓓ 14

4 Subtract. Mark the difference.

$$\begin{array}{r} 8 \\ -\ 2 \\ \hline \end{array}$$

18   17   9   6
Ⓐ   Ⓑ   Ⓒ   Ⓓ

5 Mark the related fact.

15 − 8

9 + 6 = 15   8 + 4 = 12   8 + 7 = 15   6 + 8 = 14
  Ⓐ   Ⓑ   Ⓒ   Ⓓ

Adding Doubles Plus 2

You can use doubles facts to find doubles-plus-2 facts.

$5 + 5 = 10$ is a doubles fact.

$$\begin{array}{r} 5 \\ + 5 \\ \hline 10 \end{array}$$

$5 + 7$ is a doubles-plus-2 fact.

$$\begin{array}{r} 5 \\ + 7 \\ \hline 12 \end{array}$$

5, 10, 11, 12

Add the double.

Then count on 2.

Write each sum. Use cubes if you need to.

1
$$\begin{array}{r} 3 \\ + 3 \\ \hline \end{array} \qquad \begin{array}{r} 3 \\ + 5 \\ \hline \end{array}$$

2
$$\begin{array}{r} 4 \\ + 4 \\ \hline \end{array} \qquad \begin{array}{r} 6 \\ + 4 \\ \hline \end{array}$$

3
$$\begin{array}{r} 7 \\ + 7 \\ \hline \end{array} \qquad \begin{array}{r} 9 \\ + 7 \\ \hline \end{array}$$

4
$$\begin{array}{r} 6 \\ + 6 \\ \hline \end{array} \qquad \begin{array}{r} 8 \\ + 6 \\ \hline \end{array}$$

5
$$\begin{array}{r} 8 \\ + 8 \\ \hline \end{array} \qquad \begin{array}{r} 8 \\ + 10 \\ \hline \end{array}$$

6
$$\begin{array}{r} 2 \\ + 4 \\ \hline \end{array} \quad \begin{array}{r} 6 \\ + 4 \\ \hline \end{array} \quad \begin{array}{r} 5 \\ + 3 \\ \hline \end{array} \quad \begin{array}{r} 10 \\ + 8 \\ \hline \end{array} \quad \begin{array}{r} 7 \\ + 9 \\ \hline \end{array} \quad \begin{array}{r} 6 \\ + 8 \\ \hline \end{array}$$

7 **Writing in Math**

Find the missing numbers.

What pattern do you see?

$3 + 5 = 4 + \square$

$6 + 8 = 7 + \square$

$9 + 7 = 8 + \square$

Home Connection Your child learned how to solve doubles-plus-two facts. **Home Activity** Ask your child which doubles fact he or she used to solve each problem.

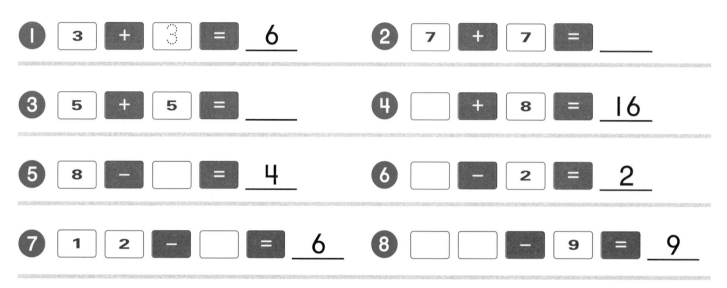

Learning with Technology

Learn Doubles Facts Using a Calculator

Press ON/C each time you begin.

1 | 3 | + | 3 | = | _6_

2 | 7 | + | 7 | = | ___

3 | 5 | + | 5 | = | ___

4 | ☐ | + | 8 | = | _16_

5 | 8 | − | ☐ | = | _4_

6 | ☐ | − | 2 | = | _2_

7 | 1 | 2 | − | ☐ | = | _6_

8 | ☐ ☐ | − | 9 | = | _9_

Complete each number sentence. Find the pattern.

9 | 2 | + | 2 | = | ___

10 | 4 | + | 4 | = | ___

11 | 8 | + | 8 | = | ___

12 | 1 | 6 | + | ☐ ☐ | = | ___

13 | ☐ ☐ | + | 3 | 2 | = | ___

14 | ☐ ☐ | + | ☐ ☐ | = | ___

Think About It Reasoning

What pattern do you notice in Exercises 9–14?

Home Connection Your child used a calculator to complete number sentences involving doubles. **Home Activity** Ask your child to explain how he or she solved Exercise 5. (Sample answer: Since I know 4 + 4 = 8, I pressed 8 − 4 = on my calculator.)

Chapter 2

Name _____

Get Information for the Answer

Many math problems have tables. You can get information from these tables to help you solve the problems.

Test-Taking Strategies

Understand the Question

Get Information for the Answer

Plan How to Find the Answer

Make Smart Choices

Use Writing in Math

The table below shows scores for three card games. Use the information in the table to answer the question below the table. Then fill in the answer bubble.

Card Game Points			
	David	Chris	Ann
Game 1	8	6	3
Game 2	4	9	6
Game 3	5	3	7

 Which addition sentence tells how many points Ann scored in all three games?

Ⓐ $3 + 6 + 7 = 16$ Ⓒ $6 + 9 + 3 = 18$

Ⓑ $8 + 6 + 3 = 17$ Ⓓ $5 + 3 + 7 = 15$

Your Turn

Use information from the same table to answer this question:

2 How many points did all three players score in Game 2?

Ⓐ $8 + 4 + 5 = 17$ Ⓒ $5 + 3 + 7 = 15$

Ⓑ $6 + 9 + 3 = 18$ Ⓓ $4 + 9 + 6 = 19$

Home Connection Your child prepared for standardized tests by using information from a table to solve math problems. **Home Activity** Ask your child to explain how he or she used the table to answer the question in Exercise 2.

Name _____

What's the Buzz?

Have you ever heard a bee buzzing around your ear?
Sometimes people are afraid of bees,
but bees help flowers and plants form seeds.
Then the seeds can grow into new plants.

wing

head

antenna

leg

thorax

abdomen

"Bee" Part of It

Write a number sentence to solve each problem.

1 A bee has 1 antenna on each side of its body.
How many antennae does it have in all?

_____ + _____ = _____ antennae in all

2 A bee has 3 legs on each side of its body.
How many legs does it have in all?

_____ + _____ = _____ legs in all

3 How many legs do 3 bees have?

_____ + _____ + _____ = _____ legs

Take It to the NET
Video and Activities
www.scottforesman.com

Home Connection Your child wrote number sentences to solve problems about bees. **Home Activity** Ask your child to write a number sentence that shows how many wings a bee has and then a number sentence to show how many wings 2 bees have.

Add or subtract.

1 $5 + 5 = \boxed{}$

11	10	5	0
Ⓐ	Ⓑ	Ⓒ	Ⓓ

2 $8 - 4 = \boxed{}$

4	5	7	8
Ⓐ	Ⓑ	Ⓒ	Ⓓ

3 $5 + 6 = \boxed{}$

1	9	10	11
Ⓐ	Ⓑ	Ⓒ	Ⓓ

4 $4 + 3 = \boxed{}$

7	8	9	10
Ⓐ	Ⓑ	Ⓒ	Ⓓ

Subtract. Use the number line to help you.

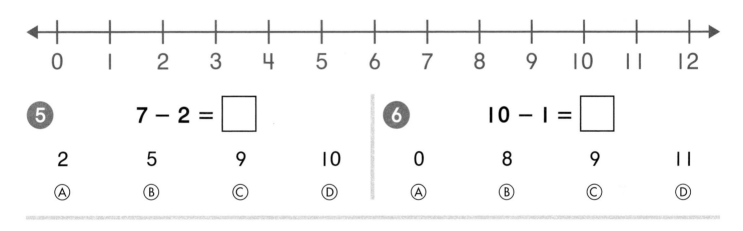

0 1 2 3 4 5 6 7 8 9 10 11 12

5 $7 - 2 = \boxed{}$

2	5	9	10
Ⓐ	Ⓑ	Ⓒ	Ⓓ

6 $10 - 1 = \boxed{}$

0	8	9	11
Ⓐ	Ⓑ	Ⓒ	Ⓓ

7   Which sentence tells how many pieces of popcorn IN ALL?

Ⓐ 9 take away 7 is 2.

Ⓑ 7 and 7 is 14.

Ⓒ 7 and 9 is 16.

Ⓓ 9 and 9 is 18.

8   Look at this number sentence:

$$12 - 5 = \boxed{}$$

Which number fact will help you find the number to go in the box?

Ⓐ $5 + 5 = 10$

Ⓑ $7 + 5 = 12$

Ⓒ $7 + 7 = 14$

Ⓓ $12 - 12 = 0$

Name _____

9 How many eggs IN ALL?

Ⓐ 3

Ⓑ 8

Ⓒ 9

Ⓓ 10

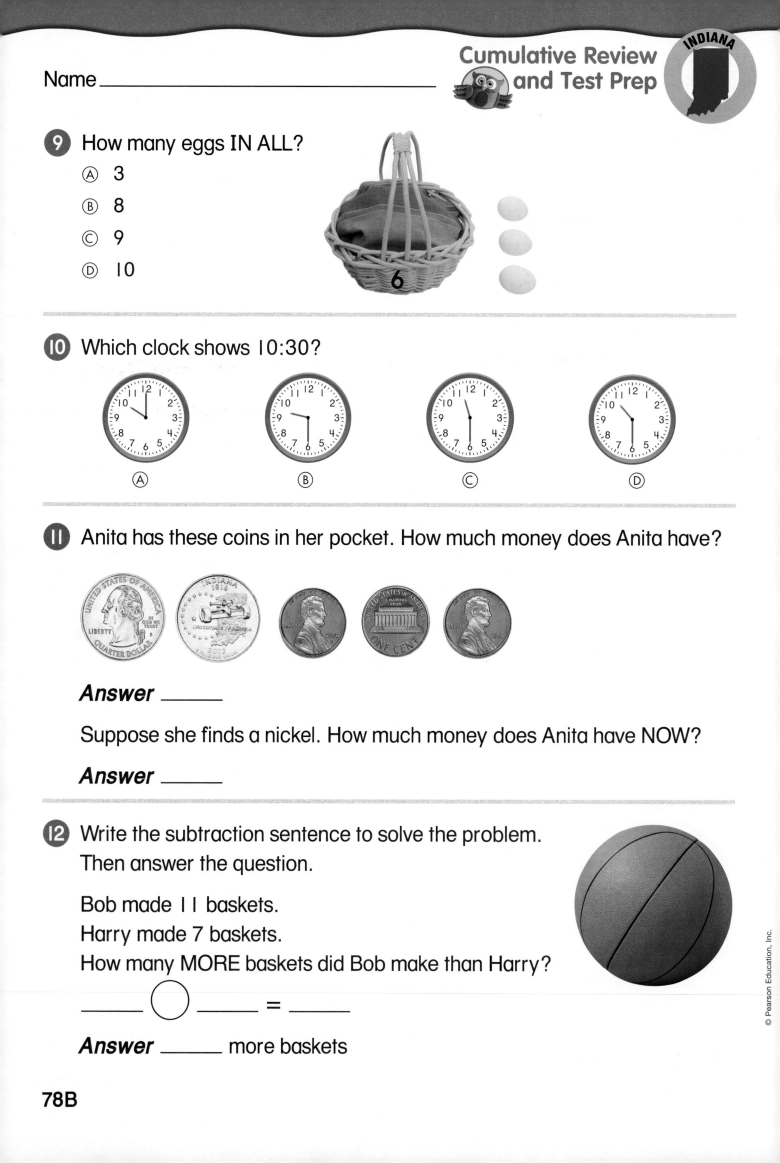

6

---

10 Which clock shows 10:30?

Ⓐ   Ⓑ   Ⓒ   Ⓓ

---

11 Anita has these coins in her pocket. How much money does Anita have?

Answer _____

Suppose she finds a nickel. How much money does Anita have NOW?

Answer _____

---

12 Write the subtraction sentence to solve the problem.
Then answer the question.

Bob made 11 baskets.
Harry made 7 baskets.
How many MORE baskets did Bob make than Harry?

_____ ◯ _____ = _____

Answer _____ more baskets

78B

All Kinds of Stones

Written by Tara Lane

This Math Storybook belongs to

_____

3A

Collecting stones is what we like.
We think it's so much fun!
We like them big.
We like them small.
Let's count them, everyone.

We gathered all the shiny stones.
They look so smooth and round.
We filled 1 box of 10, and
5 more are on the ground.

How many do we have in all?

Look at all the thin, flat stones! We found some at the shore. We filled **3** buckets of **10**, and here we have **2** more.

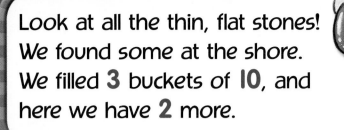

How many do we have in all?

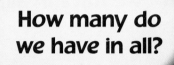

We have some rough and bumpy stones.
We found them far and near.
We filled **2** baskets of **10**, and
oh, there's **1** more here.

How many do
we have in all?

10

10

3E

Shiny, flat, or bumpy stones—
which kind do you like best?
Let's count the groups of 10 we have
and then count all the rest.

Home-School Connection

Dear Family,

Today my class started Chapter 3, **Place Value to 100 and Money.** I will learn about tens and ones, even numbers and odd numbers, and how the numbers from 1 through 100 fit together. I will also learn how to count different combinations of coins. Here are some of the math words I will be learning and some things we can do to help me with my math.

Love,

_____

Math Activity to Do at Home

Collect 100 buttons or bottle caps. Count them by 1s. Group them by 10s. Count the sets by 10s. Break apart one of the sets and count the entire 100 by 10s and then by 1s (when you get to the broken-apart set). Count by 2s and 5s; count forward and backward. Have fun!

Books to Read Together

Reading math stories reinforces concepts. Look for these books in your local library:

From One to One Hundred
by Teri Sloat
(Puffin, 1995)

The King's Commissioners
by Aileen Friedman
Scholastic, 1994)

Take It to the NET
More Activities
www.scottforesman.com

My New Math Words

even numbers If every part has a match, the number is even.

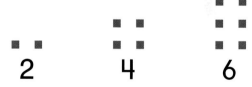

odd numbers If one part has no match, the number is odd.

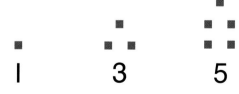

ordinal numbers Ordinal numbers (e.g., *first, second, third, fourth*) show the order of things.

dollar A bill or coin worth 100 cents (100¢).

100 cents *or* 100¢ *or* $1.00

How Many in All?

How to Play

1. Place your marker on a pile of stones marked START.
2. When it is your turn, say the number on the pile, toss the cube, and count the dots.
3. Add that number to the number on your pile of stones.
4. Put a marker on the stone that has the correct sum on it.
5. Continue playing until all of the stones are covered.

Player 1 START

10

15

11

22

25

23

26

Player 2 START

14

24

20

13

21

16

12

© Pearson Education, Inc.

Name _____

Learn!

The number 35 has 2 **digits**.

Number __35__

3 and 5 are digits in __35__ .

Number word

thirty-five

Ones	Teens	Tens
1 one	11 eleven	10 ten
2 two	12 twelve	20 twenty
3 three	13 thirteen	30 thirty
4 four	14 fourteen	40 forty
5 five	15 fifteen	50 fifty
6 six	16 sixteen	60 sixty
7 seven	17 seventeen	70 seventy
8 eight	18 eighteen	80 eighty
9 nine	19 nineteen	90 ninety

Word Bank

digit
number word

Check ✓

Write the number.

1 ninety-four __94__   sixteen _____   forty _____

2 thirty-one _____   twenty-three _____   eighty-nine _____

Write the number word.

3 70 _____   32 _____

4 65 _____   11 _____

Think About It   Number Sense

Name the ones digits in seventy-nine and eighty-two.
Name the tens digits in thirty and fifty-six.

Write the number.

5   nine _____   thirty-three _____   eighty-two _____

6   seventy _____   seventeen _____   fifty-eight _____

7   forty-five _____   ninety-one _____   twenty-six _____

Write the number word.

8   12 _____

9   90 _____

10 84 _____

11 49 _____

12 2 tens _____

13 1 ten 6 ones _____

14 15 ones _____

15 6 tens _____

16 9 tens 3 ones _____

17 5 tens 7 ones _____

Problem Solving   Number Sense

What is the number?

18 It is greater than thirty-five and less than forty-five. If you add the two digits, the sum is five.

    Write the number word.

    _____

19 It is less than 70 and greater than 65. If you add the two digits, the sum is 14.

    Write the number.

    _____

Home Connection Your child learned number words.
Home Activity Name a number between 10 and 99 and ask your child to write it as a number word.

Reading for Math Success

Understand Graphic Sources: Lists

1 Making a list is a good way to think things through.

A mysterious suitcase fell off the train and popped open. "Hmm," said the detective. "No name. How can we find the owner?"

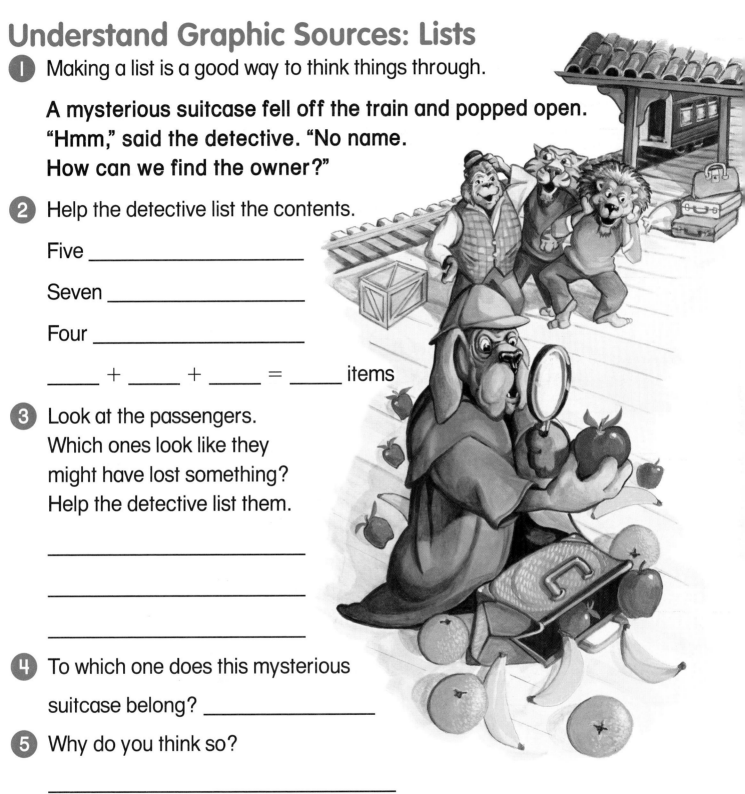

2 Help the detective list the contents.

Five _____

Seven _____

Four _____

_____ + _____ + _____ = _____ items

3 Look at the passengers. Which ones look like they might have lost something? Help the detective list them.

_____

_____

_____

4 To which one does this mysterious suitcase belong? _____

5 Why do you think so?

_____

Think About It   Number Sense

You can make a list for just about anything.
Make a list of your three favorite names for girls
and your three favorite names for boys.

Here are two lists of names. They show 10 popular names for girls and 10 popular names for boys.

6 Beside each name, write down the number
of people you know who have that name.
If you don't know anyone with that name, write 0.
If **your** name is on the list, don't forget to count yourself!

1. Emily   6. Hailey   1. Jacob   6. Andrew

2. Hannah   7. Ashley   2. Michael   7. Joseph

3. Kaitlyn   8. Brianna   3. Nicholas   8. Christopher

4. Madison   9. Samantha   4. Matthew   9. Anthony

5. Sarah   10. Jasmine   5. Joshua   10. Dylan

7 Add up the total number of girls.
Then add up the total number of boys.

Girls _____   Boys _____

Home Connection Your child looked at lists as a way of organizing
information. **Home Activity** Show your child lists you use in everyday life,
for example, a grocery list or an address book.

88 eighty-eight

1 Make 100 as many ways as you can by using groups of ten.

What two groups of ten make 100?

Read and Understand

You need to find groups of ten that make 100.

Plan and Solve

Make an **organized list** to keep track of the groups. Use cubes and Workmat 1 if you need to.

Complete the first row. The first row says that 0 tens and 10 tens make 100.

Write the missing numbers in the chart.

Look Back and Check

Do your answers make sense? Does each row have a total of 10 tens (or 100)?

Tens	Tens	Total
0	10	100
1	9	100
2	8	100
		100
		100
		100
		100
		100
		100
		100
		100

Word Bank

organized list

Think About It Reasoning

How does making an organized list help you?

Use cubes and Workmat 1 if you need to.

2 Make 60.

Tens	Tens	Total
0	6	60
		60
		60
		60
		60
		60
		60

3 Make 50.

Tens	Tens	Total
		50
		50
		50
		50
		50
		50

4 Make 90.

Tens	Tens	Total
0	9	90
		90
		90
		90
		90
5	4	
		90
7	2	
		90

I see number patterns!

© Pearson Education, Inc.

Home Connection Your child made organized lists with groups of ten to make given multiples of ten. **Home Activity** Ask your child to make an organized list identifying the different ways to make 70 using groups of ten.

Name_____

Learn! Algebra

We can compare numbers by using >, <, and =.

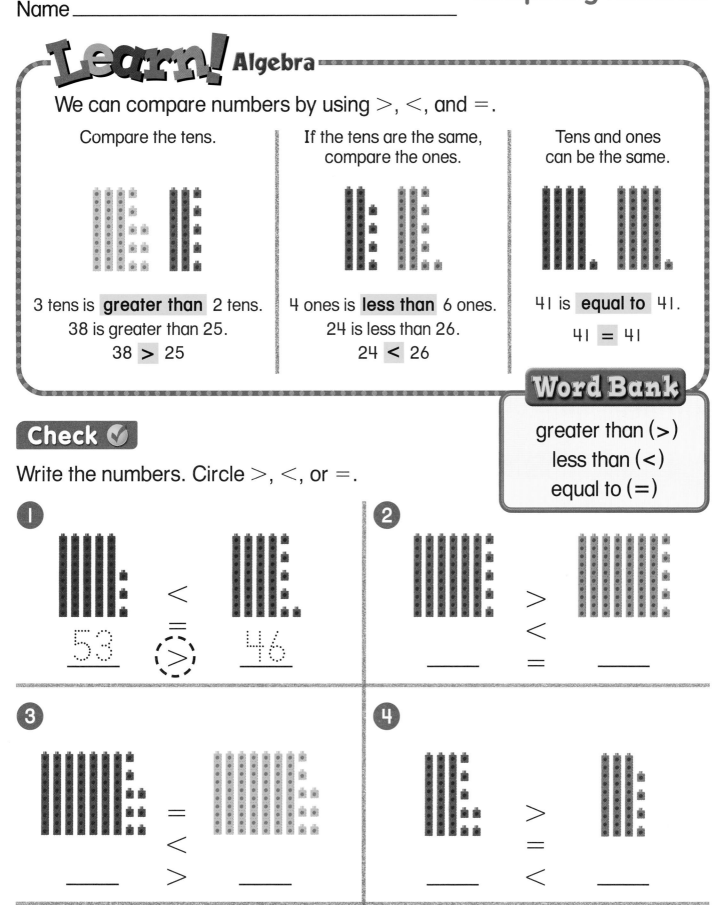

Compare the tens.	If the tens are the same, compare the ones.	Tens and ones can be the same.
3 tens is **greater than** 2 tens.	4 ones is **less than** 6 ones.	41 is **equal to** 41.
38 is greater than 25.	24 is less than 26.	41 = 41
38 > 25	24 < 26	

Word Bank

greater than (>)
less than (<)
equal to (=)

Check ✓

Write the numbers. Circle >, <, or =.

1 53 (>) 46

2 ____ (> < =) ____

3 ____ (= < >) ____

4 ____ (> = <) ____

Think About It Number Sense

Which number is greater, 46 or 64? How do you know?

Write >, <, or =.

Compare the tens first!

⑤ 21 ⊙> 14   28 ◯ 82   73 ◯ 68

⑥ 90 ◯ 86   57 ◯ 61   43 ◯ 43

⑦ 39 ◯ 95   84 ◯ 84   65 ◯ 56

⑧ 6 ◯ 36   99 ◯ 100   49 ◯ 35

Write a number that makes the statement true.

⑨ ____ < 41   77 = ____   100 > ____

⑩ ____ = 16   ____ > 80   ____ > 25

Problem Solving   Reasoning

What number am I?

⑪ My tens digit is 2 more
than my ones digit.
I am less than 100.
I am greater than 89.

____

⑫ My ones digit is
double my tens digit.
I am less than 42.
I am greater than 30.

____

Home Connection Your child compared numbers using >, <, and =.
Home Activity Select pairs of two-digit numbers for your child to compare.

Circle groups of ten. Count the tens and ones.
Write the numbers.

1 _____ tens and _____ ones is _____ in all.

Write the number of tens and ones.

2

Tens	Ones

_____ tens _____ ones =

3 Use groups of ten to make 80.

Tens	Tens	Total
0	8	80
	7	80
2		80
3	5	
		80
6		
		80
8		

Write the number.

4 eleven _____

seventy-nine _____

Write the number word.

5 68 _____

13 _____

80 _____

Write >, <, or =.

6 40 ◯ 20   **7** 31 ◯ 48

100 ◯ 90   61 ◯ 16

69 ◯ 70   24 ◯ 24

Name _____

Mark the related **addition** fact.

①   **5 + 3 = 8**

5 + 2 = 7   3 + 5 = 8   8 − 5 = 3   2 + 3 = 5
Ⓐ   Ⓑ   Ⓒ   Ⓓ

Mark the fact that does not belong in the fact family.

②   12 − 5 = 7   5 + 7 = 12   12 − 7 = 5   5 + 2 = 7
Ⓐ   Ⓑ   Ⓒ   Ⓓ

Subtract.

③ $13 - 4 = \square$ **④** $\square = 11 - 3$

10   8   9   17   14   13   10   8
Ⓐ   Ⓑ   Ⓒ   Ⓓ   Ⓐ   Ⓑ   Ⓒ   Ⓓ

Add.

⑤ $9 + 8 = \square$ **⑥** $\square = 5 + 8$

17   16   15   1   12   17   3   13
Ⓐ   Ⓑ   Ⓒ   Ⓓ   Ⓐ   Ⓑ   Ⓒ   Ⓓ

Writing in Math

⑦ Write the missing number. $9 + \square = 15$

Then write a number story that tells about this number sentence.

_____

_____

_____

_____

Name _____

Learn! Algebra

You can use tens to tell **about** how many.
Find the **closest ten**.

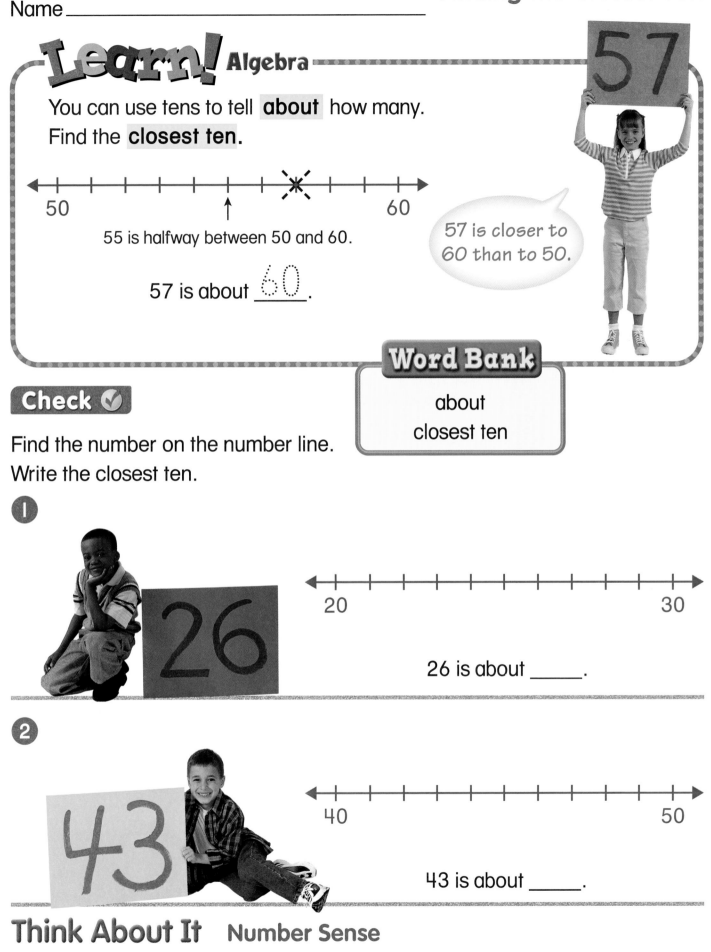

55 is halfway between 50 and 60.

57 is about __60__.

57 is closer to 60 than to 50.

Word Bank

about

closest ten

Check ✓

Find the number on the number line.
Write the closest ten.

1

20   30

26 is about _____.

2

40   50

43 is about _____.

Think About It   Number Sense

Is 45 closer to 40 or to 50?

Find the number on the number line.
Write the closest ten.

3 ←——|——|——|——|——|——|——|——|——|——|——|——→
     80   90

88 is closest to _____.

4 ←——|——|——|——|——|——|——|——|——|——|——|——|——→
     60   70

64 is closest to _____.

5 ←——|——|——|——|——|——|——|——|——|——|——|——|——→
     30   40

39 is closest to _____.

Write the closest ten.

6 _____

7 _____

8 _____

9 _____

Problem Solving Reasonableness

10 Which could be the exact number
of children?

68   55   39   22

_____ children

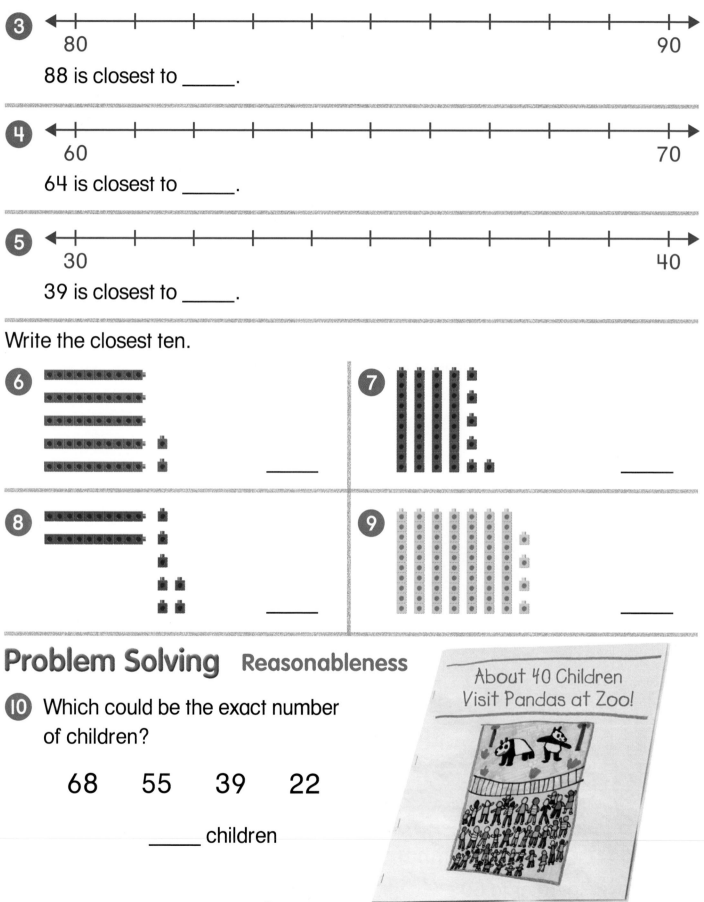

About 40 Children
Visit Pandas at Zoo!

 Home Connection Your child found the closest ten to tell about how
many. **Home Activity** Ask your child to find the closest ten for 34 and
to explain his or her thinking.

96 ninety-six

Name_____

Learn!

What is the number?

1	2	3	4	5	6	7	8	9	10
11	12	13	14	15	16	17	18	19	20
21	22	23	24	25	26	27	28	29	30
31	32	33	34	35	36	37	38	39	40
41	42	43	44	45	46	47	48	49	50
51	52	53	54	55	56	57	58	59	60
61	62	63	64	65	66	67	68	69	70
71	72	73	74	75	76	77	78	79	80
81	82	83	84	85	86	87	88	89	90
91	92	93	94	95	96	97	98	99	100

Use the hundred chart to help you.

One **before** 56 is __55__.

One **after** 53 is __54__.

__46__ is **between** 45 and 47.

Word Bank

before

after

between

Check ✓

Write the missing numbers.
Answer the questions.

1

16	
27	28
37	39

One after 16 is __17__.

One before 28 is _____.

The number between 37 and 39 is _____.

2

	74
82	84
92	

One before 74 is _____.

One after 92 is _____.

The number between 82 and 84 is _____.

Think About It   Number Sense

Use the words **before**, **after**, and **between** to describe 47.

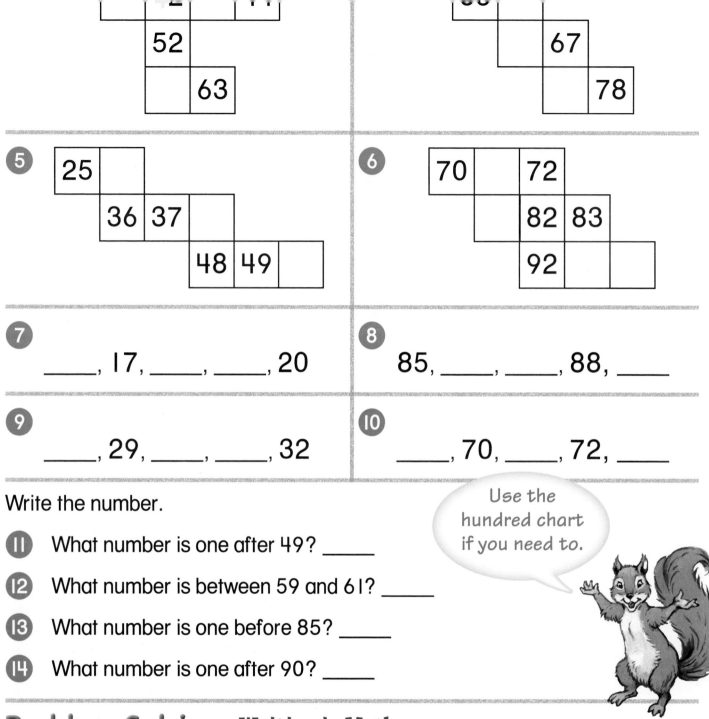

52	
	63

67	
	78

5

25		
36	37	
	48	49

6

70		72
	82	83
	92	

7 ____, 17, ____, ____, 20

8 85, ____, ____, 88, ____

9 ____, 29, ____, ____, 32

10 ____, 70, ____, 72, ____

Write the number.

Use the hundred chart if you need to.

11 What number is one after 49? _____

12 What number is between 59 and 61? _____

13 What number is one before 85? _____

14 What number is one after 90? _____

Problem Solving   Writing in Math

15  Use the words **one greater than** and **one less than** to describe the number between 51 and 53.

© Pearson Education, Inc.

 Home Connection Your child identified which numbers come before, after, and between given numbers. **Home Activity** Ask your child to select a number—1 to 99—and to describe it by using *before, after,* and *between.*

Name ________________________________

Skip Counting on the Hundred Chart

Learn! Algebra

Skip counting makes **patterns** on the hundred chart.
What pattern do you see?

1	2	(3)	4	5	(6)	7	8	(9)	10
11	(12)	13	14	(15)	16	17	(18)	19	20
(21)	22	23	(24)	25	26	(27)	28	29	(30)
31	32	(33)	34	35	(36)	37	38	(39)	40
41	(42)	43	44	(45)	46	47	(48)	49	50
(51)	52	53	(54)	55	56	(57)	58	59	(60)
61	62	(63)	64	65	(66)	67	68	(69)	70
71	(72)	73	74	(75)	76	77	(78)	79	80
(81)	82	83	(84)	85	86	(87)	88	89	(90)
91	92	(93)	94	95	(96)	97	98	(99)	100

I circled the skip counts by 3s.

Word Bank

skip counting
pattern

Check

1. Finish coloring skip counts by 2s.
2. Circle skip counts by 4s.

1	2	3	(4)	5	6	7	8	9	10
11	12	13	14	15	16	17	18	19	20
21	22	23	24	25	26	27	28	29	30
31	32	33	34	35	36	37	38	39	40
41	42	43	44	45	46	47	48	49	50
51	52	53	54	55	56	57	58	59	60
61	62	63	64	65	66	67	68	69	70
71	72	73	74	75	76	77	78	79	80
81	82	83	84	85	86	87	88	89	90
91	92	93	94	95	96	97	98	99	100

Think About It Reasoning

Look at the chart. What patterns do you see?

Practice

3 Finish coloring skip counts by 5s.

4 Circle skip counts by 10s.

5 What patterns do you see with skip counts by 5s and 10s?

_____

_____

_____

1	2	3	4	5	6	7	8	9	10
11	12	13	14	15	16	17	18	19	20
21	22	23	24	25	26	27	28	29	30
31	32	33	34	35	36	37	38	39	40
41	42	43	44	45	46	47	48	49	50
51	52	53	54	55	56	57	58	59	60
61	62	63	64	65	66	67	68	69	70
71	72	73	74	75	76	77	78	79	80
81	82	83	84	85	86	87	88	89	90
91	92	93	94	95	96	97	98	99	100

Problem Solving   Number Sense

6 Count by 2s. 2, 4, 6, 8, ____, ____, ____, ____

7 Count by 3s. 12, 15, 18, 21, ____, ____, ____, ____

8 Count by 5s. 30, 35, 40, 45, ____, ____, ____, ____

9 Count by 10s. 10, 20, 30, 40, ____, ____, ____, ____

10 Count backward by 2s. 20, 18, 16, 14, ____, ____, ____, ____

11 Count backward by 3s. 60, 57, 54, 51, ____, ____, ____, ____

12 Count backward by 5s. 50, 45, 40, 35, ____, ____, ____, ____

13 Count backward by 10s. 100, 90, 80, 70, ____, ____, ____, ____

Home Connection Your child learned that skip counting makes number patterns. **Home Activity** Ask your child to skip count by 2s and 4s, forward and backward, using the hundred chart.

Name _____

Learn! Algebra

If all parts of a number match, the number is **even**.

6

_3_ _3_

6 is an ___even___ number.

If one part of a number has no match, the number is **odd**.

7

_3_ _4_

7 is an ___odd___ number.

Word Bank

even

odd

Check ✓

Write each part of the number.
Is the number odd or even?
Draw objects to show the number if you need to.

❶ 15   _7_ _8_

15 is an ___odd___ number.

❷ 14   ___ ___

14 is an _____ number.

❸ 17   ___ ___

17 is an _____ number.

❹ 18   ___ ___

18 is an _____ number.

Think About It   Number Sense

If you add two odd numbers, will the sum be odd or even?
Explain.

Practice

5 Circle the even numbers.

6 The ones digit in an even number can be
2 _____.

7 The ones digit in an odd number can be
_____.

1	(2)	3	(4)	5	6	7	8	9	10
11	12	13	14	15	16	17	18	19	20
21	22	23	24	25	26	27	28	29	30
31	32	33	34	35	36	37	38	39	40
41	42	43	44	45	46	47	48	49	50
51	52	53	54	55	56	57	58	59	60

Circle the numbers that are odd.

8 27   28   29   30

Circle the numbers that are even.

9 33   52   66   41

Write **even** or **odd**.

10 16 _____   34 _____   49 _____

11 71 _____   82 _____   57 _____

12 28 _____   100 _____   95 _____

Problem Solving   Algebra

13 The same shapes weigh the same amount. How much does each solid figure weigh?

25 pounds   **20 pounds**

⬜ weighs _____ pounds.

⬛ weighs _____ pounds.

Home Connection Your child learned about odd and even numbers.
Home Activity Say a number from 1 to 100 and ask your child to tell you whether it is odd or even. Then ask, "How do you know?"

Name _____

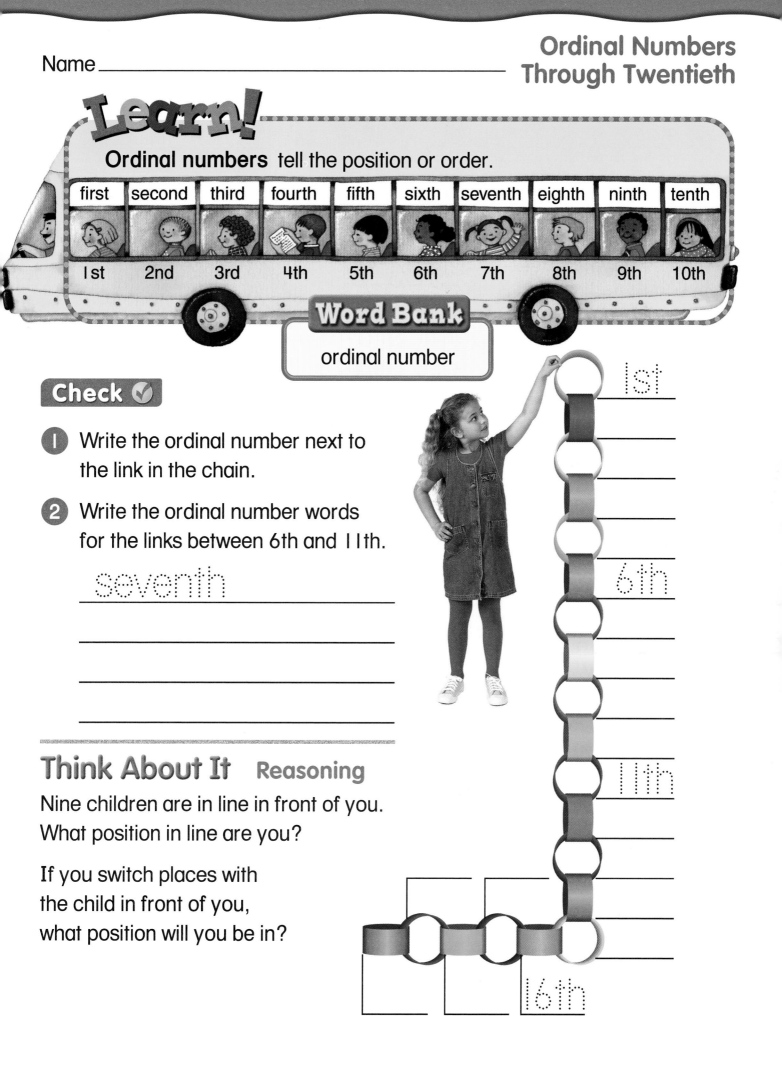

Learn!

Ordinal numbers tell the position or order.

first	second	third	fourth	fifth	sixth	seventh	eighth	ninth	tenth
1st	2nd	3rd	4th	5th	6th	7th	8th	9th	10th

Word Bank

ordinal number

Check ✓

1 Write the ordinal number next to the link in the chain.

2 Write the ordinal number words for the links between 6th and 11th.

seventh

_____

_____

_____

Think About It   Reasoning

Nine children are in line in front of you. What position in line are you?

If you switch places with the child in front of you, what position will you be in?

1st

6th

11th

16th

Use the pencils to solve. Write the letter or number.

A B C D E F G H I J K L M N O P Q R S T

| | | | | | | | | | | | | | | | | | | |

1st   10th   20th

3 The sixth pencil is F____.

4 The 3rd pencil is ____.

5 The second pencil is ____.

6 The tenth pencil is ____.

7 The 17th pencil is ____.

8 The 15th pencil is ____.

9 How many pencils are before the 12th pencil? ____

10 How many pencils are after the 15th pencil? ____

11 How many pencils are before the 20th pencil? ____

12 How many pencils are after the 11th pencil? ____

Mark your answers on the bottle caps.

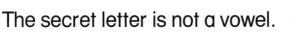

13 Write an **X** on the fifth bottle cap.

14 Circle the tenth bottle cap.

15 Write a ✓ on the 14th bottle cap.

16 Put a box around the 18th bottle cap.

Problem Solving   Reasonableness

Solve the riddle.

17 The secret letter comes after the second letter.
It comes before the 6th letter.
This letter is not the letter C.
The secret letter is not a vowel.

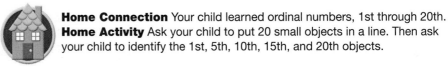

What is the secret letter? ____

© Pearson Education, Inc.

Home Connection Your child learned ordinal numbers, 1st through 20th.
Home Activity Ask your child to put 20 small objects in a line. Then ask your child to identify the 1st, 5th, 10th, 15th, and 20th objects.

Use Data from a Chart

Learn!

What is the secret number?

Cross out numbers on the chart that do not fit each clue.

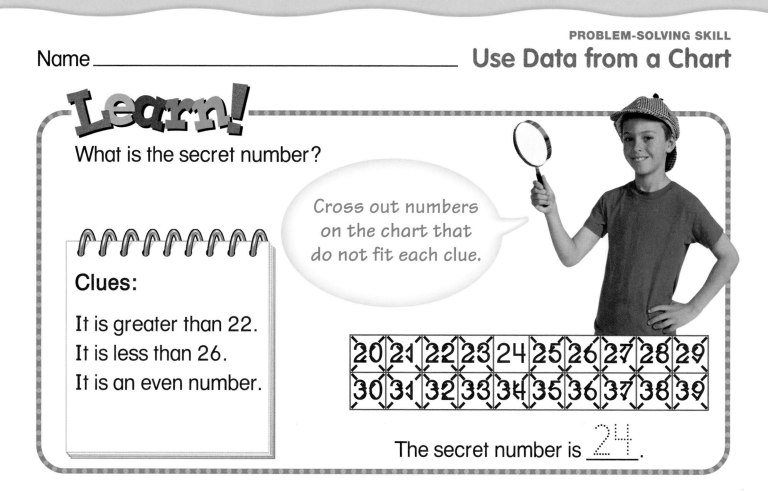

Clues:

It is greater than 22.
It is less than 26.
It is an even number.

The secret number is __24__.

Check ✓

Use clues to find the secret number.
Cross out the numbers on the chart
that do not fit the clues.

1. It is less than 40.
   It is more than 31.
   It has 3 in the ones place.

30	31	32	33	34	35	36	37	38	39
40	41	42	43	44	45	46	47	48	49

   The secret number is _____.

2. It is greater than 67.
   It is less than 70.
   It is an odd number.

60	61	62	63	64	65	66	67	68	69
70	71	72	73	74	75	76	77	78	79

   The secret number is _____.

Think About It   Reasoning

How does using clues help you find the answer?

Use clues to find the secret number.

3 It is less than 53.
It has 5 in the tens place.
It is an odd number.

40	41	42	43	44	45	46	47	48	49
50	51	52	53	54	55	56	57	58	59
60	61	62	63	64	65	66	67	68	69

The secret number is _____.

4 It is greater than 69.
It has 7 ones.

50	51	52	53	54	55	56	57	58	59
60	61	62	63	64	65	66	67	68	69
70	71	72	73	74	75	76	77	78	79

The secret number is _____.

5 It has 8 tens.
It is greater than 86.
It is an even number.

70	71	72	73	74	75	76	77	78	79
80	81	82	83	84	85	86	87	88	89
90	91	92	93	94	95	96	97	98	99

The secret number is _____.

Writing in Math

6 Choose a secret number
from the chart. Write 3 clues.
Ask a friend to find your
secret number.

70	71	72	73	74	75	76	77	78	79
80	81	82	83	84	85	86	87	88	89
90	91	92	93	94	95	96	97	98	99

Clues: _____

_____

_____

Home Connection Your child used clues to help find a secret number.
Home Activity Give your child 6 number choices and 3 clues. Ask your
child to select the secret number from the 6 choices.

Find the number on the number line.
Write the closest ten.

1

30 ————————————————————————————— 40

37 is closest to _____ .

Use clues to find the secret number.

2 It is less than 60.
It is more than 57.
It is an even number.

| 50 | 51 | 52 | 53 | 54 | 55 | 56 | 57 | 58 | 59 |
| 60 | 61 | 62 | 63 | 64 | 65 | 66 | 67 | 68 | 69 |

The secret number is _____ .

3 Circle 55. Beginning with 55, circle skip counts by 5s.

4 Write an **X** on the even numbers that are circled.

5 Color the odd numbers that are circled.

51	52	53	54	55	56	57	58	59	60
61	62	63	64	65	66	67	68	69	70
71	72	73	74	75	76	77	78	79	80
81	82	83	84	85	86	87	88	89	90
91	92	93	94	95	96	97	98	99	100

Write the missing numbers.

6

21			24
	32		
	42		

7

| 56 | | 58 |
| | 77 | |

8 Write the letter for each block.

A B C D E F G H I J K L M N O P Q R S T

1st   20th

ninth block _____   18th block _____   fifth block _____

Mark the statement that is true.

1
| 15 > 51 | 47 < 37 | 19 = 18 | 68 > 63 |
| Ⓐ | Ⓑ | Ⓒ | Ⓓ |

Mark the missing number.

2 $\square + 5 = 10$

| 4 | 15 | 5 | 10 |
| Ⓐ | Ⓑ | Ⓒ | Ⓓ |

3 $7 + \square = 10$

| 17 | 3 | 2 | 1 |
| Ⓐ | Ⓑ | Ⓒ | Ⓓ |

Add.

4 $7 + 7 = \square$

| 14 | 15 | 16 | 17 |
| Ⓐ | Ⓑ | Ⓒ | Ⓓ |

5 $9 + 9 = \square$

| 16 | 17 | 18 | 0 |
| Ⓐ | Ⓑ | Ⓒ | Ⓓ |

Subtract.

6 $12 - 6 = \square$

| 18 | 6 | 5 | 7 |
| Ⓐ | Ⓑ | Ⓒ | Ⓓ |

7 $16 - 8 = \square$

| 9 | 24 | 7 | 8 |
| Ⓐ | Ⓑ | Ⓒ | Ⓓ |

Writing in Math

8 Add to find the sum. $2 + 6 + 8 = \square$

Then explain how you solved the problem.

_____

_____

_____

_____

Name _____

Read Together

Plan How to Find the Answer

To solve some math problems, you need to decide whether you will **add** or **subtract**.

1 12 children are swimming.
5 children get out of the water.
Which number sentence tells
how many children are still swimming?

Ⓐ $12 + 5 = 17$ Ⓒ $12 - 5 = 7$

Ⓑ $17 - 5 = 12$ Ⓓ $17 - 12 = 5$

Plan to **add** if you are joining two groups together.
Plan to **subtract** if you are separating two groups.
Also plan to subtract if you are comparing two groups.

What does this question ask you to do?
Find the number sentence that solves the problem.
Fill in the answer bubble.

Your Turn

Do you need to add or subtract?
Solve the problem and fill in the answer bubble.

2 Ted has 7 brown pencils and 4 green pencils.
Which number sentence tells how many pencils
he has altogether?

Ⓐ $11 - 7 = 4$ Ⓒ $4 + 3 = 7$

Ⓑ $7 - 4 = 3$ Ⓓ $7 + 4 = 11$

Home Connection Your child prepared for standardized tests by determining whether to add or subtract to solve math problems.
Home Activity Ask your child how he or she determined whether to add or subtract in Exercise 2.

Name _____

Discover Math in Your World

 Read Together

Made in the Mint

The coins we spend are made in the United States Mint.
At one time, people at the mint thought about making a coin in
the shape of a doughnut! That never happened, but the mint
did make gold coins that were worth $10, $5, and $2.50.

Silver and Gold

Compare the silver coins we use today with gold coins
that were used in the past. Use coins and bills
to help you solve each problem.

$10

$5

$2.50

1 How many half-dollars show the same amount as one

gold $2.50 coin? _____ half-dollars

How many quarters show this same amount? _____ quarters

2 Which amount of money is worth more: a gold $5 coin
or 3 dollar coins and 7 quarters? Explain your answer.

_____

_____

3 Show $10 in three different ways.

Dollar	Half-Dollar	Quarter	Dime
5	4		
4			
3			

 **Take It to the NET**
Video and Activities
www.scottforesman.com

Home Connection Your child solved problems by comparing the values
of coins used today with the values of gold coins used in the past.
Home Activity Ask your child to tell you three ways to show the same
amount as a gold coin worth $2.50 using dollars, half-dollars, and quarters.

© Pearson Education, Inc.

Name _____

Circle groups of ten. Count the tens and ones. Write the numbers.

1 ❋❋❋❋❋❋❋❋❋
_____ tens and _____ ones is _____ in all.

Write <, >, or =.

2 4 ◯ 6

53 ◯ 27

81 ◯ 84

Draw lines to match the numbers.

3 16   sixty-one

61   sixteen

Tens	Ones
6	1

Tens	Ones
1	6

4 Use groups of ten to make 30. Write the missing numbers.

Tens	Tens	Total
0	3	30
		30
		30
		30

Find the number on the number line. Write the closest ten.

5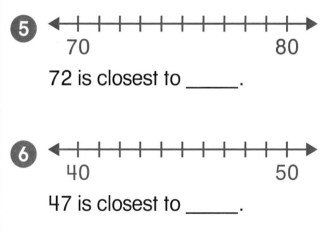
70   80
72 is closest to _____.

6
40   50
47 is closest to _____.

Use clues to find the secret number.

7 It is greater than 70.
It is less than 74.
It is an even number.
The secret number is _____.

61	62	63	64	65	66	67	68	69	70
71	72	73	74	75	76	77	78	79	80
81	82	83	84	85	86	87	88	89	90

8 Write the missing numbers on the chart.

9 The number between 79 and 81 is _____.

10 Circle the odd numbers in the third row.

11 Begin with 72 and skip count by 2s. Write an **X** on each of these numbers.

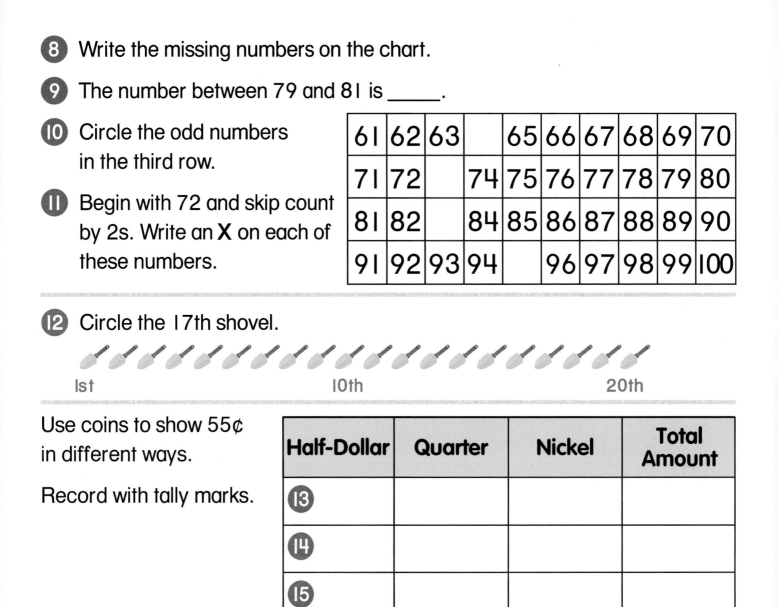

61	62	63		65	66	67	68	69	70
71	72		74	75	76	77	78	79	80
81	82		84	85	86	87	88	89	90
91	92	93	94		96	97	98	99	100

12 Circle the 17th shovel.

1st   10th   20th

Use coins to show 55¢ in different ways.

Record with tally marks.

Half-Dollar	Quarter	Nickel	Total Amount
13			
14			
15			

Draw coins from the greatest to the least value.
Count on to find the total amount.

16

				Total Amount
_____	_____	_____	_____	

Draw the coins you would get for change.
Write the amount of change.

	Price:	You give:	You get:	Change:
17	92¢	$1.00	92¢	

Read Together

It's All in Your Head

Written by Cal Q. Late Illustrated by Martha Avilés

This Math Storybook belongs to

_____

Carlos helped his father at the flea market.

A man bought a cup and saucer for **30** cents.

He gave Carlos two quarters.

Carlos knew that he owed the man change.

"Oh, no! I forgot to bring a pencil and paper," said Carlos.

"Use your head," said Papi.

"How much money did the man give you?"

"Two quarters," said Carlos. "He gave me **50** cents."

"That's right," said Papi. "How many dimes make **50** cents?"

"**5** dimes make **50** cents," said Carlos.

"And **5** dimes take away **3** dimes is **2** dimes. That means that I owe the man **20** cents in change."

Carlos turned to the man.

"The cup and saucer cost **30** cents.
You gave me **50** cents.
50 take away **30** is **20**.

"So here is your cup and saucer,
and your **20** cents in change."

A woman bought a set of salt-and-pepper shakers for **55** cents. She gave Carlos two quarters and a dime.

"Can you give the lady the correct change?" asked Papi.

"Sure!" said Carlos. "It's all in my head."

"That's my boy!" said Papi.

4F

Dear Family,

Today my class started Chapter 4, **Mental Math: Addition and Subtraction.** I will learn how to use models for tens and ones, mental math, and estimation to add and subtract two-digit numbers. And I will learn how to add on to a number to make the nearest ten and even 100! Here are some of the math words I will be learning and some things we can do to help me with my math.

Love,

_____

Math Activity to Do at Home

Play "Moving on Up." Give your child a number between 1 and 99 and challenge him or her to add on to that number to "move on up" to the next-higher ten (e.g., 10, 20, 30—or even 100). Ask your child to write each answer as a number sentence (e.g., $33 + 7 = 40$).

Books to Read Together

Reading math stories reinforces concepts. Look for these titles in your local library:

A Fair Bear Share
By Stuart J. Murphy
(HarperCollins, 1997)

One Hundred Hungry Ants
By Elinor J. Pinczes
(Scholastic, 1994)

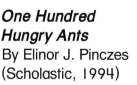

Take It to the NET
More Activities
www.scottforesman.com

My New Math Words

Let's see. 45 and 3 more tens. That's 55, 65, 75— the sum is 75.

mental math Use this strategy when estimating or when working with numbers that end in 0 or 5.

estimate To find an answer that is close to an exact answer.

pattern One kind of pattern is a repeating pattern: one in which a central unit, or part, is repeated again and again. A numeric repeating pattern:

$$5 + 7 = 12$$
$$12 + 7 = 19$$
$$19 + 7 = 26$$
$$\vdots$$
and so on

Spin for Change

How to Play

1. Put one marker on **FREE**. Put your other markers on one of the $1.00 bills.
2. Take turns spinning. Name the object and its cost.
3. Pretend that you are paying for the object with your $1.00 bill. Place a marker on the square that shows the correct change.
4. The first player to get 3 markers in a straight line is the winner.

20¢	75¢	30¢
50¢	FREE	70¢
45¢	90¢	5¢

Change Due

30¢ 95¢
80¢ 25¢
70¢ 55¢
10¢ 50¢

Player 1

Player 2

Name _____

Learn!

How many cubes are there in all?
You can use cubes or **mental math**.

Think:
Start at 43.
Count on 53, 63, or
40 and 20 is 60 and
3 more is 63.

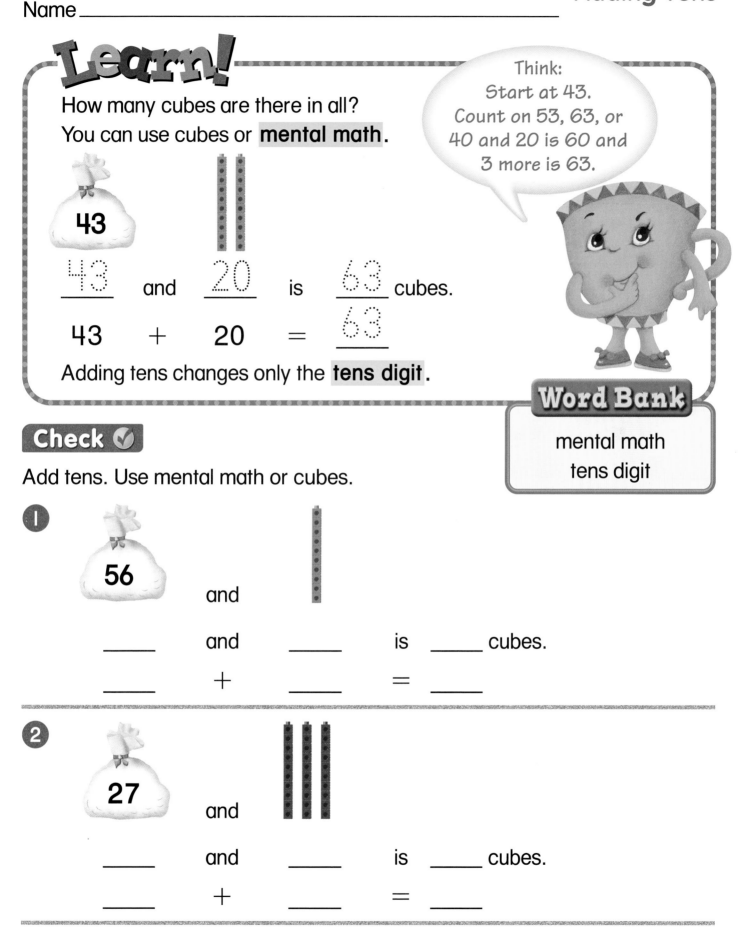

43

43   and   20   is   63   cubes.

43   +   20   =   63

Adding tens changes only the **tens digit**.

Word Bank

mental math
tens digit

Check ✓

Add tens. Use mental math or cubes.

1.   56   and

____   and   ____   is   ____ cubes.

____   +   ____   =   ____

2.   27   and

____   and   ____   is   ____ cubes.

____   +   ____   =   ____

Think About It   Number Sense

What number and 40 is 83? Explain.

Practice

Add tens. Use mental math or cubes.

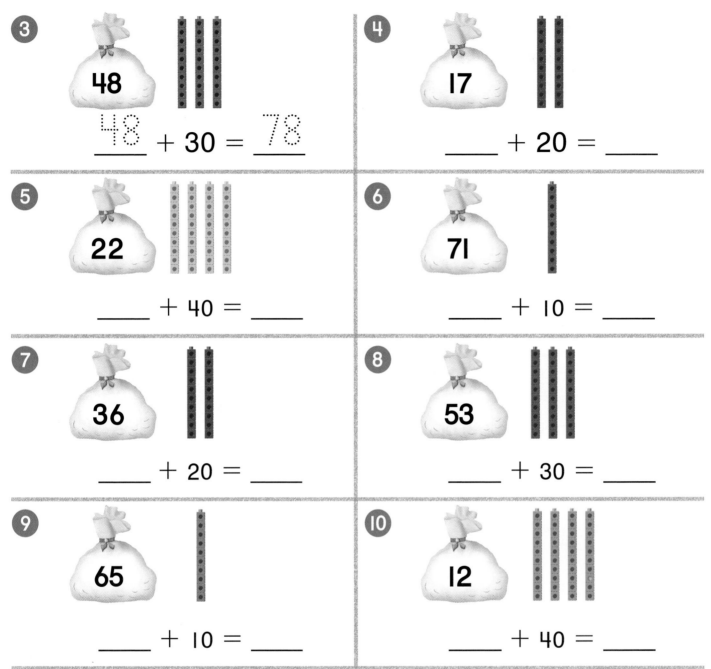

3   48 $\underline{48} + 30 = \underline{78}$

4   17   ____ + 20 = ____

5   22   ____ + 40 = ____

6   71   ____ + 10 = ____

7   36   ____ + 20 = ____

8   53   ____ + 30 = ____

9   65   ____ + 10 = ____

10   12   ____ + 40 = ____

Problem Solving   Number Sense

11   Aidan had 27¢ in his bank.
Grandpa gave him 10¢ a day on Monday,
Tuesday, and Wednesday. How much
money does Aidan have now?

____

© Pearson Education, Inc.

Home Connection Your child added multiples of ten to given numbers by using mental math and/or by using cubes. **Home Activity** Ask your child to tell you the sums of 63 and 30, 27 and 20, and 45 and 10. *(93, 47, 55)*

Name_____

Learn!

How many cubes are there in all?
You can use cubes or mental math.

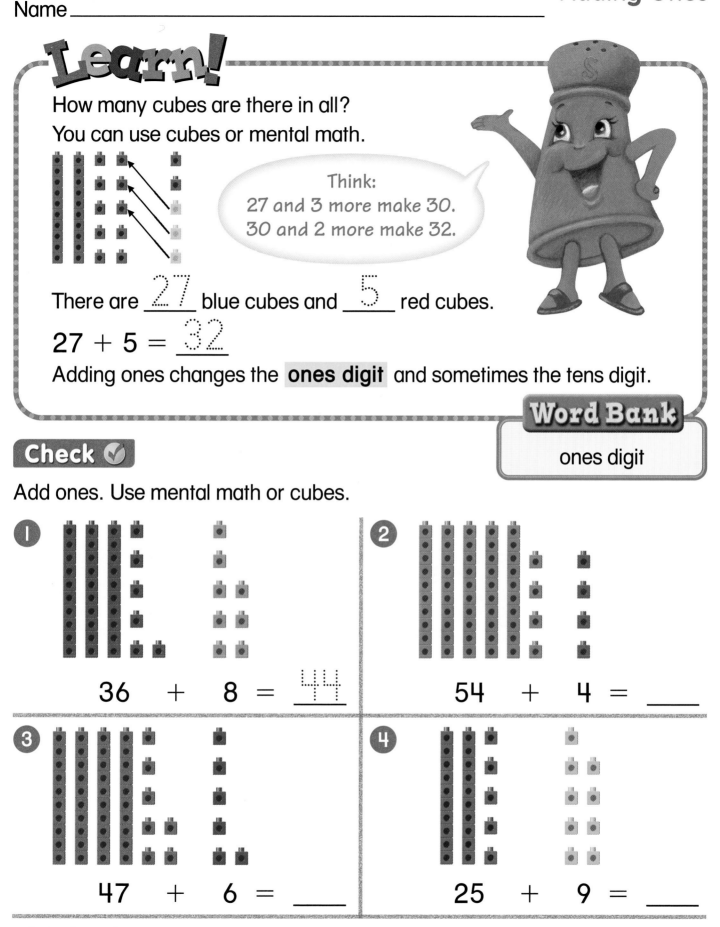

Think:
27 and 3 more make 30.
30 and 2 more make 32.

There are __27__ blue cubes and __5__ red cubes.

$27 + 5 = $ __32__

Adding ones changes the **ones digit** and sometimes the tens digit.

Word Bank

ones digit

Check ✓

Add ones. Use mental math or cubes.

❶ $36 + 8 = $ __44__

❷ $54 + 4 = $ ___

❸ $47 + 6 = $ ___

❹ $25 + 9 = $ ___

Think About It   Reasoning

How does making ten help you add ones?

Add ones. Use mental math or cubes.

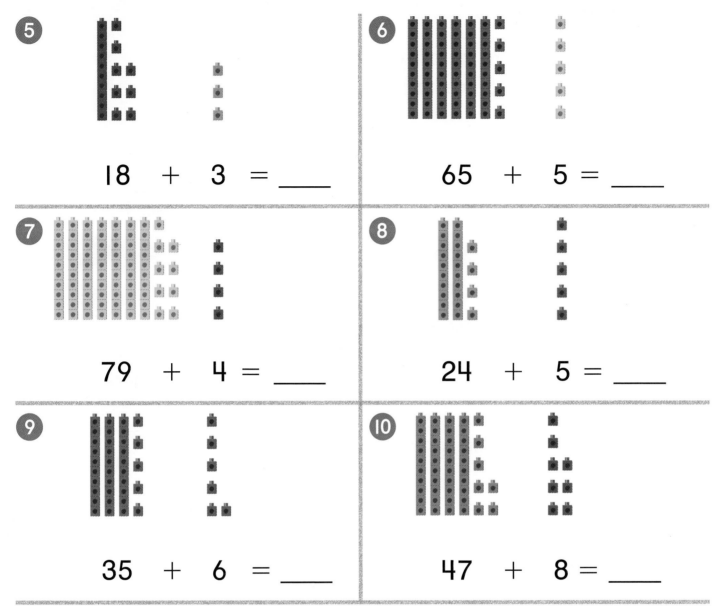

5 18 + 3 = _____

6 65 + 5 = _____

7 79 + 4 = _____

8 24 + 5 = _____

9 35 + 6 = _____

10 47 + 8 = _____

Problem Solving Algebra

Circle the weights that answer the question.

11 Which weights can you put on the scale to make it balance?

Home Connection Your child added ones to a number by using mental math and/or by using cubes. **Home Activity** Ask your child to tell you how he or she solved some of the problems on this page.

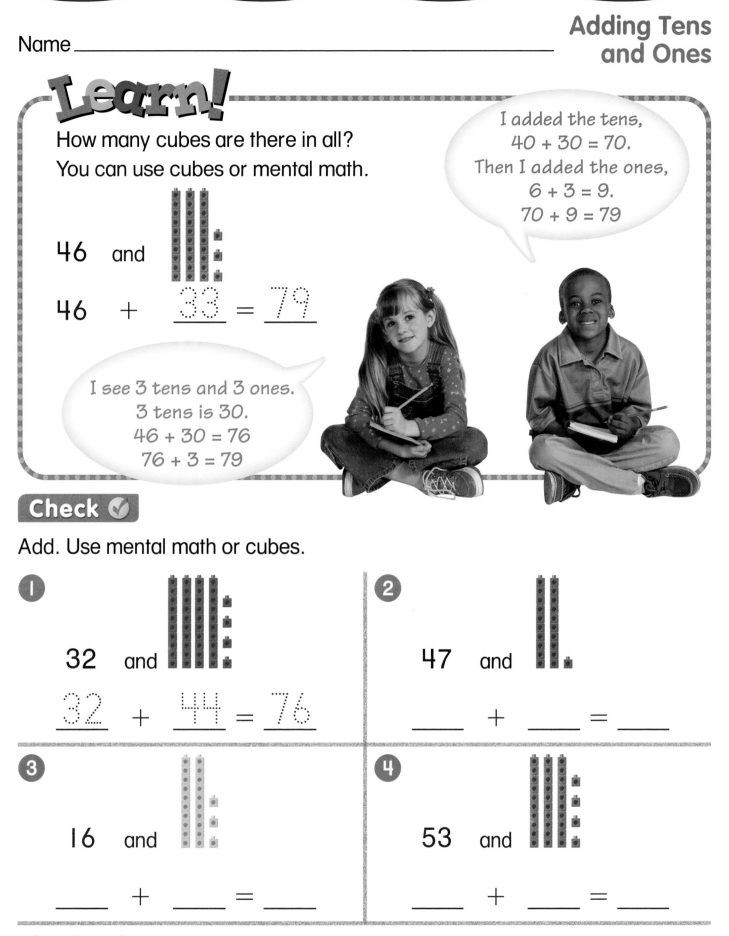

Learn!

How many cubes are there in all?
You can use cubes or mental math.

46 and

$46 + 33 = 79$

I see 3 tens and 3 ones.
3 tens is 30.
$46 + 30 = 76$
$76 + 3 = 79$

I added the tens,
$40 + 30 = 70$.
Then I added the ones,
$6 + 3 = 9$.
$70 + 9 = 79$

Check ✓

Add. Use mental math or cubes.

1 32 and

$32 + 44 = 76$

2 47 and

___ + ___ = ___

3 16 and

___ + ___ = ___

4 53 and

___ + ___ = ___

Think About It   Number Sense

Add $24 + 12$, $24 + 22$, and $24 + 32$.
What do you notice about the sums?

Add. Use mental math or cubes.

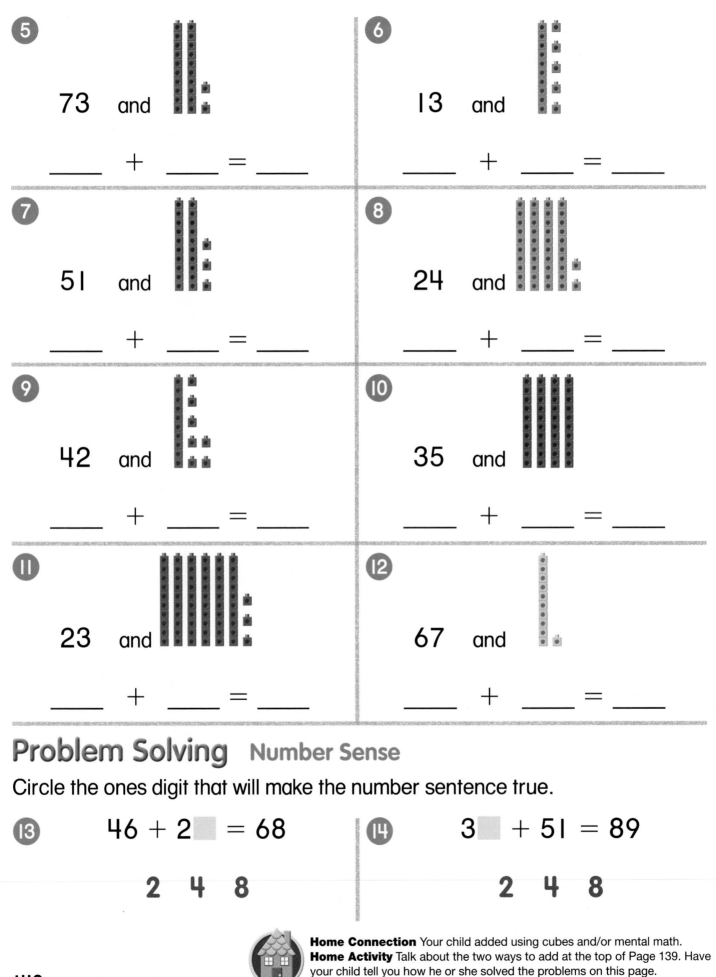

5 73 and

___ + ___ = ___

6 13 and

___ + ___ = ___

7 51 and

___ + ___ = ___

8 24 and

___ + ___ = ___

9 42 and

___ + ___ = ___

10 35 and

___ + ___ = ___

11 23 and

___ + ___ = ___

12 67 and

___ + ___ = ___

Problem Solving Number Sense

Circle the ones digit that will make the number sentence true.

13   46 + 2⬛ = 68

2   4   8

14   3⬛ + 51 = 89

2   4   8

Home Connection Your child added using cubes and/or mental math.
Home Activity Talk about the two ways to add at the top of Page 139. Have your child tell you how he or she solved the problems on this page.

Name_____

Learn! Algebra

Can I buy the top and the boat?

To **estimate**, add the tens first.
If you need to, then add the ones.

17¢

35¢

> I have 50¢.
> The boat is about 20¢.
> 20¢ and 35¢ is more
> than 50¢. I can't buy
> both toys.

Word Bank

estimate

Check ✓

Estimate. Circle **yes** or **no** to answer the question in each exercise.

49¢   33¢   15¢   34¢

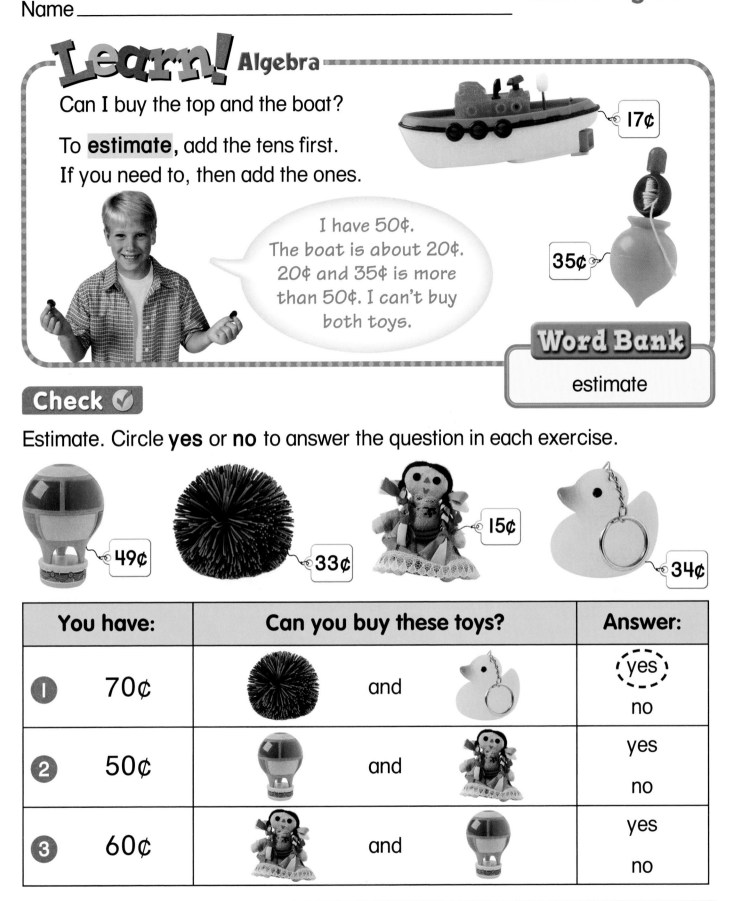

You have:	Can you buy these toys?		Answer:
❶ 70¢	(pom-pom) and	(duck)	(yes) / no
❷ 50¢	(balloon) and	(doll)	yes / no
❸ 60¢	(doll) and	(balloon)	yes / no

Think About It   Reasoning

What is the difference between estimating and adding?

44¢

16¢

35¢

22¢

46¢

Estimate.

Circle **yes** or **no** to answer the question in each exercise.

You have:	Can you buy these toys?			Answer:
4 60¢	🦀	and	🪅	yes no
5 90¢	🪅	and	🧶	yes no
6 80¢	🤖	and	🐕	yes no
7 70¢	🐕	and	🧶	yes no

Problem Solving   Reasoning

8 José has 70¢. He has exactly enough money to buy both robots. How much does the blue robot cost?

_____

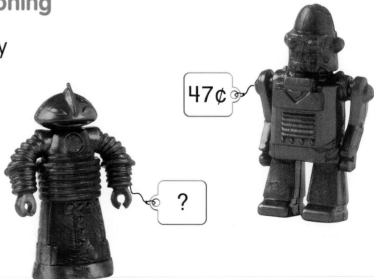

47¢

?

Home Connection Your child estimated whether a sum was more or less than a multiple of ten. **Home Activity** Choose two toys from above. Ask your child to estimate and to explain whether he or she could buy the toys with 50¢.

Add tens. Use mental math or cubes.

1 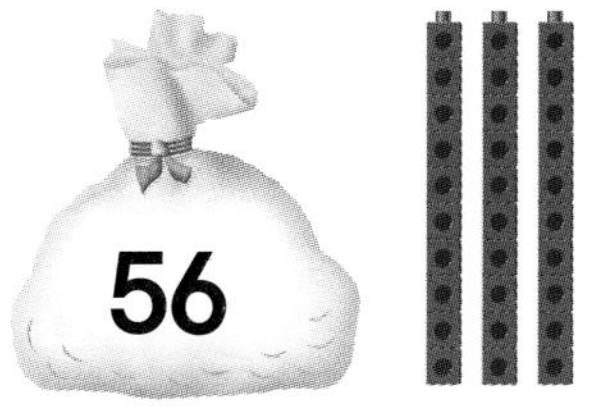 56

___ + 30 = ___

2 23

___ + 40 = ___

Add ones. Use mental math or cubes.

3 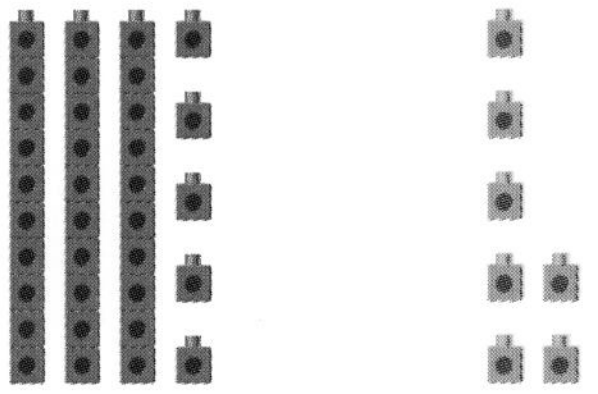 35 + 7 = ___

4 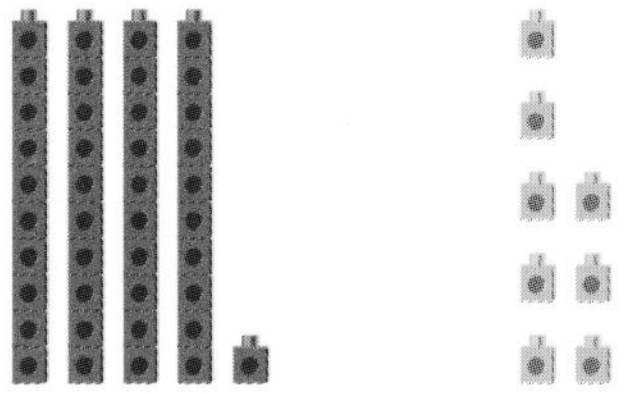 41 + 8 = ___

Add. Use mental math or cubes.

5 52 and

___ + ___ = ___

6 74 and

___ + ___ = ___

Estimate. Circle **yes** or **no** to answer the question.

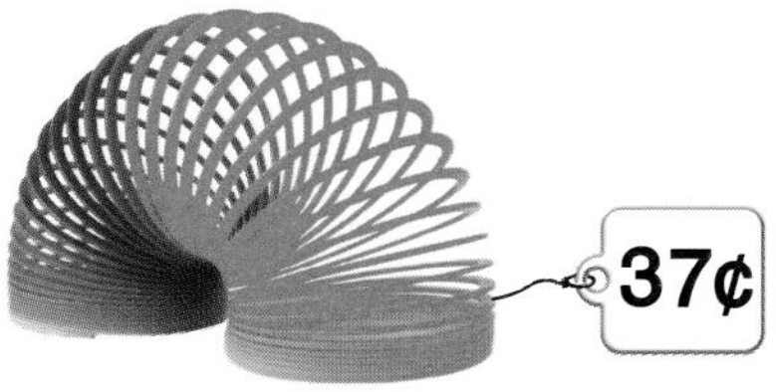

37¢ 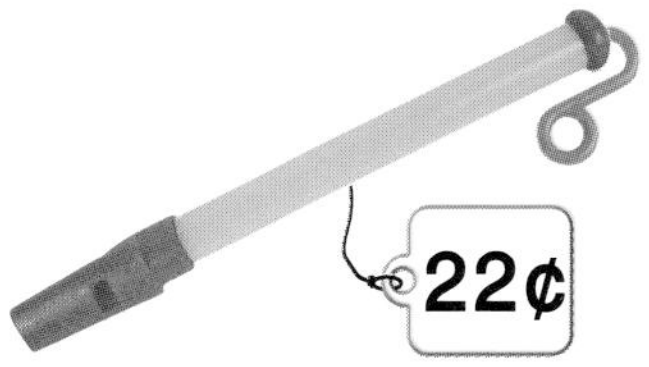   22¢

You have:	Can you buy these toys?	Answer:
7 60¢	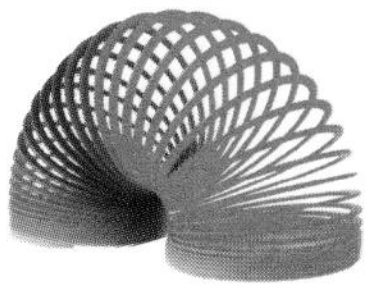 and 	yes no

Mark the number sentence that tells how many kittens there are in all.

1 6 orange kittens are playing. 3 brown kittens join them.

6   3

$3 + 3 = 6$ $6 + 3 = 9$ $6 + 6 = 12$ $6 - 3 = 3$

Ⓐ   Ⓑ   Ⓒ   Ⓓ

Mark the number that shows how many more red cubes there are.

2

5	18	4	11
Ⓐ	Ⓑ	Ⓒ	Ⓓ

Count on to find each sum.

3   5
      + 3

Ⓐ 9
Ⓑ 3
Ⓒ 8
Ⓓ 10

4   4
      + 1

Ⓐ 3
Ⓑ 5
Ⓒ 6
Ⓓ 10

Count back to find each difference.

5   10
      − 2

Ⓐ 6
Ⓑ 7
Ⓒ 12
Ⓓ 8

6   7
      − 1

Ⓐ 9
Ⓑ 8
Ⓒ 6
Ⓓ 4

Mark the missing number.

7   _____, 33, 34

30	32	33	35
Ⓐ	Ⓑ	Ⓒ	Ⓓ

8   59, _____, 61

60	58	62	63
Ⓐ	Ⓑ	Ⓒ	Ⓓ

Name_____

Learn!

Take away 30. How many cubes are left?

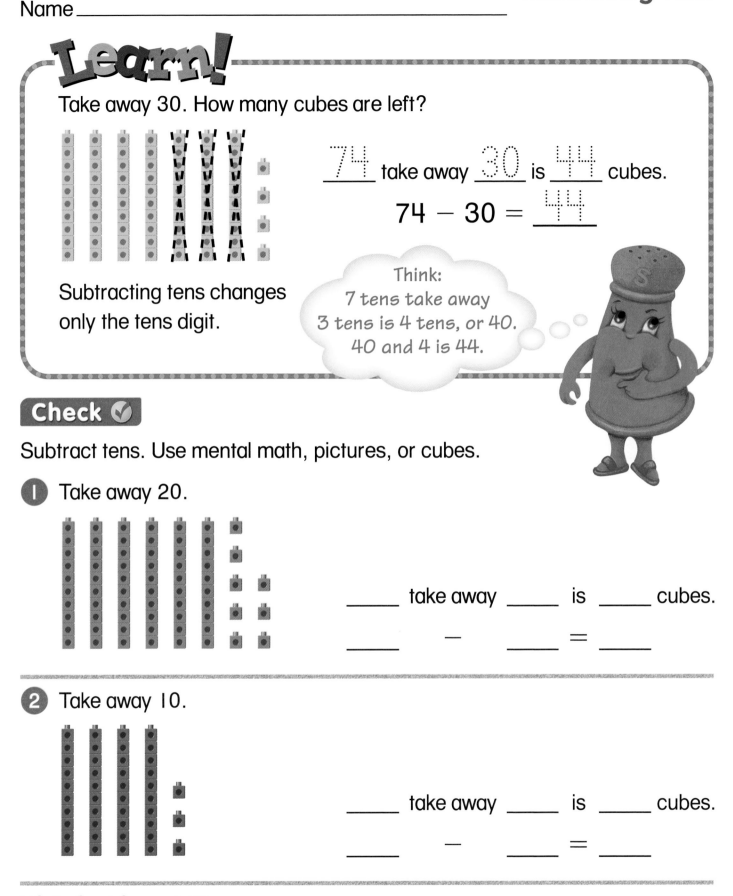

Subtracting tens changes only the tens digit.

__74__ take away __30__ is __44__ cubes.

74 − 30 = __44__

Think:
7 tens take away
3 tens is 4 tens, or 40.
40 and 4 is 44.

Check ✓

Subtract tens. Use mental math, pictures, or cubes.

1 Take away 20.

_____ take away _____ is _____ cubes.

_____ − _____ = _____

2 Take away 10.

_____ take away _____ is _____ cubes.

_____ − _____ = _____

Think About It   Number Sense

What do you take away from 88 to get 58? Explain.

Subtract tens. Use mental math, pictures, or cubes.

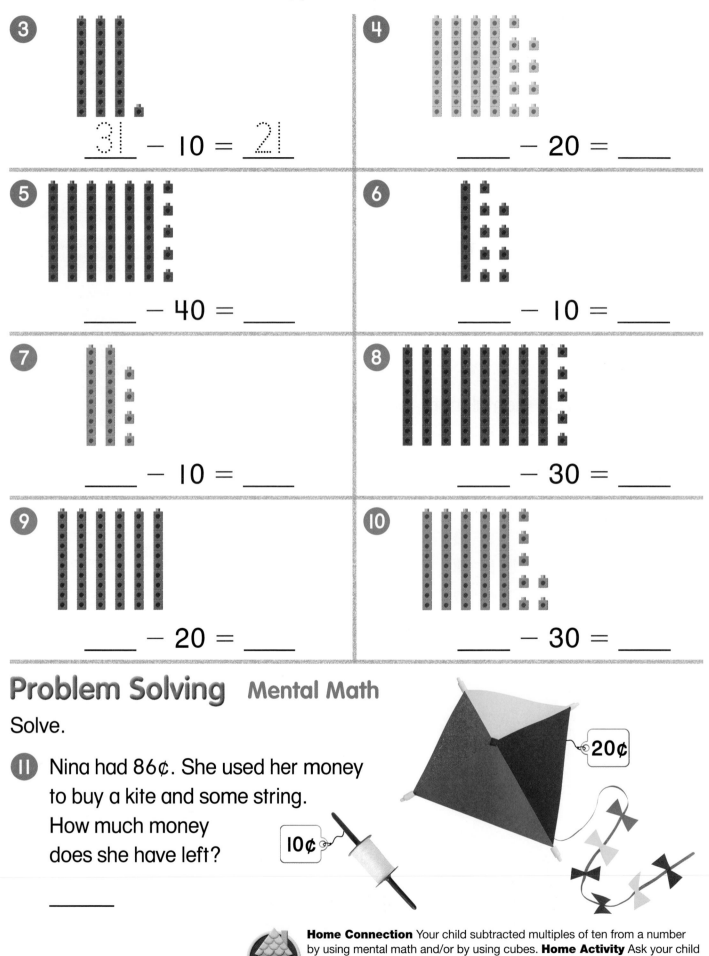

3 _31_ – 10 = _21_

4 ___ – 20 = ___

5 ___ – 40 = ___

6 ___ – 10 = ___

7 ___ – 10 = ___

8 ___ – 30 = ___

9 ___ – 20 = ___

10 ___ – 30 = ___

Problem Solving   Mental Math

Solve.

11 Nina had 86¢. She used her money to buy a kite and some string. How much money does she have left?

20¢

10¢

_____

© Pearson Education, Inc.

Home Connection Your child subtracted multiples of ten from a number by using mental math and/or by using cubes. **Home Activity** Ask your child to tell you the difference between 87 and 40, 63 and 20, and 35 and 10 (47, 43, 25).

Learn!

How many are left?

There are different ways to subtract tens and ones.

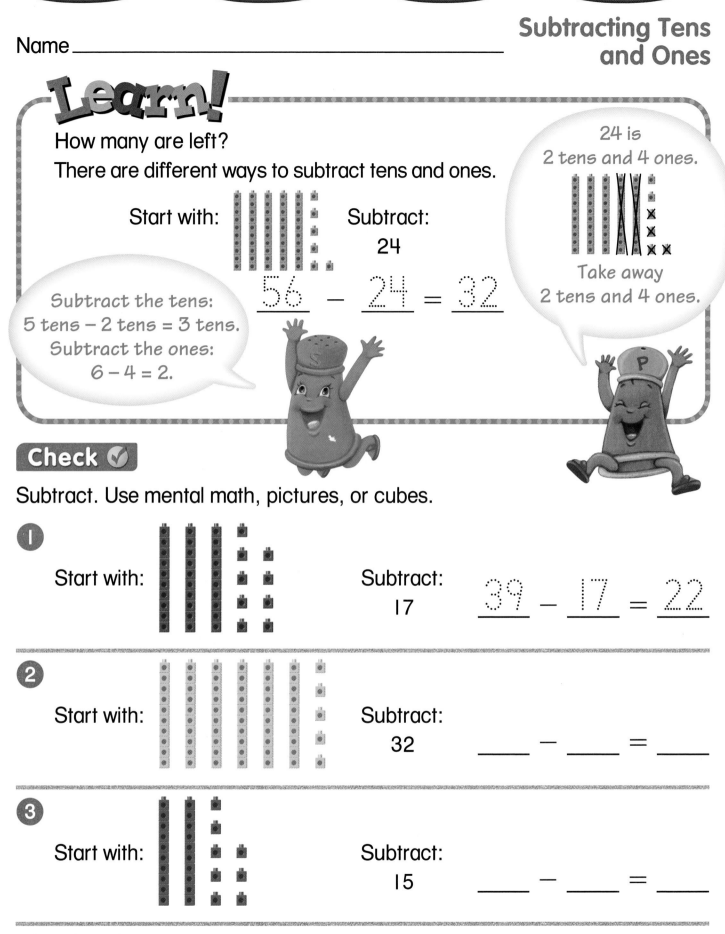

Start with: Subtract:
24

24 is
2 tens and 4 ones.

$$56 - 24 = 32$$

Subtract the tens:
5 tens − 2 tens = 3 tens.
Subtract the ones:
6 − 4 = 2.

Take away
2 tens and 4 ones.

Check ✓

Subtract. Use mental math, pictures, or cubes.

1. Start with: Subtract:
17

$$39 - 17 = 22$$

2. Start with: Subtract:
32

$$\underline{\quad} - \underline{\quad} = \underline{\quad}$$

3. Start with: Subtract:
15

$$\underline{\quad} - \underline{\quad} = \underline{\quad}$$

Think About It   Reasoning

Look for a pattern: 29 − 11 = 18, 29 − 12 = 17, 29 − 13 = 16.

What does 29 − 14 equal? How do you know?

Subtract. Use mental math, pictures, or cubes.

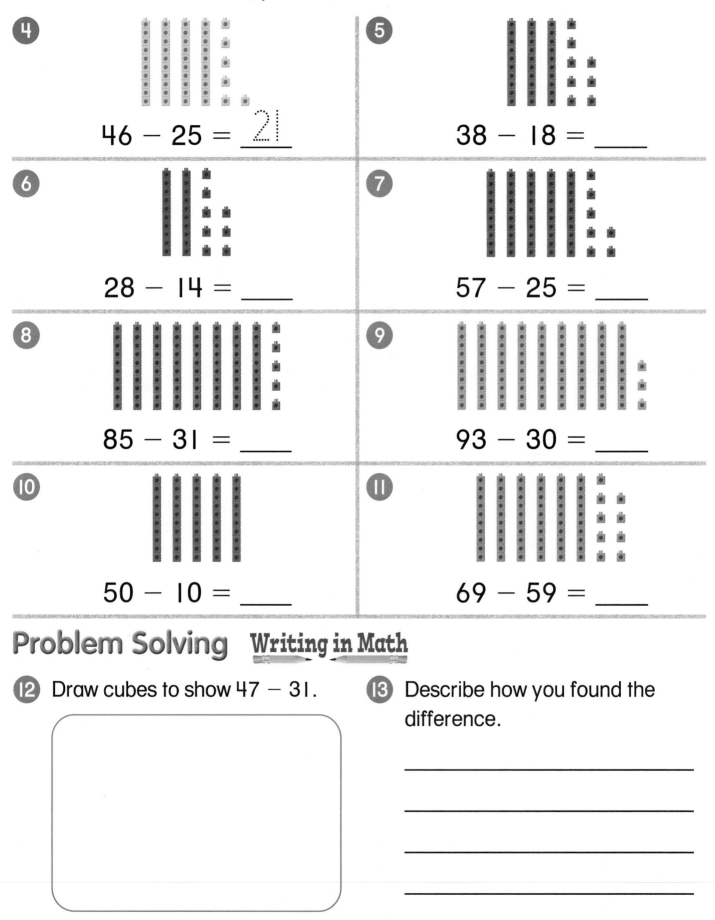

④ 46 − 25 = __21__

⑤ 38 − 18 = _____

⑥ 28 − 14 = _____

⑦ 57 − 25 = _____

⑧ 85 − 31 = _____

⑨ 93 − 30 = _____

⑩ 50 − 10 = _____

⑪ 69 − 59 = _____

Problem Solving Writing in Math

⑫ Draw cubes to show 47 − 31.

⑬ Describe how you found the difference.

_____

_____

_____

_____

Home Connection Your child subtracted tens and ones by using mental math and/or by using cubes. **Home Activity** Ask your child to tell you how he or she found some of the answers on this page.

Learn! Algebra

How much money will I have left?
Will I have **more** or **less** than 20¢ left?

To estimate, subtract the tens.
Think about the ones.

I have 50¢.
50 − 30 = 20.
So 50¢ − 33¢ will be
less than 20¢. I'll have
less than 20¢ left.

33¢

Word Bank

more

less

Check ✓

Estimate. Circle **more** or **less** to answer each question.

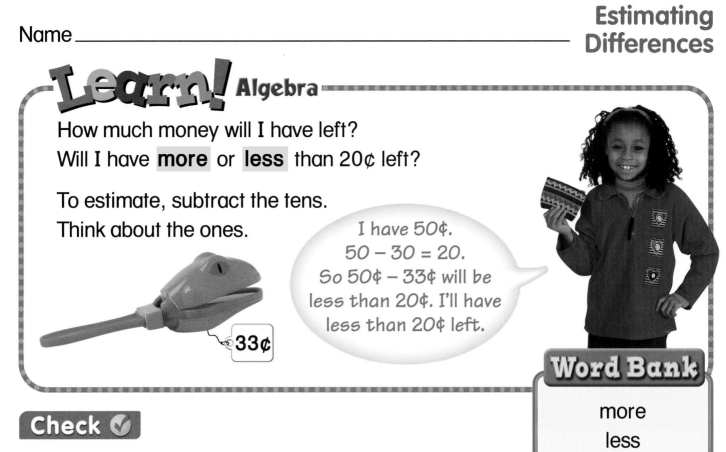

You have:	You buy:	Answer:
❶ 80¢	42¢	Will you have more or less than 30¢ left? (more) less
❷ 60¢	28¢	Will you have more or less than 40¢ left? more less
❸ 70¢	51¢	Will you have more or less than 10¢ left? more less

Think About It Reasoning

45 + 30 = 75. Is 73 − 45 more or less than 30? Explain.

Estimate. Circle **more** or **less** to complete each sentence.

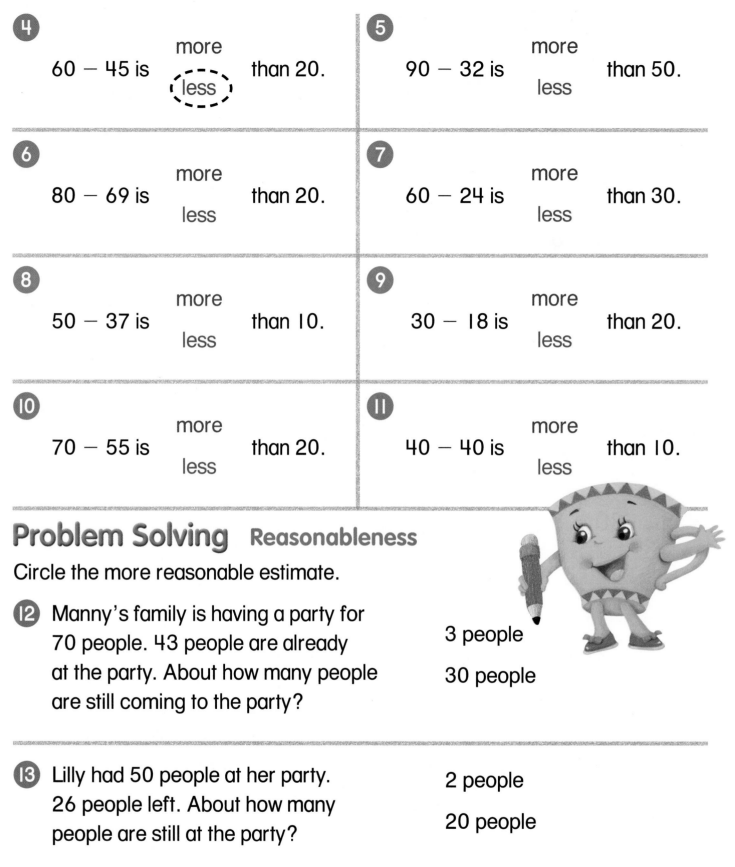

4

60 − 45 is   more   than 20.
               (less)

5

90 − 32 is   more   than 50.
               less

6

80 − 69 is   more   than 20.
               less

7

60 − 24 is   more   than 30.
               less

8

50 − 37 is   more   than 10.
               less

9

30 − 18 is   more   than 20.
               less

10

70 − 55 is   more   than 20.
               less

11

40 − 40 is   more   than 10.
               less

Problem Solving Reasonableness

Circle the more reasonable estimate.

12 Manny's family is having a party for
70 people. 43 people are already
at the party. About how many people
are still coming to the party?

3 people

30 people

13 Lilly had 50 people at her party.
26 people left. About how many
people are still at the party?

2 people

20 people

 Home Connection Your child estimated whether a difference was more or less than a multiple of 10. **Home Activity** Ask your child to estimate and explain whether 90 − 37 is more or less than 60.

Subtract tens. Use mental math, pictures, or cubes.

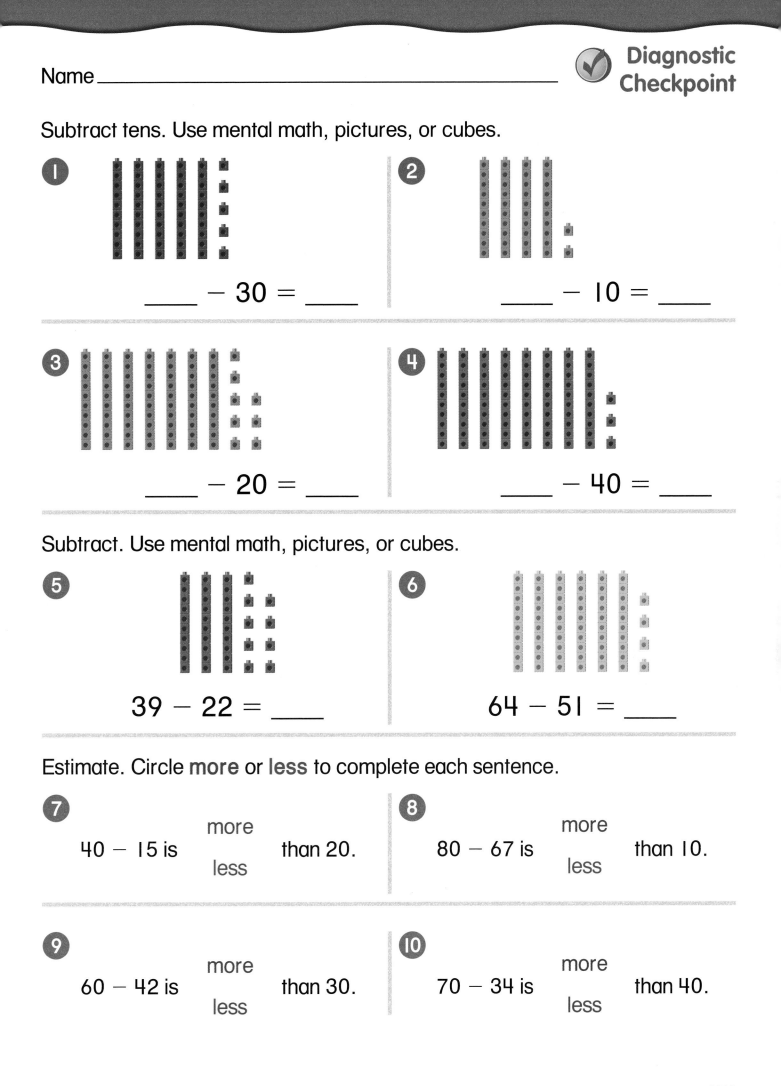

1 ___ − 30 = ___

2 ___ − 10 = ___

3 ___ − 20 = ___

4 ___ − 40 = ___

Subtract. Use mental math, pictures, or cubes.

5 39 − 22 = ___

6 64 − 51 = ___

Estimate. Circle **more** or **less** to complete each sentence.

7 40 − 15 is more / less than 20.

8 80 − 67 is more / less than 10.

9 60 − 42 is more / less than 30.

10 70 − 34 is more / less than 40.

Count backward by 5s. Mark the number that comes next.

1   50, 45, 40, 35, ___

40   34   30   25

Ⓐ   Ⓑ   Ⓒ   Ⓓ

Add.

2
$$\begin{array}{r} 9 \\ + 9 \\ \hline \end{array}$$

    Ⓐ 14
    Ⓑ 16
    Ⓒ 18
    Ⓓ 20

3
$$\begin{array}{r} 6 \\ + 6 \\ \hline \end{array}$$

    Ⓐ 11
    Ⓑ 12
    Ⓒ 13
    Ⓓ 0

4
$$\begin{array}{r} 5 \\ 7 \\ + 5 \\ \hline \end{array}$$

    Ⓐ 12
    Ⓑ 10
    Ⓒ 16
    Ⓓ 17

5
$$\begin{array}{r} 8 \\ 4 \\ + 1 \\ \hline \end{array}$$

    Ⓐ 13
    Ⓑ 12
    Ⓒ 9
    Ⓓ 14

Mark the number sentence that tells how many birds are left.

6 **There are 9 birds eating. 3 birds fly away.**

9   3

$6 - 3 = 3$ $9 - 3 = 6$ $9 - 6 = 3$ $3 - 3 = 0$

Ⓐ   Ⓑ   Ⓒ   Ⓓ

Writing in Math

7 Add to find the sum.

Then write a story about this addition sentence.

$$56 + 20 = \underline{}$$

Predict and Verify

1 Read the story of The Boy Who Cried Wolf.
Try to **predict** what will happen next.
(Count the sheep before you read the story.)

A shepherd boy thought sheep were boring.
So he decided to have some fun.

"Help! Help!" he cried. "Wolf! Wolf!"
The villagers came running to help.

When the villagers saw that there was no wolf,
they were very mad. "Stop playing tricks!" they said.
"No more tricks," agreed the shepherd boy.

2 Do you think the boy will keep his promise?

Circle **Yes** or **No.**   Yes   No

Again, the shepherd boy cried, "Wolf! Wolf!"
Again, the villagers came to help.
Again, there was no wolf.

Think About It   Reasoning

How do you think this story might end?

3 Write an ending to The Boy Who Cried Wolf.

_____

_____

_____

4 Did the wolf eat any sheep? What do you think?

Circle **Yes** or **No.**   Yes   No

5 How many sheep did the shepherd have to begin with? _____ sheep
(Check back if you don't remember.)

6 Now circle the hidden sheep in the picture below.

7 How many sheep did the wolf eat? _____ sheep

Home Connection Your child predicted the outcome of a story that involves numbers. **Home Activity** Read a story with your child. Stop from time to time to ask what might happen next.

PROBLEM-SOLVING STRATEGY
Try, Check, and Revise

Learn!

Read and Understand

Look at the four numbers in the bubbles below.
Which two of them have a sum of 50?

50

? ?

Plan and Solve

I need to add two numbers with a sum of 50.

Try: Pick two numbers: **12** and **27.**
The sum of the ones digits
must be 0 or 10.

Check: $2 + 7 = 9$,
so 12 plus 27 does not equal 50.

Revise: Pick two different numbers.

Try: Add the ones digits of **12** and **38.**

Check:

$$\underline{2} + \underline{8} = \underline{10}$$

Now add the tens digits.

$$\underline{10} + \underline{30} = \underline{40}$$

10 and 40 is $\underline{50}$,

so 12 and 38 is $\underline{50}$.

Numbers with a sum of 50

$\underline{12}$ and $\underline{38}$

_____ and _____

38

23

12

27

Look Back and Check

Try and check other number pairs.
Revise your list if needed. Make sure
the sum of the ones digits is 0 or 10
and the sum of the tens digits is 50 or 40.

Word Bank

revise

Think About It   Reasoning

You are finding two numbers with a sum of 70.
What is the sum of the ones digits?
What is the sum of the tens digits? Explain.

Find pairs of numbers with the given sum.
The sum of the ones digits must be 0 or 10.

1 19 10 30 21

Numbers with a sum of
40

__19__ and __21__

____ and ____

2 24 55 25 56

Numbers with a sum of
80

____ and ____

____ and ____

3 37 31 23 29

Numbers with a sum of
60

____ and ____

____ and ____

4 28 14 16 2

Numbers with a sum of
30

____ and ____

____ and ____

5 65 47 25 43

Numbers with a sum of
90

____ and ____

____ and ____

Home Connection Your child found pairs of numbers with a given sum.
Home Activity Write these numbers: 25, 43, 35, 17. Have your child find
two number pairs with a sum of 60. *(25 and 35, 43 and 17)*

Learn! Algebra

What **pattern** do you see?
You can use the hundred chart.

12, 17, 22, 27, _32_, _37_

The pattern rule is ___add 5___.

Look at the ones digits. What is the
pattern? The pattern is **2, 7, 2, 7, 2, 7,**
and so on. Look at the tens digits.
What is the pattern? The pattern
is **1, 1, 2, 2, 3, 3,** and so on.

1	2	3	4	5	6	7	8	9	10
11	12	13	14	15	16	17	18	19	20
21	22	23	24	25	26	27	28	29	30
31	32	33	34	35	36	37	38	39	40
41	42	43	44	45	46	47	48	49	50
51	52	53	54	55	56	57	58	59	60
61	62	63	64	65	66	67	68	69	70
71	72	73	74	75	76	77	78	79	80
81	82	83	84	85	86	87	88	89	90
91	92	93	94	95	96	97	98	99	100

Word Bank

pattern

Check ✓

What is the pattern? Write the numbers.
Use a hundred chart if you need to.

1 33, 43, 53, 63, _____, _____, _____

The pattern rule is _____.

What is the pattern in the ones digits? _____

What is the pattern in the tens digits? _____

2 69, 65, 61, 57, 53, 49, 45, 41, 37, 33, _____, _____

The pattern rule is _____.

What is the pattern in the ones digits? _____

What is the pattern in the tens digits? _____

Think About It   Number Sense

Write a series of numbers that shows a pattern rule of add 7.
Explain how you did it.

What is the pattern? Write the numbers.

3 20, 24, 28, 32, 36, _____, _____, _____, _____, _____, _____, _____,

_____, _____, _____

What is the pattern rule? _____

Look at the ones digits. What is the pattern?

_____

Look at the tens digits. What is the pattern?

_____

4 94, 88, 82, 76, 70, _____, _____, _____, _____, _____, _____, _____,

_____, _____, _____

What is the pattern rule? _____

Look at the ones digits. What is the pattern?

_____

Look at the tens digits. What is the pattern?

_____

Problem Solving Algebra

Find the pattern. Write the missing numbers.

5 25 and 10 is 35.

35 and 10 is _____.

45 and _____ is _____.

_____ and _____ is _____.

_____ and _____ is _____.

6 60 take away 10 is 50.

60 take away 20 is _____.

60 take away _____ is _____.

_____ take away _____ is _____.

_____ take away _____ is _____.

Home Connection Your child identified and extended number patterns.
Home Activity Have your child start with 7 and write the number pattern that is made by adding 4 and explain the number pattern.

Name _____

Learn! Algebra

What do I need to make 100? I have 65 cubes.

Use mental math and add on to make 100.
65 and 10 is 75.
75 and 10 is 85.
85 and 10 is 95.
95 and 5 is 100.

and ?

65 and 35 is 100.

Check ✓

Add on to find the other part of 100.
Use mental math or cubes.

1 Show 55.

and ?

55 and 45 is 100.

2 Show 75.

and ?

_____ and _____ is 100.

3 Show 15.

and ?

_____ and _____ is 100.

Think About It   Reasoning

How can you tell that 60 and 45 together
do not make 100?

Add on to find the other part of 100.
Use mental math or cubes.

④ 60 and __40__ is 100.

⑤ 30 and _____ is 100.

⑥ 85 and _____ is 100.

⑦ 5 and _____ is 100.

⑧ 50 and _____ is 100.

⑨ 25 and _____ is 100.

⑩ 45 and _____ is 100.

⑪ 80 and _____ is 100.

⑫ 10 and _____ is 100.

⑬ 35 and _____ is 100.

Problem Solving Algebra

Use mental math or cubes to solve.

⑭ If 35 and __65__ is 100,

then 100 take away 35 is __65__.

and ?

⑮ If 20 and _____ is 100,

then 100 take away 20 is _____.

and ?

⑯ If 85 and _____ is 100,

then 100 take away 85 is _____.

and ?

Home Connection Your child found the missing part of 100 by using mental math and/or by using cubes. **Home Activity** Have your child complete and explain the following: 20 and ____ is 100.

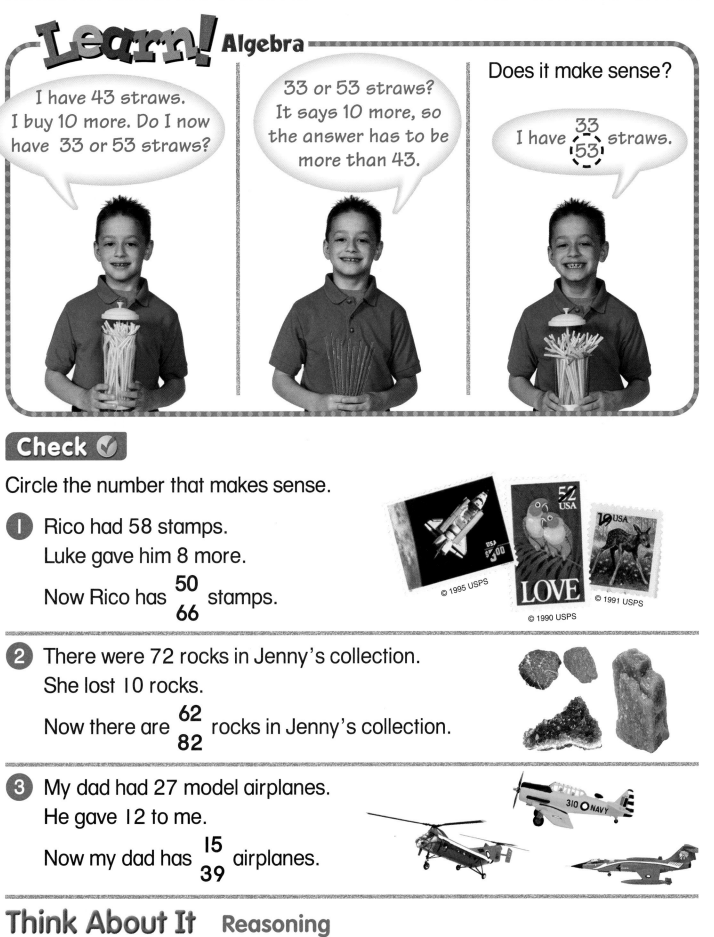

Learn! Algebra

I have 43 straws. I buy 10 more. Do I now have 33 or 53 straws?

33 or 53 straws? It says 10 more, so the answer has to be more than 43.

Does it make sense?

I have ~~33~~ (53) straws.

Check ✓

Circle the number that makes sense.

1. Rico had 58 stamps.
   Luke gave him 8 more.
   Now Rico has **50 / 66** stamps.

   © 1995 USPS
   LOVE
   © 1991 USPS
   © 1990 USPS

2. There were 72 rocks in Jenny's collection.
   She lost 10 rocks.
   Now there are **62 / 82** rocks in Jenny's collection.

3. My dad had 27 model airplanes.
   He gave 12 to me.
   Now my dad has **15 / 39** airplanes.

   310 NAVY

Think About It   Reasoning

Tell how you decided which number made sense in Exercise 3.

Circle the number that makes sense.

4 Carrie has 44 stickers.
Her friend gives her 30 more.

Now Carrie has $\begin{matrix} 14 \\ 74 \end{matrix}$ stickers.

5 Pablo had 42 marbles.
He gave 12 marbles to his brother.

Now Pablo has $\begin{matrix} 30 \\ 54 \end{matrix}$ marbles.

6 Judy read 14 books last month.
Harry read 7 books.

Together, Judy and Harry read $\begin{matrix} 7 \\ 21 \end{matrix}$ books.

7 Mom made 48 biscuits for the party.
The people ate 20 biscuits.

There were $\begin{matrix} 28 \\ 68 \end{matrix}$ biscuits left.

Visual Thinking

How many cubes are there in all? Circle your answer.

8

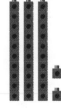 and  is  or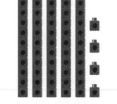

Home Connection Your child solved problems and looked back and checked to make sure the answers made sense. **Home Activity** Have your child tell you how he or she solved Exercise 4 and why the answer makes sense.

Name _____

Dorling Kindersley

THE YOUNG BASEBALL PLAYER
FOREWORD BY EDUARDO PEREZ

Do You Know...

that baseball is the top sport in the United States? It is also played in more than 100 countries around the world.

1 Baseball players usually use bats that are between 32 and 36 inches long. Write the missing numbers.

_____, 33, _____, _____, 36 inches

Fun Fact!

During a Major League game, each baseball is used for only about 6 pitches.

2 A baseball game usually lasts 9 innings. If a game lasted 12 innings, how many extra innings were played?

_____ ◯ _____ = _____ extra innings

3 At the end of a baseball game, the Reds had 4 more runs than the Blues. How many runs did the Reds have?

Scoreboard	
Blues	Reds
5	?

_____ ◯ _____ = _____

The Reds had _____ runs.

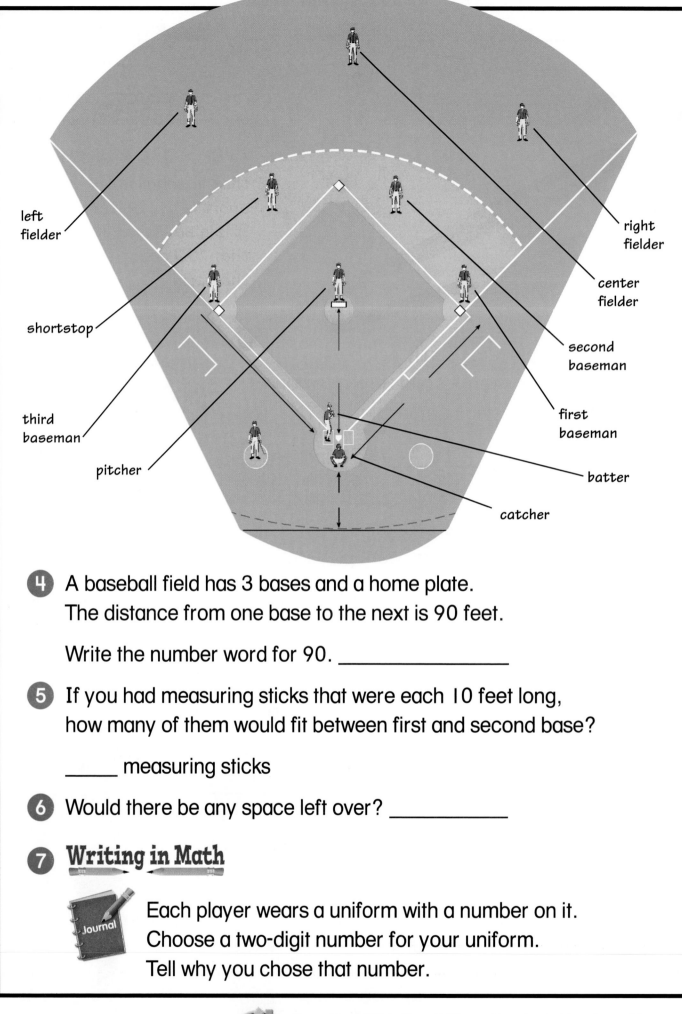

left
fielder

right
fielder

center
fielder

shortstop

second
baseman

third
baseman

first
baseman

pitcher

batter

catcher

4 A baseball field has 3 bases and a home plate.
The distance from one base to the next is 90 feet.

Write the number word for 90. _____

5 If you had measuring sticks that were each 10 feet long,
how many of them would fit between first and second base?

_____ measuring sticks

6 Would there be any space left over? _____

7 **Writing in Math**

Each player wears a uniform with a number on it.
Choose a two-digit number for your uniform.
Tell why you chose that number.

164 one hundred sixty-four

Home Connection Your child learned to solve problems by applying
his or her math skills. **Home Activity** Talk to your child about how he
or she solved the problems on these two pages.

Find pairs of numbers with a sum of 70.
The sum of the ones digits must be 0 or 10.

1 21   55   49   15

Numbers with a sum of **70**
_____ and _____
_____ and _____

What is the pattern? Write the numbers.

2 13, 18, 23, 28, _____, _____, _____, _____

What is the pattern rule? _____

Look at the ones digits. What is the pattern?

_____

Look at the tens digits. What is the pattern?

_____

Circle the number that makes sense.

3 I have 36 markers.
I buy 12 more.
Now I have 48
24 markers.

Add on to find the other part of 100.
Use mental math or cubes.

4 70 and _____ is 100.

5 45 and _____ is 100.

Add. Use doubles to help you.

1   5
      + 6

  Ⓐ 10
  Ⓑ 12
  Ⓒ 11
  Ⓓ 1

2   4
      + 3

  Ⓐ 8
  Ⓑ 7
  Ⓒ 6
  Ⓓ 1

There are 8 books in all. Mark the number that tells how many books are in the bag.

3

1 + ___ = 8

6 books	9 books	7 books	10 books
Ⓐ	Ⓑ	Ⓒ	Ⓓ

Mark the one that tells how many cubes there are.

4

Tens	Ones
4	9

Ⓐ

Tens	Ones
9	4

Ⓑ

Tens	Ones
3	9

Ⓒ

Tens	Ones
4	8

Ⓓ

Mark the total amount.

5

  Ⓐ 45¢
  Ⓑ 51¢
  Ⓒ 66¢
  Ⓓ 56¢

Mark the related addition fact.

6 7 + 3 = 10

8 + 2 = 10	3 + 7 = 10	10 − 3 = 7	7 + 4 = 11
Ⓐ	Ⓑ	Ⓒ	Ⓓ

Mark the related addition fact.

7 2 + 9 = 11

9 + 1 = 10	7 + 4 = 11	11 − 9 = 2	9 + 2 = 11
Ⓐ	Ⓑ	Ⓒ	Ⓓ

Function Tables Algebra

Think of a number. Then add 10 to it.

7 ... 17

68 ... 78

The **Start** numbers are given.

Follow the rule. Write the **Finish** numbers.

①

Add 10.

Start	Finish
7	17
27	
36	
70	

②

Add 5.

Start	Finish
10	
20	
45	
65	

③

Subtract 10.

Start	Finish
90	
80	
70	
60	

Write the rule.

④

_____

Start	23	33	75	95
Finish	13	23	65	85

⑤

_____

Start	84	64	34	19
Finish	94	74	44	29

⑥ **Writing in Math**

How did you get your answers in Exercises 4 and 5?

Home Connection Your child completed tables by adding or subtracting 5 or 10. **Home Activity** Say 10 numbers less than 90. Ask your child to add 5 to each number.

Name _____

Find Missing Parts Using a Calculator

You can use a calculator to find missing parts of numbers.
Use a calculator to complete each number sentence.

Press ON/C each time you begin.

Write the letter that matches each
missing number in the correct space below.
Then solve the riddle.

> What kind of dog likes cows?

1. | 1 | 0 | 0 | − | 75 | = | 2 | 5 |

2. | 7 | 8 | + | ___ | = | 1 | 0 | 0 |

3. | 5 | 3 | + | ___ | = | 8 | 0 |

4. | ___ | + | 3 | 5 | = | 1 | 0 | 0 |

5. | ___ | − | 4 | 0 | = | 5 | 0 |

6. If 30 and _____ is 100, then 100 minus 30 is _____.

7. If 62 and _____ is 100, then 100 minus 62 is _____.

8. If 17 and _____ is 50, then 50 minus 17 is _____.

90	70	65	33	27	38	75	22
L	D	L	G	U	O	A	B

A ___ ___ ___ ___ ___ ___ ___
1   2   3   4   5   6   7   8

Think About It   Reasoning

Tell how you used a calculator to find the missing numbers
in Exercise 6.

Home Connection Your child used a calculator to find the
missing parts of 100 and other numbers. **Home Activity**
Ask your child to explain how to complete the following
using a calculator: 15 and ____ is 100.

Name_____

Read Together

Make Smart Choices

After you choose your answer on a test, you can estimate to find out if your answer is reasonable.

Test-Taking Strategies
Understand the Question
Get Information for the Answer
Plan How to Find the Answer
Make Smart Choices
Use Writing in Math

1 Max has 80¢. Which two toys does he have enough money to buy? Fill in the answer bubble.

 48¢    53¢    36¢   42¢

Ⓐ   the train and the bus   Ⓒ   the tractor and the bus

Ⓑ   the tractor and the car   Ⓓ   the tractor and the train

The price of the tractor is 36¢. The price of the car is 42¢.

30¢ and 40¢ is 70¢.

6¢ and 2¢ is 8¢ more.

70¢ and 8¢ is 78¢.

Is Choice B a reasonable answer?

Your Turn

Solve. Estimate. Fill in the answer bubble.

2 Jennifer has 70¢. Which art supply can she buy and have more than 30¢ left?

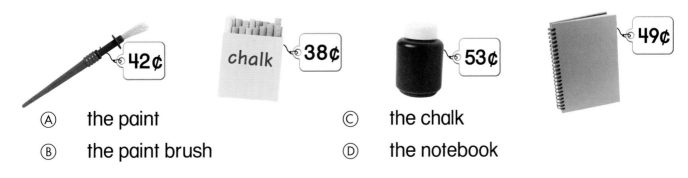

42¢   chalk 38¢   53¢   49¢

Ⓐ   the paint   Ⓒ   the chalk

Ⓑ   the paint brush   Ⓓ   the notebook

Home Connection Your child prepared for standardized tests by estimating to find out whether his or her answer is reasonable.
Home Activity Ask your child to explain how he or she solved Exercise 2 and estimated to check the reasonableness of the answer.

Name _____

Planning a Menu

The people in your neighborhood
are having a picnic. There will be 30 people.
Will there be enough food?
Use tens to estimate.

Estimating Sums and Differences

1 Your family is bringing sandwiches for
everybody. You have 8 turkey sandwiches
and 12 cheese sandwiches. About how
many more sandwiches do you need?

We need about _____ more sandwiches.

2 Your friend Juan asks you to estimate the number
of apples he has. One bag has 12 apples. Another
bag has 28 apples. About how many apples
does Juan have?

Juan has about _____ apples.

3 Each person will get 1 juice box. Marie's family is bringing
28 boxes. Sam's family is bringing 11 boxes. About how
many juice boxes will be left over?

About _____ juice boxes will be left over.

Take It to the NET
Video and Activities
www.scottforesman.com

Home Connection Your child estimated sums and differences by
finding the nearest ten. **Home Activity** Ask your child to explain how
he or she found the answer to Exercise 3. *(Sample response: 28 is about
30. 11 is about 10. 30 + 10 = 40. So 40 boxes − 30 boxes needed =
10 boxes left over.)*

Name _____

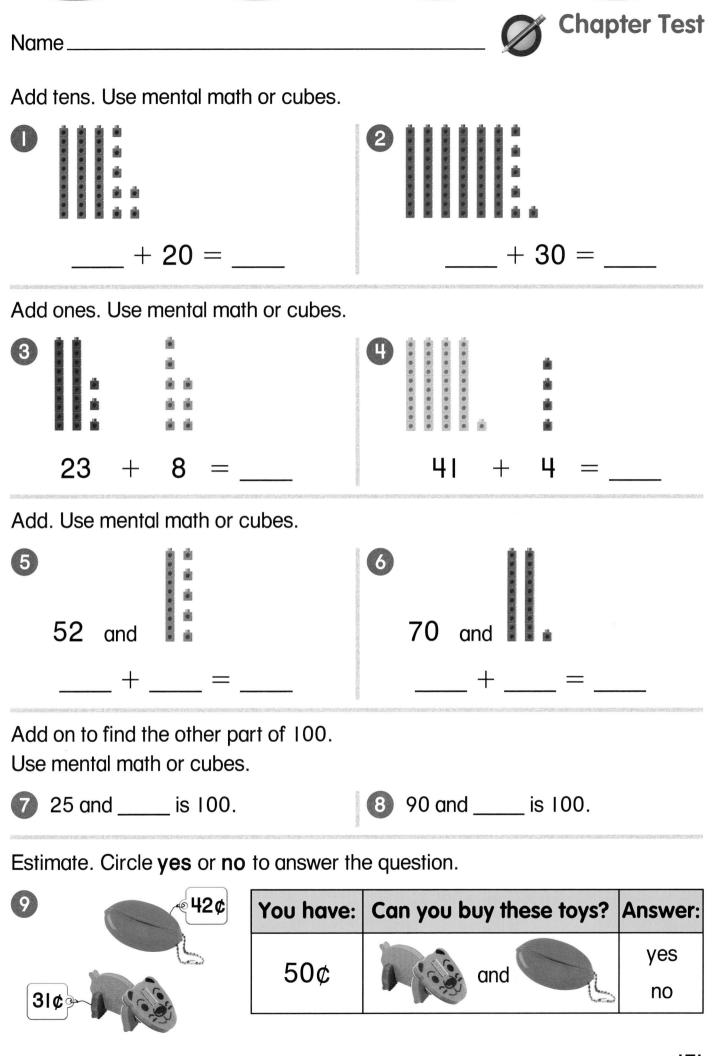

Chapter Test

Add tens. Use mental math or cubes.

1 ___ + 20 = ___

2 ___ + 30 = ___

Add ones. Use mental math or cubes.

3 23 + 8 = ___

4 41 + 4 = ___

Add. Use mental math or cubes.

5 52 and ___ + ___ = ___

6 70 and ___ + ___ = ___

Add on to find the other part of 100.
Use mental math or cubes.

7 25 and _____ is 100.

8 90 and _____ is 100.

Estimate. Circle **yes** or **no** to answer the question.

9 42¢ 31¢

You have:	Can you buy these toys?	Answer:
50¢	and	yes / no

Chapter 4

one hundred seventy-one   **171**

Circle the number that makes sense.

⑩ Kelly had 62 buttons in her collection.
She gave 20 to Sammi Jo.

Now Kelly has 42
              82 buttons.

Subtract. Use mental math, pictures, or cubes.

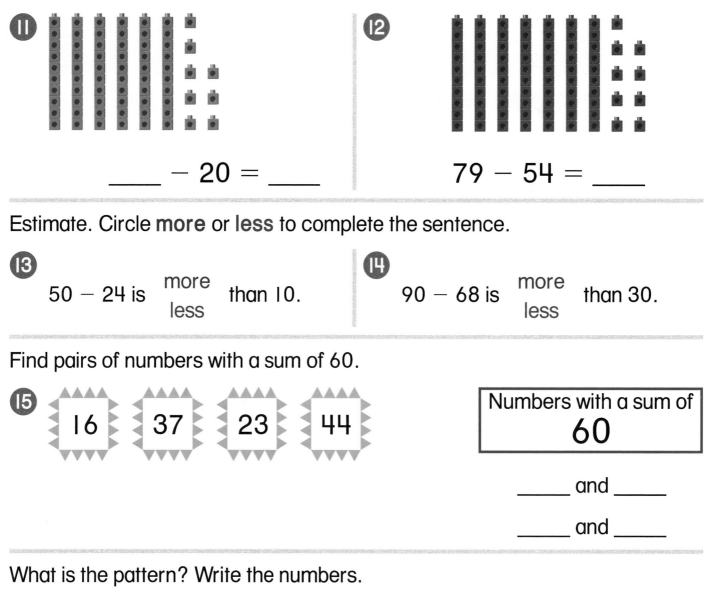

⑪ _____ − 20 = _____

⑫ 79 − 54 = _____

Estimate. Circle **more** or **less** to complete the sentence.

⑬ 50 − 24 is   more
              less   than 10.

⑭ 90 − 68 is   more
              less   than 30.

Find pairs of numbers with a sum of 60.

⑮ 16   37   23   44

Numbers with a sum of 60

_____ and _____

_____ and _____

What is the pattern? Write the numbers.

⑯ 86, 76, 66, 56, _____, _____, _____, _____

What is the pattern rule? _____

Look at the ones digits. What is the pattern? _____

Look at the tens digits. What is the pattern? _____

Cumulative Review and Test Prep

INDIANA

1 Which number is 10 LESS than 64?

54	63	65	74
Ⓐ	Ⓑ	Ⓒ	Ⓓ

2 Which number is even?

37	49	53	60
Ⓐ	Ⓑ	Ⓒ	Ⓓ

3 Which number makes the statement true?

☐ < 25

25	37	16	51
Ⓐ	Ⓑ	Ⓒ	Ⓓ

4 What is another name for 7 tens and 6 ones?

13	17	67	76
Ⓐ	Ⓑ	Ⓒ	Ⓓ

Add or subtract.

5
$$\begin{array}{r} 73 \\ -\ 20 \\ \hline \end{array}$$

50	53	90	93
Ⓐ	Ⓑ	Ⓒ	Ⓓ

6
$$\begin{array}{r} 68 \\ +\ 31 \\ \hline \end{array}$$

37	90	99	109
Ⓐ	Ⓑ	Ⓒ	Ⓓ

7 Which ball has stars?

Ⓐ first
Ⓑ second
Ⓒ sixth
Ⓓ seventh

8 There are 5 tens and 2 ones. Add 1 MORE ten.

Ⓐ 6 tens and 2 ones
Ⓑ 6 tens and 3 ones
Ⓒ 5 tens and 3 ones
Ⓓ 4 tens and 2 ones

How many are there now?

Name _____

Cumulative Review and Test Prep

9 What is the pattern?

21, 31, 41, 51, 61, 71, 81, 91

(A) add one
(B) add ten
(C) subtract one
(D) subtract ten

10 Look at this number sentence:

$16 - 9 = \boxed{}$

Which addition fact will help you find the number to go in the box?

(A) $9 + 7 = 16$ (C) $9 + 9 = 18$
(B) $8 + 8 = 16$ (D) $16 + 2 = 18$

11 Ming has these coins in her pocket. How much money does she have?

59¢   74¢   94¢   99¢
(A)   (B)   (C)   (D)

12 Add on to find the other part of 100. Use mental math or cubes.

Show All Work

Answer 35 and _____ is 100.

13 Write the numbers. Then circle >, <, or =.

<   =   >

_____   _____

172B

King Adam Upp

Written by Anne Miranda

Illustrated by John Steven Gurney

This Math Storybook belongs to

_____

5A

Once upon a time...
in a kingdom far away in the north, there lived a very kind king.

It was a very cold winter, so the king called for the Royal Sock Maker. "Make new, warm socks for the **12** knights in my kingdom," said the king.

"And for the **25** squires?" asked the Royal Sock Maker.

"Yes, that's right. They need warm socks too," answered the king.

12 knights
25 Squires

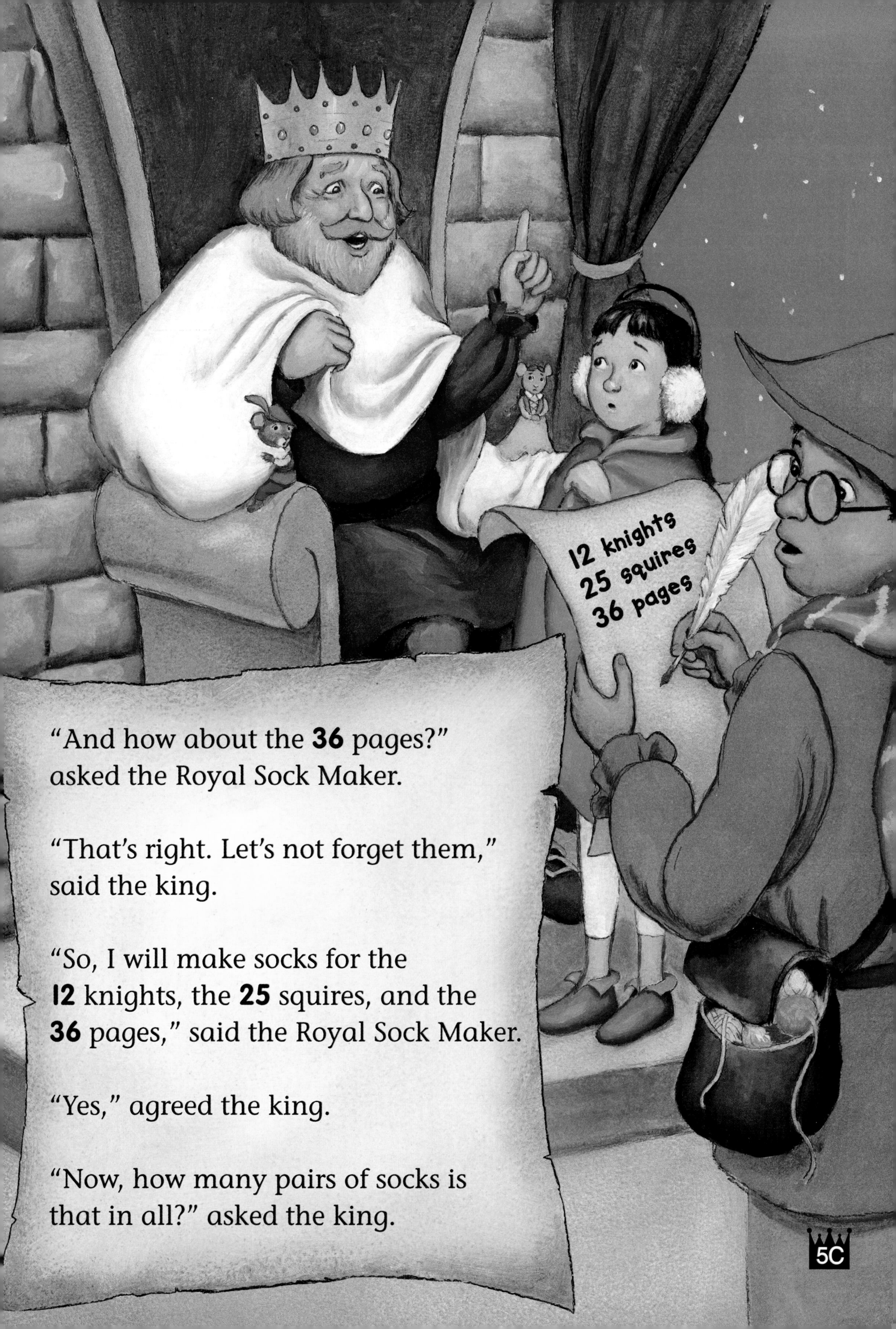

The label on the scroll reads:

12 knights
25 squires
36 pages

"And how about the **36** pages?" asked the Royal Sock Maker.

"That's right. Let's not forget them," said the king.

"So, I will make socks for the **12** knights, the **25** squires, and the **36** pages," said the Royal Sock Maker.

"Yes," agreed the king.

"Now, how many pairs of socks is that in all?" asked the king.

12 knights
25 squires
+ 36 pages
_____
◯ pairs of socks in all

"How can we find the total, so that you will know exactly how many pairs of socks to make?"

"Why don't you ask the Royal Adder?" suggested the Royal Sock Maker.

So the king called the Royal Adder.

He came into the room.

He listened to the king.

"There are **12** knights, **25** squires, and **36** pages in my kingdom. Now, how many pairs of socks should I tell the Royal Sock Maker to make for them?" asked the king.

12 knights
25 squires
+36 pages
_____
◯ pairs of
socks
in all

The Royal Adder said, "Well, **12** plus **25** is **37**. That part is easy. And **37** plus **36** equals **73**. So, **73** pairs of socks, plus another **3** pairs for the three of us will do very nicely. Very nicely, indeed. That will be **76** pairs of socks in all, sire."

"Jolly good!" said the king. "Well done, Royal Adder."

And so it was that the Royal Sock Maker made **76** pairs of new, warm, fuzzy socks.

"Thanks to you, Royal Sock Maker and Royal Adder, we will all have warm feet this winter!" proclaimed the king.

Home-School Connection

Dear Family,

Today my class started Chapter 5, **Two-Digit Addition.** I will learn how to trade 10 ones for 1 ten to solve problems like 27 + 43, where there are too many ones to fit in the ones part of the answer. And I will also learn how to solve money problems. Here are some of the math words I will be learning and some things we can do to help me with my math.

Love,

_____

Math Activity to Do at Home

Play "Pennies and Dimes." Spread coins out on a table and invite your child to display 29¢ three different ways (as 29 pennies; as 2 dimes 9 pennies; and as 1 dime 19 pennies).

Books to Read Together

Reading math stories reinforces concepts. Look for these titles in your local library:

17 Kings and 42 Elephants
By Margaret Mahy
(Dial Books for Young Readers, 1990)

26 Letters and 99 Cents
By Tana Hoban
(Greenwillow, 1997)

My New Math Words

regroup To add 46 and 29, regroup the 15 ones as 1 ten 5 ones. The sum is then understood as 7 tens 5 ones, or 75.

two-digit number Any number from 10 to 99. Each is a combination of tens and ones.

data Children learn that data means information. Data can be gathered, organized, and analyzed.

Take It to the NET
More Activities
www.scottforesman.com

Sock Addition

How to Play

1. Place a square on each sock.
2. Both players pick up 2 squares each, add the numbers, and call out the sum.
3. The person with the higher sum takes all 4 squares.
4. Keep playing until all of the socks have been uncovered.
5. The person who has the most squares wins the game.

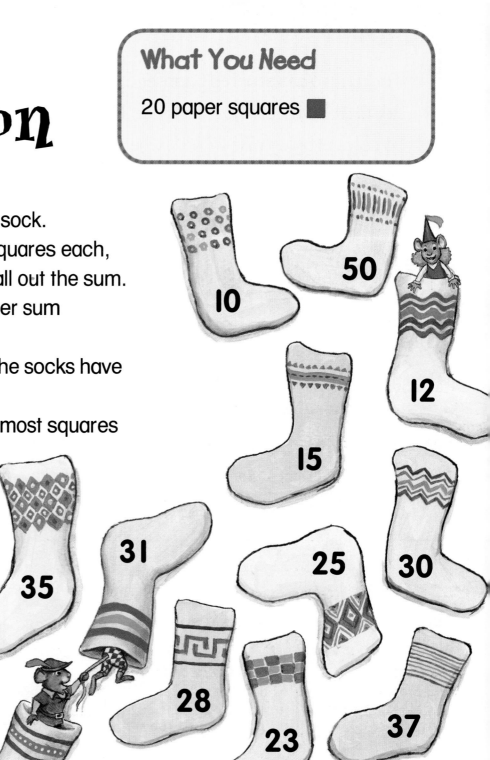

10   50   12   15

14   35   31   25   30

41   28   23   37

45   20   16

40   18   34   49

174   one hundred seventy-four

© Pearson Education, Inc.

Name_____

Adding With and Without Regrouping

Learn!

How do you add 7 to 25? **25 + 7 = ?**

1 Show 25.
Then **add** 7.

2 **Regroup** 10 ones as 1 ten
to find the **sum**.

Tens	Ones

Tens	Ones

Tens	Ones

10 ones = 1 ten

25 + 7 = 32

Word Bank
add
regroup
sum

Check ✓

Use cubes and Workmat 4.
Add. Regroup if you need to.

Show.	Add.	Do you need to regroup?	Find the sum.
1 47	6	yes	47 + 6 = 53
2 64	5	_____	64 + 5 = ___
3 32	8	_____	32 + 8 = ___

Think About It   Reasoning

When adding two numbers, how do you know
if you need to regroup?

Chapter 5 ★ Lesson 1

one hundred seventy-five   **175**

Practice

Use cubes and Workmat 4.
Add. Regroup if you need to.

Show.	Add.	Do you need to regroup?	Find the sum.
4 18	5	yes	18 + 5 = 23
5 54	2	_____	54 + 2 = ___
6 36	6	_____	36 + 6 = ___
7 41	9	_____	41 + 9 = ___
8 85	7	_____	85 + 7 = ___
9 70	8	_____	70 + 8 = ___
10 64	7	_____	64 + 7 = ___

Problem Solving Writing in Math

11 Which one-digit numbers can be added to 26 without having to regroup?

_____

_____

12 Which one-digit numbers can be added to 26 if you regroup?

_____

Home Connection Your child identified when it is necessary to regroup 10 ones as 1 ten when adding. **Home Activity** Ask your child to explain whether it is necessary to regroup when finding the sums of 36 and 9, and 52 and 3.

Name_____

Learn!

Add 6 to 48. **48 + 6 = ?**

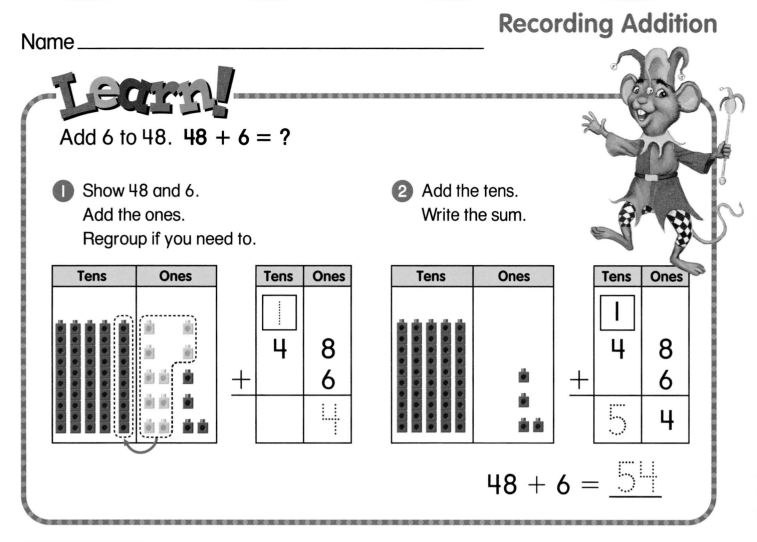

① Show 48 and 6.
Add the ones.
Regroup if you need to.

② Add the tens.
Write the sum.

48 + 6 = 54

Check ✓

Use cubes and Workmat 4. Add.
Did you need to regroup? Circle **Yes** or **No.**

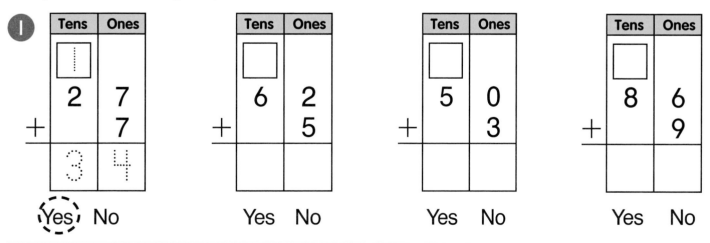

①

Tens	Ones
1	
2	7
+	7
3	4

Yes   No

Tens	Ones
6	2
+	5

Yes   No

Tens	Ones
5	0
+	3

Yes   No

Tens	Ones
8	6
+	9

Yes   No

Think About It   Number Sense

Now look at 86 + 9 in Exercise 1.
What number do you write in the box above the 8?
How many tens do you add to 8 tens?

Chapter 5 ★ Lesson 2

Add. Regroup if you need to. Use cubes and Workmat 4 if needed.

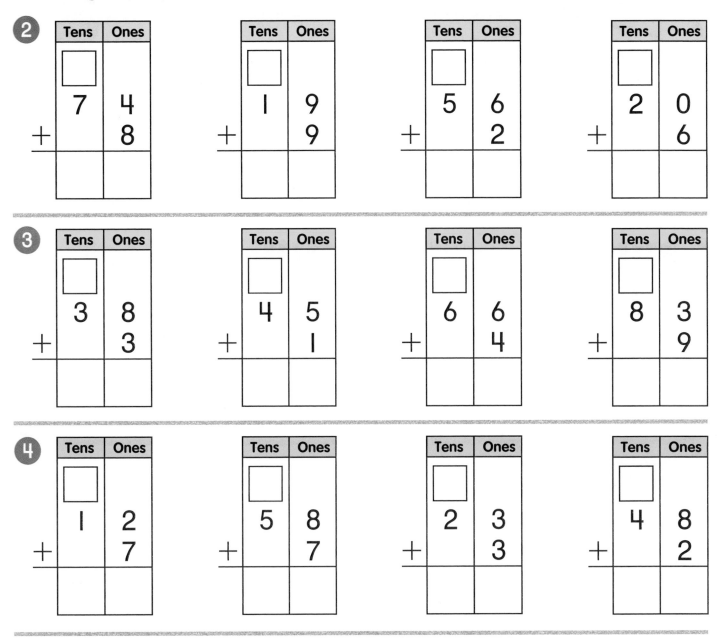

2

Tens	Ones
☐	
7	4
+	8

Tens	Ones
☐	
1	9
+	9

Tens	Ones
☐	
5	6
+	2

Tens	Ones
☐	
2	0
+	6

3

Tens	Ones
☐	
3	8
+	3

Tens	Ones
☐	
4	5
+	1

Tens	Ones
☐	
6	6
+	4

Tens	Ones
☐	
8	3
+	9

4

Tens	Ones
☐	
1	2
+	7

Tens	Ones
☐	
5	8
+	7

Tens	Ones
☐	
2	3
+	3

Tens	Ones
☐	
4	8
+	2

Problem Solving   Number Sense

Use the numbers shown. Make the sum of the numbers across
equal the sum of the numbers down.

5   4   2   5   6   3

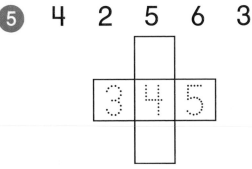

6   5   11   9   7   3

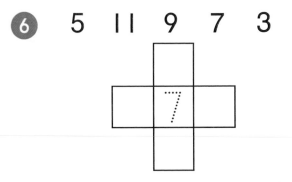

Home Connection Your child practiced solving two-digit addition
problems. **Home Activity** Ask your child to add 36 + 8, explaining
each step aloud, including how to record the regrouping.

Name _____

Learn!

Add the **two-digit numbers** 34 and 28. **34 + 28 = ?**

1 Show 34 and 28.
Add the ones.
Regroup 10 ones as 1 ten.

Tens	Ones

Tens	Ones
1	
3	4
+ 2	8
	2

2 Add the tens.
Write the sum.

Tens	Ones

Tens	Ones
1	
3	4
+ 2	8
6	2

34 + 28 = 62

Word Bank

two-digit number

Check ✓

Use cubes and Workmat 4.
Add. Regroup if you need to.

1

Tens	Ones
2	6
+ 3	9

Tens	Ones
3	7
+ 1	8

Tens	Ones
5	4
+ 2	4

Tens	Ones
4	3
+ 3	8

Think About It   Reasoning

How are these problems alike?
How are these problems different?

Tens	Ones
4	7
+	6

Tens	Ones
4	7
+ 3	6

Add. Regroup if you need to.
Use cubes and Workmat 4 if needed.

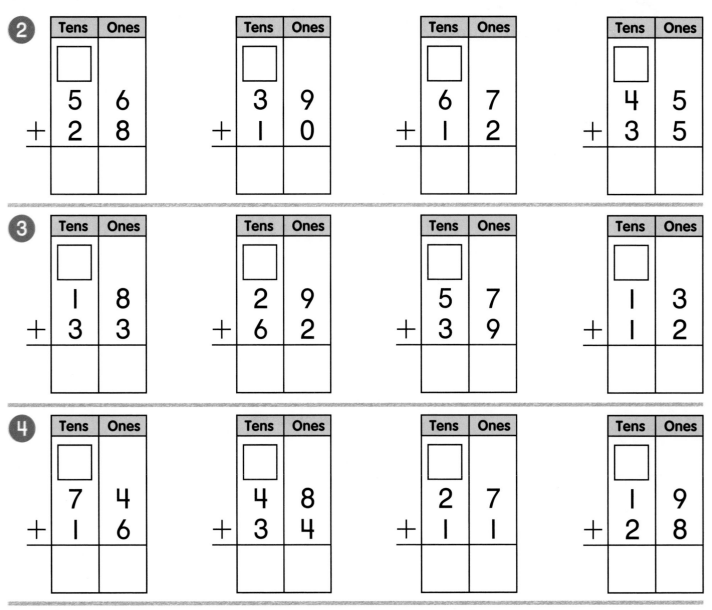

2

Tens	Ones
5	6
+ 2	8

Tens	Ones
3	9
+ 1	0

Tens	Ones
6	7
+ 1	2

Tens	Ones
4	5
+ 3	5

3

Tens	Ones
1	8
+ 3	3

Tens	Ones
2	9
+ 6	2

Tens	Ones
5	7
+ 3	9

Tens	Ones
1	3
+ 1	2

4

Tens	Ones
7	4
+ 1	6

Tens	Ones
4	8
+ 3	4

Tens	Ones
2	7
+ 1	1

Tens	Ones
1	9
+ 2	8

Problem Solving   Reasonableness

5   Use the numbers and clues below.
Find out how long the fire truck is.

85   45   20   90   55

It is less than 70 feet long.
It is more than 25 feet long.
It is not 25 + 30 feet long.

The fire truck is _____ feet long.

Home Connection Your child learned to add two-digit numbers where regrouping 10 ones as 1 ten was necessary. **Home Activity** Have your child show you how to add 35 + 48.

Learn!

26 + 48 = ?

How many collars does the pet store have?

Creature Comforts
26 cat collars
48 dog collars

1 Add the ones.
Regroup if needed.

Tens	Ones
1	
2	6
+ 4	8
	4

2 Add the tens.

Tens	Ones
1	
2	6
+ 4	8
7	4

The pet store has __74__ collars.

Check ✓

Write the addition problem. Find the sum.

1   54 + 29   31 + 22   78 + 19   42 + 43

Tens	Ones
1	
5	4
+ 2	9
8	3

Tens	Ones
+	

Tens	Ones
+	

Tens	Ones
+	

Think About It   Number Sense

This is how Lauren solved a problem.
What would you do differently? Explain.

```
  56
+ 27
-----
 713
```

Write the addition problem. Find the sum.

2 35 + 18

Tens	Ones
☐	

$$\begin{array}{r} 3\ 5 \\ +\ 1\ 8 \\ \hline 5\ 3 \end{array}$$

62 + 24

Tens	Ones
☐	

$+$

47 + 43

Tens	Ones
☐	

$+$

30 + 17

Tens	Ones
☐	

$+$

3 22 + 65

Tens	Ones
☐	

$+$

15 + 46

Tens	Ones
☐	

$+$

25 + 21

Tens	Ones
☐	

$+$

28 + 46

Tens	Ones
☐	

$+$

4 19 + 15

Tens	Ones
☐	

$+$

39 + 18

Tens	Ones
☐	

$+$

72 + 20

Tens	Ones
☐	

$+$

24 + 35

Tens	Ones
☐	

$+$

Problem Solving   Algebra

5 Write the missing numbers.
What pattern do you see?

$$55 + 9 = 45 + \boxed{19}$$
$$65 + 9 = 45 + \boxed{}$$
$$75 + 9 = 45 + \boxed{}$$
$$85 + 9 = 45 + \boxed{}$$

Home Connection Your child practiced adding two-digit numbers without using pictures or cubes. **Home Activity** Have your child show how to add 28 + 43.

Add. Regroup if you need to.

Show.	Add.	Do you need to regroup?	Find the sum.
① 19	6	_____	19 + 6 = ___
② 27	4	_____	27 + 4 = ___
③ 75	2	_____	75 + 2 = ___
④ 54	8	_____	54 + 8 = ___

Add. Regroup if you need to.

⑤

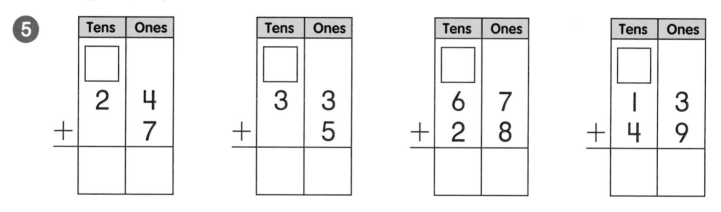

Tens	Ones
2	4
+	7

Tens	Ones
3	3
+	5

Tens	Ones
6	7
+ 2	8

Tens	Ones
1	3
+ 4	9

Write the addition problem. Find the sum.

⑥ 77 + 16   36 + 45   21 + 29   58 + 10

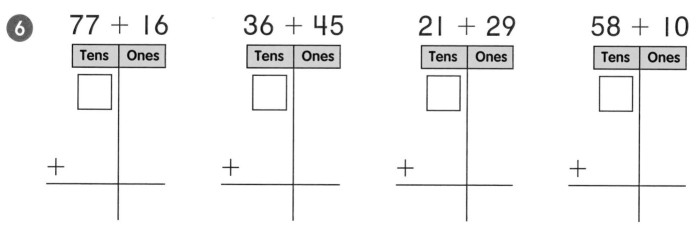

Mark the number sentence that tells about the picture.

1

Start with:

Subtract:
12

Ⓐ $35 + 12 = 47$

Ⓑ $35 - 12 = 23$

Ⓒ $35 - 12 = 47$

Ⓓ $35 + 10 = 35$

Add or subtract. Mark the answer.

2 $8 + 9$

Ⓐ 16
Ⓑ 1
Ⓒ 17
Ⓓ 89

3 $11 - 2$

Ⓐ 13
Ⓑ 10
Ⓒ 8
Ⓓ 9

4
$$\begin{array}{r} 5 \\ 6 \\ + 4 \\ \hline \end{array}$$

Ⓐ 20
Ⓑ 10
Ⓒ 15
Ⓓ 14

5
$$\begin{array}{r} 16 \\ - 8 \\ \hline \end{array}$$

Ⓐ 8
Ⓑ 7
Ⓒ 9
Ⓓ 12

Mark the total amount.

6

50¢
Ⓐ

95¢
Ⓑ

$1.00
Ⓒ

75¢
Ⓓ

There are 8 socks in all. How many socks are in the box?

7

1 sock
Ⓐ

2 socks
Ⓑ

3 socks
Ⓒ

5 socks
Ⓓ

Learn!

Zach has 57¢. Tanya has 26¢.
How much money do they have altogether?

57¢ + 26¢ = ?

```
  ☐
  5 7¢
+ 2 6¢
──────
  8 3¢
```

They have __83¢__.

Check ✓

Add to find the total amount.

❶
```
  ☐
  2 8¢
+ 4 7¢
──────
```
```
  ☐
  5 6¢
+ 3 2¢
──────
```
```
  ☐
  1 9¢
+   6¢
──────
```
```
  ☐
  1 7¢
+ 3 0¢
──────
```

❷
```
  ☐
  6 4¢
+ 2 9¢
──────
```
```
  ☐
  1 8¢
+   8¢
──────
```
```
  ☐
  1 0¢
+ 4 2¢
──────
```
```
  ☐
  8 6¢
+   5¢
──────
```

Think About It Number Sense

How are these problems the same? How are they different?
How will the sums be the same? How will they be different?

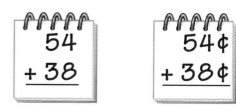

```
  54
+ 38
────
```
```
  54¢
+ 38¢
─────
```

Add to find the total amount.

3

☐	☐	☐	☐
2 0¢	4 1¢	8 8¢	1 3¢
+ 6 2¢	+ 1 5¢	+ 7¢	+ 2 8¢

4

☐	☐	☐	☐
5 9¢	1 7¢	4 6¢	2 0¢
+ 1 5¢	+ 7 3¢	+ 8¢	+ 7 0¢

5

☐	☐	☐	☐
3 0¢	8 4¢	3 1¢	3 5¢
+ 5 2¢	+ 9¢	+ 5 9¢	+ 3 5¢

Problem Solving Visual Thinking

6 Marla wants to buy two bracelets. She has 50¢.
Which two bracelets can she buy? Circle them.

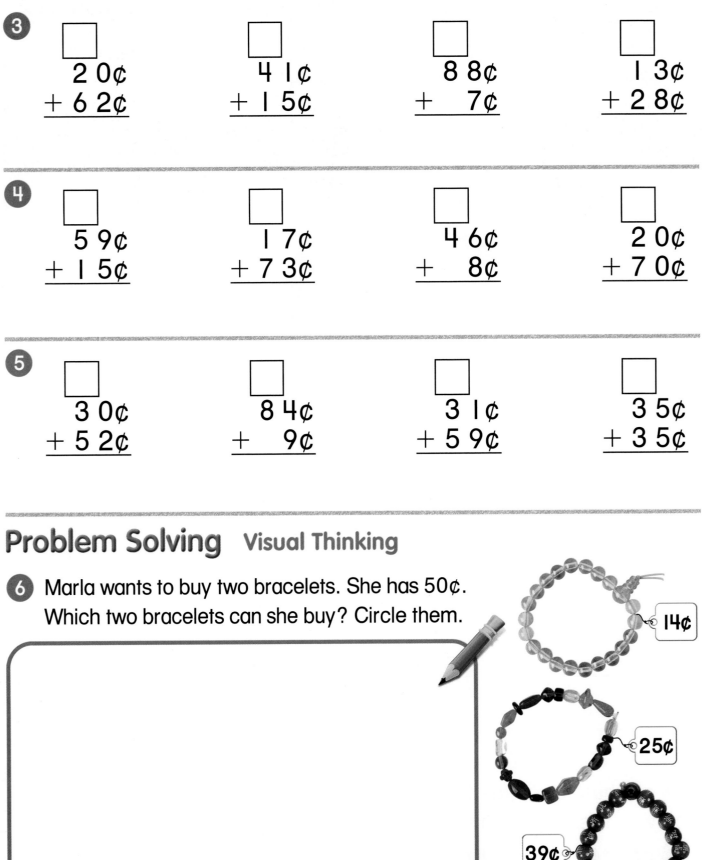

14¢

25¢

39¢

Home Connection Your child practiced adding two-digit monetary
amounts. **Home Activity** Show your child two sets of coins, each set's
total value being less than 50¢, and ask him or her to use paper and pencil
to add the two values.

© Pearson Education, Inc.

Learn! Algebra

You can add in any order.
Use the fact strategies you know to add 3 numbers.

Use Doubles Facts.	Use Counting On.	Use Making 10.

Use Doubles Facts.

```
 1
 28
 22
+18
 68
```

$8 + 8 = 16$
$16 + 2 = 18$

Use Counting On.

```
 1
 28
 22
+18
 68
```

$8 + 2 = 10$
$10 + 8 = 18$

Use Making 10.

```
 1
 28
 22
+18
 68
```

$2 + 8 = 10$
$10 + 8 = 18$

Check ✓

Add. Circle the two numbers you added first.

1

```
  23
  14
+ 47
  84
```

```
  31
  24
+ 14
```

```
  15
  33
+  5
```

```
  49
  13
+ 21
```

```
  25
  54
+ 16
```

2

```
  34
  16
+  8
```

```
  14
  16
+ 15
```

```
  18
  12
+ 21
```

```
  13
  37
+ 43
```

```
  24
  30
+ 26
```

Think About It   Reasoning

In Exercise 2, circle the two numbers you added first
in each problem. Is there a pattern?

Add in any order.

3

15	26	32	14	67
10	17	56	33	19
+ 43	+ 24	+ 8	+ 23	+ 2

4

18	37	85	25	34
41	12	4	25	12
+ 4	+ 38	+ 10	+ 25	+ 25

5

23	16	4	52	35
27	14	15	16	21
+ 23	+ 68	+ 25	+ 26	+ 4

Problem Solving   Reasoning

6 Find the value of the letters E and F. Use the chart to help you.

_____   _____

A = 1¢
B = 2¢
C = 3¢
D = 4¢

7 How much are these words worth?

bed $2¢ + 5¢ + 4¢ = 11¢$

bead   _____

feed   _____

8 Make a word worth more than 30¢.

_____

Home Connection Your child has learned to add 3 two-digit numbers. **Home Activity** Have your child explain two ways to add 27 + 13 + 4.

© Pearson Education, Inc.

Learn!

This **table** shows **data** about second-grade book orders.

Book Orders	
Kind	**Number**
Jokes	52
Games	9
Animals	47
Famous people	39
Famous places	28

The table helps me keep track of book orders.

How many orders are there in all for joke books and game books?

_52_ joke books   _9_ game books

$$\begin{array}{r} 52 \\ + 9 \\ \hline 61 \end{array}$$

_61_ books

Word Bank

table

data

Check ✓

Use data from the table to solve the problem.

1 How many books about famous people and famous places were ordered in all?

_____ famous-people books

_____ famous-places books

_____ books

Think About It   Reasoning

Use two numbers from the table.
Write an addition story problem.

Use the data from the table to solve the problems.

Craft Books in the Library					
Kind	Puppets	Mobiles	Flowers	Masks	Car Models
Number	44	27	63	38	9

2 How many books about puppets and masks are there in all?

_____ books

3 How many books about mobiles and flowers are there in all?

_____ books

4 How many books about mobiles, flowers, and car models are there in all?

_____ books

5 If the library added 12 more books about masks, how many mask books would there be?

_____ books

Home Connection Your child learned to solve problems using information from a table. **Home Activity** Have your child add two-digit numbers, each less than 50, found on nutrition labels of cereal boxes.

© Pearson Education, Inc.

Name_____

 Algebra

Estimate the sum of 28 and 43.

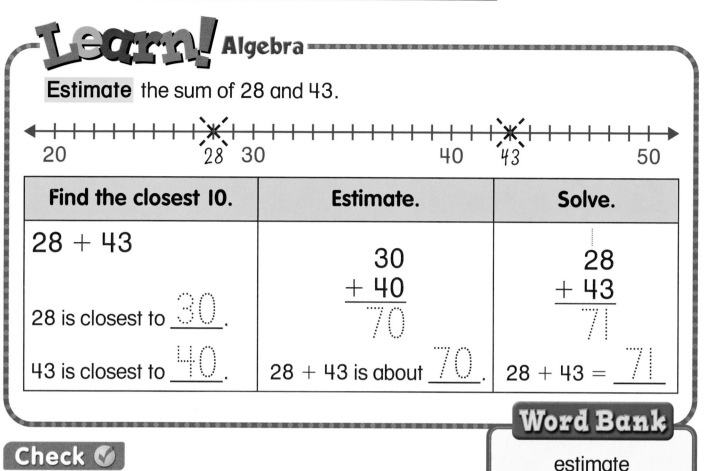

Find the closest 10.	Estimate.	Solve.
28 + 43 28 is closest to __30__. 43 is closest to __40__.	$$\begin{array}{r} 30 \\ + 40 \\ \hline 70 \end{array}$$ 28 + 43 is about __70__.	$$\begin{array}{r} 28 \\ + 43 \\ \hline 71 \end{array}$$ 28 + 43 = __71__

Word Bank

estimate

Check ✓

Estimate the sum. Then solve and compare.

Find the closest 10.	Estimate.	Solve.
❶ 11 + 47 11 is closest to _____. 47 is closest to _____.	11 + 47 is about _____.	11 + 47 = _____
❷ 52 + 39 52 is closest to _____. 39 is closest to _____.	52 + 39 is about _____.	52 + 39 = _____

Think About It   Number Sense

Are the estimates the same for 52 + 39 and 59 + 32?
Are the exact sums the same? Explain.

Estimate the sum. Then solve and compare.

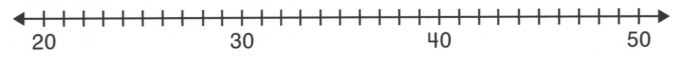

Find the closest 10.	Estimate.	Solve.
③ 23 + 39 23 is closest to _____. 39 is closest to _____.	23 + 39 is about _____.	23 + 39 = _____
④ 78 + 14 78 is closest to _____. 14 is closest to _____.	78 + 14 is about _____.	78 + 14 = _____
⑤ 42 + 47 42 is closest to _____. 47 is closest to _____.	42 + 47 is about _____.	42 + 47 = _____

Problem Solving Estimation

⑥ Estimate the sum of 43 and 19.
Circle each problem that has the same estimated sum.

49 + 13   52 + 13   46 + 26   32 + 32

⑦ Which problem has the same exact sum as 43 and 19?

_____

Home Connection Your child learned how to estimate the sum of 2 two-digit numbers. **Home Activity** Ask your child to estimate 31 + 47. *(30 + 50 = 80, so the estimated sum is 80.)*

© Pearson Education, Inc.

Name_____

Learn! Algebra

How will you find the answer?

Use mental math.

$$32 + 20 = ?$$

> $32 + 10 = 42$
> $42 + 10 = 52$

> $2 + 0 = 2$
> $30 + 20 = 50$
> $50 + 2 = 52$

Use cubes.

$$32 + 29 = ?$$

> The sum is 61.

Tens	Ones

Use paper and pencil.

$$32 + 28 = ?$$

> I need to regroup 10 ones as 1 ten.

$$\begin{array}{r} 1 \\ 32 \\ +\ 28 \\ \hline 60 \end{array}$$

Use a calculator.

$$32 + 59 = ?$$

> $32 + 59 = 91$

Check ✓

Circle the better way to solve the problem.
Then find the sum.

1. $\begin{array}{r} 45 \\ +\ 30 \\ \hline \end{array}$ mental math
                         paper and pencil

2. $\begin{array}{r} 24 \\ +\ 57 \\ \hline \end{array}$ mental math
                         paper and pencil

Think About It Reasoning

Explain how you solved the problems
in Exercises 1 and 2.

Chapter 5 ★ Lesson 9

Write the way you will solve the problem.
Then add and write the sum.

> • mental math
> • paper and pencil
> • cubes
> • calculator

③ $51 + 40 =$ ___91___

mental

math

④ $78 + 17 =$ ___

_____

_____

⑤ $26 + 34 =$ ___

_____

_____

⑥ $45 + 15 =$ ___

_____

_____

⑦ $85 + 9 =$ ___

_____

_____

⑧ $38 + 56 =$ ___

_____

_____

Problem Solving Mental Math

On which two different circles did
the ball land?

⑨ Meg's score was greater than 80.

____ and ____

⑩ George scored between 30 and 60.

____ and ____

50

31

18

Home Connection Your child learned to choose a method for solving
an addition problem. **Home Activity** Have your child explain which
method he or she will use to solve $28 + 47$.

© Pearson Education, Inc.

Name _____

Predict and Verify

1 Look at these four newspaper
stories about things that are
missing. Who is missing what?
And who took all of these things?
It's all very mysterious!

Extra! Extra!
Read all about it!

2 How many things are missing altogether?

_____ + _____ + _____ + _____ = _____ things in all

3 What one thing do you see in every picture? _____

Think About It   Reasoning

What do all the missing things have in common?

4 The dot-to-dot picture below shows
who took all of these things.
Can you **predict** what the picture will show?

I think the picture will show a _____.

5 Connect the dots to **verify** your answer. Count by 5s.

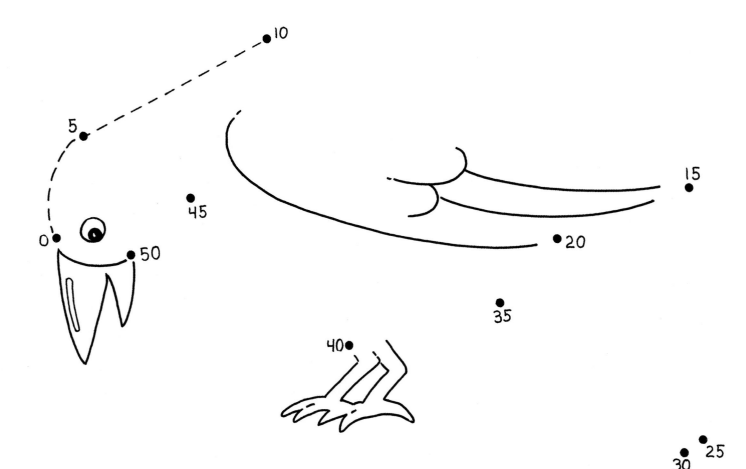

6 **Writing in Math**

Write a number story about a crow
that flies away with things.

 Home Connection Your child predicted the outcome of a four-part story,
a skill similar to estimating in math. **Home Activity** When you're shopping
with your child, look at prices. Ask her or him to estimate whether you
brought enough money with you to buy particular things, large and small.

Learn!

Read and Understand

Ben paid 74¢ for two rides.
Which rides did he choose?

Plan and Solve

Try: Choose two rides and add their costs.

Check: Is their sum 74¢?

Revise: If not, try another pair of rides.

Ben spent 74¢ to ride on the

roller coaster and the Ferris wheel .
_____   _____

Look Back and Check

Are there other pairs of rides you should check?

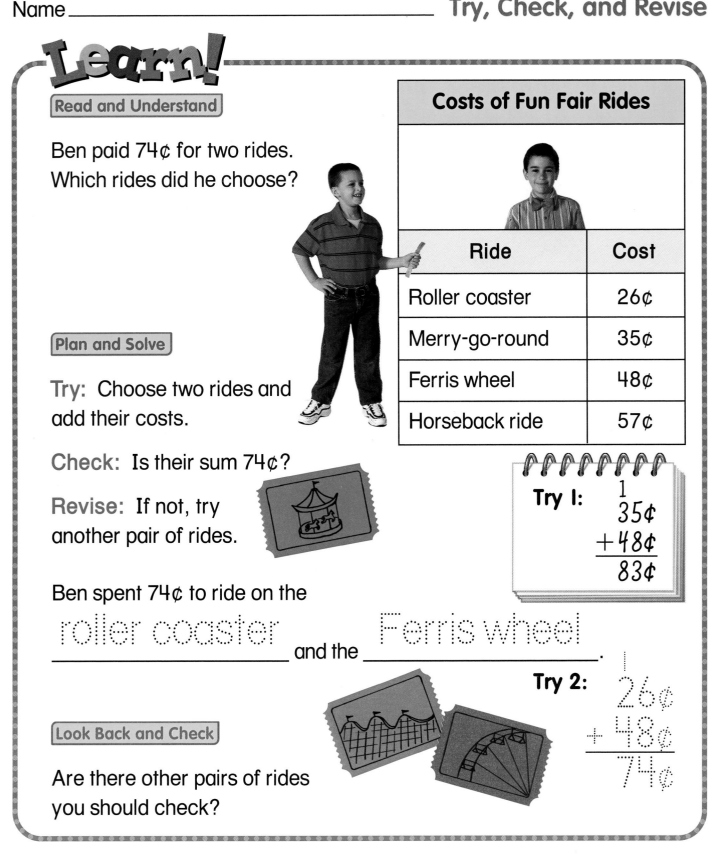

Costs of Fun Fair Rides

Ride	Cost
Roller coaster	26¢
Merry-go-round	35¢
Ferris wheel	48¢
Horseback ride	57¢

Try I:
$$\begin{array}{r} 1 \\ 35¢ \\ +48¢ \\ \hline 83¢ \end{array}$$

Try 2:
$$\begin{array}{r} 1 \\ 26¢ \\ +48¢ \\ \hline 74¢ \end{array}$$

Think About It   Reasoning

What helps you decide which pair of rides to try?

Children rode the bus to places in town. Where did they go? Try and then check to solve each problem.

Bus Fares	
Place	**Fare**
Park	13¢
Zoo	28¢
Library	33¢
Store	45¢

1 Juan paid 46¢ for 2 fares. Where did he go?

_____ and _____

2 Alissha paid 61¢ for 2 fares. Where did she go?

_____ and _____

3 Ray paid 73¢ for 2 fares. Where did he go?

_____ and _____

4 Jane paid 91¢ for 3 fares. Where did she go?

_____, _____, and _____

Problem Solving   Algebra

35¢

35¢

5 Lena spent 80¢ for two plants and a pot.

How much was the pot? _____
How do you know?

Home Connection Your child practiced solving problems using the Try, Check, and Revise strategy. **Home Activity** Have your child explain how he or she solved Exercise 5.

Name _____

DK Dorling Kindersley

PLANT

Do You Know...
that many foods you eat are parts of plants? When you eat lettuce, you are eating leaves.

① When insects land on some kinds of plants, they get stuck on the leaves.

If 15 insects got stuck on one plant and 17 insects got stuck on another plant, how many insects in all would be stuck?

____ ◯ ____ = ____ insects

② Here is a plant that does **not** eat meat. If 21 bees visited this plant in the morning and 13 bees visited it in the afternoon, how many bees in all visited this plant?

____ ◯ ____ = ____ bees

Fun Fact!
A pitcher plant has tube-like leaves that hold rainwater. Insects that get trapped in the rainwater provide nutrients for the plant.

The life cycle of a plant

3 Meat-eating plants get nutrients they need from insects they trap.

If 14 flies were trapped by plants on Monday, 24 flies were trapped on Tuesday, and 34 flies were trapped on Wednesday, how many flies in all got trapped on those 3 days?

_____ ◯ _____ ◯ _____ = _____ flies

4 Most Venus's-flytrap plants need to digest about 2 insects a month.

How many insects would the plant digest in 2 months?

_____ insects   In 6 months? _____ insects

5 Writing in Math

Write an addition story about some insects that get trapped by a plant. Try to use two-digit numbers in your story.

A Venus's-flytrap plant capturing a large insect

Home Connection Your child learned to solve problems by applying his or her math skills. **Home Activity** Talk to your child about how he or she solved the problems on these two pages.

Name _____

Add. Regroup if you need to.

1

☐
```
  4 3¢
+ 2 9¢
```

☐
```
  1 8¢
+ 6 5¢
```

☐
```
  2 7
  3 3
+ 1 7
```

☐
```
  6 2
    8
+ 1 2
```

Estimate the sum. Then solve and compare.

Find the closest 10.	Estimate.	Solve.
2 58 + 13 58 is closest to _____. 13 is closest to _____.	58 + 13 is about _____.	58 + 13 = _____

Circle the better way to solve each problem. Then find the sum.

3
```
  62    paper and pencil
+ 30    mental math
```

4
```
  47    paper and pencil
+ 16    mental math
```

Use data from the table to solve the problems.

5 How much does it cost to buy a can of chicken soup and a can of tomato soup?

_____

6 Mia paid 90¢ for two cans of soup. Which two kinds of soup did she buy?

_____ and _____

Soup Prices	
Kind	Price
Beef	52¢
Chicken	49¢
Pea	25¢
Tomato	38¢

Mark the number sentence that is NOT in the same fact family as the others.

1   Ⓐ $2 + 9 = 11$
        Ⓑ $11 - 2 = 9$
        Ⓒ $9 + 9 = 18$
        Ⓓ $11 - 9 = 2$

2   Ⓐ $10 - 6 = 4$
        Ⓑ $4 + 4 = 8$
        Ⓒ $6 + 4 = 10$
        Ⓓ $4 + 6 = 10$

Mark the statement that is true.

3   Ⓐ $16 = 16$
        Ⓑ $12 > 21$
        Ⓒ $100 < 90$
        Ⓓ $54 > 84$

4   Ⓐ $38¢ < 37¢$
        Ⓑ $100¢ = \$1.00$
        Ⓒ $65¢ > 75¢$
        Ⓓ $20¢ = 2¢$

Mark the other part of 100.

5 10 and ____ is 100.
        Ⓐ 0
        Ⓑ 100
        Ⓒ 90
        Ⓓ 10

6 85 and ____ is 100.
        Ⓐ 10
        Ⓑ 15
        Ⓒ 25
        Ⓓ 20

7 **Writing in Math**

Write and solve the number sentence that tells how many points Max scored in all.

Game Scores			
	Game 1	Game 2	Game 3
Ada	8	8	2
Max	9	7	3

____ ◯ ____ ◯ ____ = ____ points

Inequalities Algebra

You can write **greater than** or **less than** number sentences if you find the sum of the two addends.

$$27 + 35 = 62$$

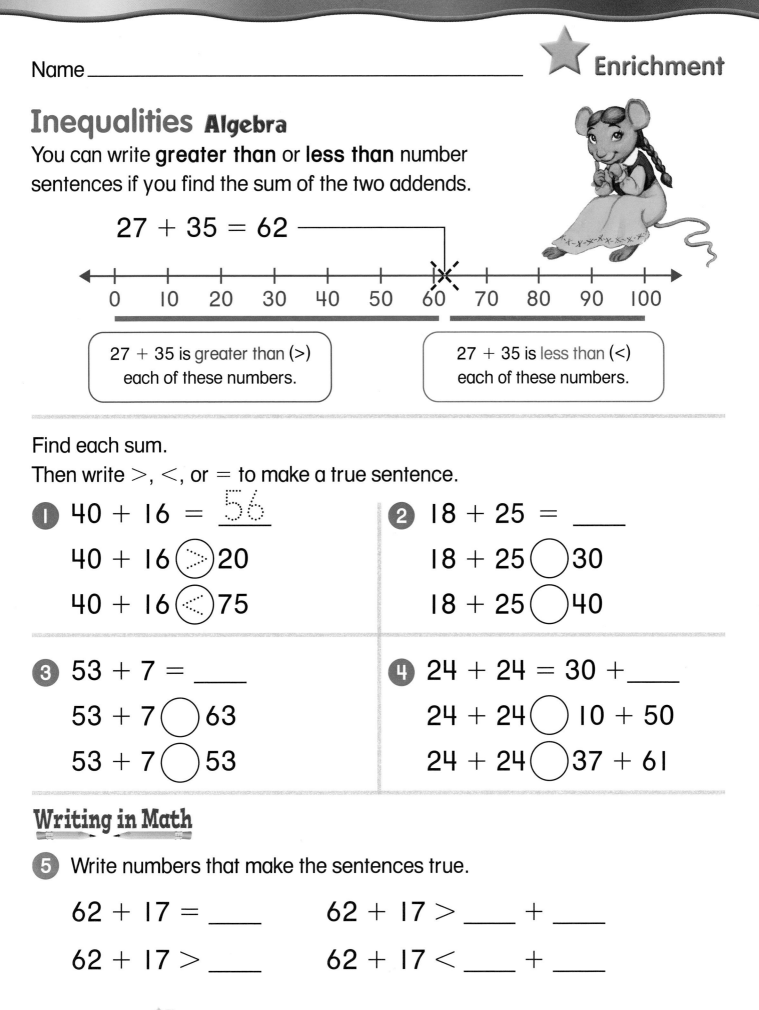

| 0 | 10 | 20 | 30 | 40 | 50 | 60 | 70 | 80 | 90 | 100 |

27 + 35 is greater than (>) each of these numbers.

27 + 35 is less than (<) each of these numbers.

Find each sum.

Then write >, <, or = to make a true sentence.

① $40 + 16 = \underline{56}$

$40 + 16 \;(>)\; 20$

$40 + 16 \;(<)\; 75$

② $18 + 25 = \underline{}$

$18 + 25 \;\bigcirc\; 30$

$18 + 25 \;\bigcirc\; 40$

③ $53 + 7 = \underline{}$

$53 + 7 \;\bigcirc\; 63$

$53 + 7 \;\bigcirc\; 53$

④ $24 + 24 = 30 + \underline{}$

$24 + 24 \;\bigcirc\; 10 + 50$

$24 + 24 \;\bigcirc\; 37 + 61$

Writing in Math

⑤ Write numbers that make the sentences true.

$62 + 17 = \underline{}$ $62 + 17 > \underline{} + \underline{}$

$62 + 17 > \underline{}$ $62 + 17 < \underline{} + \underline{}$

 Home Connection Your child used *less than* and *greater than* with two-digit numbers. **Home Activity** Ask your child: "Is 40 + 27 greater than or less than 30? 50? 70?"

Add Money Amounts Using a Calculator

You can use a calculator to add money amounts.

Draw a path from START to TARGET.
The money amounts in your path must add up to
the TARGET amount. Use your calculator to help you.

1

START $5	$38	$9
$20	$11	$1
$85	$68	TARGET $37

2

START $17	$23	$1
$75	$3	$41
$7	$64	TARGET $82

3

START $25	$4	$51
$93	$13	$48
$17	$2	TARGET $44

4

START $31	$3	$6
$42	$28	$72
$19	$8	TARGET $148

Think About It   Number Sense

In Exercise 2, how did you use a
calculator to figure out that you
were close to the target amount?

Home Connection Your child used a calculator to add several
amounts of money. **Home Activity** Ask your child to explain two
ways to find the sum of $6 + $8 + $34 on a calculator.

Name _____

Use Writing in Math

Some math tests ask you to write your answer. Remember that your answer should be **short** but **complete.**

Test-Taking Strategies

Understand the Question

Get Information for the Answer

Plan How to Find the Answer

Make Smart Choices

Use Writing in Math

1 Linnea bought two bookmarks at the book fair. One bookmark cost 27¢ and the other cost 55¢. How much money did Linnea spend on the bookmarks?

Linnea spent 82¢ on the bookmarks. _____

_____

A boy named Steve solved this problem by adding the two prices: 27¢ + 55¢ = 82¢. Then he used words from the question to help him write his answer.

Which words from the question did Steve use? If you can find some of them, raise your hand.

Your Turn

Underline the question in the problem. Solve the problem. Then write a short but complete answer to the question.

2 At the book fair, Ms. Will's class bought 43 books. Mr. Park's class bought 21 books. Ms. Larkin's class bought 35 books. How many books in all were bought by these three classes?

_____

_____

Home Connection Your child prepared for standardized tests by writing a short but complete answer to a math question. **Home Activity** Have your child explain how he or she solved the problem in Exercise 2. Then ask which words from the question he or she used in the answer.

two hundred five   **205**

Riding the Trail

In the Old West, cowboys took care of cattle. Every year they had a trail drive and brought cattle to the railroads. See how you would use addition if you were the trail boss.

Howdy, partner!

A Trail of Numbers

Solve each problem.

1. For the drive, you use crews of cowboys. One crew has 12 cowboys, and the other crew has 14 cowboys. How many cowboys are there in all?

   _____ cowboys

2. On the first day, your crews travel 17 miles. On the second day, your crews travel 15 miles. How many miles do your two crews travel in those first two days?

   _____ miles

3. For a month's work, you pay a young cowboy $25 and an older cowboy $35. How much money do you pay these two cowboys each month?

   _____

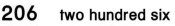

**Take It to the NET
Video and Activities**
www.scottforesman.com

Home Connection Your child solved problems about a trail drive by adding two-digit numbers. **Home Activity** Ask your child to explain how he or she found the answer to Exercise 3. *(Sample response: I added the ones: 5 + 5 = 10. Then I regrouped 10 ones as 1 ten. Then I added the tens: 1 ten + 2 tens + 3 tens = 6 tens. The answer is $60.)*

© Pearson Education, Inc.

Chapter Test

Use cubes and Workmat 4.

Add. Regroup if you need to.

Show.	Add.	Do you need to regroup?	Find the sum.
❶ 27	6	_____	27 + 6 = ___

Add. Regroup if you need to.

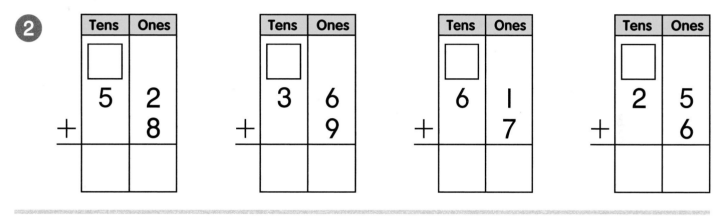

❷

Tens	Ones
□	
5	2
+	8

Tens	Ones
□	
3	6
+	9

Tens	Ones
□	
6	1
+	7

Tens	Ones
□	
2	5
+	6

Write the addition problem. Find the sum.

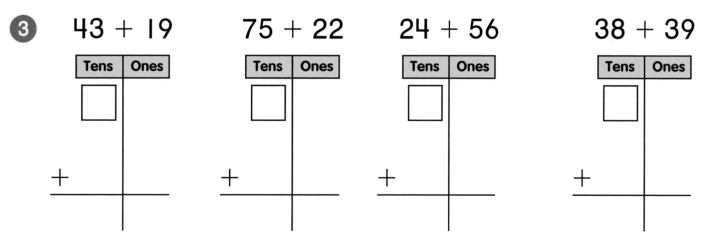

❸   43 + 19   75 + 22   24 + 56   38 + 39

Add to find the total amount.

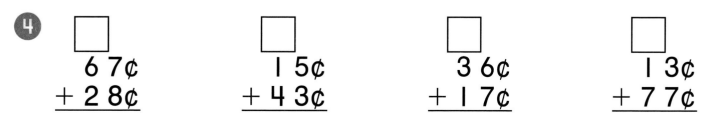

❹

  6 7¢   1 5¢   3 6¢   1 3¢
+ 2 8¢   + 4 3¢   + 1 7¢   + 7 7¢

Add in any order.

5

11	32	44	64
29	20	17	13
+ 15	+ 8	+ 23	+ 16

Estimate the sum. Then solve and compare.

Find the closest 10.	Estimate.	Solve.
6 18 + 41 18 is closest to ____. 41 is closest to ____.	18 + 41 is about ____.	18 + 41 = ____

Circle the better way to solve each problem.
Then find the sum.

7 22   paper and pencil
   + 36   mental math

8 65   paper and pencil
   + 20   mental math

Use data from the table to solve the problems.

9 How many dogs and cats
are there in all?

____ dogs and cats

Pet Show	
Kind	Number
Dog	48
Cat	22
Bird	9
Fish	13

10 There are 61 pets in the big
tent. Which two kinds of pets
are in the big tent?

_____ and _____

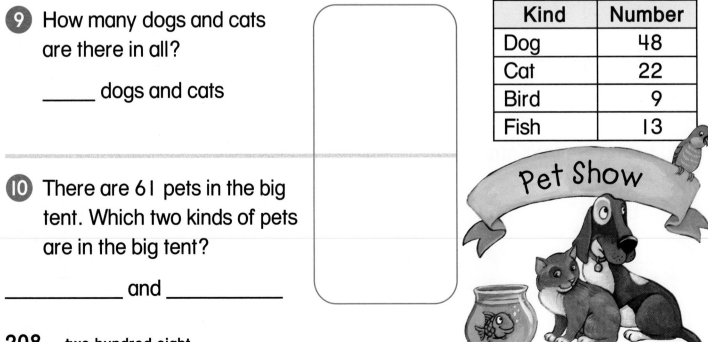

Too Many Marbles!

Written by Anne Miranda

Illustrated by Cathi Mingus

This Math Storybook belongs to

_____

Tom had too many marbles!
Marbles here, marbles there,
marbles, marbles everywhere!

"What can we do with all these marbles?"
asked Tom's mom.

"I know," answered Tom.
"I'll have a sidewalk sale."

Tom got ready for his big sale.

He put **25** blue marbles in one box.
He put **36** yellow marbles in another box.
He put **52** red marbles in a third box.

Then he made a big sign.

Tom's friend Michael read the sign.
He bought **11** of the blue marbles.

"Let's see," said Tom. "That leaves me
with **14** blue ones."

Michael turned around. "I like
the yellow ones too," he said.
"I'll buy **8** of them."

"OK," said Tom. "That leaves me
with **28** yellow ones."

Blue
Marbles

Yellow
Marbles

Red
Marbles

Tom's friend Alice liked red marbles a lot.
She bought **22** of them.

"OK," said Tom. "That leaves me
with **30** red ones."

"Wait a minute!" said Alice. "I want to
buy ALL of the red ones!"

So Tom put the remaining **30** red marbles in Alice's bag.

Tom's mom smiled. "You sold a lot of marbles today, Tom.
Now you can buy something new at the toy store."

Tom and his mom went shopping.

"What can I buy?" he wondered.
He looked around the store.

Suddenly, Tom smiled.
"Look, Mom! I found just what I need!
More marbles!"

Home-School Connection

Dear Family,

Today my class started Chapter 6, **Two-Digit Subtraction.** I will learn how to trade 1 ten for 10 ones to solve problems like 43 – 27. I will also learn how to solve money problems. Here are some of the math words I will be learning and some things we can do to help me with my math.

Love,

_____

Math Activity to Do at Home

Set 3 dimes and a pile of pennies on a table. Ask your child to display 27¢ using as many dimes as possible (2 dimes 7 pennies). Then ask him or her to subtract 9¢ from the 27¢. Give your child problems that require trading 1 dime for 10 pennies—and problems that don't.

Books to Read Together

Reading math stories reinforces concepts. Look for these titles in your local library:

Caps for Sale
By Esphyr Slobodkina
(HarperCollins, 1999)

Alexander, Who Used to Be Rich Last Sunday
By Judith Viorst
(Atheneum, 1979)

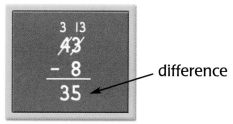

Take It to the NET
More Activities
www.scottforesman.com

My New Math Words

trade Another term for "regroup" (see below). 1 ten can be traded for 10 ones without changing the total value of the number you are subtracting from.

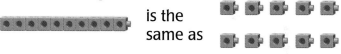 is the same as

regroup When you subtract 29 from 46, you need to regroup 1 ten as 10 ones.

$$\begin{array}{r} {\scriptstyle 3\ 16} \\ \cancel{4}\cancel{6} \\ -29 \\ \hline 17 \end{array}$$

difference The answer to a subtraction problem. "What is the difference between this number and that number?"

— difference

$$\begin{array}{r} {\scriptstyle 3\ 13} \\ \cancel{4}\cancel{3} \\ -\ \ 8 \\ \hline 35 \end{array}$$

Name _____

What's the Difference?

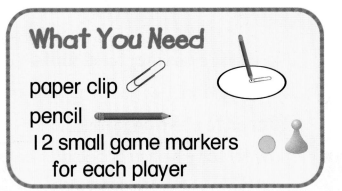

What You Need

paper clip

pencil

12 small game markers
for each player

How to Play

1. Choose one pile of marbles.
2. Take turns spinning the spinner.
3. Subtract the number on the spinner from the number on your pile.
4. Put a marker on the marble that shows the difference.
5. Continue playing until all 12 of the marbles are covered.
6. The person who covers the most marbles is the winner.

© Pearson Education, Inc.

Learn!

How do you **subtract** 6 from 34?

$34 - 6 = ?$

If you do not have enough ones, you need to regroup.

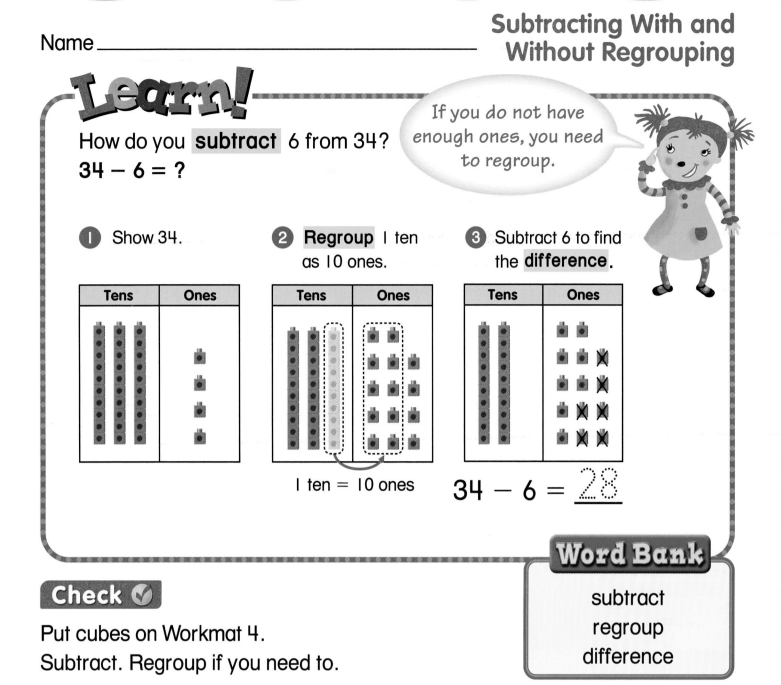

① Show 34.

② **Regroup** 1 ten as 10 ones.

③ Subtract 6 to find the **difference**.

1 ten = 10 ones

$34 - 6 = \underline{28}$

Word Bank

subtract

regroup

difference

Check ✓

Put cubes on Workmat 4.

Subtract. Regroup if you need to.

Show.	Subtract.	Do you need to regroup?	Find the difference.
❶ 35	8	yes	$35 - 8 = \underline{27}$
❷ 62	4	_____	$62 - 4 = \underline{}$
❸ 46	3	_____	$46 - 3 = \underline{}$

Think About It   Number Sense

Name a number that you can subtract from 45 without needing to regroup.

Put cubes on Workmat 4.
Subtract. Regroup if you need to.

Do you need to regroup?

Show.	Subtract.	Do you need to regroup?	Find the difference.
4️⃣ 53	7	_____	53 − 7 = ____
5️⃣ 29	1	_____	29 − 1 = ____
6️⃣ 33	3	_____	33 − 3 = ____
7️⃣ 81	2	_____	81 − 2 = ____
8️⃣ 24	9	_____	24 − 9 = ____
9️⃣ 70	8	_____	70 − 8 = ____
🔟 47	6	_____	47 − 6 = ____

Problem Solving   Visual Thinking

The path is 30 inches long. How much farther
does each snail need to crawl to get to the end?

1️⃣1️⃣ Zale crawled 10 inches. He needs to crawl _____ inches farther.

| 0 | 10 | 30 |

1️⃣2️⃣ Gail crawled 7 inches. She needs to crawl _____ inches farther.

| 0 | 7 | 30 |

Home Connection Your child identified when it is necessary to regroup in
subtraction problems. **Home Activity** Ask your child to explain whether it is
necessary to regroup when solving 68 − 7 and 38 − 4.

Name _____

Subtract 5 from 42.   **42 − 5 = ?**

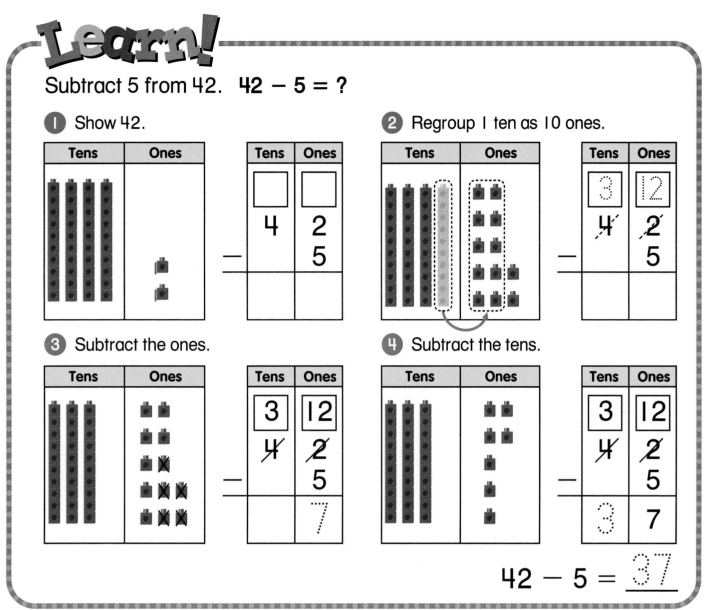

① Show 42.

Tens	Ones
4	2
	5

② Regroup 1 ten as 10 ones.

Tens	Ones
3	12
4̸	2̸
	5

③ Subtract the ones.

Tens	Ones
3	12
4̸	2̸
	5
	7

④ Subtract the tens.

Tens	Ones
3	12
4̸	2̸
	5
3	7

42 − 5 = 37

Check ✓

Put cubes on Workmat 4. Subtract. Regroup if you need to.

①

Tens	Ones
5	4
	9

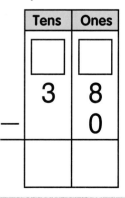

Tens	Ones
2	7
	5

Tens	Ones
3	8
	0

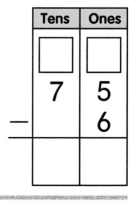

Tens	Ones
7	5
	6

Think About It   Number Sense

Look at 75 − 6 in Exercise 1. How did you decide
what number to write above the 5 in the ones column?

Subtract. Regroup if you need to.
Use cubes and Workmat 4 if you need to.

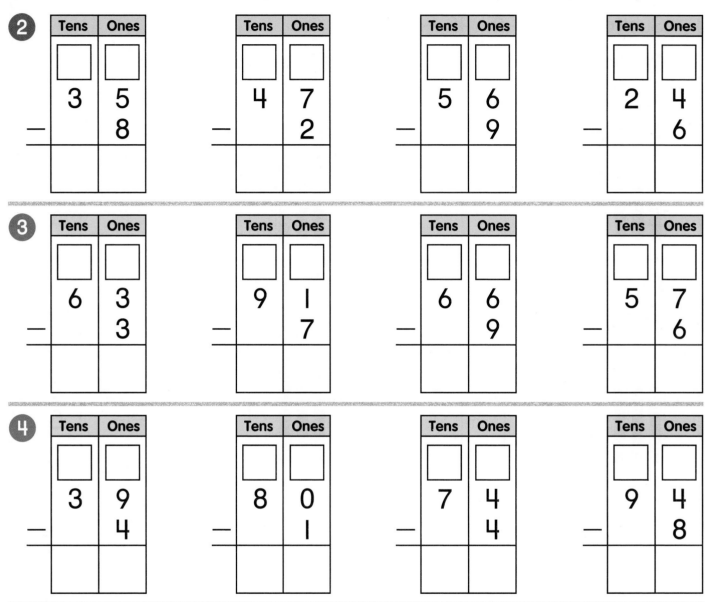

2

Tens	Ones
3	5
−	8

Tens	Ones
4	7
−	2

Tens	Ones
5	6
−	9

Tens	Ones
2	4
−	6

3

Tens	Ones
6	3
−	3

Tens	Ones
9	1
−	7

Tens	Ones
6	6
−	9

Tens	Ones
5	7
−	6

4

Tens	Ones
3	9
−	4

Tens	Ones
8	0
−	1

Tens	Ones
7	4
−	4

Tens	Ones
9	4
−	8

Problem Solving   Reasonableness

Draw a line to match
each person with his or her age.

5 Adam is 7 years younger
than Kendra.
Ravi is 5 years older
than Kendra.

Adam

Kendra

Ravi

45 years old   40 years old   33 years old

Home Connection Your child practiced subtracting a one-digit number
from a two-digit number. **Home Activity** Ask your child to explain how he
or she solved the problems in Exercise 4.

Name _____

Learn!

Subtract 18 from 31.   31 − 18 = ?

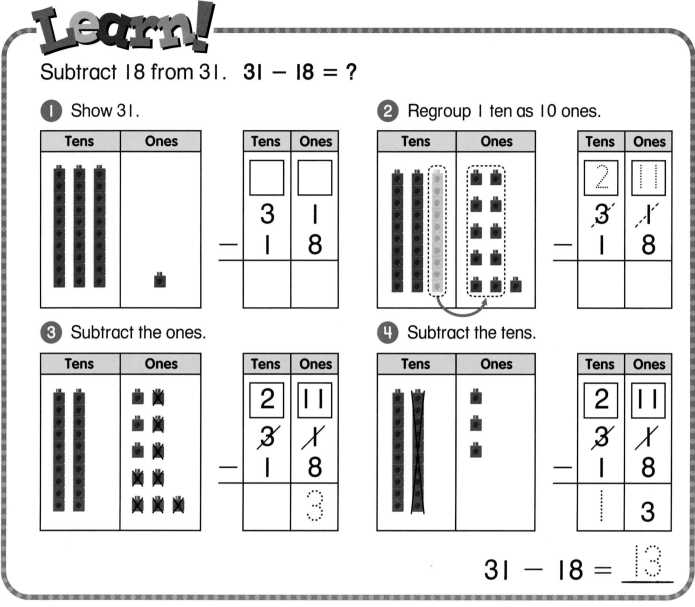

① Show 31.

Tens	Ones
3	1
− 1	8

② Regroup 1 ten as 10 ones.

Tens	Ones
2	11
3	1
− 1	8

③ Subtract the ones.

Tens	Ones
2	11
3	1
− 1	8
	3

④ Subtract the tens.

Tens	Ones
2	11
3	1
− 1	8
1	3

31 − 18 = __13__

Check ✓

Put cubes on Workmat 4. Subtract. Regroup if you need to.

①
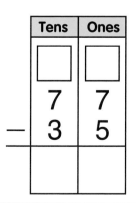

Tens	Ones
5	2
− 1	4

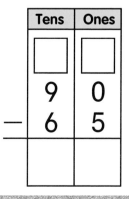

Tens	Ones
7	7
− 3	5

Tens	Ones
9	0
− 6	5

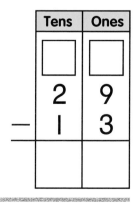

Tens	Ones
2	9
− 1	3

Think About It   Number Sense

Look at Exercise 1. Which problems did you **not** need
to regroup? Explain why you did not need to regroup.

Subtract. Regroup if you need to.

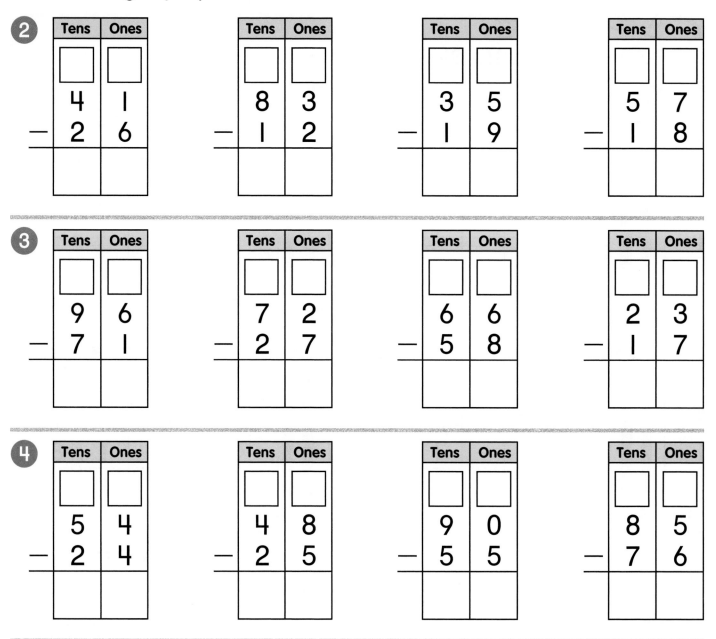

2

Tens	Ones
4	1
− 2	6

Tens	Ones
8	3
− 1	2

Tens	Ones
3	5
− 1	9

Tens	Ones
5	7
− 1	8

3

Tens	Ones
9	6
− 7	1

Tens	Ones
7	2
− 2	7

Tens	Ones
6	6
− 5	8

Tens	Ones
2	3
− 1	7

4

Tens	Ones
5	4
− 2	4

Tens	Ones
4	8
− 2	5

Tens	Ones
9	0
− 5	5

Tens	Ones
8	5
− 7	6

Problem Solving Algebra

Write a number in each number sentence to make it true.

5 $40 - 20 = 50 - \underline{\hspace{1cm}}$

$70 - 30 = 40 - \underline{\hspace{1cm}}$

$50 - 10 = 60 - \underline{\hspace{1cm}}$

6 $60 - 50 = 70 - \underline{\hspace{1cm}}$

$90 - 60 = 40 - \underline{\hspace{1cm}}$

$80 - 30 = 90 - \underline{\hspace{1cm}}$

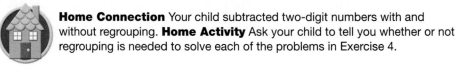

Home Connection Your child subtracted two-digit numbers with and without regrouping. **Home Activity** Ask your child to tell you whether or not regrouping is needed to solve each of the problems in Exercise 4.

216   two hundred sixteen

Name _____

Learn!

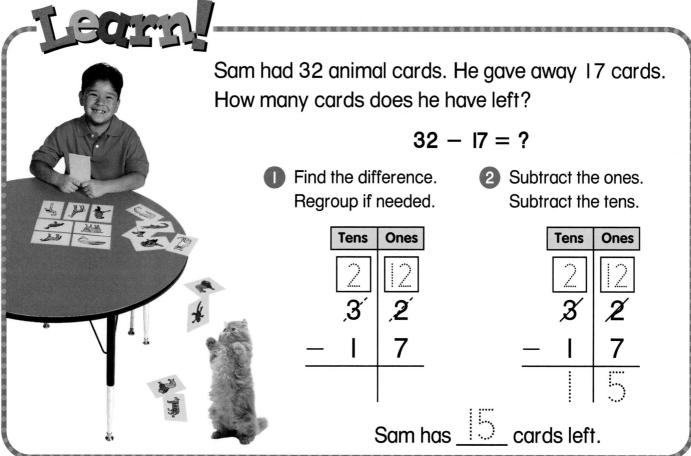

Sam had 32 animal cards. He gave away 17 cards. How many cards does he have left?

$$32 - 17 = ?$$

1 Find the difference. Regroup if needed.

Tens	Ones
2	12
3̷	2̷
− 1	7

2 Subtract the ones. Subtract the tens.

Tens	Ones
2	12
3̷	2̷
− 1	7
	5

Sam has __15__ cards left.

Check ✓

Write the subtraction problem. Find the difference.

1

54 − 26	31 − 20	85 − 79	60 − 37

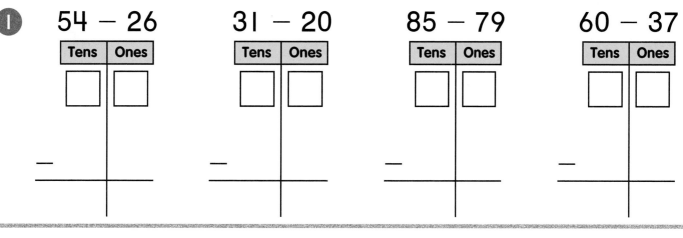

Tens	Ones
☐	☐

Tens	Ones
☐	☐

Tens	Ones
☐	☐

Tens	Ones
☐	☐

Think About It   Number Sense

Look at how Pat solved this subtraction problem. What is wrong?

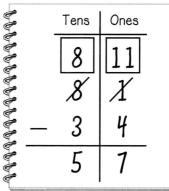

Tens	Ones
8	11
8̷	1̷
− 3	4
5	7

Write the subtraction problem. Find the difference.

2

52 − 36

Tens	Ones

−

94 − 54

Tens	Ones

−

41 − 25

Tens	Ones

−

33 − 8

Tens	Ones

−

3

65 − 42

Tens	Ones

−

70 − 48

Tens	Ones

−

96 − 37

Tens	Ones

−

87 − 45

Tens	Ones

−

Problem Solving   Number Sense

For each problem, use each number only once.

5   3   2   4

4 Make the greatest sum.

Tens	Ones

+

5 Make the greatest difference.

Tens	Ones

−

Home Connection Your child practiced subtracting two-digit numbers with and without regrouping. **Home Activity** Ask your child to explain why he or she needed to regroup in order to solve one of the problems.

Identify the Main Idea

1 Read the story of the Five Foolish Fishermen.
See if you can tell what counting mistake was made.

Once there were five fishermen
who went to the river to fish.
"Are we all here?" asked the first fisherman.
He pointed at each of his friends and counted.
"One. Two. Three. Four."

"Oh, no! Oh, no! Oh, no!" cried the fisherman.
"There were five of us.
And now there are only four!
One of us must have fallen into the river!"

2 What mistake did the fisherman make?

_____

Think About It   Reasoning

What did the fisherman and his friends think had happened?
Write a number sentence that shows this.

3 A group of fish is sometimes called a **school.**
Two schools of fish have gotten all mixed up. Help them out.
Color the fish that have one dot red.
Color the fish that have two dots blue.
How many fish are red? How many fish are blue?

4 What is the main idea of this number story?

   a. Fish go to school.

   b. Two groups of fish have gotten mixed up.

   c. All fish have dots on them.

5 Count the fish. There are _____ red fish and _____ blue fish.

Home Connection Your child identified the main idea in a folktale and wrote a number sentence about it. **Home Activity** Talk with your child about the main idea of a number sentence: the numbers before the equal sign and the number after the equal sign are different ways of naming the same amount.

Learn! Algebra

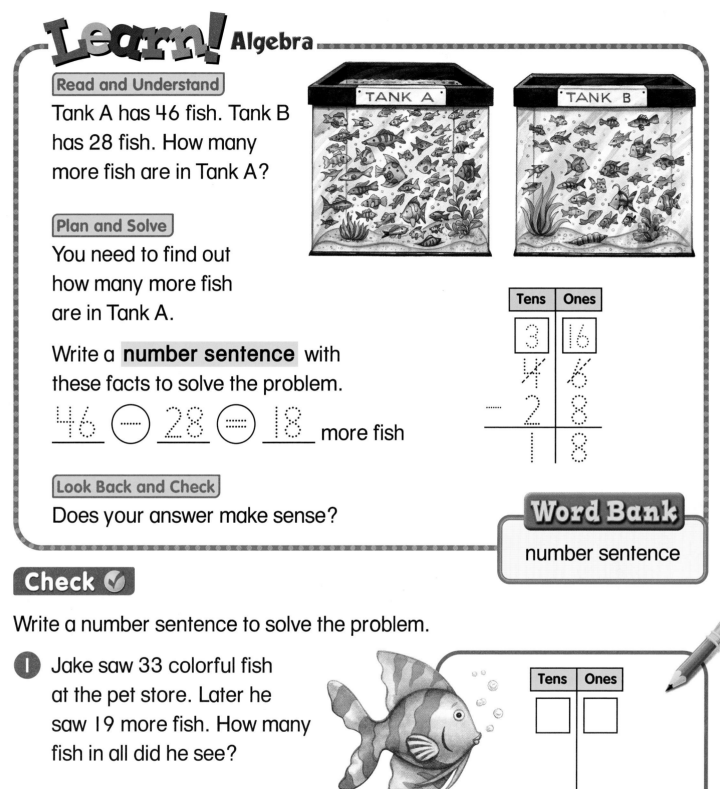

Read and Understand

Tank A has 46 fish. Tank B has 28 fish. How many more fish are in Tank A?

Plan and Solve

You need to find out how many more fish are in Tank A.

Write a **number sentence** with these facts to solve the problem.

$46 \bigcirc 28 \bigcirc 18$ more fish

Look Back and Check

Does your answer make sense?

Tens	Ones
3	16
4̸	6̸
− 2	8
1	8

Word Bank

number sentence

Check ✓

Write a number sentence to solve the problem.

1. Jake saw 33 colorful fish at the pet store. Later he saw 19 more fish. How many fish in all did he see?

Tens	Ones

 fish

Think About It   Reasoning

How did you decide whether to add or subtract in Exercise 1?

2 There are 74 water plants.
There are 66 tanks.
How many more water plants
than tanks are there?

Tens	Ones

$-$

____ ◯ ____ ◯ ____ more plants

3 Eri has 23 clown fish and
49 angelfish. How many
fish does he have in all?

Tens	Ones

$+$

____ ◯ ____ ◯ ____ fish in all

4 Maria fed the fish 65 flakes.
Paul fed the fish 50 flakes.
How many more flakes did
Maria feed the fish?

Tens	Ones

$-$

____ ◯ ____ ◯ ____ more flakes

5 Kwame gave Lauren
32 zebra fish. Lauren
gave Jack 16 of these fish.
How many zebra fish does
Lauren have left?

Tens	Ones

$-$

____ ◯ ____ ◯ ____ zebra fish

© Pearson Education, Inc.

Home Connection Your child wrote number sentences to solve
problems. **Home Activity** Using two-digit numbers, make up a problem
for your child to solve. Ask how he or she will solve the problem.

Name _____

Put cubes on Workmat 4.
Subtract. Regroup if you need to.

Show.	Subtract.	Do you need to regroup?	Find the difference.
① 41	6	_____	41 − 6 = ___
② 78	8	_____	78 − 8 = ___

Subtract. Regroup if you need to.

③
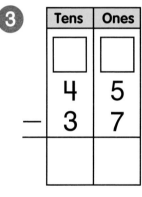

Tens	Ones
4	5
− 3	7

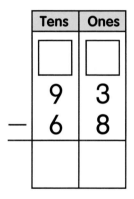

Tens	Ones
9	3
− 6	8

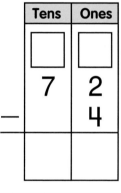

Tens	Ones
7	2
−	4

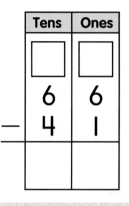

Tens	Ones
6	6
− 4	1

Write the subtraction problem. Find the difference.

④ 91 − 63

Tens	Ones

48 − 14

Tens	Ones

53 − 29

Tens	Ones

74 − 61

Tens	Ones

Write a number sentence to solve the problem.

Tens	Ones

⑤ Ben counted 34 blocks.
Kay counted 27 blocks. How many
blocks did they count altogether?

____ ◯ ____ ◯ ____ blocks

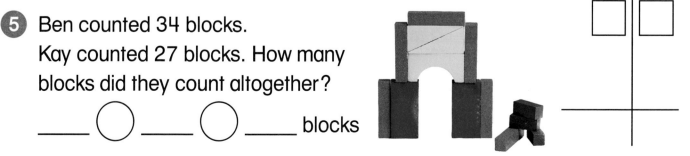

Count and mark the number of tens.

1

- Ⓐ 6
- Ⓑ 4
- Ⓒ 3
- Ⓓ 1

Count and mark the number.

2

- Ⓐ 40
- Ⓑ 55
- Ⓒ 41
- Ⓓ 51

Mark the sum.

3

15 + 20

- Ⓐ 45
- Ⓑ 35
- Ⓒ 30
- Ⓓ 15

4

10 + 9

- Ⓐ 10
- Ⓑ 9
- Ⓒ 11
- Ⓓ 19

Add. Mark the sum.

5

```
   5
   6
 + 2
```

- Ⓐ 8
- Ⓑ 11
- Ⓒ 13
- Ⓓ 7

6

```
  24
  19
+ 56
```

- Ⓐ 99
- Ⓑ 919
- Ⓒ 89
- Ⓓ 79

Writing in Math

Write the number sentence that solves the problem.
Then write the answer.

7 There are 8 plates on the table.
4 plates are on the shelf.
How many plates are there in all?

_____ ◯ _____ = _____ plates

Name_____

Learn! Algebra

Estimate the difference between 42 and 28.

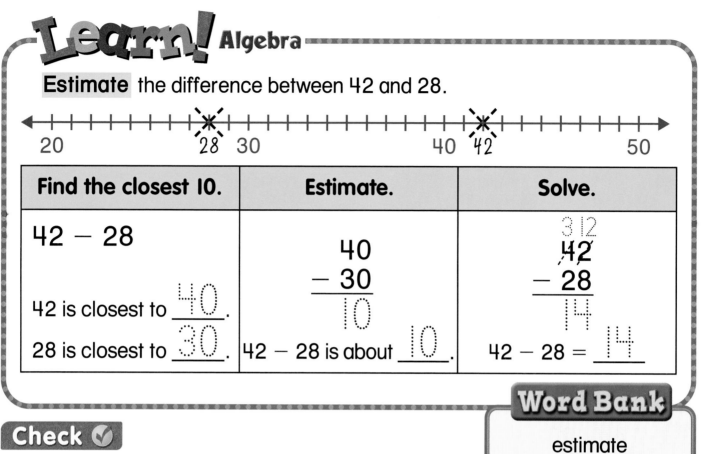

Find the closest 10.	Estimate.	Solve.
42 − 28 42 is closest to __40__. 28 is closest to __30__.	40 − 30 ‾‾‾ 10 42 − 28 is about __10__.	$\begin{array}{r} 3\,12 \\ \cancel{4}\,\cancel{2} \\ -\ 28 \\ \hline 14 \end{array}$ 42 − 28 = __14__

Word Bank

estimate

Check ✓

Estimate the difference. Then solve and compare.

Find the closest 10.	Estimate.	Solve.
① 78 − 31 78 is closest to _____. 31 is closest to _____.	78 − 31 is about _____.	78 − 31 = _____
② 53 − 19 53 is closest to _____. 19 is closest to _____.	53 − 19 is about _____.	53 − 19 = _____

Think About It   Reasoning

Why is it helpful to estimate the answer
before you solve the problem?

Estimate the difference. Then solve and compare.

Find the closest 10.	Estimate.	Solve.
③ 61 − 27 61 is closest to ____. 27 is closest to ____.	61 − 27 is about ____.	61 − 27 = ____
④ 93 − 42 93 is closest to ____. 42 is closest to ____.	93 − 42 is about ____.	93 − 42 = ____
⑤ 77 − 28 77 is closest to ____. 28 is closest to ____.	77 − 28 is about ____.	77 − 28 = ____

Problem Solving   Estimation

Estimate to solve the problem.

Number of Houses			
Street	1st	2nd	3rd
Number	47	68	____

⑥ 3rd Street has about 30 more houses
than 1st Street. About how many houses
are on 3rd Street?

about ____ houses

Home Connection Your child practiced estimating before subtracting
two-digit numbers. **Home Activity** Ask your child to estimate 92 − 49.
(*90 − 50 = 40, so the answer is about 40.*)

Name _____

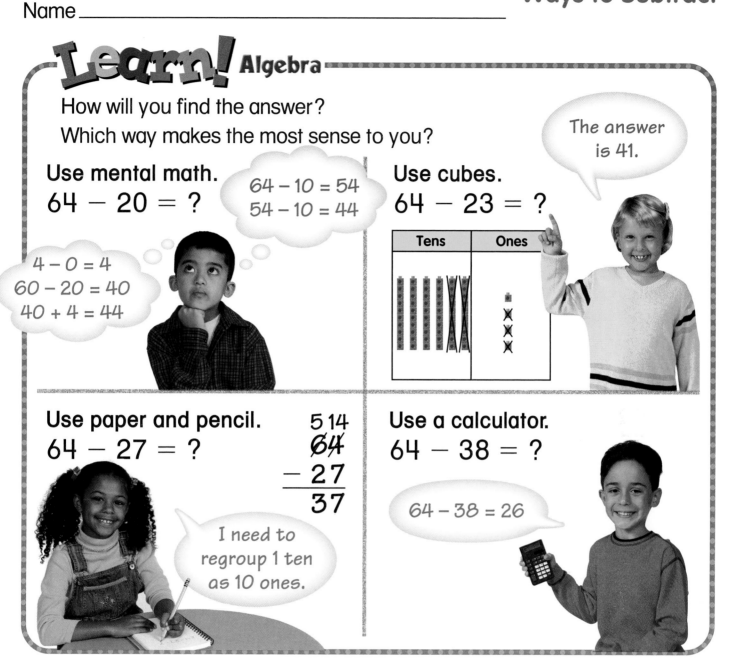

Learn! Algebra

How will you find the answer?
Which way makes the most sense to you?

Use mental math.
64 − 20 = ?

64 − 10 = 54
54 − 10 = 44

4 − 0 = 4
60 − 20 = 40
40 + 4 = 44

Use cubes.
64 − 23 = ?

The answer is 41.

Tens	Ones

Use paper and pencil.
64 − 27 = ?

$$\begin{array}{r} 5\ 14 \\ \cancel{6}\cancel{4} \\ -\ 27 \\ \hline 37 \end{array}$$

I need to regroup 1 ten as 10 ones.

Use a calculator.
64 − 38 = ?

64 − 38 = 26

Check ✓

Circle what you think is the better way to solve each problem.
Then subtract.

1
$$\begin{array}{r} 54 \\ -\ 40 \\ \hline \end{array}$$
   mental math
   calculator

2
$$\begin{array}{r} 63 \\ -\ 57 \\ \hline \end{array}$$
   paper and pencil
   mental math

Think About It   Reasoning

Explain how you solved the problems in Exercises 1 and 2.

Practice

Write the letter that tells how you
will solve the problem.

Then subtract and write the difference.

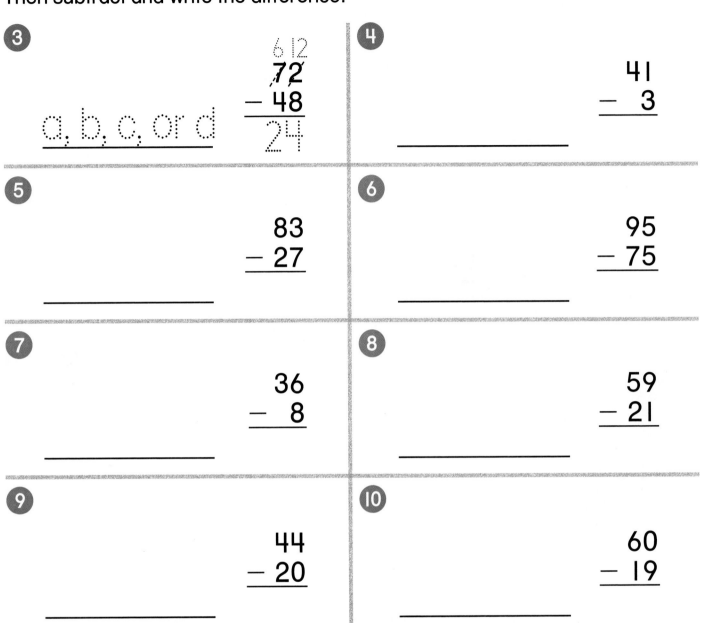

3

a, b, c, or d

$$\overset{6\ 12}{\cancel{7}2}$$
$$-\ 48$$
$$\overline{\ 24}$$

4

$$41$$
$$-\ \ 3$$

5

$$83$$
$$-\ 27$$

6

$$95$$
$$-\ 75$$

7

$$36$$
$$-\ \ 8$$

8

$$59$$
$$-\ 21$$

9

$$44$$
$$-\ 20$$

10

$$60$$
$$-\ 19$$

Problem Solving   Writing in Math

11 Write 2 new subtraction problems
that you can use mental math
to solve.

Home Connection Your child chose a way to solve each problem.
Home Activity Ask your child to explain which method he or she will
use to solve 91 − 50.

232   two hundred thirty-two

Learn!

Cross out the extra **information**. Solve the problem.

The boys packed 32 milk boxes and 15 juice cans. ~~Amanda packed 28 sandwiches.~~ How many more milk boxes than juice cans were there?

I do not need to know how many sandwiches Amanda packed.

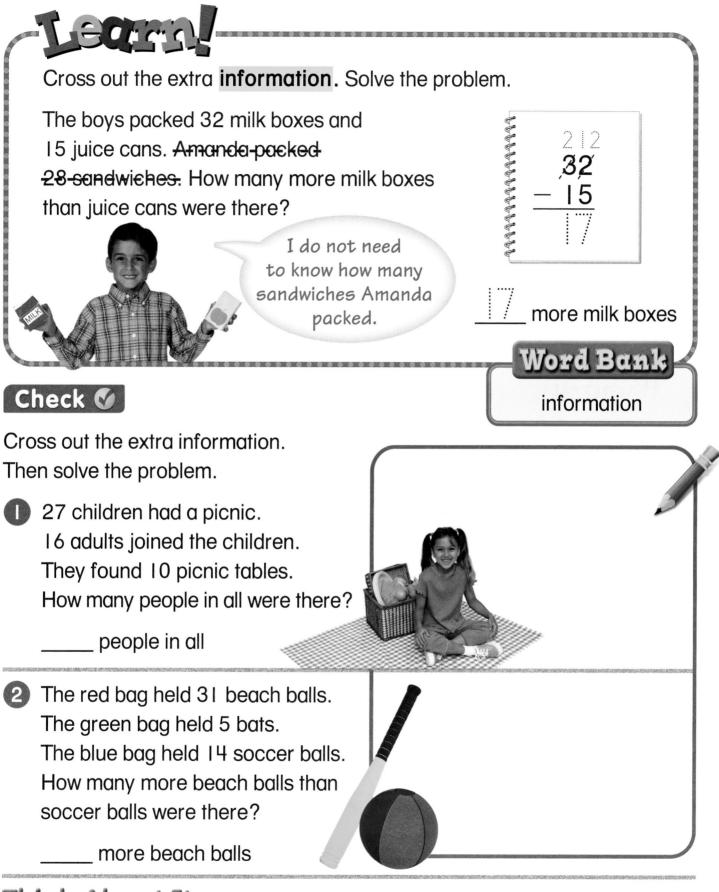

$$\begin{array}{r} 2\ 12 \\ \cancel{3}\cancel{2} \\ -\ 15 \\ \hline 17 \end{array}$$

___17___ more milk boxes

Word Bank

information

Check ✓

Cross out the extra information.
Then solve the problem.

1. 27 children had a picnic.
   16 adults joined the children.
   They found 10 picnic tables.
   How many people in all were there?

   _____ people in all

2. The red bag held 31 beach balls.
   The green bag held 5 bats.
   The blue bag held 14 soccer balls.
   How many more beach balls than soccer balls were there?

   _____ more beach balls

Think About It Number Sense

Tell a subtraction story that has extra information in it.
Use the numbers 31, 27, and 10.

Cross out the extra information.
Then solve the problem.

3 82 sandwiches were made.
The people ate 76 of them.
They also ate 20 apples.
How many sandwiches are left?

_____ sandwiches

4 25 children played games
with 15 adults.
2 children went hiking.
How many people played games?

_____ people

5 The children found 63 shells.
They saw 11 birds.
Then they found 47 feathers.
How many more shells than
feathers did they find?

_____ more shells

6 There were 19 kites in the sky.
There were also 74 red balloons
and 59 yellow balloons.
How many more red balloons
than yellow balloons were there?

_____ more red balloons

Home Connection Your child identified information that is not needed
to solve a problem. **Home Activity** Ask your child to write a problem
about a picnic—a story problem that has extra information.

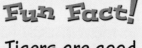

Dorling Kindersley

Do You Know...

that Siberian tigers are the world's biggest cats? Some of them weigh as much as 675 pounds!

1 One tiger's tail is 37 inches long.
Another tiger's tail is 29 inches long.
How much longer is the first tiger's tail?

_____ ◯ _____ = _____ inches longer

2 Tigers have 5 claws on each of their front paws. They have 4 claws on each of their back paws. How many claws do they have in all?

_____ ◯ _____ = _____ front claws

_____ ◯ _____ = _____ back claws

_____ ◯ _____ = _____ claws in all

Fun Fact!

Tigers are good swimmers. They can even swim across rivers.

Siberian tigers are very rare. There may be only about 400 of them alive.

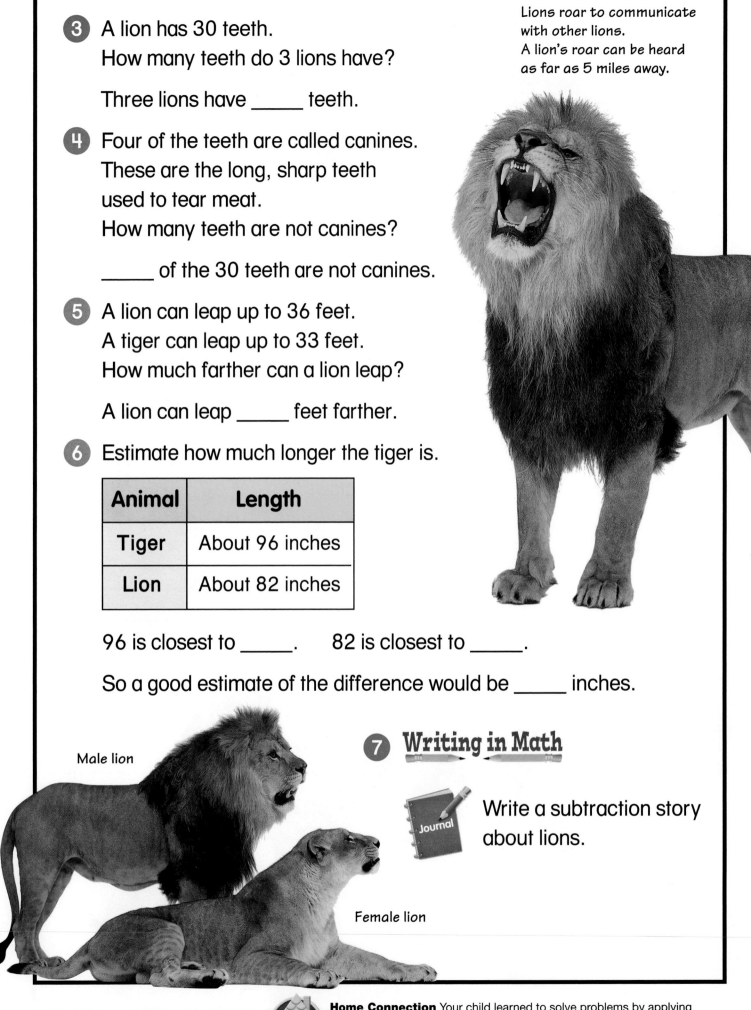

3 A lion has 30 teeth.
How many teeth do 3 lions have?

Three lions have _____ teeth.

4 Four of the teeth are called canines.
These are the long, sharp teeth
used to tear meat.
How many teeth are not canines?

_____ of the 30 teeth are not canines.

5 A lion can leap up to 36 feet.
A tiger can leap up to 33 feet.
How much farther can a lion leap?

A lion can leap _____ feet farther.

6 Estimate how much longer the tiger is.

Animal	Length
Tiger	About 96 inches
Lion	About 82 inches

96 is closest to _____.   82 is closest to _____.

So a good estimate of the difference would be _____ inches.

Lions roar to communicate
with other lions.
A lion's roar can be heard
as far as 5 miles away.

Male lion

Female lion

7 **Writing in Math**

Write a subtraction story
about lions.

© Pearson Education, Inc.

Home Connection Your child learned to solve problems by applying
his or her math skills. **Home Activity** Talk to your child about how he
or she solved the problems on these two pages.

Name_____

Subtract to find the difference.

①

	7	7¢
−	5	1¢

②

	4	2¢
−	1	8¢

Subtract.
Check your answer by adding.

③

```
   54
 − 25
```

Write the letter that tells how you will solve the problem. Then subtract and write the difference.

> a. mental math   c. cubes
> b. paper and pencil   d. calculator

④

```
   87
 − 30
```

_____

⑤

```
   61
 − 43
```

_____

Estimate the difference. Then solve and compare.

Find the closest 10.	Estimate.	Solve.
⑥ 57 − 29 57 is closest to _____. 29 is closest to _____.	57 − 29 is about _____.	57 − 29 = _____

Cross out the extra information. Then solve the problem.

⑦ Abby saw 37 moths. Mike saw 48 moths. Jenna saw 19 spiders. How many moths in all did Abby and Mike see?

_____ moths

Name _____

Mark the true statement.

1   73 > 69   49 > 50   32 = 23   94 < 90

　　　Ⓐ　　　　　　　Ⓑ　　　　　　　Ⓒ　　　　　　　Ⓓ

Add. Mark the sum.

2 36 + 9
Ⓐ 54
Ⓑ 36
Ⓒ 45
Ⓓ 46

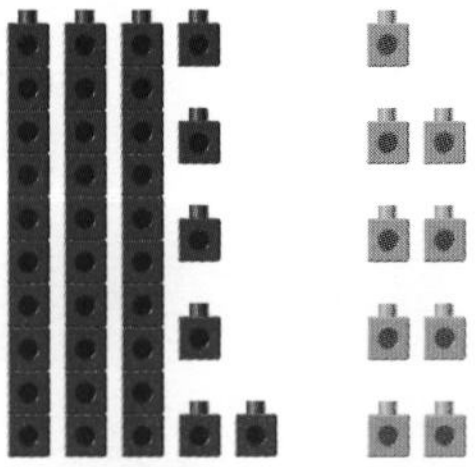

3 21 + 5
Ⓐ 25
Ⓑ 21
Ⓒ 15
Ⓓ 26

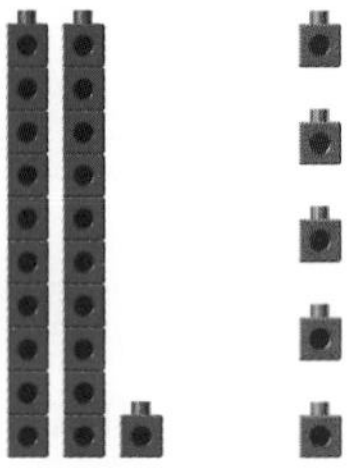

Add. Mark the sum.

4
　47¢
+ 22¢
Ⓐ 67¢
Ⓑ 69¢
Ⓒ 60¢
Ⓓ 77¢

5
　56¢
+ 39¢
Ⓐ 86¢
Ⓑ 85¢
Ⓒ 95¢
Ⓓ 59¢

Mark the other part of 100.

6   50 and ____ is 100.

25   50   75   0
Ⓐ   Ⓑ   Ⓒ   Ⓓ

7   60 and ____ is 100.

30   20   50   40
Ⓐ   Ⓑ   Ⓒ   Ⓓ

Writing in Math

8 Draw a set of coins that has the value of $1.00.

Name_____  **Enrichment**

Finding Numbers to Subtract
for a Given Difference **Algebra**

The difference between two of the four numbers is 30.
Find these two numbers.

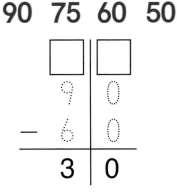

1 The first number is greater than the second
number. So the first number can't be 50.

2 80 − 50 = 30, but 80 is not a number
choice. So the second number can't be 50.

3 The difference between the ones digits is 0.
So 75 can't be the first or second number.

4 The two numbers are 90 and 60.

90 75 60 50

```
  9 │ 0
−   │
  6 │ 0
────┼────
  3 │ 0
```

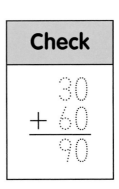

Check
```
  30
+ 60
────
  90
```

Find the two numbers for which the difference is given. Then check.

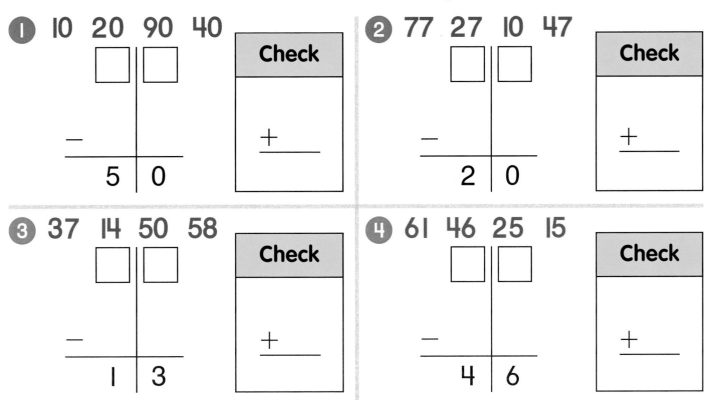

1 10 20 90 40

```
    │
−   │
────┼────
  5 │ 0
```

Check

+ ___

2 77 27 10 47

```
    │
−   │
────┼────
  2 │ 0
```

Check

+ ___

3 37 14 50 58

```
    │
−   │
────┼────
  1 │ 3
```

Check

+ ___

4 61 46 25 15

```
    │
−   │
────┼────
  4 │ 6
```

Check

+ ___

Writing in Math

5 Write a different problem for Exercise 2. Give four numbers.
Make sure that only two of them have a difference of 20.

Home Connection Your child chose pairs of numbers
for which the differences were given. **Home Activity**
Ask your child, "Which two of these numbers have a
difference of 15: 80, 35, 45, 50?"

Name_____

Subtract Two-Digit Numbers Using a Calculator

You can use a calculator to subtract two-digit numbers. Press ON/C each time you begin.
Find number pairs that have the same difference.
Write the letters of the matches on the blanks below.

A	B	C	D
43 − 16	51 − 48	20 − 9	110 − 55
E	**F**	**G**	**H**
84 − 63	75 − 68	54 − 27	15 − 12
I	**J**	**K**	**L**
175 − 85	150 − 95	165 − 75	34 − 17
M	**N**	**O**	**P**
94 − 87	65 − 54	70 − 49	100 − 83

My Matches

__A__ and __G__   _____ and _____

_____ and _____   _____ and _____

_____ and _____   _____ and _____

_____ and _____   _____ and _____

Think About It   Reasoning

Tell how you used a calculator to find a match for B.

Home Connection Your child used a calculator to subtract two-digit numbers. **Home Activity** Ask your child to explain how he or she would use a calculator to find out whether or not 75 − 34 and 50 − 9 have the same difference.

Name _____

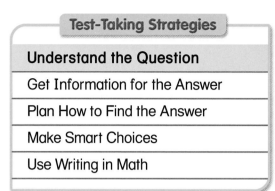

 Read Together

Understand the Question

Some math problems have special words such as NOT and EXCEPT.

These words can change the meaning of a math problem.

1 Which number sentence is not true?

Ⓐ $60 + 10 = 80 - 10$

Ⓑ $40 + 40 = 90 - 30$

Ⓒ $20 + 30 = 70 - 20$

Ⓓ $10 + 40 = 60 - 10$

Find the word NOT in the question.
Check each number sentence.
Find the one that is **not** true.
Then fill in the correct answer bubble.

Test-Taking Strategies
Understand the Question
Get Information for the Answer
Plan How to Find the Answer
Make Smart Choices
Use Writing in Math

Your Turn

Underline the words EXCEPT and NOT in Exercise 2.
Then solve the problem and fill in the answer bubble.

2 You need to regroup to solve all of these subtraction problems except one. Which problem does not require you to regroup?

Ⓐ
Tens	Ones
5	7
− 2	9

Ⓑ
Tens	Ones
7	3
− 3	4

Ⓒ
Tens	Ones
9	4
− 3	8

Ⓓ
Tens	Ones
8	5
− 6	2

 Home Connection Your child prepared for standardized tests by identifying important words and by thinking about their meanings.
Home Activity Ask your child what the words EXCEPT and NOT mean in Exercise 2.

Name _____

Discover Math in Your World

How Tall Is Tall?

Three kinds of great apes are **orangutans, gorillas,** and **chimpanzees.** Some great apes can be very tall. Use subtraction to compare your height with the heights of these great apes.

Measuring Up

1 Use a measuring tape to find your height in inches.

2 Find the difference between the height of each ape and your height. Fill in the table.

	Orangutan	Gorilla	Chimpanzee
Ape's Height	60 inches	72 inches	48 inches
Your Height			
Difference			

3 How much taller is the orangutan than you are?

It is _____ inches taller than I am.

4 How much taller is the gorilla than you are?

It is _____ inches taller than I am.

5 Are you taller or shorter than the chimpanzee?

I am _____ than the chimpanzee.

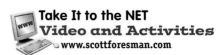
Take It to the NET
Video and Activities
www.scottforesman.com

Home Connection Your child solved problems about height by subtracting two-digit numbers. **Home Activity** Ask your child to find the difference between his or her height and the height of another family member.

Chapter 6

Name _____

Put cubes on Workmat 4.

Subtract. Regroup if you need to.

Show.	Subtract.	Do you need to regroup?	Find the difference.
1 28	6	_____	28 − 6 = ___
2 63	7	_____	63 − 7 = ___

Subtract. Regroup if you need to.

3

Tens	Ones
☐	☐
9	4
− 7	6

Tens	Ones
☐	☐
5	3
− 2	7

Tens	Ones
☐	☐
4	7
− 3	1

Tens	Ones
☐	☐
8	8
−	8

Write the subtraction problem. Find the difference.

4   75 − 36   24 − 19   83 − 55   42 − 23

Tens	Ones
☐	☐

Tens	Ones
☐	☐

Tens	Ones
☐	☐

Tens	Ones
☐	☐

Write a number sentence to solve the problem.

5 Nora found 64 books on a cart.
Kevin found 49 books on a cart.
How many more books did Nora find?

Tens	Ones
☐	☐

_____ ◯ _____ ◯ _____ more books

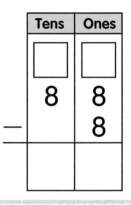

Subtract to find the difference.

6

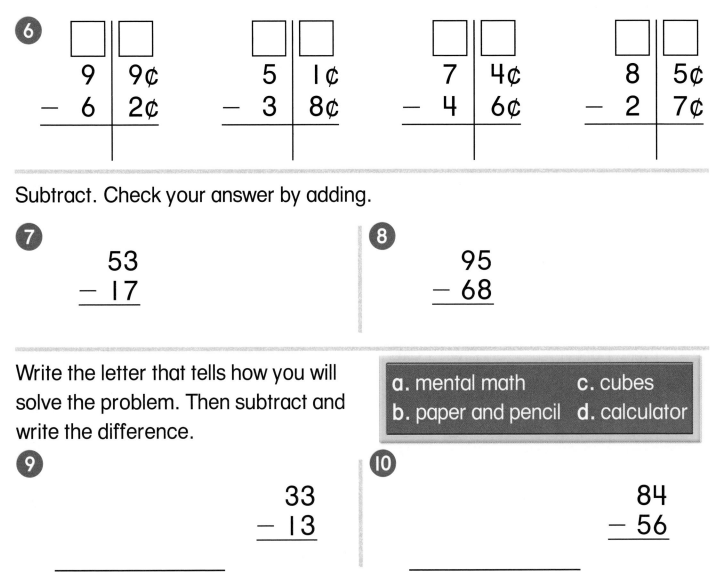

9	9¢
− 6	2¢

5	1¢
− 3	8¢

7	4¢
− 4	6¢

8	5¢
− 2	7¢

Subtract. Check your answer by adding.

7

      53
    − 17

8

      95
    − 68

Write the letter that tells how you will solve the problem. Then subtract and write the difference.

> **a.** mental math   **c.** cubes
> **b.** paper and pencil   **d.** calculator

9

      33
    − 13

_____

10

      84
    − 56

_____

Estimate the difference. Then solve and compare.

Find the closest 10.	Estimate.	Solve.
11 72 − 49 72 is closest to _____. 49 is closest to _____.	72 − 49 is about _____.	72 − 49 = _____

Cross out the extra information. Then solve the problem.

12 38 shoes are in the closet. 12 shoes are on the floor. 19 hats are on the shelf. How many shoes are there in all?

_____ shoes

Add or subtract.

1

$$\begin{array}{r} 58 \\ + 34 \\ \hline \end{array}$$

24   63   84   92
Ⓐ   Ⓑ   Ⓒ   Ⓓ

2

$$\begin{array}{r} 45 \\ - 33 \\ \hline \end{array}$$

12   18   72   78
Ⓐ   Ⓑ   Ⓒ   Ⓓ

3

$$\begin{array}{r} 3 \\ 26 \\ + 47 \\ \hline \end{array}$$

83   76   66   63
Ⓐ   Ⓑ   Ⓒ   Ⓓ

4

$$\begin{array}{r} 78 \\ - 10 \\ \hline \end{array}$$

60   68   80   88
Ⓐ   Ⓑ   Ⓒ   Ⓓ

5 How many pencils are there IN ALL?

Ⓐ 47
Ⓑ 37
Ⓒ 17
Ⓓ 13

10 Pencils

10 Pencils

10 Pencils

6 Which number in the chart should be circled next?

71	72	73	74	(75)	76	77	78	79	(80)
81	82	83	84	(85)	86	87	88	89	(90)
91	92	93	94	95	96	97	98	99	100

Ⓐ 91
Ⓑ 92
Ⓒ 95
Ⓓ 100

7 Which numbers are in order from LEAST to GREATEST?

2, 5, 8	8, 2, 5	5, 2, 8	8, 5, 2
Ⓐ	Ⓑ	Ⓒ	Ⓓ

8 Which statement is true?

13 > 15	12 < 12	28 > 82	15 < 50
Ⓐ	Ⓑ	Ⓒ	Ⓓ

9 Jane added 45 and 43. She said the total was 78.
Estimate the sum. Is Jane's answer reasonable? Explain.
Show All Work

10 Ben needs $1.00 to go to The Lincoln Museum.
He has these coins.

Draw a circle around the coins Ben can use to make $1.00.

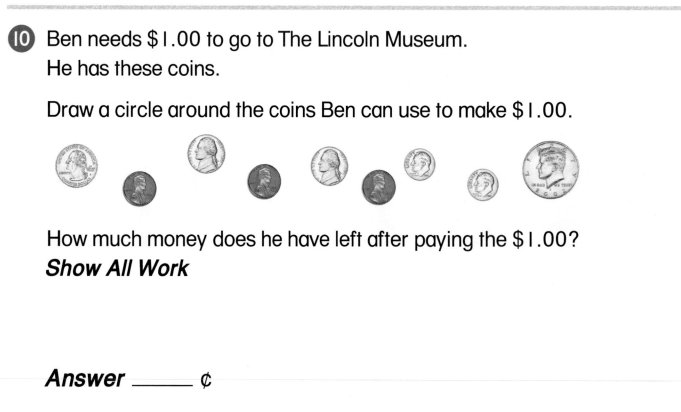

How much money does he have left after paying the $1.00?
Show All Work

Answer _____ ¢

244B

Grandma's Baskets

Photo Album

Written by
Joy Rose Dallas

Illustrated by
Daniel L. Grant

This Math Storybook belongs to

_____

Jean and her twin brother, Scott, were having a party.

"I want some cute baskets to hold the treats," said Jean. "But the baskets at the store cost too much money."

"I have a better idea," said Grandma. "We can make our own baskets."

Grandma bought some colored paper.

Make Your Own Basket!

You need ...

$2.0

Grandma looked at the paper and said, "First, I need to make a square."

She folded the paper diagonally.

Jean and Scott were puzzled. The paper didn't look like a square to them.

Then Grandma cut off the bottom. "That's a triangle, Grandma," said Scott.

"I know," answered Grandma. "When I open it, it will become a square."

Make a square.

Step 1   Step 2   Step 3

Jean and Scott watched as Grandma folded the square diagonally the other way.

Then Grandma took one corner of the square and folded it into the middle.

She did this three more times.

"Now I see four triangles and a smaller square," said Jean.

Fold each corner into the middle.

Step 4 Step 5 Step 6

Grandma turned the paper over and folded in the corners once more.

"It's another square with triangles," said Scott. "I can see lots of little triangles."

Grandma folded the little square in half.

"Now it's a rectangle," exclaimed Jean as Grandma folded the rectangle to make an even smaller square.

Step 7 Step 8 Step 9

Jean and Scott watched wide-eyed. They wondered how in the world Grandma was going to make a basket out of that tiny little square.

Grandma unfolded the little square. Then she unfolded the rectangle. Then, when she had the next square, she turned it over and pulled out the flaps.

She set it down on the table. "Is that a good basket for your treats?" she asked Jean and Scott.

"Oh, Grandma, that's a great basket! That will work very well," cried Jean.

"I'm going to put some stickers on mine!" said Scott.

Step 10

Step 11

Step 12

Home-School Connection

Dear Family,

Today my class started Chapter 7, **Geometry and Fractions.** I will learn how to describe solid figures (such as spheres) and plane shapes (such as squares). I will also learn how to name fractions. Here are some of the math words I will be learning and some things we can do to help me with my math.

Love,

_____

Math Activity to Do at Home

Go on a "Shapes Hunt." Search for objects that approximate geometric solids (such as cylinders and cones) and geometric shapes (such as circles and triangles). Encourage your child to describe the features of each.

Books to Read Together

Reading math stories reinforces concepts. Look for these titles in your local library:

The Greedy Triangle
By Marilyn Burns
(Scholastic, 1995)

The Amazing Book of Shapes
By Lydia Sharman
(Dorling Kindersley, 1994)

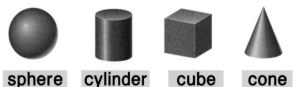

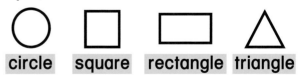

Take It to the NET
More Activities
www.scottforesman.com

My New Math Words

solid figures Three-dimensional geometric solids, such as …

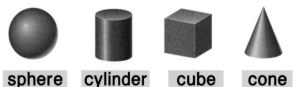

sphere   cylinder   cube   cone

plane shapes Two-dimensional geometric shapes, such as …

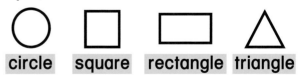

circle   square   rectangle   triangle

fraction When a shape or a set is divided into equal parts, we say that each part is a fraction of the whole.

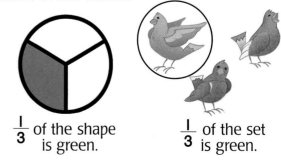

$\frac{1}{3}$ of the shape is green.

$\frac{1}{3}$ of the set is green.

Solid Concentration

What You Need

20 paper squares

How to Play

1. Place the squares on the gameboard.
2. Take turns. Turn over 2 squares.
3. If you find a match, keep the squares.
4. If you do not find a match, put the squares back.
5. The person who has the most squares wins the game.

(circle shape)	circle	(sphere shape)	(rectangle shape)	cylinder
sphere	(cylinder shape)	cube	triangle	(square shape)
pyramid	(triangle shape)	square	(rectangular prism shape)	(cone shape)
(cube shape)	rectangle	cone	(pyramid shape)	rectangular prism

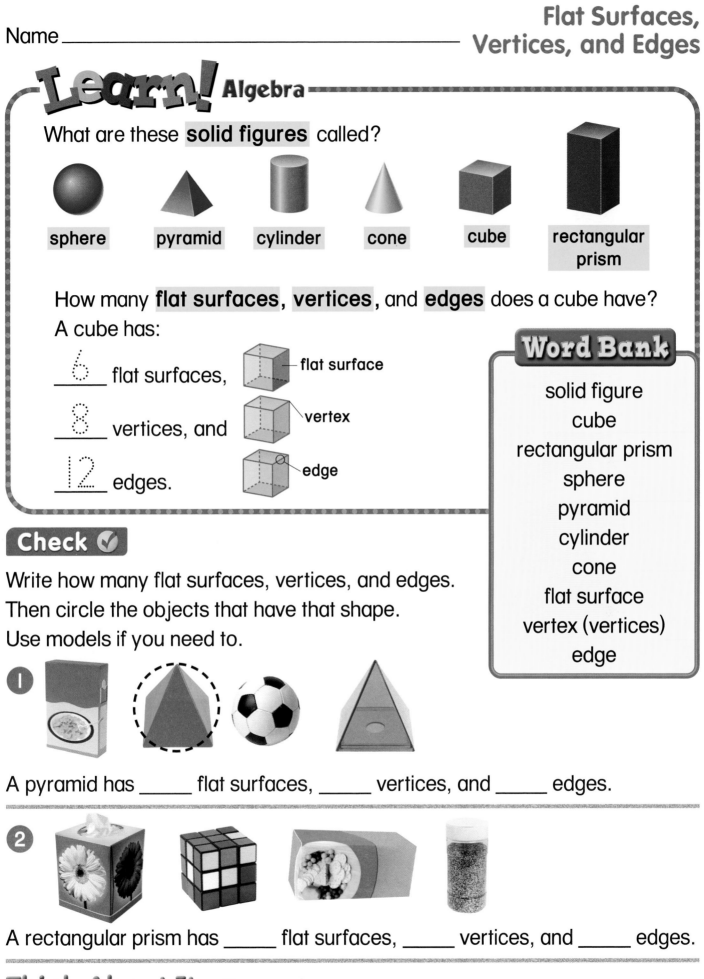

Learn! Algebra

What are these **solid figures** called?

sphere   pyramid   cylinder   cone   cube   rectangular prism

How many **flat surfaces**, **vertices**, and **edges** does a cube have?

A cube has:

___6___ flat surfaces,   — flat surface

___8___ vertices, and   — vertex

___12___ edges.   — edge

Word Bank

solid figure
cube
rectangular prism
sphere
pyramid
cylinder
cone
flat surface
vertex (vertices)
edge

Check ✓

Write how many flat surfaces, vertices, and edges.
Then circle the objects that have that shape.
Use models if you need to.

1

A pyramid has _____ flat surfaces, _____ vertices, and _____ edges.

2

A rectangular prism has _____ flat surfaces, _____ vertices, and _____ edges.

Think About It Reasoning

Name an object that is shaped like a cylinder.

Write how many flat surfaces, vertices, and edges.
Then circle the objects that have that shape.

3 A sphere has _____ flat surfaces, _____ vertices, and _____ edges.

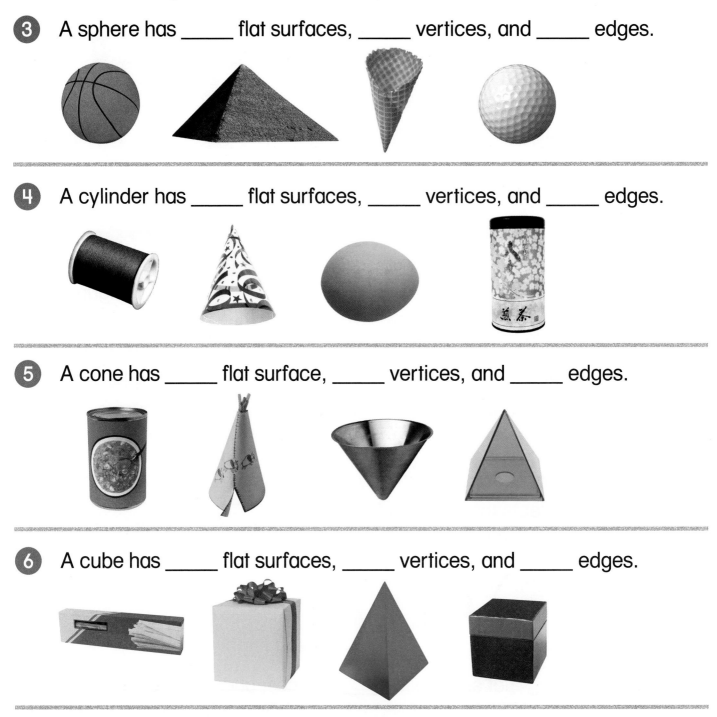

4 A cylinder has _____ flat surfaces, _____ vertices, and _____ edges.

5 A cone has _____ flat surface, _____ vertices, and _____ edges.

6 A cube has _____ flat surfaces, _____ vertices, and _____ edges.

Problem Solving Visual Thinking

Circle the answer.

7 Think about stacking two matching cubes, one on top of the other. Which shape do you make?

Home Connection Your child identified objects that have the same shapes as solid geometric figures and counted the flat surfaces, vertices, and edges on those solids. **Home Activity** Ask your child to find objects at home that have the shapes of a rectangular prism, a cylinder, a cube, a pyramid, a sphere, and a cone.

Learn! Algebra

Here are some **plane shapes** you know.

circle   square   triangle   rectangle

You can trace a pyramid to make a square
or a triangle.

Word Bank
plane shapes
circle
square
triangle
rectangle

Check ✓

Circle the plane shape or shapes you can make by
tracing the solid figure. Use models if you need to.

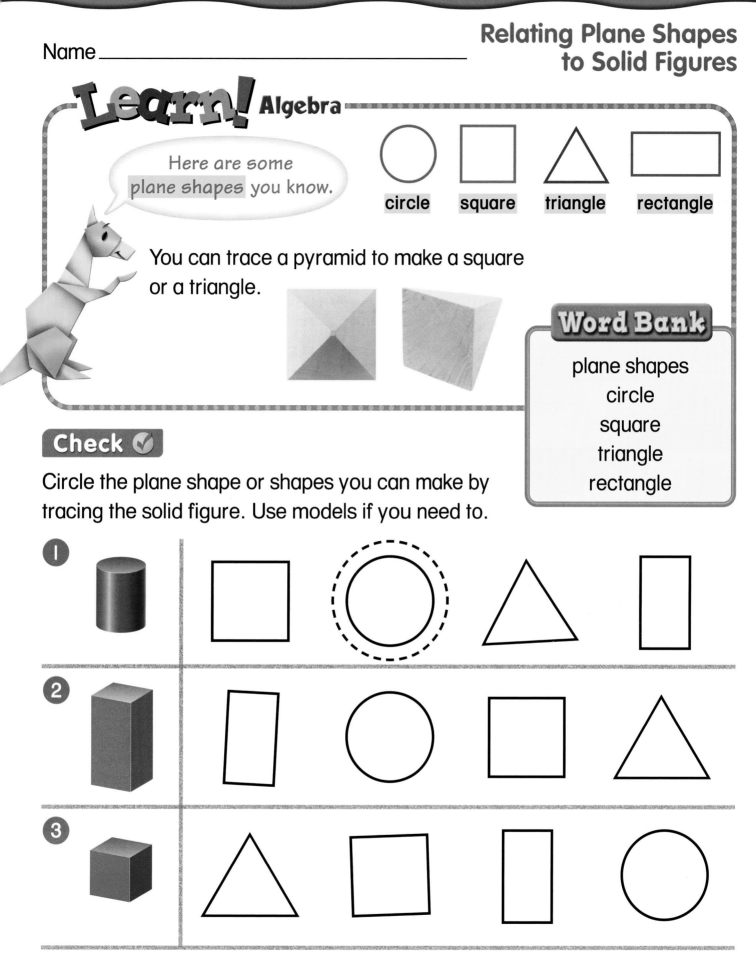

❶

❷

❸

Think About It   Reasoning

What plane shape can you make by tracing
a sphere? Explain.

Circle the solid figure or figures you can trace
to make the plane shape.

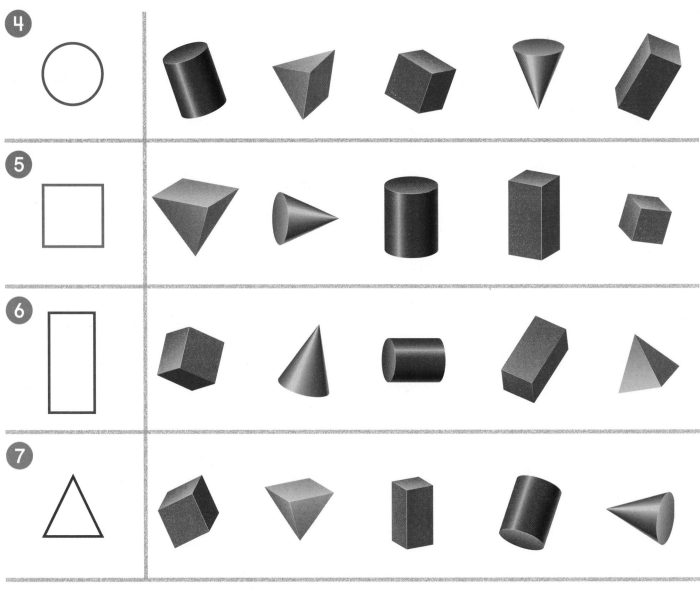

4

5

6

7

Problem Solving   Algebra

Circle the solid figure that answers the question.

8 Adam has one of these blocks.
His block has 3 more edges than flat surfaces.
Which block does Adam have?

Home Connection Your child identified shapes that can be made by
tracing solid figures. **Home Activity** Ask your child to trace around a box
and to tell you the shape he or she has made.

Learn!

This is a **net**.

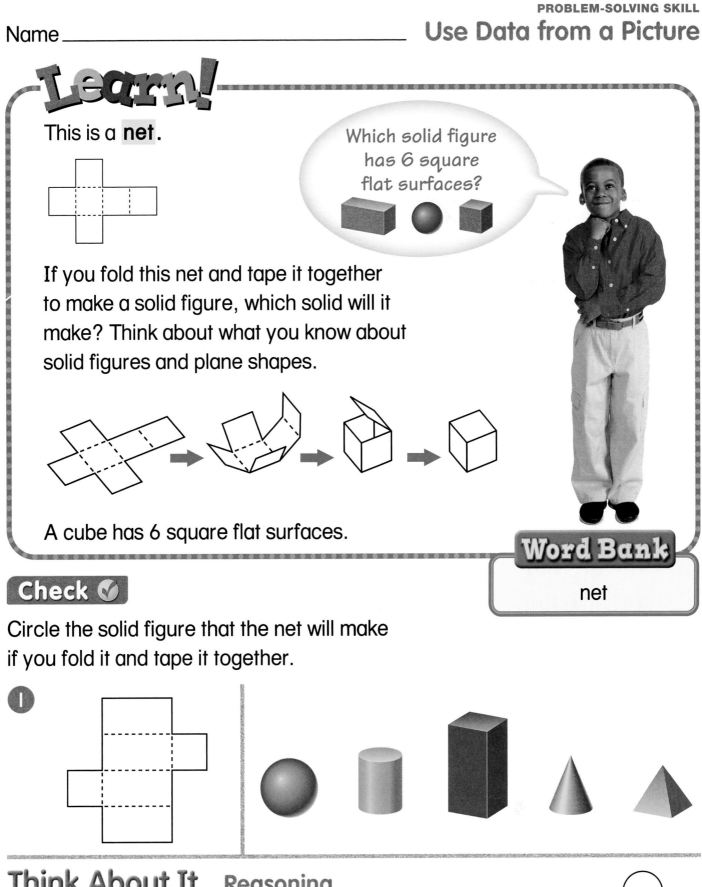

Which solid figure has 6 square flat surfaces?

If you fold this net and tape it together to make a solid figure, which solid will it make? Think about what you know about solid figures and plane shapes.

A cube has 6 square flat surfaces.

Word Bank

net

Check ✓

Circle the solid figure that the net will make if you fold it and tape it together.

1

Think About It   Reasoning

If you roll the rectangle into a tube, tape the two dark ends together, and then tape on the two circles at the ends, which solid figure will you make?

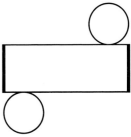

Circle the solid figure that the net will make
if you fold it and tape it together.

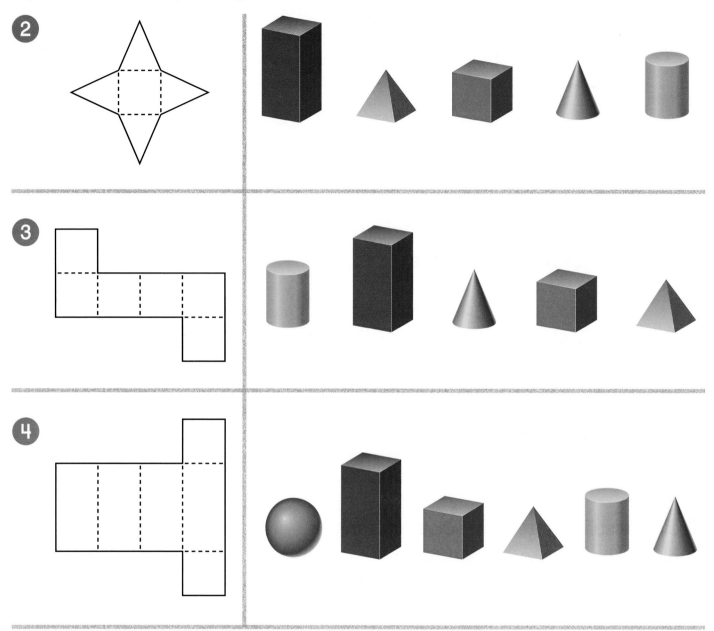

2

3

4

Visual Thinking

5 If you roll the larger part of this net
together, tape the two dark ends
together, and then tape the circle
on the bottom, which solid figure
will you make?

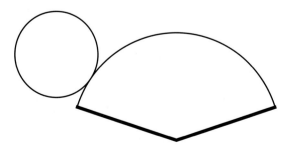

Home Connection Your child used data from pictures to solve problems.
Home Activity Have your child tell you what information in the picture in
Exercise 2 helped him or her solve the problem of which solid to circle.

Write how many flat surfaces, vertices, and edges.
Then circle the objects that have that shape.

1

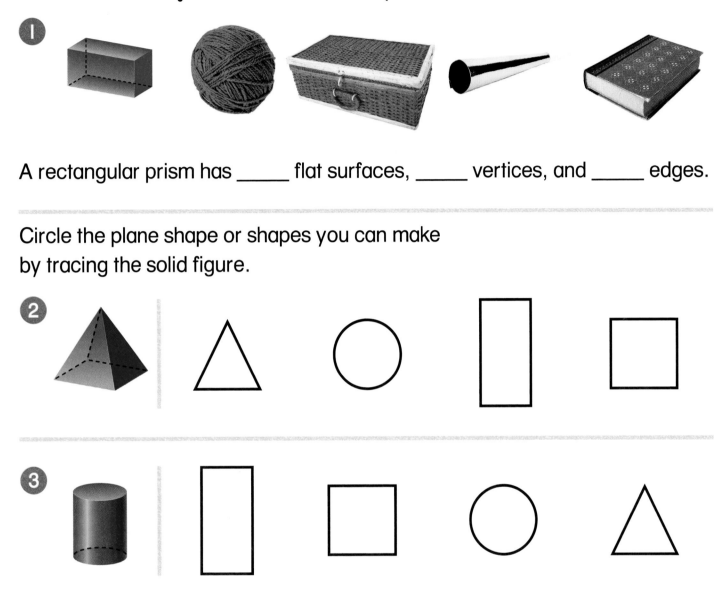

A rectangular prism has _____ flat surfaces, _____ vertices, and _____ edges.

Circle the plane shape or shapes you can make
by tracing the solid figure.

2

3

Circle the solid figure that the net will make
if you fold and tape it.

4

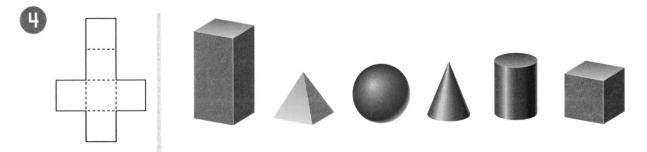

Mark the number that completes the sentence.

1   7 take away 2 is ____.

9   3   5   4

Ⓐ   Ⓑ   Ⓒ   Ⓓ

Mark the sentence that tells how many in all.

2

Ⓐ 2 tens and 3 ones is 23 in all.

Ⓑ 2 tens and 2 ones is 22 in all.

Ⓒ 3 tens and 2 ones is 32 in all.

Ⓓ I ten and 3 ones is 13 in all.

Add or subtract.

3 $\begin{array}{r} 84¢ \\ -51¢ \\ \hline \end{array}$

Ⓐ 35¢
Ⓑ 43¢
Ⓒ 32¢
Ⓓ 33¢

4 $\begin{array}{r} 68¢ \\ +23¢ \\ \hline \end{array}$

Ⓐ 85¢
Ⓑ 81¢
Ⓒ 91¢
Ⓓ 45¢

5 $\begin{array}{r} 47¢ \\ +30¢ \\ \hline \end{array}$

Ⓐ 77¢
Ⓑ 17¢
Ⓒ 67¢
Ⓓ 70¢

6 $\begin{array}{r} 75¢ \\ -38¢ \\ \hline \end{array}$

Ⓐ 27¢
Ⓑ 37¢
Ⓒ 43¢
Ⓓ 47¢

Writing in Math

7 You have 5 coins that total 47¢.
Draw and label the coins.

Name_____

Learn!

What large shape can you make
from these smaller shapes?

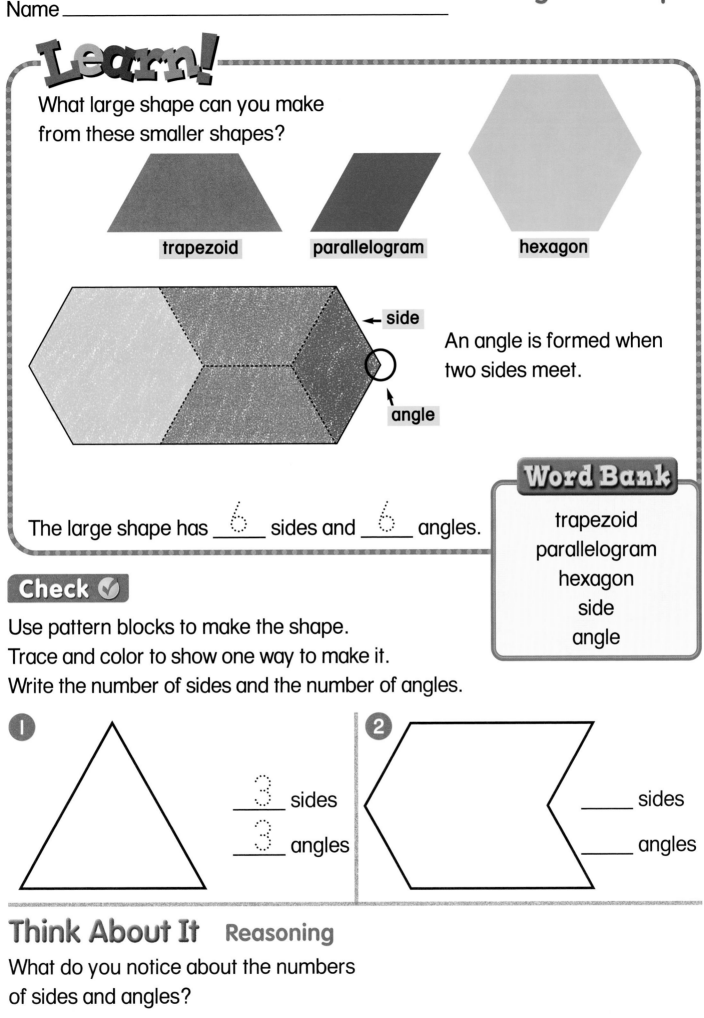

trapezoid   parallelogram   hexagon

← side

An angle is formed when
two sides meet.

angle

The large shape has __6__ sides and __6__ angles.

Word Bank

trapezoid
parallelogram
hexagon
side
angle

Check ✓

Use pattern blocks to make the shape.
Trace and color to show one way to make it.
Write the number of sides and the number of angles.

1
__3__ sides
__3__ angles

2
_____ sides
_____ angles

Think About It   Reasoning

What do you notice about the numbers
of sides and angles?

Use pattern blocks to make the shape.

Trace and color to show one way to make it.

Write the number of sides and the number of angles.

3

_____ sides _____ angles

4

_____ sides _____ angles

Problem Solving Visual Thinking

5 Make this star pattern with the number of pattern blocks shown.

6 blocks

7 blocks

Home Connection Your child used small shapes to make larger shapes and discovered that each new shape had the same numbers of sides and angles. **Home Activity** Draw shapes with 3, 4, and 5 sides, such as triangles, rectangles, and pentagons. Have your child tell you how many sides and angles each shape has.

Name _____

Learn!

These four shapes are the same size and the same shape. They are **congruent**.

> I drew two congruent shapes.

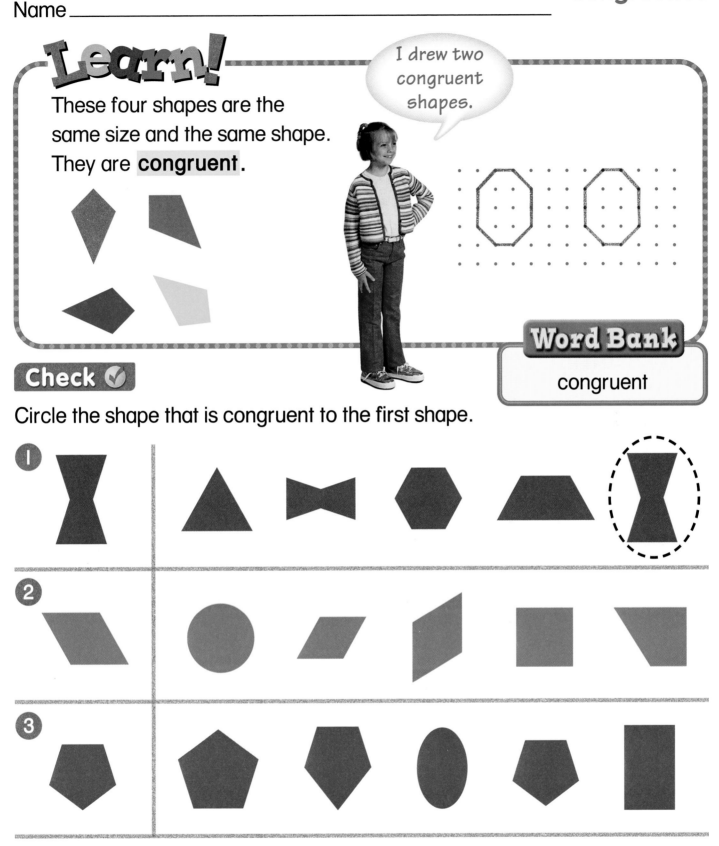

Check ✓

Circle the shape that is congruent to the first shape.

1.

2.

3.

Think About It   Reasoning

Why are the two shapes in each pair not congruent?

Practice

Draw a shape that is congruent.

4

5

6

7

Draw shapes that are congruent.

8

9

Problem Solving   Algebra

Circle all the ways in which the two shapes are alike.

10   same size   same shape   same color

11   same size   same shape   same color

12   same size   same shape   same color

Home Connection Your child identified and created congruent shapes.
Home Activity Draw two identical shapes that are the same size. Ask your child whether or not the shapes are congruent and to explain how he or she knows.

Learn!

You can **slide**, **flip**, and **turn** a shape.

Slide it.   Flip it.   Turn it.

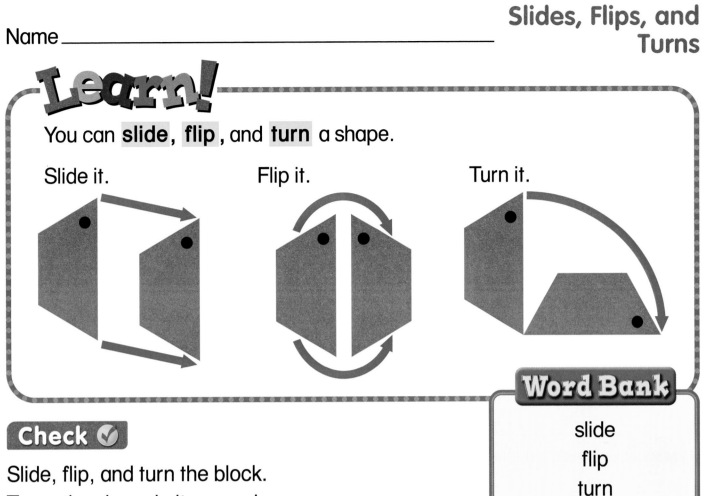

Word Bank

slide
flip
turn

Check ✓

Slide, flip, and turn the block.
Trace the shape in its new place.
Draw the dot and color the shape.

Use this block.	Slide it.	Flip it.	Turn it.
①			
②			

Think About It   Reasoning

Is this a slide or a flip?
Explain.   △ △

Is it a slide, a flip, or a turn?
Circle the answer.

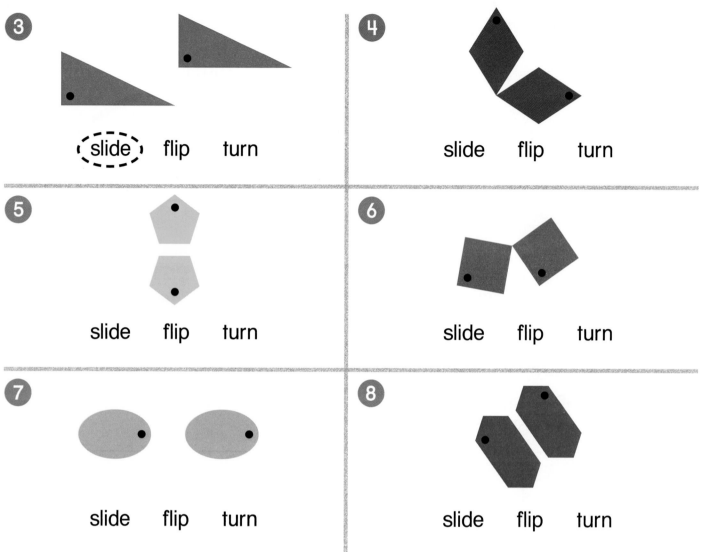

3

(slide)   flip   turn

4

slide   flip   turn

5

slide   flip   turn

6

slide   flip   turn

7

slide   flip   turn

8

slide   flip   turn

Problem Solving Visual Thinking

Look at the pattern.
Draw the shape in its next position.
Then circle the answer.

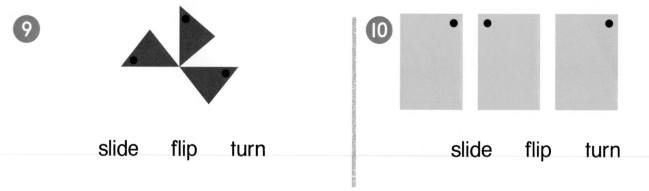

9

slide   flip   turn

10

slide   flip   turn

Home Connection Your child slid, flipped, and turned shapes and
determined whether a given shape had been slid, flipped, or turned.
Home Activity Cut out a triangle from paper. Have your child slide, flip,
and turn the shape. Then discuss each of these ways of moving a shape.

Name_____

Learn!

Does the shape have a **line of symmetry**?

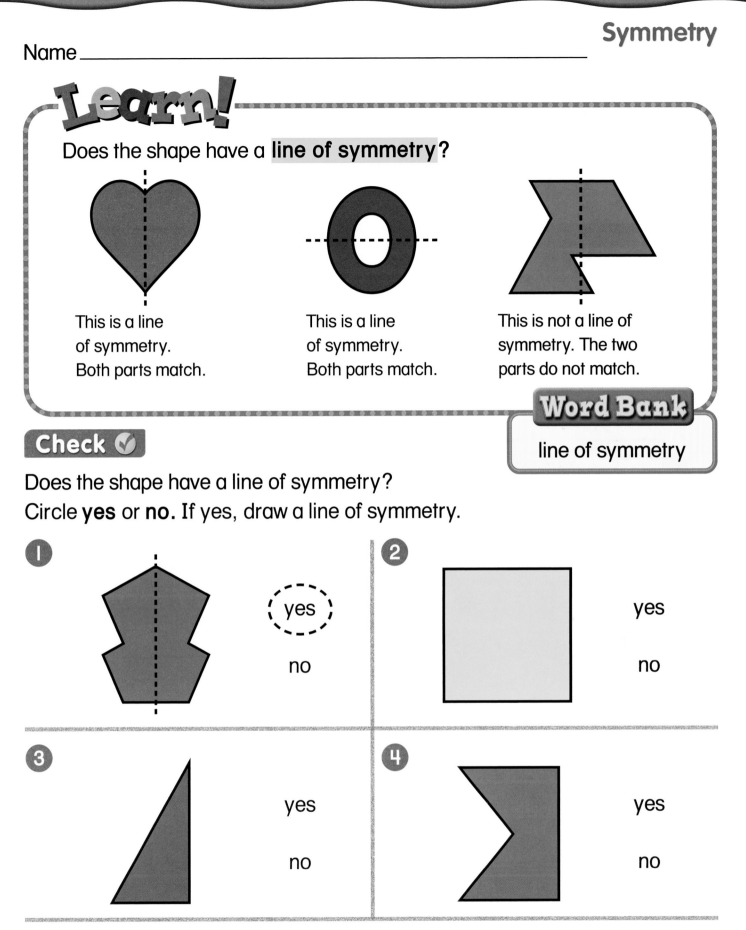

This is a line
of symmetry.
Both parts match.

This is a line
of symmetry.
Both parts match.

This is not a line of
symmetry. The two
parts do not match.

Word Bank

line of symmetry

Check ✓

Does the shape have a line of symmetry?
Circle **yes** or **no**. If yes, draw a line of symmetry.

1
yes
no

2
yes
no

3
yes
no

4
yes
no

Think About It   Reasoning

Can a shape have more than one line of symmetry?
Draw and explain.

Draw the matching part to make the shape symmetrical.

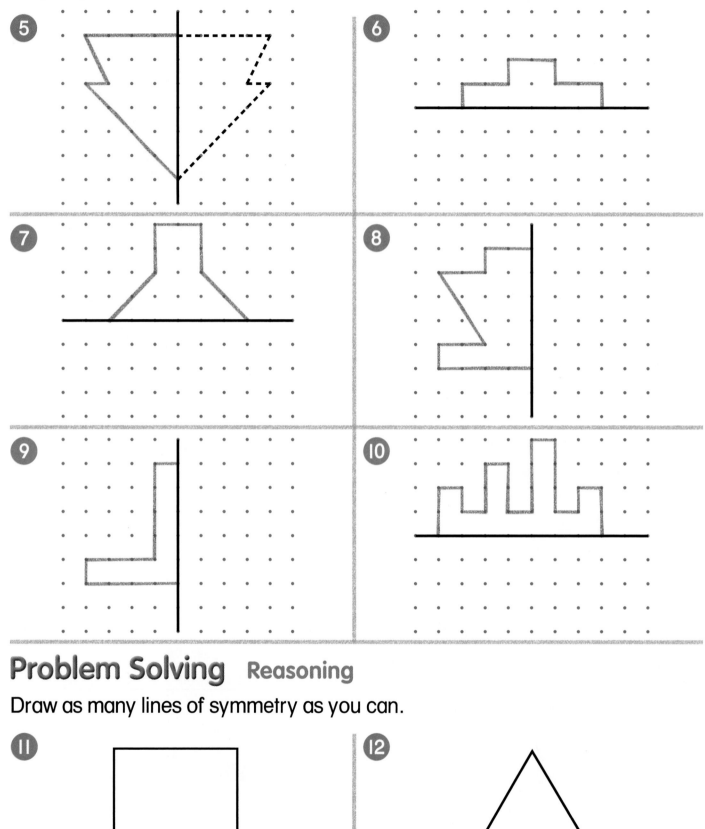

5

6

7

8

9

10

Problem Solving   Reasoning

Draw as many lines of symmetry as you can.

11

12

© Pearson Education, Inc.

Home Connection Your child identified lines of symmetry and created symmetrical shapes. **Home Activity** Have your child find several household objects that each have one or more lines of symmetry.

Name _____

Reading for Math Success

Draw Conclusions

1 Read the Mystery of Silver Blaze.

The great detective Sherlock Holmes has been asked to find a valuable horse named Silver Blaze.

Silver Blaze was stolen out of the stable at night. No one knows who took him.

A good watchdog was guarding the stable. But when the horse was stolen, the dog did nothing.

2 What conclusion might Sherlock Holmes draw from the way the dog behaved in the nighttime?

_____

_____

3 Draw a conclusion. If 3 horses are left in the stable, how many horses were there to begin with?

_____ horses were there to begin with.

4 Complete a number sentence that shows this.

_____ − _____ = 3 horses

Think About It   Reasoning

What is the difference between drawing a conclusion and jumping to a conclusion?

Chapter 7   two hundred sixty-three   **263**

A detective draws conclusions to solve a mystery.
A mystery is like a puzzle.

A **tangram** is a special kind of puzzle from China.
A tangram is a big square with 7 other shapes inside it.
If you take the shapes apart, you can make
just about anything.

5 Color the shapes in the puzzle to show where
they were used in the picture of the horse.

© Pearson Education, Inc.

Home Connection Your child drew a conclusion from the facts in a mystery
story and used logical reasoning to see how the pieces of a tangram puzzle
fit together. **Home Activity** Trace the tangram puzzle above. Then have
your child cut out the pieces and see what pictures you and your child can
make together.

Find the shape that matches the clues.

Read and Understand

Who am I?

I am purple.
I have more than 4 angles.

Plan and Solve

Cross out the shapes that do not fit the clues.

The shape that is left answers the question.

Look Back and Check

Does the answer match the clues?
Is it purple?
Does it have more than 4 angles?

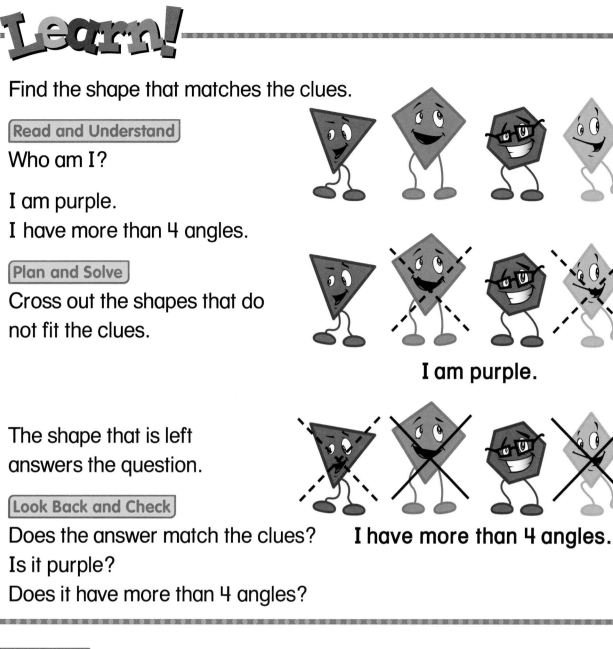

I am purple.

I have more than 4 angles.

Check

Cross out the shapes that do not match the clues.
Circle the shape that answers the question.

1 Who am I?
   I have more than 3 sides.
   I have fewer than 5 angles.

Think About It   Reasoning

How does crossing out shapes that do not match
the clues help you solve the problem?

Cross out the shapes that do not fit the clues.
Circle the shape that answers the question.

2 Who am I?
I have angles.
I am not congruent to
another shape.

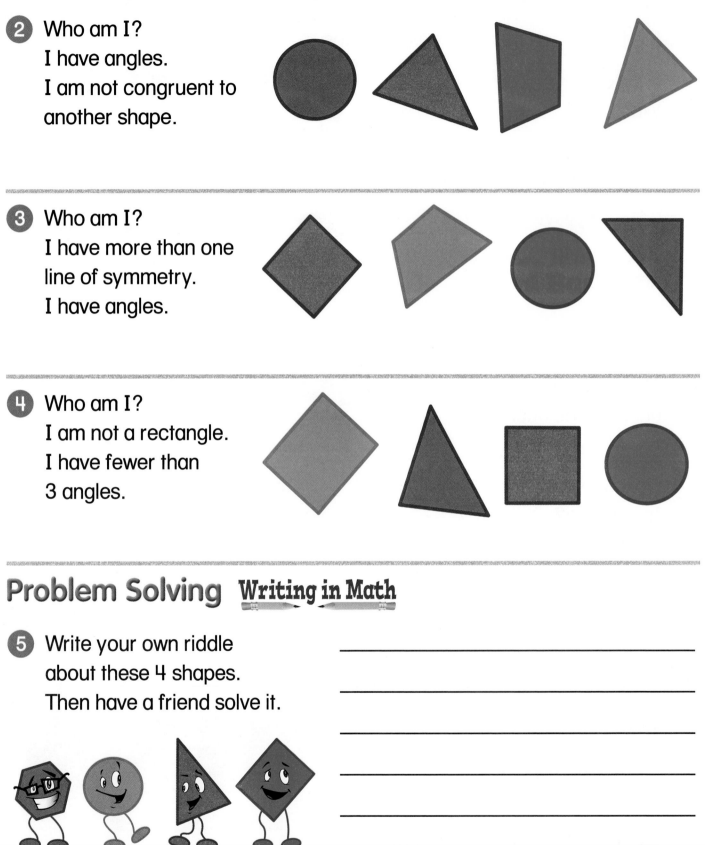

3 Who am I?
I have more than one
line of symmetry.
I have angles.

4 Who am I?
I am not a rectangle.
I have fewer than
3 angles.

Problem Solving Writing in Math

5 Write your own riddle
about these 4 shapes.
Then have a friend solve it.

_____

_____

_____

_____

_____

_____

Home Connection Your child used logical reasoning to solve problems.
Home Activity Have your child tell you how he or she solved Exercise 3.

Name _____

Use pattern blocks to make the shape. Trace and color
to show one way to make it. Write the number of sides
and the number of angles.

① 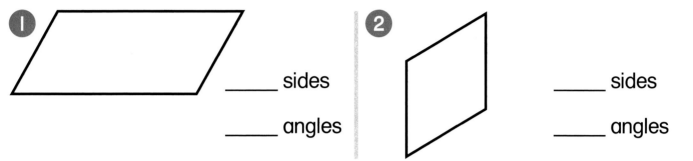 _____ sides

_____ angles

② _____ sides

_____ angles

Does the shape have a line of symmetry?
Circle **yes** or **no**. If yes, draw a line of symmetry.

③ yes

no

④ yes

no

Cross out the shapes that do not match the clues.
Circle the shape that answers the question.

⑤ Who am I?
I have fewer than 4 angles.
I have lines of symmetry.

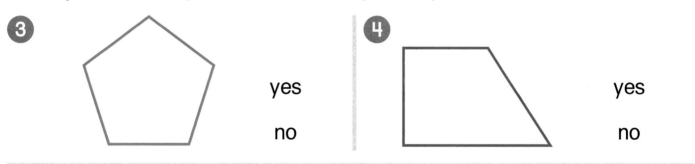

Circle the shape that is congruent to the first shape.

⑥

Is it a slide, a flip, or a turn? Circle the answer.

⑦    slide   flip   turn

Write the number sentence that solves the problem.

1 5 friends are playing at the park.
3 friends join them.
How many friends in all
are playing at the park?

Ⓐ 5 + 3 = 9 friends

Ⓑ 5 − 3 = 8 friends

Ⓒ 5 + 3 = 8 friends

Ⓓ 5 − 3 = 2 friends

Mark the number that is the closest ten.

2

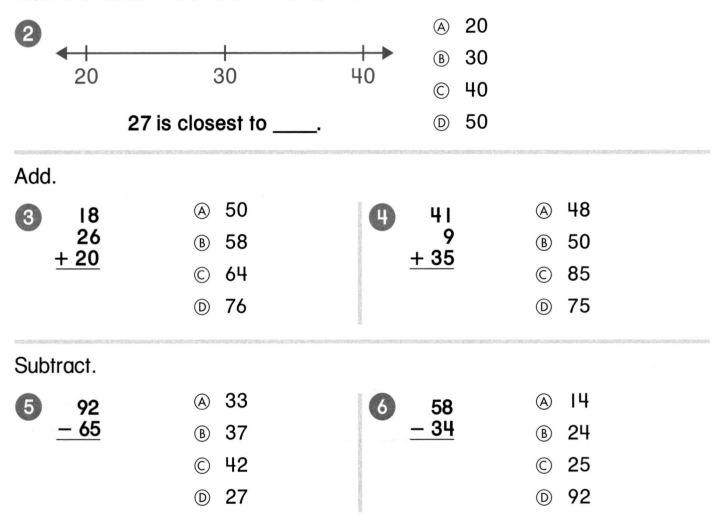

20   30   40

27 is closest to ____.

Ⓐ 20

Ⓑ 30

Ⓒ 40

Ⓓ 50

Add.

3
```
   18
   26
 + 20
```
Ⓐ 50

Ⓑ 58

Ⓒ 64

Ⓓ 76

4
```
   41
    9
 + 35
```
Ⓐ 48

Ⓑ 50

Ⓒ 85

Ⓓ 75

Subtract.

5
```
   92
 − 65
```
Ⓐ 33

Ⓑ 37

Ⓒ 42

Ⓓ 27

6
```
   58
 − 34
```
Ⓐ 14

Ⓑ 24

Ⓒ 25

Ⓓ 92

Writing in Math

7 Subtract 32 from 55.
Then show how you can use addition
to check your subtraction.

Name_____

Learn!

Are the parts equal?

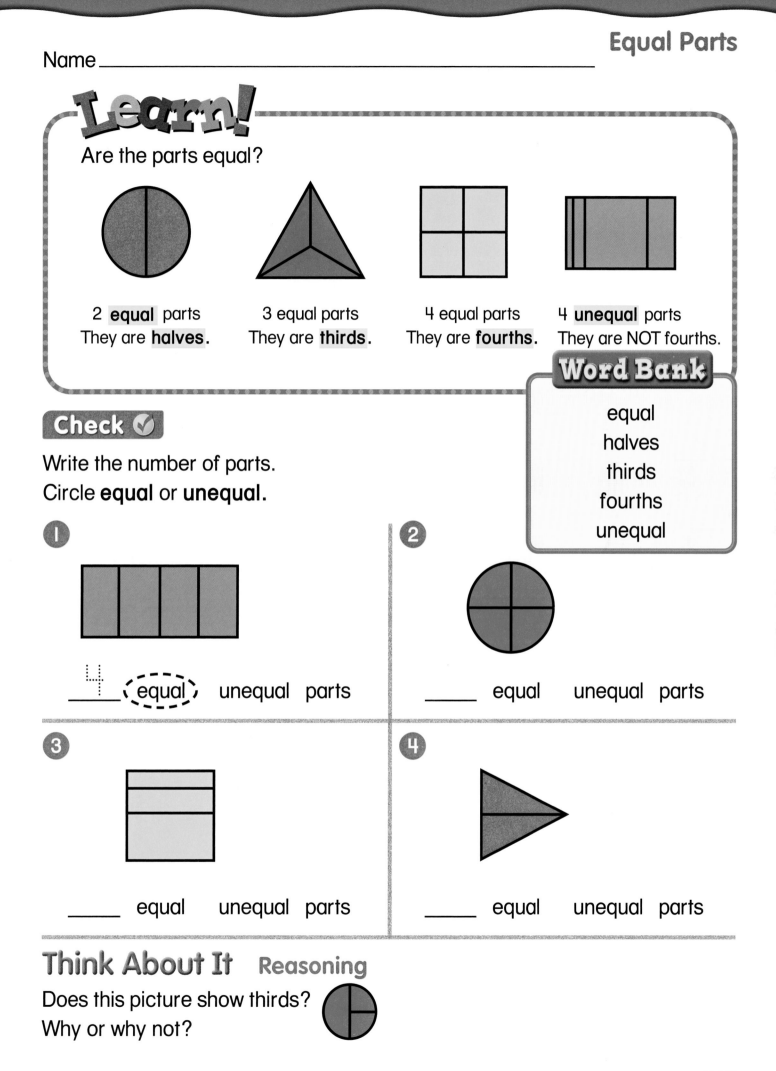

2 **equal** parts
They are **halves**.

3 equal parts
They are **thirds**.

4 equal parts
They are **fourths**.

4 **unequal** parts
They are NOT fourths.

Word Bank

equal
halves
thirds
fourths
unequal

Check ✓

Write the number of parts.
Circle **equal** or **unequal**.

1

___4___ (equal) unequal parts

2

_____ equal unequal parts

3

_____ equal unequal parts

4

_____ equal unequal parts

Think About It Reasoning

Does this picture show thirds?
Why or why not?

Draw a line or lines to show equal parts.

5 halves

6 thirds

7 fourths

8 halves

Does the picture show halves, thirds, or fourths?
Circle your answer.

9
halves
thirds
fourths

10
halves
thirds
fourths

11
halves
thirds
fourths

12
halves
thirds
fourths

Problem Solving Visual Thinking

Draw lines to show fourths in 4 different ways.

13

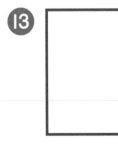

Home Connection Your child identified equal and unequal parts in shapes and named equal parts as halves, thirds, or fourths. **Home Activity** Draw a circle, square, and rectangle. Then have your child draw lines so that one shape shows halves, another shows thirds, and another shows fourths.

© Pearson Education, Inc.

Name_____

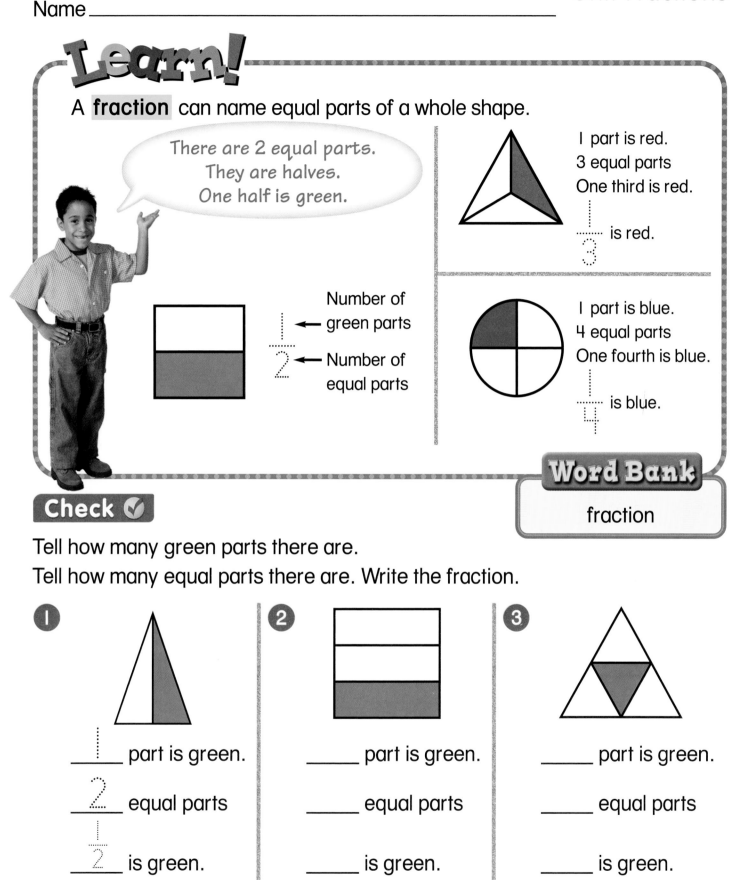

Learn!

A **fraction** can name equal parts of a whole shape.

There are 2 equal parts.
They are halves.
One half is green.

Number of ← green parts

Number of ← equal parts

1 part is red.
3 equal parts
One third is red.

‾‾ is red.
3

1 part is blue.
4 equal parts
One fourth is blue.

‾‾ is blue.
4

Word Bank

fraction

Check ✓

Tell how many green parts there are.

Tell how many equal parts there are. Write the fraction.

1
____ part is green.
_2_ equal parts
_1_ is green.
_2_

2
____ part is green.
____ equal parts
____ is green.

3
____ part is green.
____ equal parts
____ is green.

Think About It   Number Sense

Kaye Lynn ate $\frac{1}{4}$ of her sandwich. What does that mean?

Write the fraction for the shaded part of the shape.

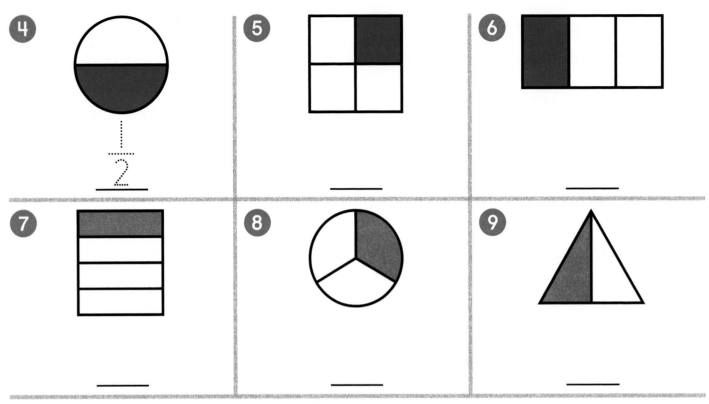

④ $\frac{1}{2}$

⑤ ___

⑥ ___

⑦ ___

⑧ ___

⑨ ___

Color to show the fraction.

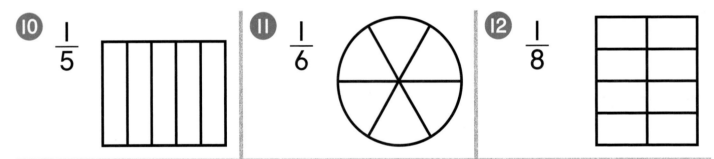

⑩ $\frac{1}{5}$

⑪ $\frac{1}{6}$

⑫ $\frac{1}{8}$

Problem Solving Visual Thinking

Draw a line or lines to show equal parts.
Then color to show the fraction.

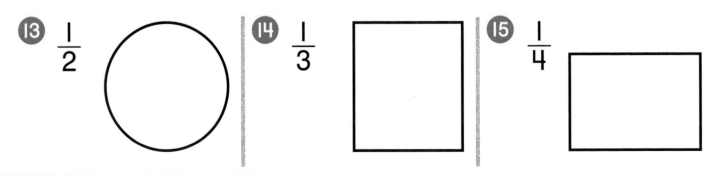

⑬ $\frac{1}{2}$

⑭ $\frac{1}{3}$

⑮ $\frac{1}{4}$

Home Connection Your child identified and showed fractions that each named one part of a whole. **Home Activity** Draw three squares. Then ask your child to divide and color them to show $\frac{1}{2}$, $\frac{1}{3}$, and $\frac{1}{4}$.

Name _____

Learn!

Fractions can also name more than one part of a whole shape.

3 parts are red.
4 equal parts

4 parts are blue.
6 equal parts

$\frac{3}{4}$ is red.

$\frac{4}{6}$ is blue.

Check ✓

Write the fraction for the shaded part of the shape.

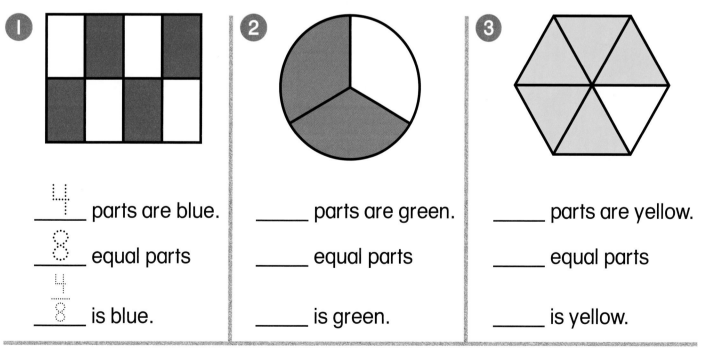

① ____4____ parts are blue.

____8____ equal parts

____$\frac{4}{8}$____ is blue.

② _____ parts are green.

_____ equal parts

_____ is green.

③ _____ parts are yellow.

_____ equal parts

_____ is yellow.

Think About It Number Sense

Johnny says that this shape shows $\frac{2}{3}$.
Is he correct? Explain.

Write the fraction for the shaded part of the shape.

④

$\frac{3}{4}$

⑤

_____

⑥

_____

⑦

_____

⑧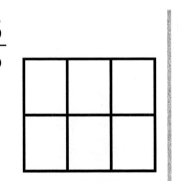

_____

⑨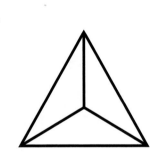

_____

Color to show the fraction.

⑩ $\frac{2}{4}$

⑪ $\frac{5}{6}$

⑫ $\frac{2}{3}$

Problem Solving   Visual Thinking

Draw a line or lines to show equal parts.
Then color to show the fraction.

⑬ $\frac{1}{2}$

⑭ $\frac{2}{4}$

⑮ $\frac{3}{6}$

Home Connection Your child identified and showed fractions that each named more than one part of a whole. **Home Activity** Draw a square and divide it into 4 equal parts. Color 3 of the parts. Have your child name the fraction that tells how much of the whole is colored.

Name _____

Learn!

About how much is left? **Estimate**.

It looks like a circle cut into 4 equal pieces. 3 of the pieces are still here. About $\frac{3}{4}$ of the pancake is left.

about $\frac{1}{2}$

about $\frac{3}{4}$

about $\frac{2}{10}$

Word Bank

estimate

Check ✓

How much is left? Circle the best estimate.

1
about $\frac{1}{3}$

about $\frac{1}{2}$

about $\frac{1}{4}$

2
about $\frac{1}{2}$

about $\frac{2}{3}$

about $\frac{3}{4}$

3
about $\frac{1}{2}$

about $\frac{1}{4}$

about $\frac{1}{3}$

4
about $\frac{1}{2}$

about $\frac{2}{4}$

about $\frac{3}{8}$

Think About It   Number Sense

If you eat $\frac{2}{3}$ of a sandwich, how much is left? How do you know?

How much is left? Circle the best estimate.

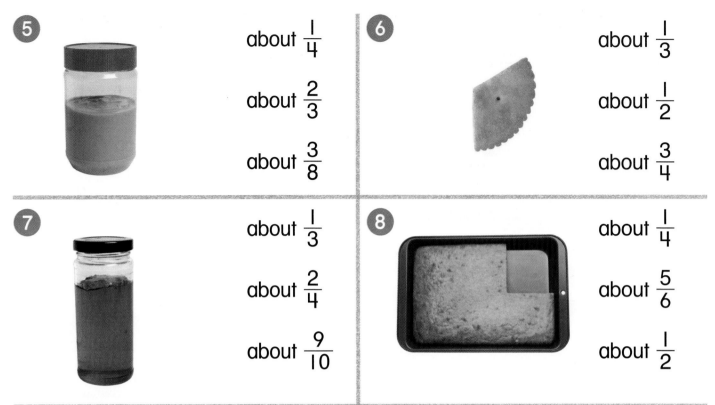

5

about $\frac{1}{4}$

about $\frac{2}{3}$

about $\frac{3}{8}$

6

about $\frac{1}{3}$

about $\frac{1}{2}$

about $\frac{3}{4}$

7

about $\frac{1}{3}$

about $\frac{2}{4}$

about $\frac{9}{10}$

8

about $\frac{1}{4}$

about $\frac{5}{6}$

about $\frac{1}{2}$

Problem Solving   Number Sense

Write the fraction for the blue part of the shape.
Then write the fraction for the red part.

9

_____ is blue.   _____ is red.

10

_____ is blue.   _____ is red.

11

_____ is blue.   _____ is red.

Home Connection Your child estimated how much of a food item was left. **Home Activity** Ask your child to tell you approximately what fraction of a food item is left after he or she has eaten part of it.

© Pearson Education, Inc.

Learn!

You can use fractions to name equal parts of a group.

There are 3 blue shirts.

There are 5 shirts in all.

$\frac{3}{5}$ of the shirts are blue.

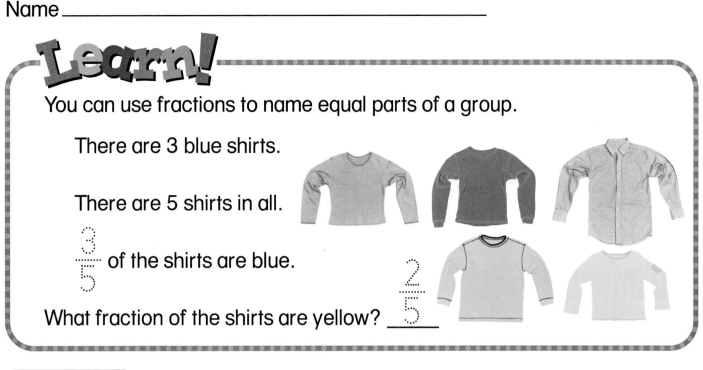

What fraction of the shirts are yellow? $\frac{2}{5}$

Check ✓

Write the fraction of the group that is blue.

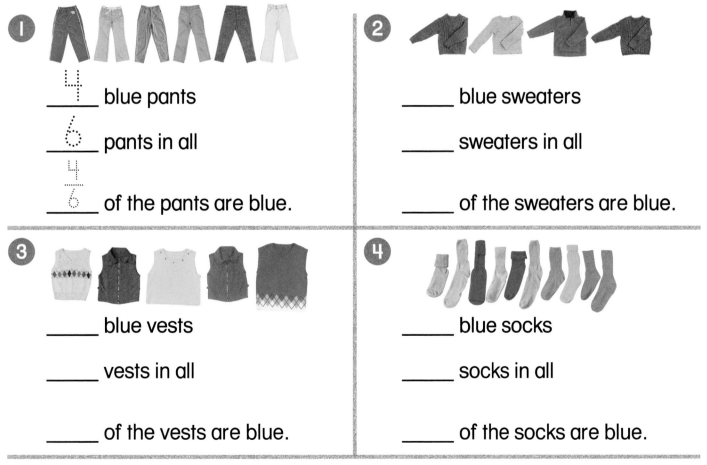

①

$\frac{4}{}$ blue pants

$\frac{6}{}$ pants in all

$\frac{4}{6}$ of the pants are blue.

②

_____ blue sweaters

_____ sweaters in all

_____ of the sweaters are blue.

③

_____ blue vests

_____ vests in all

_____ of the vests are blue.

④

_____ blue socks

_____ socks in all

_____ of the socks are blue.

Think About It   Reasoning

If $\frac{6}{8}$ of your socks are white, what fraction of

your socks are not white? How do you know?

Write the fraction of the group that is red.

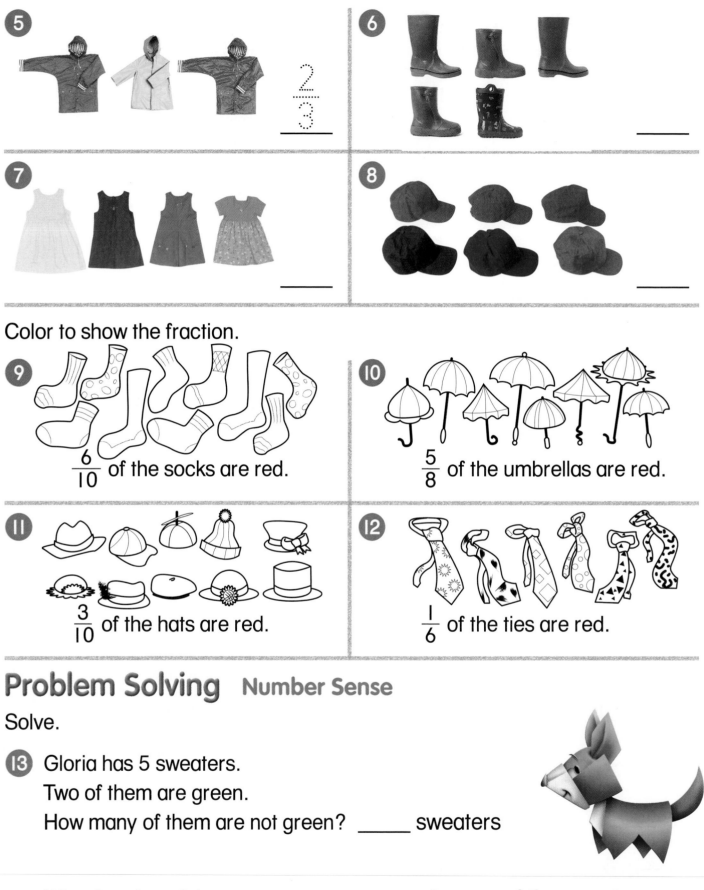

⑤ $\frac{2}{3}$

⑥ _____

⑦ _____

⑧ _____

Color to show the fraction.

⑨ $\frac{6}{10}$ of the socks are red.

⑩ $\frac{5}{8}$ of the umbrellas are red.

⑪ $\frac{3}{10}$ of the hats are red.

⑫ $\frac{1}{6}$ of the ties are red.

Problem Solving Number Sense

Solve.

⑬ Gloria has 5 sweaters.
Two of them are green.
How many of them are not green? _____ sweaters

What fraction of the sweaters are not green? _____ of the sweaters

Home Connection Your child identified and showed fractions of a set of objects. **Home Activity** Have your child draw 7 circles and then ask him or her to color $\frac{3}{7}$ of the set of 7 circles red.

Name _____

DK Dorling Kindersley

Do You Know...
that all seashells
are made by animals
that live inside them?

Fun Fact!
Have you ever seen
a spiral staircase?
It is built like a
spiral seashell!

1 Here is the inside of a nautilus shell.
It has more than two dozen sections.
If one shell had two dozen sections and
another shell had two and a half dozen sections,
how many sections would there be in all?

_____ + _____ = _____ sections in all

top

2 Here are two views of a sundial shell.
It is symmetrical. If one sundial shell is
one inch wide and another sundial shell is
one and one half inches wide, how much
wider is the bigger shell?

The bigger shell is _____ inch wider.

bottom

3 Here is a slate pencil sea urchin. Its spines are sometimes used as wind chimes or as jewelry. Which geometric shapes do you think of when you look at these spines?

When I look at these spines, I think of

_____.

4 Here is a spiny spider crab.
It has 10 legs.
If you had 10 of these creatures,
how many legs would there be in all?

There would be _____ legs in all.

Spider crabs can walk diagonally as well as sideways. But they are easy to catch because they walk very slowly.

5 **Writing in Math**

Journal

Draw a symmetrical seashell.
Then explain why it is symmetrical.

Home Connection Your child learned to solve problems by applying his or her math skills. **Home Activity** Talk to your child about how he or she solved the problems on these two pages.

Name _____

Write the number of parts.
Circle **equal** or **unequal.**

1

_____ equal   unequal   parts

2

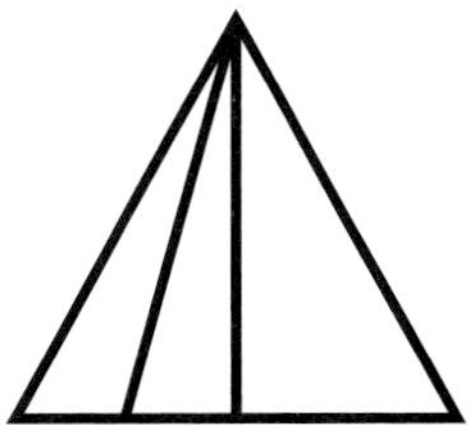

_____ equal   unequal   parts

How much is left? Circle the best estimate.

3 
about $\frac{1}{4}$

about $\frac{1}{2}$

about $\frac{3}{4}$

4 
about $\frac{1}{3}$

about $\frac{2}{4}$

about $\frac{7}{8}$

Write the fraction of the group that is red.

5

_____

6

_____

Write the fraction for the shaded part of the shape.

7

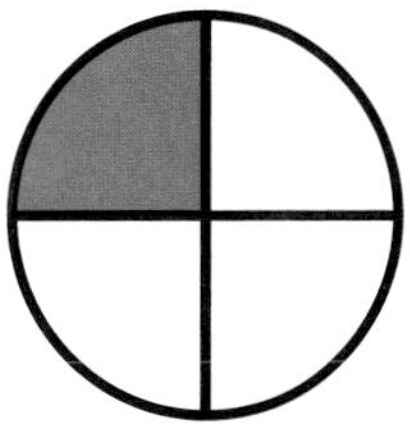

_____

8

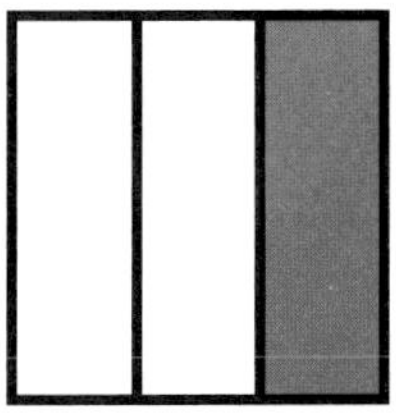

_____

9

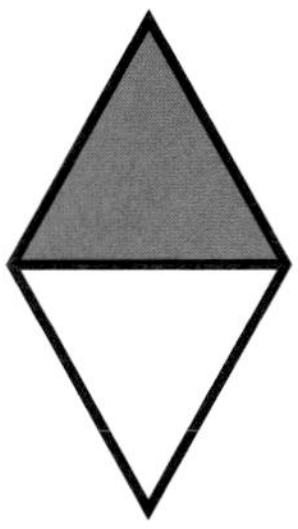

_____

10

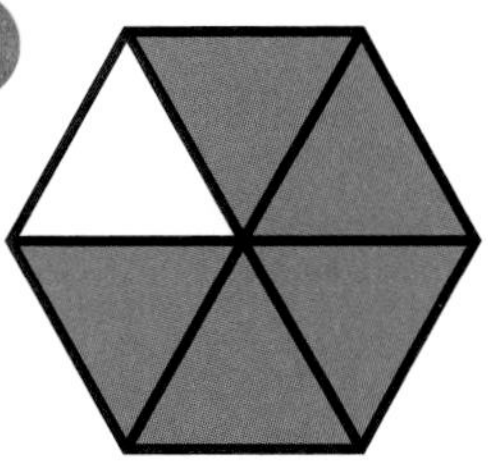

_____

11

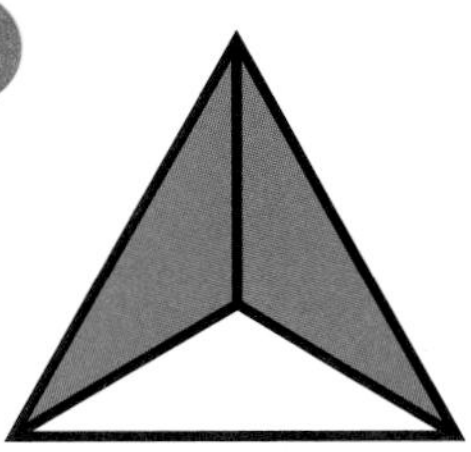

_____

12

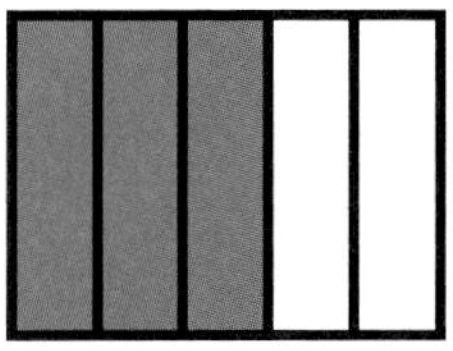

_____

Name _____

Mark the 11th wagon.

1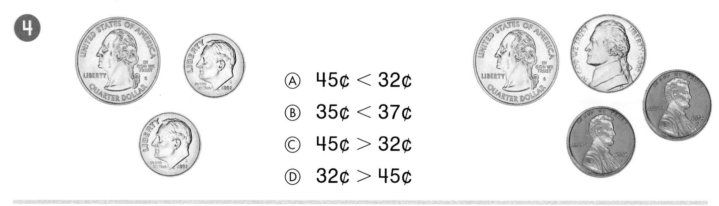

Ⓐ   Ⓑ   Ⓒ   Ⓓ

Add.

2
$$\begin{array}{r} 57 \\ + 18 \\ \hline \end{array}$$

65   75   76   85
Ⓐ   Ⓑ   Ⓒ   Ⓓ

3
$$\begin{array}{r} 24 \\ + 41 \\ \hline \end{array}$$

65   56   23   76
Ⓐ   Ⓑ   Ⓒ   Ⓓ

Compare the values of the two sets of coins.
Then mark the statement that is true.

4

Ⓐ   45¢ < 32¢

Ⓑ   35¢ < 37¢

Ⓒ   45¢ > 32¢

Ⓓ   32¢ > 45¢

Writing in Math

5 Trace pattern blocks and show one way to make this shape. Color to show which blocks you used. Then tell how many sides and how many angles this large shape has.

_____

_____

© Pearson Education, Inc.

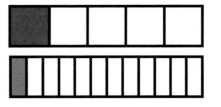 **Enrichment**

Comparing Fractions

Harry painted $\frac{1}{5}$ of his rectangle.

Emily painted $\frac{1}{12}$ of her rectangle.

Who painted more?

$\frac{1}{5}$ is greater than $\frac{1}{12}$. So Harry painted more.

Color to show both fractions.
Then circle the fraction that is greater.

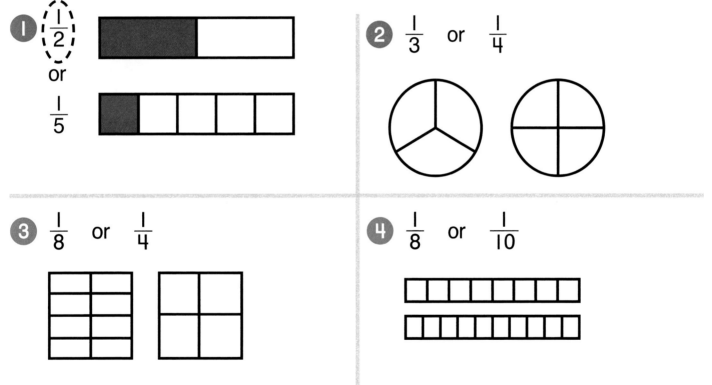

1. $\left(\frac{1}{2}\right)$

or

$\frac{1}{5}$

2. $\frac{1}{3}$ or $\frac{1}{4}$

3. $\frac{1}{8}$ or $\frac{1}{4}$

4. $\frac{1}{8}$ or $\frac{1}{10}$

---

5. **Writing in Math**

Harry and Emily each bought the same size pizza. Harry ate $\frac{1}{3}$ of his. Emily ate $\frac{1}{5}$ of hers. Explain who ate less pizza. Draw pictures if you need to.

Home Connection Your child made pictures of fractions to help him or her decide which of the two was greater. **Home Activity** Help your child draw pictures to compare $\frac{1}{2}$ with $\frac{1}{4}$ and $\frac{1}{3}$ with $\frac{1}{8}$.

Create Larger Shapes Using a Computer

You can flip, turn, and slide equilateral triangles to make different shapes. (Remember, an equilateral triangle has 3 sides that are all the same length.)

1 On a computer, go to the Geometry Shapes eTool.

2 Place 2 equilateral triangles in the workspace. Make a **parallelogram** with these triangles. In the chart below, record the number of sides and the number of angles.

3 Place 3 equilateral triangles in the workspace. Make a **trapezoid** with these triangles. Record the number of sides and the number of angles.

4 Place 6 equilateral triangles in the workspace. Make a **hexagon** with these triangles. (Hint: A hexagon can be made by using 2 trapezoids.) Record the number of sides and the number of angles.

Shape	Number of Sides	Number of Angles
Parallelogram		
Trapezoid		
Hexagon		

Think About It Reasoning

What do you notice about the number of sides and the number of angles in each of the shapes you made?

 Home Connection Your child used a computer to create larger shapes by combining equilateral triangles. He or she found a correlation between the number of sides and the number of angles for each shape. **Home Activity** Draw different shapes and have your child count the number of sides and angles for each shape.

Name _____

Get Information for the Answer

Read Together

When you are reading a math problem, look for words that give you **important information** about the answer.

Test-Taking Strategies

Understand the Question

Get Information for the Answer

Plan How to Find the Answer

Make Smart Choices

Use Writing in Math

1. I have 6 flat surfaces, 8 vertices, and 12 edges. Which solid figure am I?

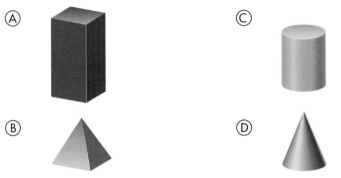

Ⓐ   Ⓒ

Ⓑ   Ⓓ

Which solid figure has **6 flat surfaces, 8 vertices, and 12 edges**? Use these three pieces of information to help you choose the correct answer. Then fill in the answer bubble.

Your Turn

Find the important information in this problem. Use the information to solve the problem. Then fill in the answer bubble.

2. I have 2 flat surfaces. I can roll. I have no vertices and no edges. Which solid figure am I?

Ⓐ   Ⓒ

Ⓑ   Ⓓ

I see 4 pieces of information!

Home Connection Your child prepared for standardized tests by identifying important information in math problems. **Home Activity** Ask your child to count the number of flat surfaces, vertices, and edges in each solid figure in Exercise 2. Then have your child check that his or her answer choice matches the information given in Exercise 2.

Name _____

 Special Symmetry

Many things in nature are **symmetrical.** Look at these pictures for some examples.

It's a Match!

1 Draw a **line of symmetry** on each picture.

2 Now look at the pictures again. Draw another line of symmetry on an object if you can.

3 Which things can you draw just one line of symmetry for?

_____

4 Which things can you draw more than one line of symmetry for?

_____

5 Find three other symmetrical objects in nature. On a separate sheet of paper, draw each object. Then draw one or more lines of symmetry for each object.

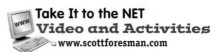 **Take It to the NET**
Video and Activities
www.scottforesman.com

 Home Connection Your child solved problems by drawing lines of symmetry for objects in nature. **Home Activity** Ask your child to explain how he or she drew one or more lines of symmetry for one of the pictures on this page.

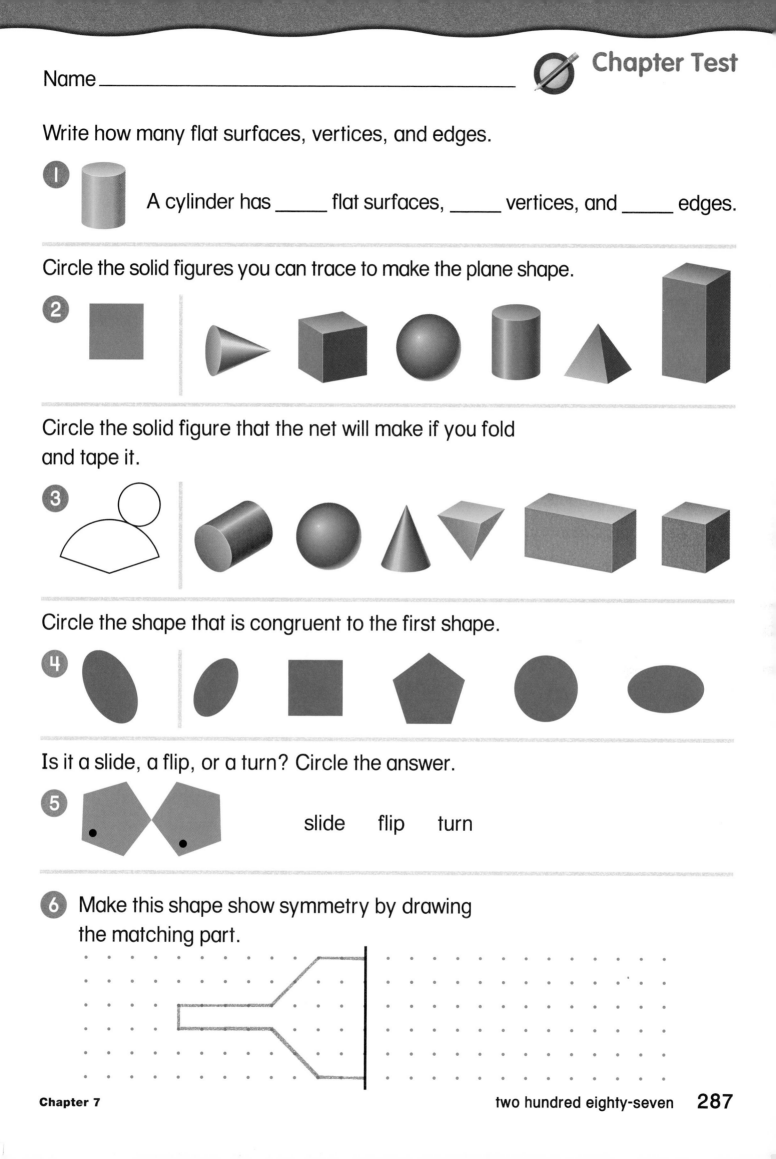

Write how many flat surfaces, vertices, and edges.

1   A cylinder has _____ flat surfaces, _____ vertices, and _____ edges.

Circle the solid figures you can trace to make the plane shape.

2

Circle the solid figure that the net will make if you fold and tape it.

3

Circle the shape that is congruent to the first shape.

4

Is it a slide, a flip, or a turn? Circle the answer.

5   slide   flip   turn

6   Make this shape show symmetry by drawing
    the matching part.

Does the picture show halves, thirds, or fourths?
Circle your answer.

7 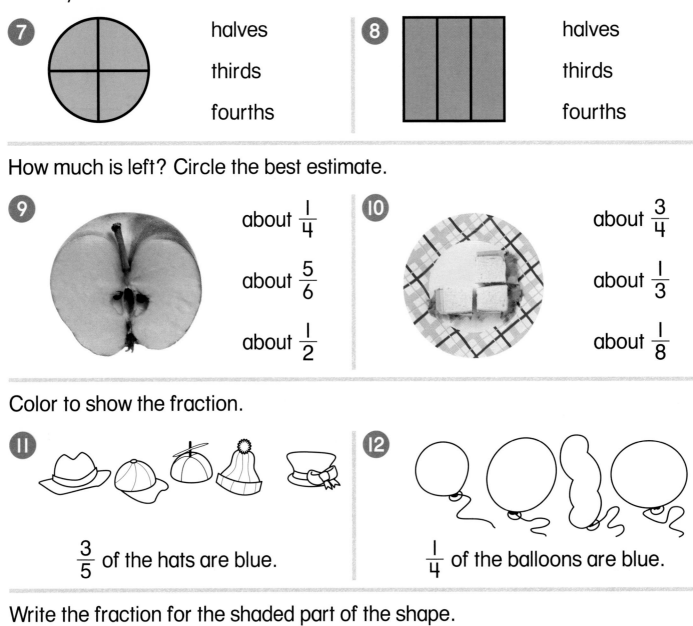 halves

thirds

fourths

8 halves

thirds

fourths

How much is left? Circle the best estimate.

9 about $\frac{1}{4}$

about $\frac{5}{6}$

about $\frac{1}{2}$

10 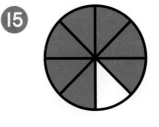 about $\frac{3}{4}$

about $\frac{1}{3}$

about $\frac{1}{8}$

Color to show the fraction.

11 $\frac{3}{5}$ of the hats are blue.

12 $\frac{1}{4}$ of the balloons are blue.

Write the fraction for the shaded part of the shape.

13 ___

14 ___

15 ___

Cross out the three shapes that do not fit the clues.
Then circle the shape that answers the question.

16 Who am I?
I have more than 3 sides.
I am not a rectangle.

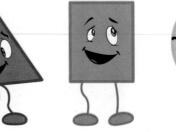

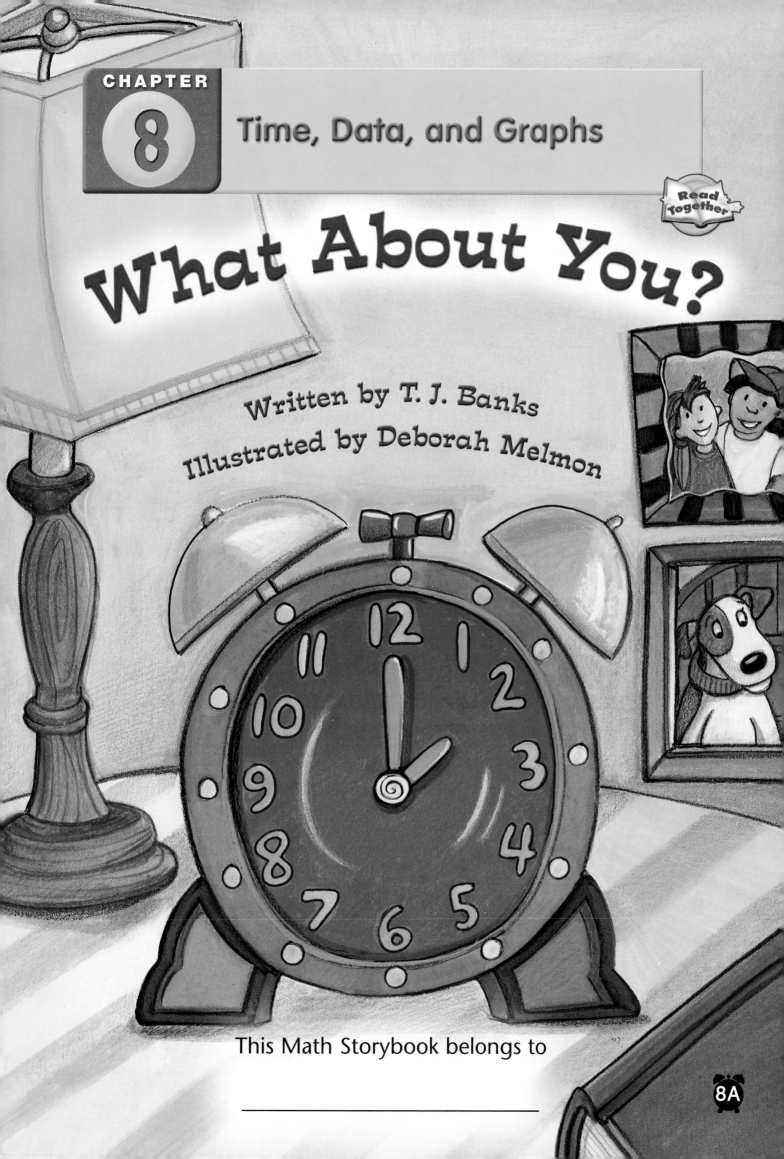

Read Together

What About You?

Written by T. J. Banks

Illustrated by Deborah Melmon

This Math Storybook belongs to

_____

When it is **7:00** in the morning, I am eating my breakfast.

What about you?

When it is **7:00** in the evening, I am playing with my dog.

What about you?

When it is **8:00** in the morning,
I am reading at school.

What about you?

When it is **8:00** in the evening,
I am going to bed.

What about you?

8C

When it is **11:00** in the morning,
I am learning math.

What about you?

When it is **11:00** at night,
I am sound asleep.

What about you?

When it is **3:00** in the afternoon,
I am leaving school and on my way home.

What about you?

When it is **3:00** in the morning,
I am dreaming sweet dreams.

What about you?

8E

When it is **6:00** in the evening,
I am eating supper with my family.

What about you?

When it is **6:00** the next morning,
I am listening to my big brother
make a lot of noise while he gets up!

What about you?

8F

Dear Family,

Today my class started Chapter 8, **Time, Data, and Graphs.** I will learn how to tell time to five minutes. And I will make different kinds of graphs to organize and display information that I collect. Here are some of the math words I will be learning and some things we can do to help me with my math.

Love,

_____

Math Activity to Do at Home

Go on a "clock hunt." Ask your child to write down the locations of clocks in your home. Then, as you go around the house, ask your child to tell you the time on each clock. Repeat the activity several times at different times of the day.

Books to Read Together

Reading math stories reinforces concepts. Look for these titles in your local library:

What Time Is It?
By Sheila Keenan
(Scholastic, 2000)

Lemonade for Sale
By Stuart J. Murphy
(HarperCollins, 1998)

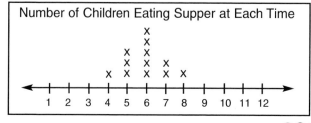
Take It to the NET
More Activities
www.scottforesman.com

My New Math Words

midnight 12 o'clock at night; the middle of the night.

noon 12 o'clock in the daytime; the middle of the day.

line plot A collection of data with an **X** placed above each number on a number line for each piece of data collected is called a line plot.

```
Number of Children Eating Supper at Each Time
                    x
                    x
                x   x
                x   x   x
            x   x   x   x   x
        ←—+—+—+—+—+—+—+—+—+—+—+—+—→
          1  2  3  4  5  6  7  8  9  10 11 12
```

Name _____

Practice Game

Tick Tock Around the Clock

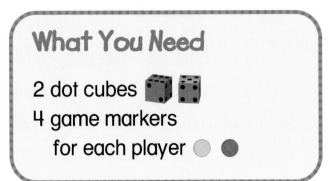
What You Need

2 dot cubes
4 game markers
for each player ⬤ ⬤

How to Play

1. Take turns tossing the cubes.
2. Add the dots. If the sum is 3, 6, 9, or 12, place a marker on that hour on your clock.
3. The first player to cover 12, 3, 6, and 9 is the winner. **Hurry up! The clock is ticking!**

© Pearson Education, Inc.

Name_____

Learn!

A calendar helps us keep track of days, weeks, months, and years!

Word Bank

calendar

Check ✓

Write the month, year, and dates for this month.

1

Month _____					Year _____	
Sunday	Monday	Tuesday	Wednesday	Thursday	Friday	Saturday

Use the calendar to answer the questions.

2 What is the last day of this month?   _____

3 What day is the 23rd of the month?   _____

Think About It   Reasoning

Do all months have the same number of days?
How do you know?

One Year

January

S	M	T	W	T	F	S
				1	2	3
4	5	6	7	8	9	10
11	12	13	14	15	16	17
18	19	20	21	22	23	24
25	26	27	28	29	30	31

February

S	M	T	W	T	F	S
1	2	3	4	5	6	7
8	9	10	11	12	13	14
15	16	17	18	19	20	21
22	23	24	25	26	27	28

March

S	M	T	W	T	F	S
1	2	3	4	5	6	7
8	9	10	11	12	13	14
15	16	17	18	19	20	21
22	23	24	25	26	27	28
29	30	31				

April

S	M	T	W	T	F	S
				1	2	3	4
5	6	7	8	9	10	11
12	13	14	15	16	17	18
19	20	21	22	23	24	25
26	27	28	29	30		

May

S	M	T	W	T	F	S
					1	2
3	4	5	6	7	8	9
10	11	12	13	14	15	16
17	18	19	20	21	22	23
24/31	25	26	27	28	29	30

June

S	M	T	W	T	F	S
	1	2	3	4	5	6
7	8	9	10	11	12	13
14	15	16	17	18	19	20
21	22	23	24	25	26	27
28	29	30				

July

S	M	T	W	T	F	S
			1	2	3	4
5	6	7	8	9	10	11
12	13	14	15	16	17	18
19	20	21	22	23	24	25
26	27	28	29	30	31	

August

S	M	T	W	T	F	S
						1
2	3	4	5	6	7	8
9	10	11	12	13	14	15
16	17	18	19	20	21	22
23/30	24/31	25	26	27	28	29

September

S	M	T	W	T	F	S
		1	2	3	4	5
6	7	8	9	10	11	12
13	14	15	16	17	18	19
20	21	22	23	24	25	26
27	28	29	30			

October

S	M	T	W	T	F	S
				1	2	3
4	5	6	7	8	9	10
11	12	13	14	15	16	17
18	19	20	21	22	23	24
25	26	27	28	29	30	31

November

S	M	T	W	T	F	S
1	2	3	4	5	6	7
8	9	10	11	12	13	14
15	16	17	18	19	20	21
22	23	24	25	26	27	28
29	30					

December

S	M	T	W	T	F	S
		1	2	3	4	5
6	7	8	9	10	11	12
13	14	15	16	17	18	19
20	21	22	23	24	25	26
27	28	29	30	31		

Use the calendar to answer the questions.

4 How many months have 30 days? _____

5 What month is the sixth month of the year? _____

6 What month comes just before November? _____

7 What day is October 6th on this calendar? _____

8 Which month has neither 30 nor 31 days? _____

Problem Solving Reasoning

Solve.

9 Ann and Rachel are both 7 years old. Ann's birthday is in August.
Rachel's birthday is in May. It is April now. Who is older?
How do you know?

_____

_____

© Pearson Education, Inc.

Name_____

Learn! Algebra

Equivalent Times	
one quarter hour	15 minutes
one half hour	30 minutes
one hour	60 minutes

Equivalent Times	
1 day	24 hours
1 week	7 days
1 year	12 months

"Equivalent" means "same."

How many hours are in 1 day?

Word Bank

equivalent

Check ✓

Use the tables to solve each problem.

1. My bus ride home is 30 minutes long. Is my ride one quarter hour long or one half hour long?

_____

2. Aunt Sandy lived in Canada for 12 months. Did she live there for 1 day, 1 week, or 1 year?

_____

3. Sam and Ken went camping for 3 days. Is that more than a week or less than a week?

_____

4. I played volleyball for one and a half hours today. How many minutes did I play?

_____

Think About It   Reasoning

How many minutes are in 2 hours?
Explain.

Morning Schedule		
8:30– 9:30	Reading	
9:30–10:30	Math	10 + 2 = 12
10:30–10:45	Recess	
10:45–11:30	Art	
11:30–12:15	Lunch	

Use the schedule to answer these questions.

5 How many hours long is Reading? _____

How many minutes is this? _____

6 Which other class is as long as Reading? _____

7 Which two activities are each 45 minutes long? _____

_____

8 Which activity is 15 minutes long? _____

Problem Solving Visual Thinking

9 Write the time for each clock. Find the pattern.
What will the last clock show?
Draw the hands and write the time.

_____   _____   _____

© Pearson Education, Inc.

 Home Connection Your children answered questions involving equivalent times. **Home Activity** Name the times listed in the first column of each table on Student Book Page 305. Have your child name an equivalent time.

Name_____

Write the time. Then circle another way to say the time.

1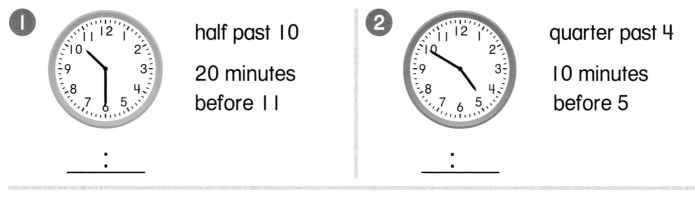

half past 10

20 minutes before 11

____:____

2

quarter past 4

10 minutes before 5

____:____

Circle the amount of time each activity would take.

3

about 30 minutes

about 30 hours

about 30 days

4

about 2 minutes

about 2 hours

about 2 days

Write the times. Then circle how long the activity lasted.

5 Pick vegetables.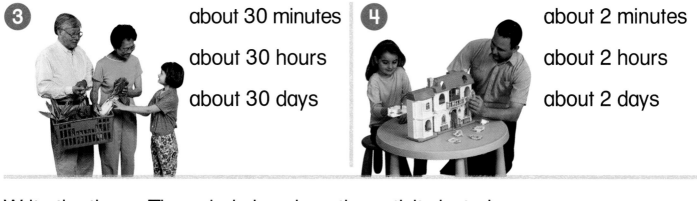

Start	End

_____   _____

3 hours

4 hours

Use the calendar to answer the questions.

6 How many days are in the month? _____

7 What day is the 18th of the month? _____

8 How many days are in 1 week? _____

November						
S	M	T	W	T	F	S
			1	2	3	4
5	6	7	8	9	10	11
12	13	14	15	16	17	18
19	20	21	22	23	24	25
26	27	28	29	30		

Add or subtract.

1
$$\begin{array}{r} 9 \\ + 3 \\ \hline \end{array}$$

Ⓐ 6
Ⓑ 9
Ⓒ 21
Ⓓ 12

2
$$\begin{array}{r} 79 \\ - 59 \\ \hline \end{array}$$

Ⓐ 20
Ⓑ 19
Ⓒ 29
Ⓓ 59

Which is the closest ten?

3

70   80

77 is closest to ____.

70   75   80   10
Ⓐ   Ⓑ   Ⓒ   Ⓓ

Which shape is congruent to this shape?

4

Ⓐ   Ⓑ   Ⓒ   Ⓓ

5 Mark the pair of numbers that has the sum of 50.

20 and 15   32 and 18   14 and 70   50 and 50
Ⓐ   Ⓑ   Ⓒ   Ⓓ

Writing in Math

6 Explain which is the better way to add.

$$\begin{array}{r} 79 \\ + 19 \\ \hline \end{array}$$

paper and pencil

mental math

_____

_____

Name_____

The Nice Doggy School Bus

The Nice Doggy School of Cute Tricks

Understand Graphic Sources: Tables

Look at the table of Saturday classes.
Then answer the questions.

1 Which class starts after lunch?

_____

2 Which class is longest?

_____

3 Which class is shortest?

_____

4 Which class is earliest?

_____

5 Which class starts at the
same time as Sitting Up?

_____

Class	Starts	Ends
Rolling Over	10:00	12:00
Shaking Paws	8:00	10:00
Sitting Up	10:00	11:00
Fetching Sticks	1:00	3:00
Jumping Through Hoops	9:00	12:00

Think About It   Reasoning

What is the greatest number of classes a dog
could take in one day? Explain your thinking.

6 Read the information about dogs and look at the pictures.

There are more than 300 kinds or breeds of dogs.
The breeds can be placed in 7 groups.
Here are some examples.

Breed: St. Bernard
Group: Working dogs
Height: 26–30 inches
Weight: 140–200 pounds

Breed: Chihuahua
Group: Toy dogs
Height: 5 inches
Weight: 1–6 pounds

Breed: Beagle
Group: Hounds
Height: 13–15 inches
Weight: 18–30 pounds

Breed: Scottish Terrier
Group: Terriers
Height: 9–10 inches
Weight: 18–22 pounds

Breed: Golden Retriever
Group: Sporting dogs
Height: 22–24 inches
Weight: 55–75 pounds

Breed: Collie
Group: Herding dogs
Height: 22–26 inches
Weight: 50–75 pounds

Breed: Dalmatian
Group: Nonsporting dogs
Height: 19–23 inches
Weight: 40–50 pounds

7 Pick your 3 favorite breeds. Write their information in the table.
Then answer questions about your favorites.

Breed	Group	Height	Weight

8 Which of your picks is the tallest? _____

9 Which of your picks weighs the least? _____

Home Connection Your child organized information in a table.
Home Activity With your child, look for a table used in everyday life—
for example, a train schedule, a table of television programs, or a schedule
of sporting events, showing home and away games.

Name

Read and Understand

What kinds of plants did the children plant in the class garden?
How many of each kind of plant?

First you need to find out the kinds of plants.
Then find out how many of each kind.

Plan and Solve

You can make a table. Make tally marks to show how many of each kind.

What kinds of plants are in the garden?

There are __8__ bean plants, __3__ radish plants, _____ lettuce plants, _____ marigold plants, and _____ sunflower plants.

Look Back and Check

How did making a table help you answer the questions?

| Classroom 2A's Garden ||
Kind	Number
Bean	卌 |||
Radish	|||
Lettuce	卌
Marigold	卌	
Sunflower	|||||

Think About It   Number Sense

Are there more bean plants and radish plants or bean plants and sunflower plants?

The children in Class 2B drew crayons to show their favorite colors.
Complete the table. Use tally marks.

1

Favorite Colors					
Color	Red				
Number	l				

2 How many children are in Class 2B?   _____ children

3 How many children named red
as their favorite color?   _____ children

4 Do more children like green or yellow?   _____

How many more?   _____ more children

5 What color is the favorite of
most children?   _____

6 What color did two children name
as their favorite?   _____

Visual Thinking

Use the table to solve the problem.

7 How many children in all
are in Grades 2 and 3?

_____ children

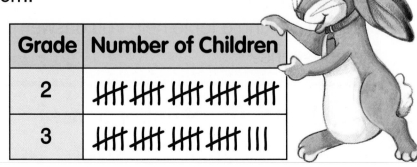

Grade	Number of Children
2	卌 卌 卌 卌 卌
3	卌 卌 卌 卌 lll

Home Connection Your child used tally marks to record data in a chart and used the chart to answer questions. **Home Activity** Ask your child questions that can be answered using the above tables, such as: "How many more children are in Grade 2 than are in Grade 3?"

Name _____

Learn!

Taking a **survey** is one way to collect information, or **data**.

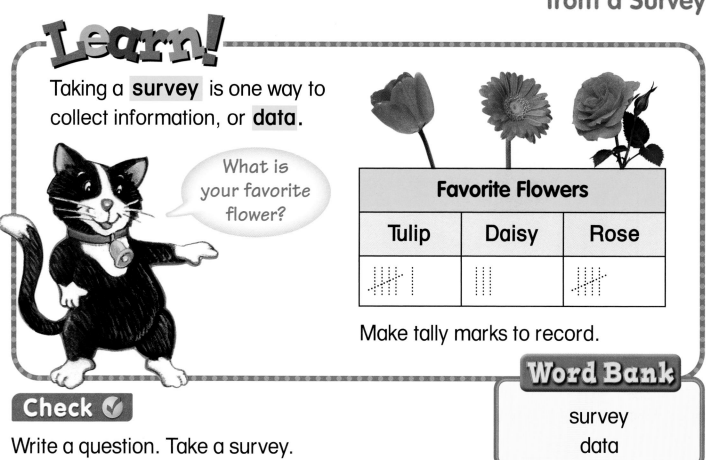

What is your favorite flower?

Favorite Flowers		
Tulip	Daisy	Rose
卌丨	丨丨丨	卌

Make tally marks to record.

Word Bank

survey

data

Check ✓

Write a question. Take a survey.
Complete the chart.

What is your favorite _____?		
_____	_____	_____

1. What did most people choose as their favorite? _____

2. What did the least number of people choose as their favorite? _____

3. How many people did you survey? _____

Think About It   Reasoning

Would you get the same data if you asked your parents the survey question instead of your classmates? Explain.

Use the survey to answer the questions.

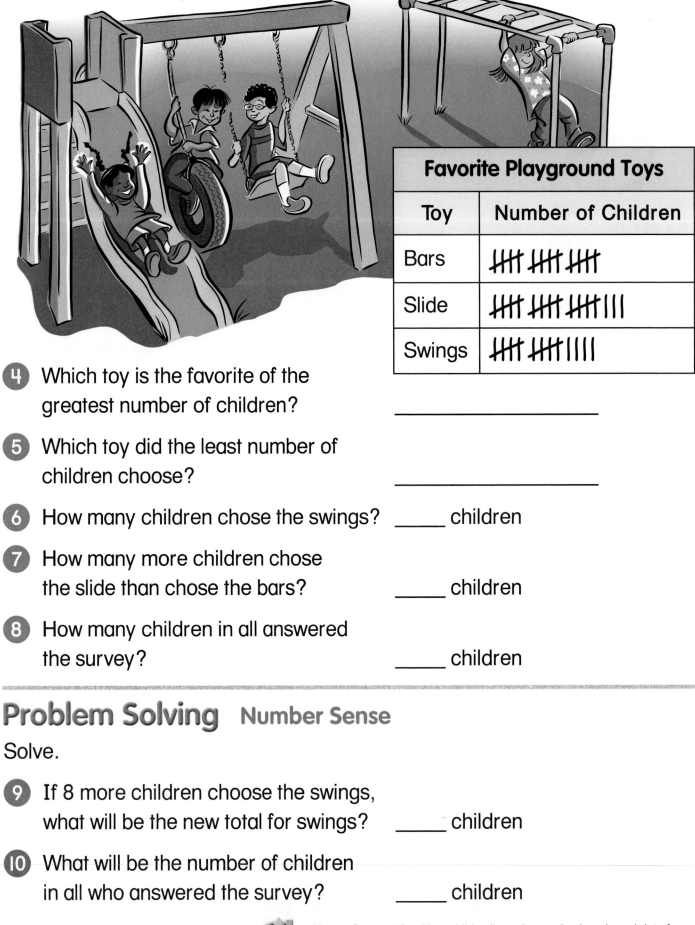

Favorite Playground Toys	
Toy	Number of Children
Bars	$\cancel{||||}$ $\cancel{||||}$ $\cancel{||||}$
Slide	$\cancel{||||}$ $\cancel{||||}$ $\cancel{||||}$ |||
Swings	$\cancel{||||}$ $\cancel{||||}$ ||||

4 Which toy is the favorite of the greatest number of children? _____

5 Which toy did the least number of children choose? _____

6 How many children chose the swings? _____ children

7 How many more children chose the slide than chose the bars? _____ children

8 How many children in all answered the survey? _____ children

Problem Solving Number Sense

Solve.

9 If 8 more children choose the swings, what will be the new total for swings? _____ children

10 What will be the number of children in all who answered the survey? _____ children

Home Connection Your child collected, organized, and used data from a survey to solve problems. **Home Activity** Have your child survey family members and record results using tally marks.

Learn!

You can collect and show data using a **Venn diagram**.

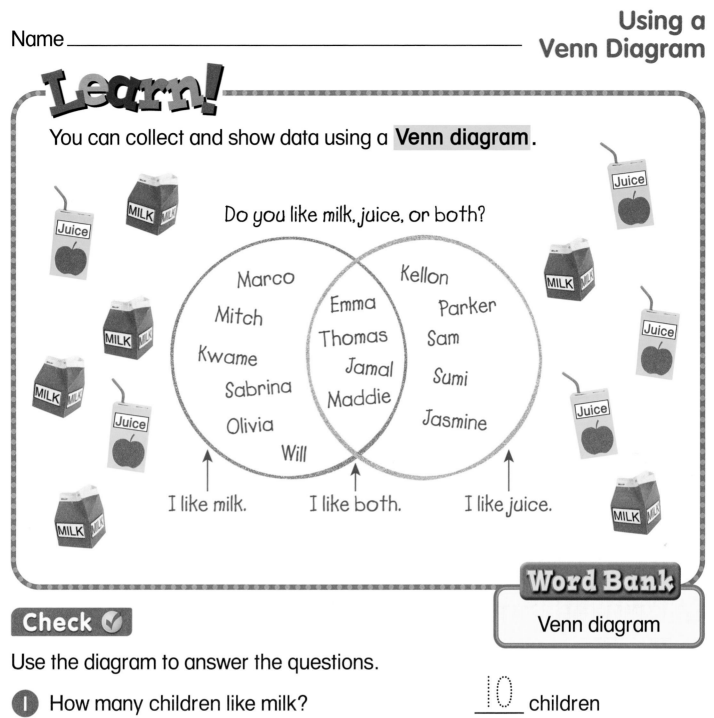

Do you like milk, juice, or both?

Marco
Mitch
Kwame
Sabrina
Olivia
Will

Emma
Thomas
Jamal
Maddie

Kellon
Parker
Sam
Sumi
Jasmine

↑ I like milk.　　↑ I like both.　　↑ I like juice.

Word Bank

Venn diagram

Check ✓

Use the diagram to answer the questions.

1 How many children like milk?   _10_ children

2 How many children like juice?   ____ children

3 How many children like both milk and juice?   ____ children

4 How many children like milk but **not** juice?   ____ children

5 How many children like juice but **not** milk?   ____ children

6 How many children were surveyed?   ____ children

Think About It　Number Sense

How many more children like milk than like juice?
Explain.

7 Ask seven children the question below. Record the data.

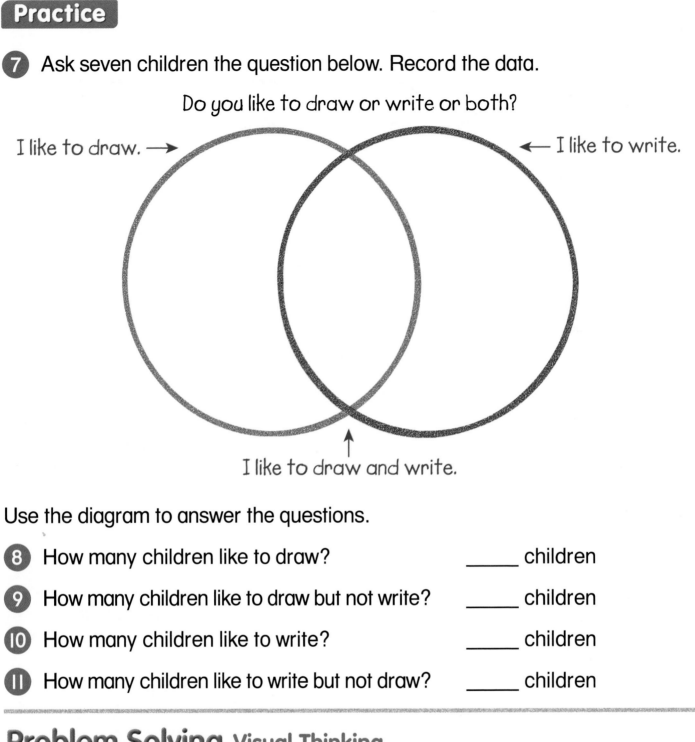

Do you like to draw or write or both?

I like to draw. →   ← I like to write.

↑
I like to draw and write.

Use the diagram to answer the questions.

8 How many children like to draw?   _____ children

9 How many children like to draw but not write?   _____ children

10 How many children like to write?   _____ children

11 How many children like to write but not draw?   _____ children

Problem Solving Visual Thinking

12 Who likes all 3 kinds of fruit?

_____

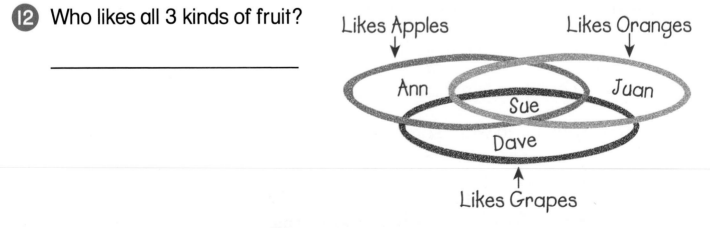

Likes Apples   Likes Oranges
↓   ↓

Ann   Juan
Sue
Dave

↑
Likes Grapes

Home Connection Your child collected and organized data and then used this information to solve problems. **Home Activity** Look for various kinds of diagrams and graphs in the newspaper and discuss them with your child.

Name _____

Use the table to solve the problems.

Favorite Zoo Animals	
Kind	**Number**
Lion	|||
Tiger	||||
Elephant	HHI I
Giraffe	
Polar bear	||

1 Make tally marks to show that 5 children chose the giraffe as their favorite zoo animal.

2 Which animal is the favorite of the most children?

_____

3 Which animal is the favorite of the fewest children?

_____

Use the survey to answer the questions.

What is your favorite season?	
Winter	HHI I
Spring	||||
Summer	HHI HHI I
Fall	||

4 How many children chose winter as their favorite season?

_____ children

5 How many more children like spring than like fall?

_____ more children

Use the diagram to answer the questions.

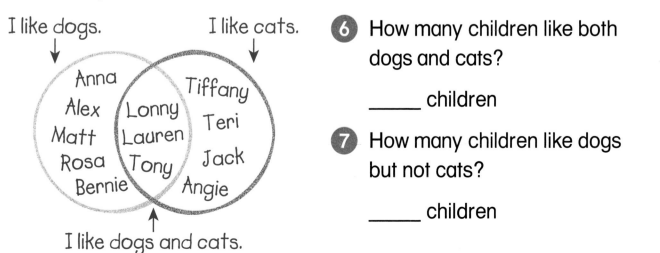

I like dogs.   I like cats.

Anna
Alex   Lonny   Tiffany
Matt   Lauren   Teri
Rosa   Tony   Jack
Bernie   Angie

I like dogs and cats.

6 How many children like both dogs and cats?

_____ children

7 How many children like dogs but not cats?

_____ children

1 What number is shown?

Ⓐ 64

Ⓑ 70

Ⓒ 74

Ⓓ 47

2 What amount of money do both sets show?

$1.00
Ⓐ

75¢
Ⓑ

90¢
Ⓒ

50¢
Ⓓ

3 What solid figure could you trace to make this plane shape?

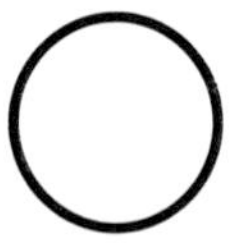

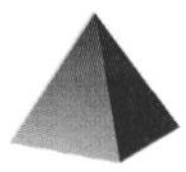

Ⓐ   Ⓑ   Ⓒ   Ⓓ

Find the difference.

4
```
   □
  52¢
- 29¢
```
Ⓐ 12¢

Ⓑ 10¢

Ⓒ 31¢

Ⓓ 23¢

5
```
   □
  26¢
- 17¢
```
Ⓐ 9¢

Ⓑ 19¢

Ⓒ 43¢

Ⓓ 11¢

Writing in Math

6 Write 3 ways to say the time shown.

_____

Name _____

Learn!

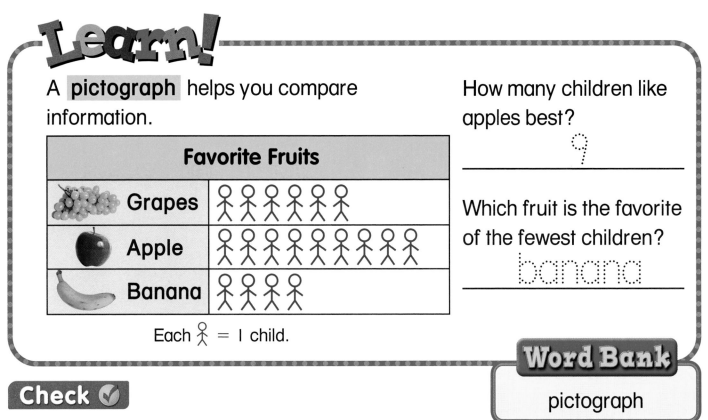

A **pictograph** helps you compare information.

Favorite Fruits

Grapes	☺☺☺☺☺☺
Apple	☺☺☺☺☺☺☺☺☺
Banana	☺☺☺☺

Each ☺ = I child.

How many children like apples best?

9

Which fruit is the favorite of the fewest children?

banana

Word Bank

pictograph

Check ✓

1 Which food does your class like best?
Make a pictograph to find out. Complete the graph.

Favorite Foods	
Hamburger	
Pizza	
Taco	

Each ☺ = I child.

2 Which food is favored by the most children? _____

3 Which food is favored by the fewest children? _____

4 How many children chose tacos? _____ children

Think About It Reasoning

What if 5 more children choose tacos as their favorite food?
Would the class's favorite food be the same?

Use the graph to answer the questions.

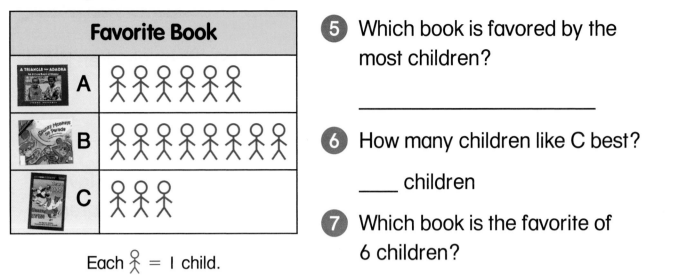

Favorite Book

A

B

C

Each 👤 = 1 child.

5 Which book is favored by the most children?

_____

6 How many children like C best?

____ children

7 Which book is the favorite of 6 children?

_____

Use the graph to answer the questions.

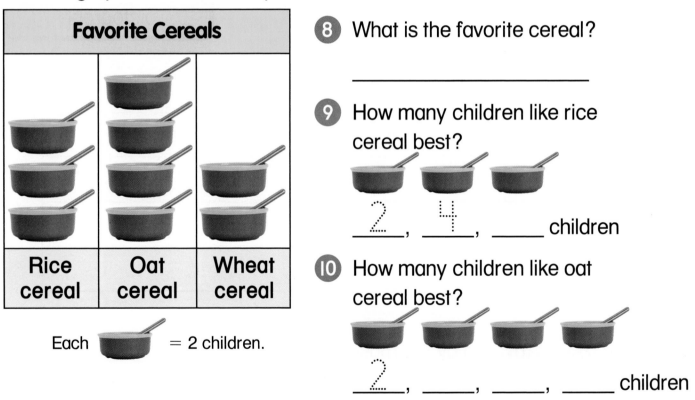

Favorite Cereals

| Rice cereal | Oat cereal | Wheat cereal |

Each 🍲 = 2 children.

8 What is the favorite cereal?

_____

9 How many children like rice cereal best?

__2__, __4__, _____ children

10 How many children like oat cereal best?

__2__, _____, _____, _____ children

Problem Solving Number Sense

11 Write the number sentence that tells how many more children chose oat cereal than chose wheat cereal. Solve.

_____

_____ more children

Home Connection Your child created and analyzed pictographs.
Home Activity Have your child compare rice cereal and wheat cereal in the above pictograph. How many children like each kind of cereal? How many more children like rice cereal than like wheat cereal?

Name _____

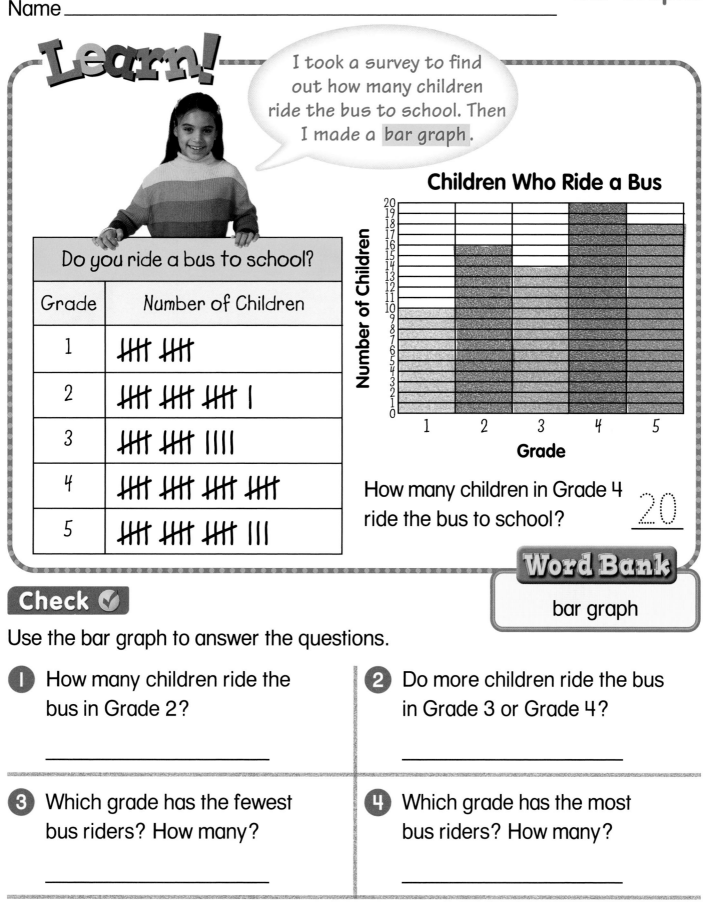

Learn!

I took a survey to find out how many children ride the bus to school. Then I made a bar graph.

Do you ride a bus to school?

Grade	Number of Children
1	ЖЖ ЖЖ
2	ЖЖ ЖЖ ЖЖ I
3	ЖЖ ЖЖ IIII
4	ЖЖ ЖЖ ЖЖ ЖЖ
5	ЖЖ ЖЖ ЖЖ III

Children Who Ride a Bus

How many children in Grade 4 ride the bus to school? _20_

Word Bank

bar graph

Check ✓

Use the bar graph to answer the questions.

1. How many children ride the bus in Grade 2?

   _____

2. Do more children ride the bus in Grade 3 or Grade 4?

   _____

3. Which grade has the fewest bus riders? How many?

   _____

4. Which grade has the most bus riders? How many?

   _____

Think About It Number Sense

How many bus riders are there in all?
Tell how you know.

5. Take a survey. Ask classmates what they most like to do outside. Make tally marks to keep track of what each classmate says.

Favorite Outside Activities	
Ride bike	
Skateboard	
Play games	
Jump rope	

6. Make a bar graph. Color one box for each time an activity was chosen.

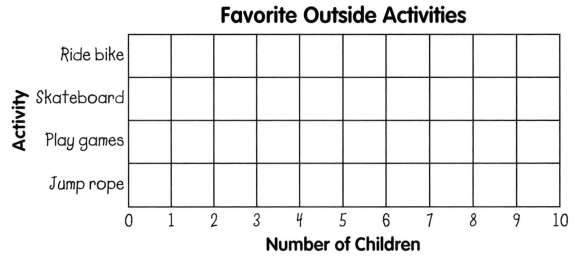

Favorite Outside Activities

Activity: Ride bike, Skateboard, Play games, Jump rope

Number of Children (0 1 2 3 4 5 6 7 8 9 10)

Use the graph to answer each question.

7. Which activity is favored by the most children? _____

8. Which activity is favored by the fewest children? _____

9. Do more children like to ride a bike or play games? _____

Problem Solving Writing in Math

10. Write one way that tally charts and bar graphs are alike and one way that they are different.

Home Connection Your child gathered and used data from tally charts and bar graphs. **Home Activity** Ask your child a question that can be answered using the above graph.

Name _____

Line Plots

Learn!

How many books did you read this month?

Books	0	1	2	3	4	5	6	7	8	9	10
Tallies	I	II	II	I	卌	卌	卌I	III	IIII	I	I
Children	1	2	2	1	5	5	6	3	4	1	1

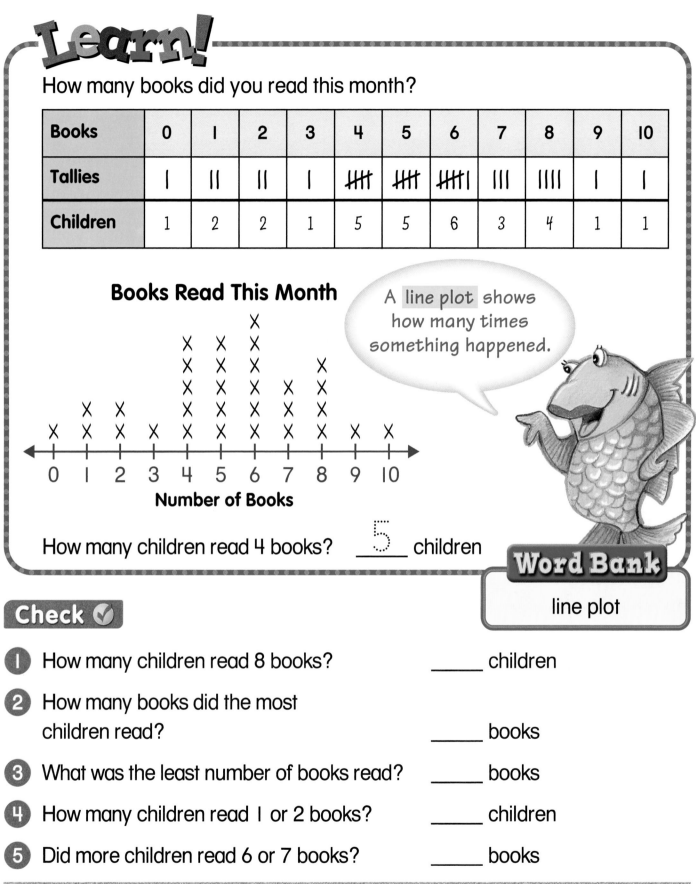

Books Read This Month

A line plot shows how many times something happened.

How many children read 4 books? __5__ children

Word Bank

line plot

Check ✓

1. How many children read 8 books? _____ children

2. How many books did the most children read? _____ books

3. What was the least number of books read? _____ books

4. How many children read 1 or 2 books? _____ children

5. Did more children read 6 or 7 books? _____ books

Think About It Number Sense

How many children were surveyed?
Tell your strategy for figuring this out.

Chapter 8 ★ Lesson 14

three hundred twenty-three **323**

Practice

Use the line plot to answer the questions.

Bouncing a Ball for 15 Seconds

```
                                            X
                                            X
                                            X
                        X                   X
              X         X         X         X
        X     X    X    X    X    X    X    X    X
   X    X     X    X    X    X    X    X    X    X    X
  ◄──┼────┼────┼────┼────┼────┼────┼────┼────┼────┼────┼──►
    18   19   20   21   22   23   24   25   26   27   28
```

Number of Bounces

---

6 How many children bounced the ball 20 times?

_____ children

7 What is the greatest number of times a child bounced the ball?

_____ times

---

8 What is the least number of times a child bounced the ball?

_____ times

9 How many children bounced the ball 25 or more times?

_____ children

---

10 How many children bounced the ball 22 or fewer times?

_____ children

11 How many children in all bounced the ball?

_____ children

Problem Solving Reasonableness

Circle the answer that is more reasonable.

12 Ginny bounced the ball for 15 seconds.
She bounced the ball _____ times.   2   22

13 Tyrone bounced the ball for 30 seconds.
He bounced the ball _____ times.   45   450

Home Connection Your child analyzed line plots to answer questions.
Home Activity Have family members bounce a ball for 15 seconds and record the number of bounces. Add the data to the graph above. Discuss how the graph changed when you added the new data.

Name _____

Learn! Algebra

Look at the coordinate graph. Can you tell me which musical instrument is located at (C, 3)?

Find the Musical Instruments

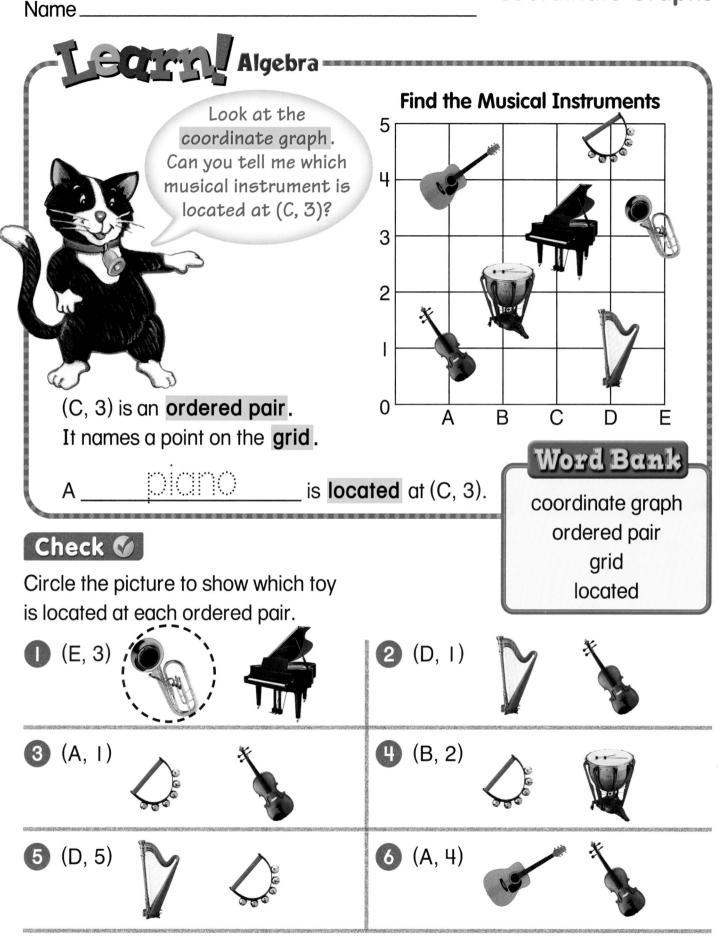

(C, 3) is an **ordered pair**.
It names a point on the **grid**.

A ___piano___ is **located** at (C, 3).

Word Bank

coordinate graph
ordered pair
grid
located

Check ✓

Circle the picture to show which toy is located at each ordered pair.

1 (E, 3)

2 (D, 1)

3 (A, 1)

4 (B, 2)

5 (D, 5)

6 (A, 4)

Think About It Reasoning

Draw a new instrument on the grid. Name its location using an ordered pair.

Find the Farm Animals

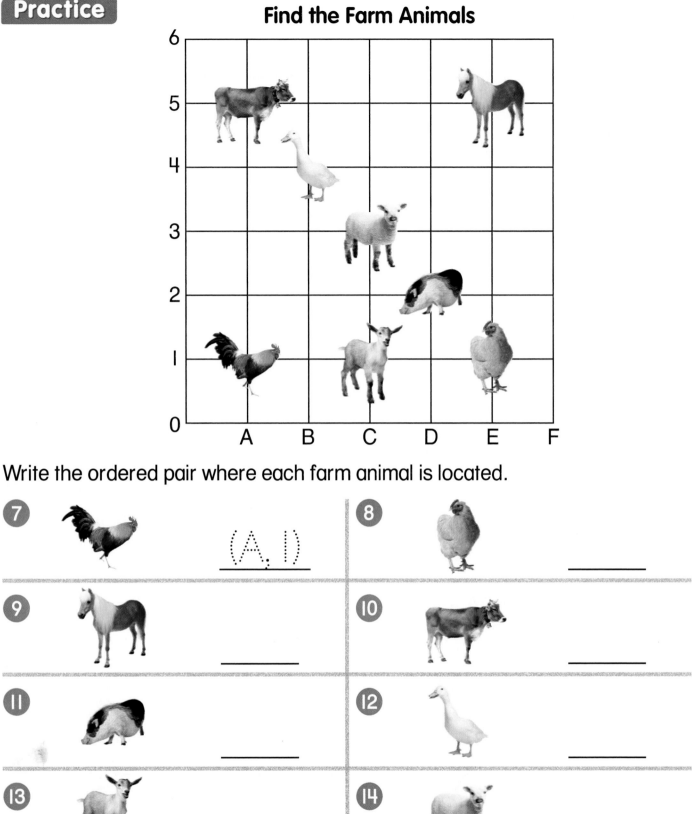

Write the ordered pair where each farm animal is located.

7 _____(A, 1)_____

8 _____

9 _____

10 _____

11 _____

12 _____

13 _____

14 _____

Problem Solving Writing in Math

15 Tell how you would find the ordered pair that tells the location of the pig.

 Home Connection Your child used ordered pairs to locate points on a grid. **Home Activity** Name an ordered pair, such as (D, 5), and have your child locate it with his or her finger.

Name_____

Learn!

How many butterfly cards does Eva have? There are 7 cards next to "Butterfly." Each picture stands for 5 cards. Count by 5s.

Eva's Insect Cards							
Butterfly	🦋	🦋	🦋	🦋	🦋	🦋	🦋
Grasshopper	🦗	🦗	🦗	🦗			
Beetle	🪲	🪲	🪲				

I 🦋 = 5 cards.

5 , 10 , 15 , ____ , ____ , ____ , ____

Eva has 35 butterfly cards.

Check ✓

Use the graph to answer the questions.

1 How many grasshopper cards does Eva have?

_____

2 Does Eva have more grasshopper cards or butterfly cards?

_____

3 How many more butterfly cards than grasshopper cards does Eva have?

_____

4 Eva bought 5 more butterfly cards. How many butterfly cards does she have now?

_____

Think About It   Reasoning

How many more beetle cards does Eva need to buy to have 20 beetle cards in all? Tell how you know.

Coin Collections

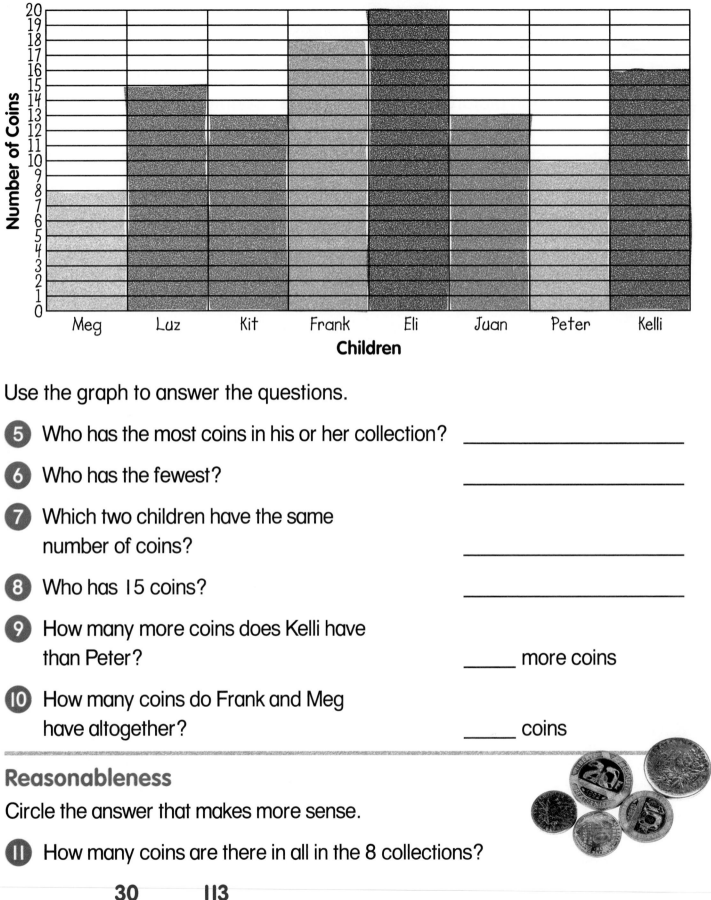

Use the graph to answer the questions.

5 Who has the most coins in his or her collection? _____

6 Who has the fewest? _____

7 Which two children have the same
number of coins? _____

8 Who has 15 coins? _____

9 How many more coins does Kelli have
than Peter? _____ more coins

10 How many coins do Frank and Meg
have altogether? _____ coins

Reasonableness

Circle the answer that makes more sense.

11 How many coins are there in all in the 8 collections?

30   **113**

Home Connection Your child used data from a pictograph and
a bar graph to solve problems. **Home Activity** Have your child
ask you a question that can be answered using one of the graphs.

328 three hundred twenty-eight

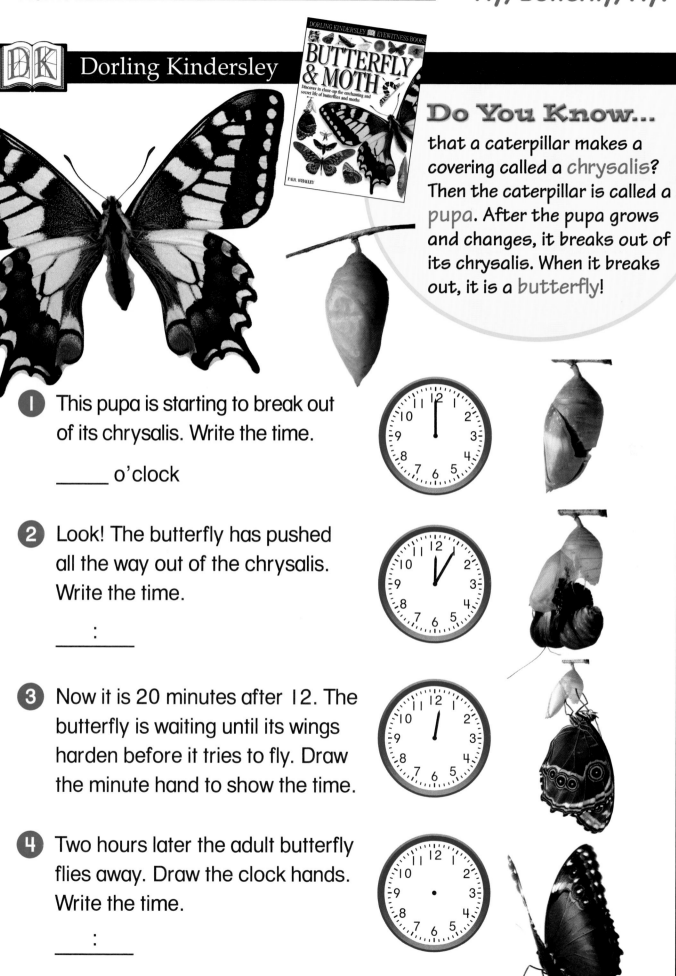

DK Dorling Kindersley

DORLING KINDERSLEY EYEWITNESS BOOKS
BUTTERFLY & MOTH
Discover in close-up the enchanting and secret life of butterflies and moths
PAUL WHALLEY

Do You Know...
that a caterpillar makes a covering called a chrysalis? Then the caterpillar is called a pupa. After the pupa grows and changes, it breaks out of its chrysalis. When it breaks out, it is a butterfly!

1 This pupa is starting to break out of its chrysalis. Write the time.

_____ o'clock

2 Look! The butterfly has pushed all the way out of the chrysalis. Write the time.

_____ : _____

3 Now it is 20 minutes after 12. The butterfly is waiting until its wings harden before it tries to fly. Draw the minute hand to show the time.

4 Two hours later the adult butterfly flies away. Draw the clock hands. Write the time.

_____ : _____

5 This butterfly landed on a flower at 4:00. It rested there for 5 minutes. Then it flew away. It flew away at

____ : ____.

6 There are 11 butterflies in the garden. 6 more break out of their chrysalises. How many butterflies are in the garden now?

____ + ____ = ____ butterflies

7 22 children in a class voted for their favorite butterflies. If 12 children chose painted ladies, how many children chose other kinds of butterflies?

____ ◯ ____ = ____ children

Writing in Math

8 Write a story about time. Tell about a caterpillar changing into a butterfly.

© Pearson Education, Inc.

Home Connection Your child learned how to solve problems by applying his or her math skills. **Home Activity** Talk to your child about how he or she solved the problems on these two pages.

Name_____

Answer each question.

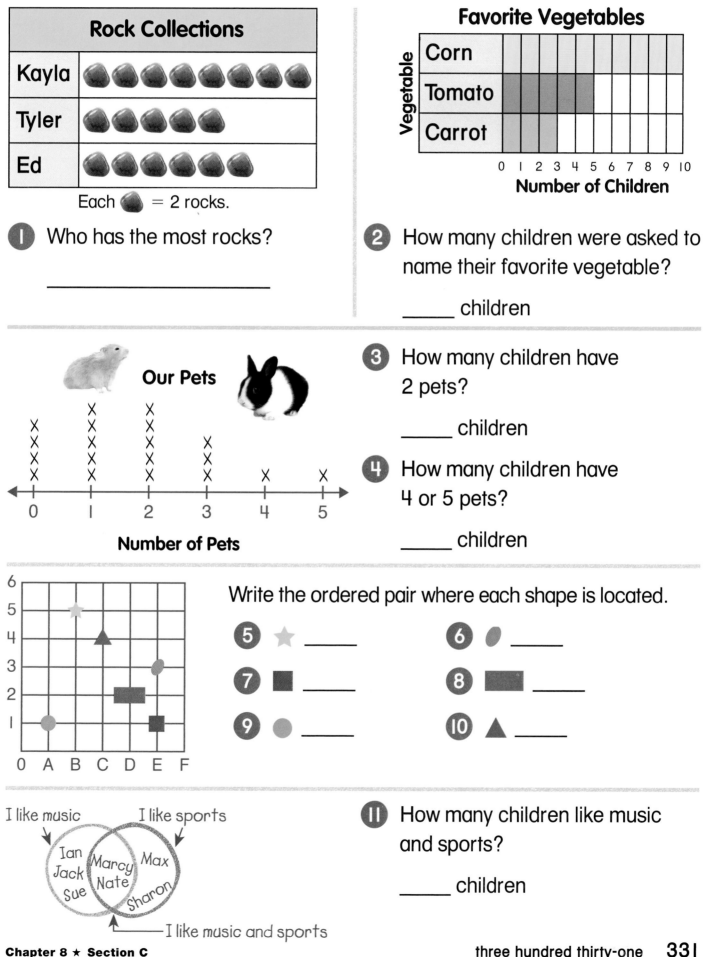

Rock Collections	
Kayla	🪨🪨🪨🪨🪨🪨🪨🪨
Tyler	🪨🪨🪨🪨
Ed	🪨🪨🪨🪨🪨

Each 🪨 = 2 rocks.

1 Who has the most rocks?

_____

Favorite Vegetables

Vegetable

	Corn									
	Tomato									
	Carrot									

0 1 2 3 4 5 6 7 8 9 10
Number of Children

2 How many children were asked to name their favorite vegetable?

_____ children

Our Pets

0 1 2 3 4 5
Number of Pets

3 How many children have 2 pets?

_____ children

4 How many children have 4 or 5 pets?

_____ children

6
5
4
3
2
1
0 A B C D E F

Write the ordered pair where each shape is located.

5 ★ _____

6 ⬮ _____

7 ◼ _____

8 ▬ _____

9 ● _____

10 ▲ _____

I like music   I like sports

Ian
Jack   Marcy   Max
Sue   Nate
       Sharon

I like music and sports

11 How many children like music and sports?

_____ children

Name _____

1 Which number sentence completes the fact family?

$$4 + 5 = 9 \qquad\qquad 5 + 4 = 9 \qquad\qquad 9 - 4 = 5$$

$9 - 5 = 4$ $8 - 4 = 4$ $5 + 5 = 10$ $9 - 0 = 9$

   Ⓐ   Ⓑ   Ⓒ   Ⓓ

2 Which picture shows a line of symmetry?

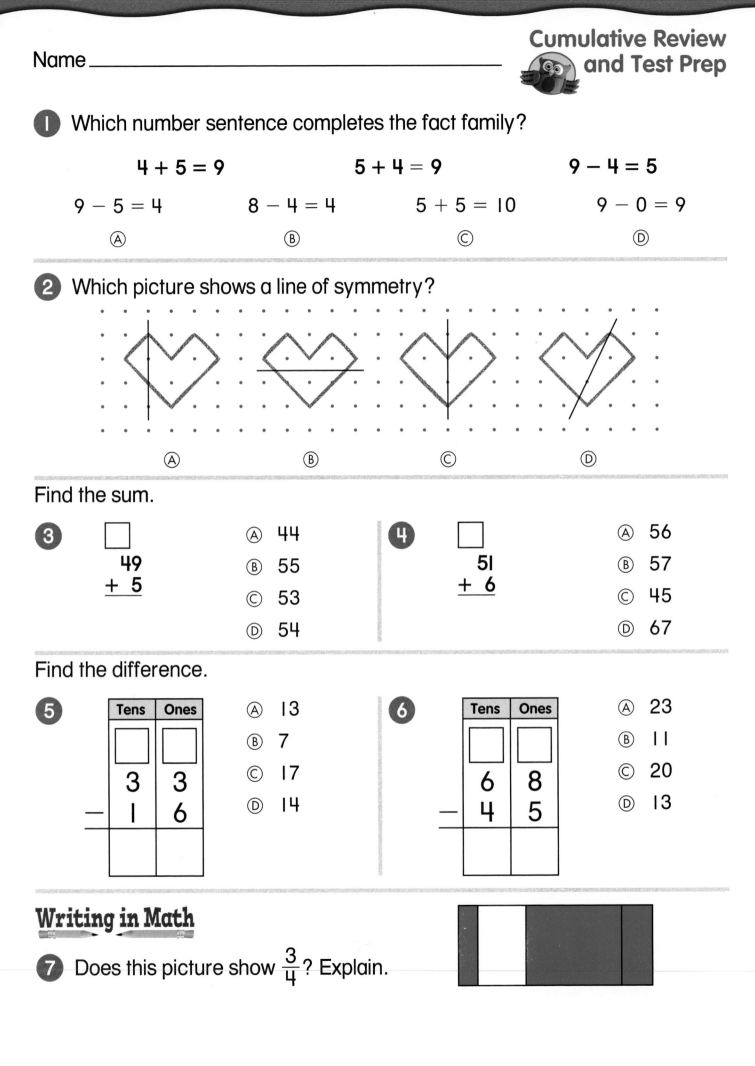

   Ⓐ   Ⓑ   Ⓒ   Ⓓ

Find the sum.

3
$$\begin{array}{r} \square \\ 49 \\ +\ 5 \\ \hline \end{array}$$

  Ⓐ 44
  Ⓑ 55
  Ⓒ 53
  Ⓓ 54

4
$$\begin{array}{r} \square \\ 51 \\ +\ 6 \\ \hline \end{array}$$

  Ⓐ 56
  Ⓑ 57
  Ⓒ 45
  Ⓓ 67

Find the difference.

5

Tens	Ones
□	□
3	3
− 1	6

  Ⓐ 13
  Ⓑ 7
  Ⓒ 17
  Ⓓ 14

6

Tens	Ones
□	□
6	8
− 4	5

  Ⓐ 23
  Ⓑ 11
  Ⓒ 20
  Ⓓ 13

Writing in Math

7 Does this picture show $\frac{3}{4}$? Explain.

Range and Mode

How many pets would you like to have in your classroom?

The girls in Room 110 said:
3, 1, 3, 1, 1, 2, 3, 3, 1, 3, 2

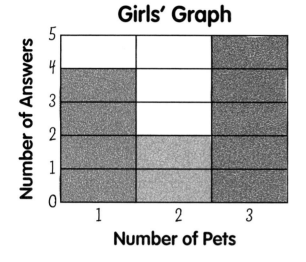

Girls' Graph

Number of Answers

Number of Pets

The girls' graph shows the girls' answers. The most popular answer is the **mode.**

The mode is __3__.

The **range** is the difference between the greatest answer and the least answer.

The range is 3 − 1, or __2__.

The boys in Room 110 said:
3, 7, 7, 2, 2, 3, 1, 3, 7, 7, 7, 7

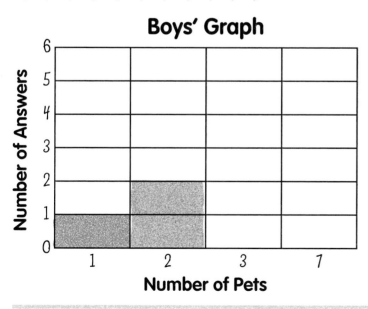

Boys' Graph

Number of Answers

Number of Pets

① Complete the boys' graph.

② What is the mode? _____

③ What is the range?

_____ − _____, or _____

④ How could you change the mode in the girls' graph by adding two more answers?

_____

Writing in Math

⑤ Put all of the girls' and boys' answers together. Make a new graph. How do the mode and the range change?

Name_____

Use a Computer to Find Elapsed Time

1 Under **Rides** in the table below, make a list of rides you want to go on at the amusement park.

2 Under **Elapsed Time,** write how many minutes you think it will take to go on each ride. 10 minutes? 15 minutes? 20 minutes?

Rides	Elapsed Time	Starting Time	Ending Time
Ferris wheel	10 minutes	6:00 P.M.	6:10 P.M.
		6:10 P.M.	

3 On a computer, go to the Time eTool. Set the clock to 6:00 P.M.

4 Set the elapsed time to the time you think your ride will last.

5 In your table, write down the ending time for this ride.

6 Now, set the starting time of the clock to the ending time of the first ride you went on.

7 Follow the same steps for all of the rides on your list.

Think About It   Reasoning

If you have to leave the amusement park at 7:00 P.M., will you have enough time to go on all of your rides?

Home Connection Your child made a table of amusement park rides and used a computer to show the starting time and ending time for each ride.
Home Activity Ask your child to explain how he or she used a computer to find the starting time and the ending time for one of the rides listed in his or her table.

Chapter 8

Read Together

Plan How to Find the Answer

You can use problem-solving strategies to help you find answers on tests.

Test-Taking Strategies
Understand the Question
Get Information for the Answer
Plan How to Find the Answer
Make Smart Choices
Use Writing in Math

One strategy is reading a table. Another strategy is writing a number sentence.

1 How many more children chose running than chose swimming?

Ⓐ 3 more children

Ⓑ 4 more children

Ⓒ 5 more children

Ⓓ 7 more children

Read the table.
Compare the two numbers:

____ − ____ = ____

Fill in the answer bubble.

4 more children chose running than chose swimming.

Our Favorite Sports	
Sport	**Number of Children**
Swimming	|||
Running	卌 ||
Basketball	卌

Your Turn

Choose a strategy to solve the problem. Then fill in the answer bubble.

2 How many children voted for their favorite sport?

Ⓐ 10 children   Ⓒ 15 children

Ⓑ 12 children   Ⓓ 16 children

3 How many fewer children chose basketball than chose running?

Ⓐ 1 fewer child   Ⓒ 3 fewer children

Ⓑ 2 fewer children   Ⓓ 5 fewer children

Home Connection Your child prepared for standardized tests by using problem-solving strategies to answer math questions.
Home Activity Ask your child to describe the strategy he or she used to solve Exercise 2.

three hundred thirty-five **335**

Name _____

Discover Math in Your World

 # Be a Weather Watcher

We all like to know when it is going to rain or snow,
and whether it is going to be hot or cold. Can you use
a thermometer to find out what the temperature is?

Measuring Temperature

1 For five days, measure the temperature once in the morning
and once in the afternoon.

2 Write the morning temperature and the afternoon temperature
for each day in the table below.

3 Find the difference between the morning temperature
and the afternoon temperature each day.

Temperature	Day 1	Day 2	Day 3	Day 4	Day 5
Morning					
Afternoon					
Difference					

 **Take It to the NET**
Video and Activities
www.scottforesman.com

 Home Connection Your child measured air temperature
twice a day and found the difference between the two readings.
Home Activity Watch a weather report on TV or look in the
newspaper with your child to find the high and low temperatures
for the day. Ask your child to find the difference between the two.

© Pearson Education, Inc.

Chapter 8

Write the time. Circle another way to say the time.

1

half past 1

quarter to 2

Circle the amount of time each activity would take.

2

about 1 minute

about 1 hour

about 1 day

3

about 1 minute

about 1 hour

about 1 day

Draw the clock hands and write the end time.

4 Go to the amusement park.

| Starts | Lasts | Ends |

3 hours

12:00 _____

_____

Answer the questions.

5 How many minutes are in one half hour? _____

6 How many days are in one week? _____

Use the survey to answer the questions.

What Should We Do?	
Go to movie	ЖЖ I
Go to park	III
Go swimming	ЖЖ ЖЖ II

7 Which activity do most children want to do?

_____

8 Do more children want to go to a movie or to a park?

_____

Use the graph to answer the questions.

Favorite Sandwiches	
Egg	🍞🍞🍞🍞🍞
Tomato	🍞🍞🍞🍞
Cheese	🍞🍞🍞🍞🍞🍞🍞🍞

Each 🍞 = 1 child.

Favorite Ball Games

Number of Children

6
5
4
3
2
1
0

Soccer   Baseball   Football   Basketball

Game

9 Which sandwich is the least favorite?

_____

10 How many children were asked to name their favorite ball game?

_____ children

Answer the questions.

Fruit Snack Time

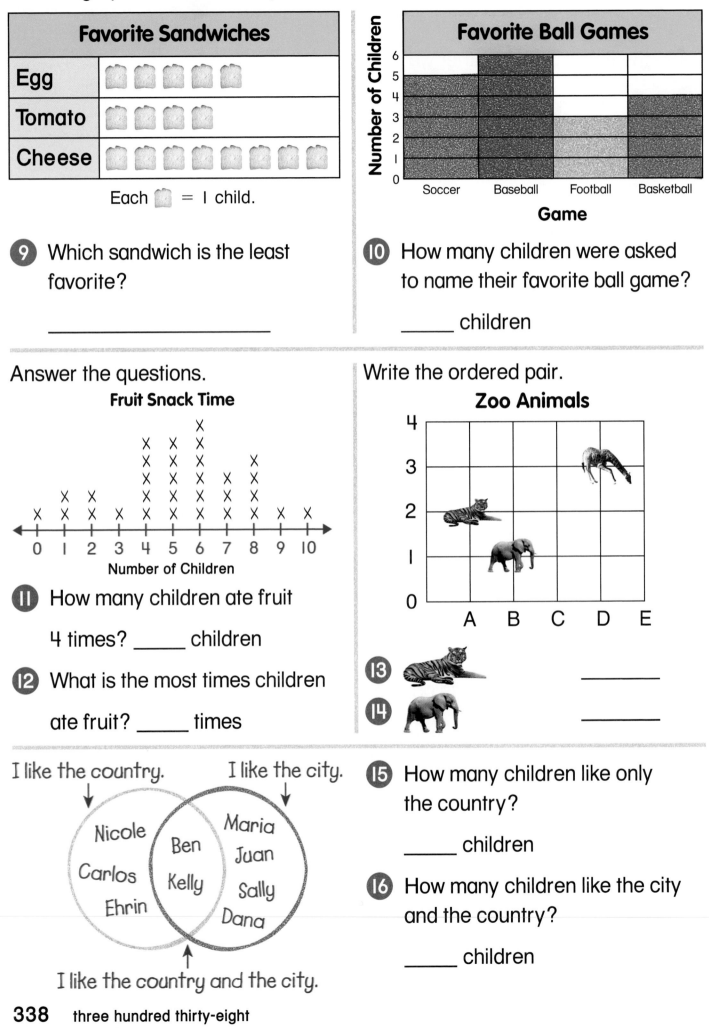

Number of Children

11 How many children ate fruit 4 times? _____ children

12 What is the most times children ate fruit? _____ times

Write the ordered pair.

Zoo Animals

4
3
2
1
0

A   B   C   D   E

13 🐅 _____

14 🐘 _____

I like the country.   I like the city.

Nicole   Ben   Maria
Carlos   Kelly   Juan
Ehrin   Sally
              Dana

I like the country and the city.

15 How many children like only the country?

_____ children

16 How many children like the city and the country?

_____ children

338 three hundred thirty-eight

© Pearson Education, Inc.

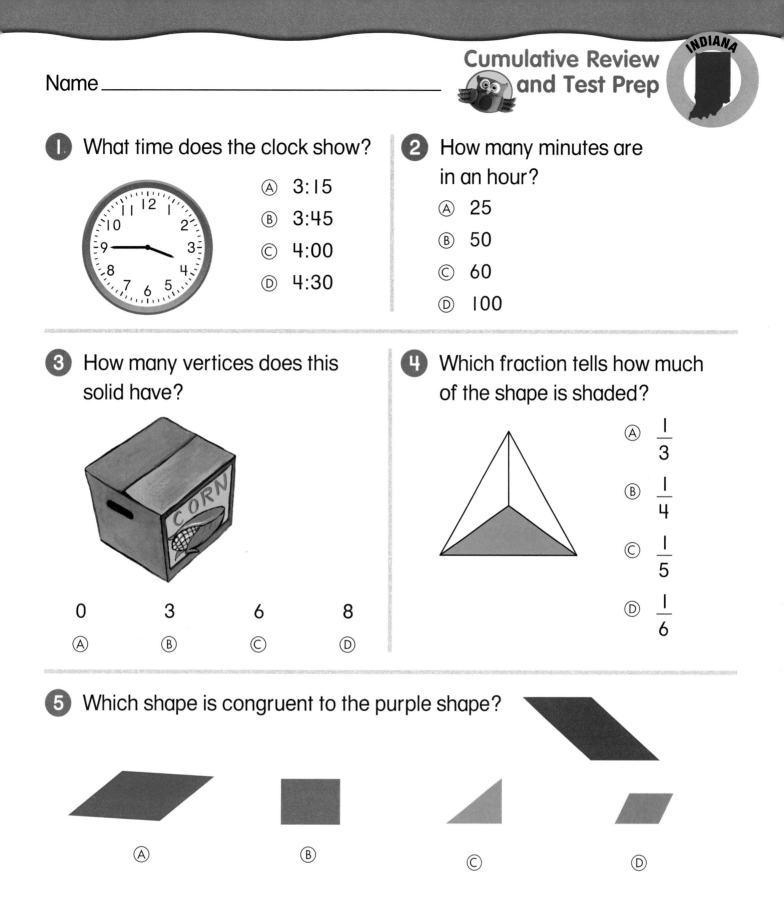

1. What time does the clock show?

Ⓐ 3:15

Ⓑ 3:45

Ⓒ 4:00

Ⓓ 4:30

2 How many minutes are in an hour?

Ⓐ 25

Ⓑ 50

Ⓒ 60

Ⓓ 100

3 How many vertices does this solid have?

0	3	6	8
Ⓐ	Ⓑ	Ⓒ	Ⓓ

4 Which fraction tells how much of the shape is shaded?

Ⓐ $\frac{1}{3}$

Ⓑ $\frac{1}{4}$

Ⓒ $\frac{1}{5}$

Ⓓ $\frac{1}{6}$

5 Which shape is congruent to the purple shape?

Ⓐ   Ⓑ   Ⓒ   Ⓓ

6 You have the coins shown. How much money do you have?

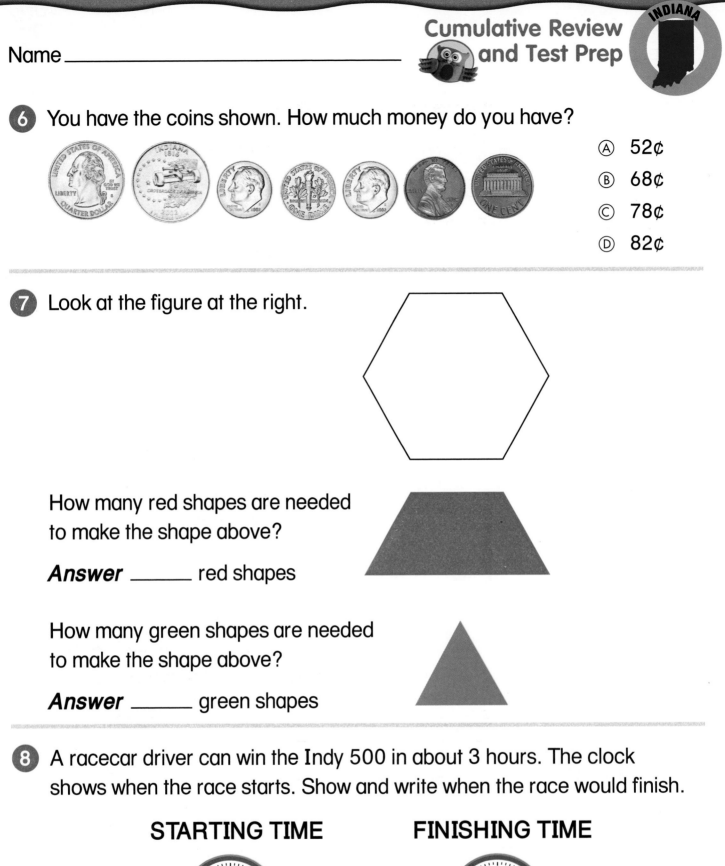

Ⓐ 52¢

Ⓑ 68¢

Ⓒ 78¢

Ⓓ 82¢

7 Look at the figure at the right.

How many red shapes are needed
to make the shape above?

Answer _____ red shapes

How many green shapes are needed
to make the shape above?

Answer _____ green shapes

8 A racecar driver can win the Indy 500 in about 3 hours. The clock
shows when the race starts. Show and write when the race would finish.

STARTING TIME

FINISHING TIME

Answer The race would finish at _____.

338B

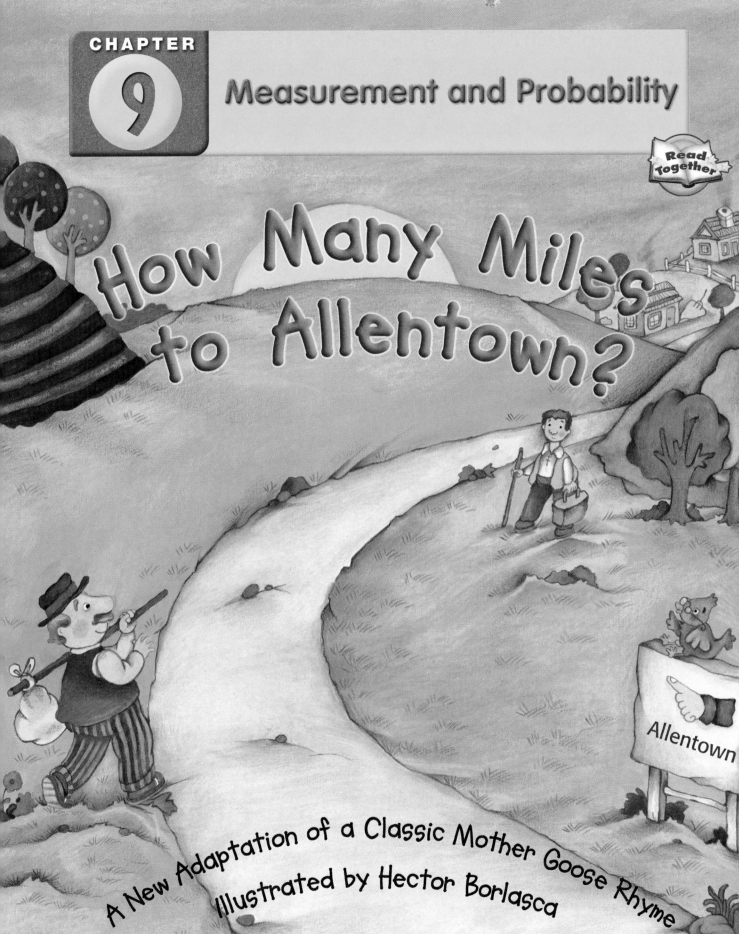

How Many Miles to Allentown?

Allentown

A New Adaptation of a Classic Mother Goose Rhyme

Illustrated by Hector Borlasca

This Math Storybook belongs to

_____

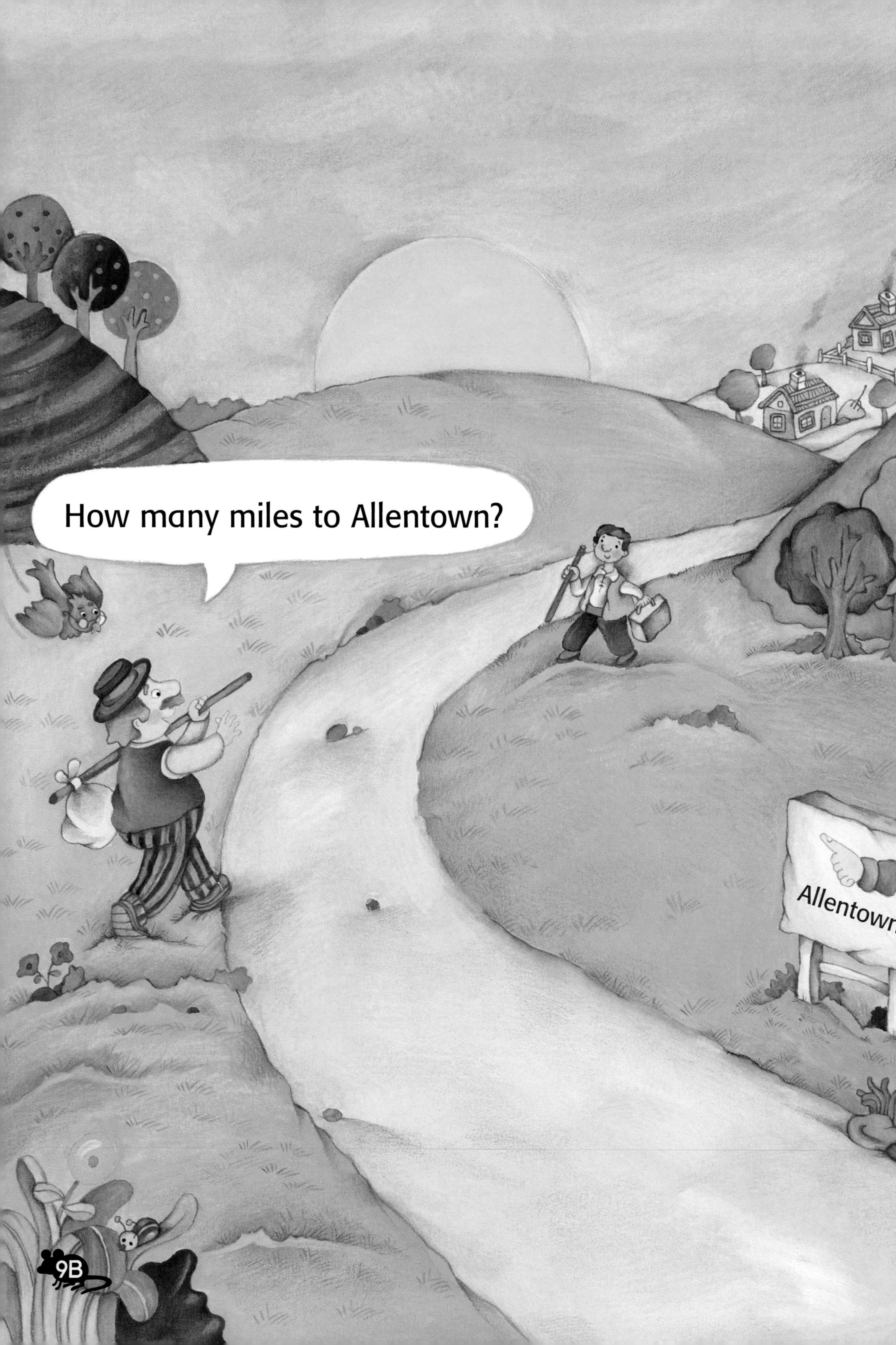

9B

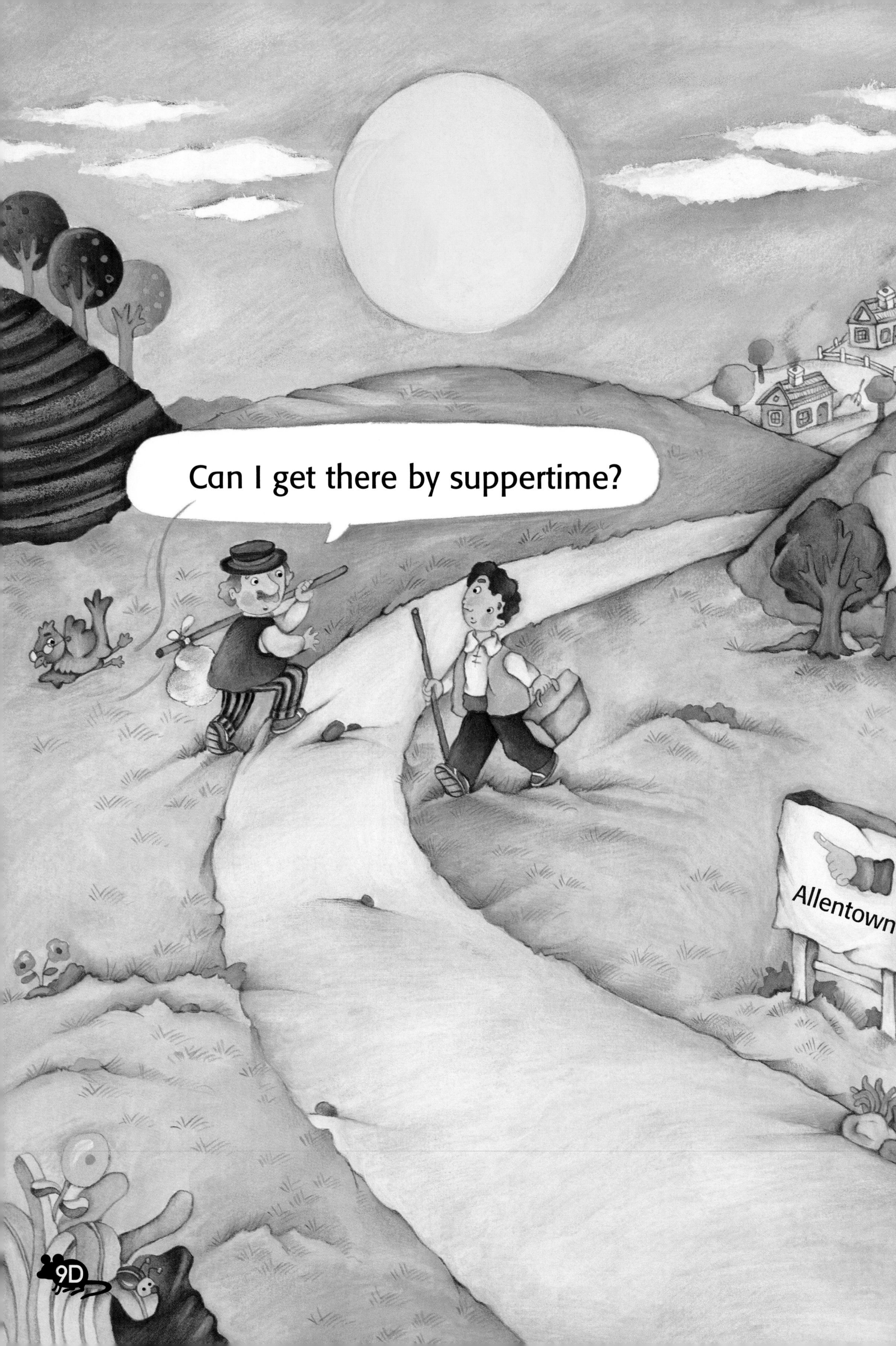
Can I get there by suppertime?
Allentown
9D

9F

Home-School Connection

Dear Family,

Today my class started Chapter 9, **Measurement and Probability.** I will learn about ways to measure length, weight, and how much something holds. I will also learn how to predict how likely or unlikely it is that certain things will happen. Here are some of the math words I will be learning and some things we can do to help me with my math.

Love,

_____

Math Activity to Do at Home

Go on a measuring tool hunt with your child. Look for rulers, tape measures, yardsticks, measuring cups and spoons, and scales. You also may want to have your child look at the measurements listed on various food products.

Books to Read Together

Reading math stories reinforces concepts. Look for these titles in your local library:

Measuring Penny
By Loreen Leedy
(Holt, 2000)

If You Hopped Like a Frog
By David M. Schwartz
(Scholastic, 1999)

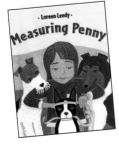

Take It to the NET
More Activities
www.scottforesman.com

My New Math Words

inch A unit of measure used to measure the lengths of small objects.

foot A unit of length equal to 12 inches.

yard A unit of length equal to 36 inches, or 3 feet.

cup A unit of volume for liquids.

pint A unit of volume for liquids, equal to 2 cups.

quart A unit of volume for liquids, equal to 4 cups or 2 pints.

three hundred thirty-nine **339**

Can You Get Home by Suppertime?

How to Play

1. Place your marker on START.
2. Toss the cube. In this game,

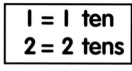

> 1 = 1 ten
> 2 = 2 tens

3. You need 1 to move 10 miles to the next marker.
4. You need 2 to move 20 miles to the next marker.
5. If you get 3, 4, 5, or 6, you have to toss again!
6. How many tosses do you think it will take you to get to each marker? Write your predictions and record your tosses on the chart.

What You Need

I dot cube
I small game marker

Recording Chart		
Mile Marker	Number of Tosses to Get There (Predictions)	Number of Tosses to Get There (Tally Marks)
20 miles		
40 miles		
60 miles		
70 miles Allentown!		
90 miles		
110 miles		
130 miles		
140 miles Suppertime!		
	TOTAL:	TOTAL:

START
20 miles
40 miles
60 miles
70 Miles
Allentown!
90 miles
110 miles
130 miles
140 Miles
Home by Suppertime!

Learn!

How tall is the key? Measure its **height**.

You can measure using cubes or paper clips.

The key is about __3__ cubes tall.

How long is the pencil? Measure its **length**.

The pencil is about __5__ paper clips long.

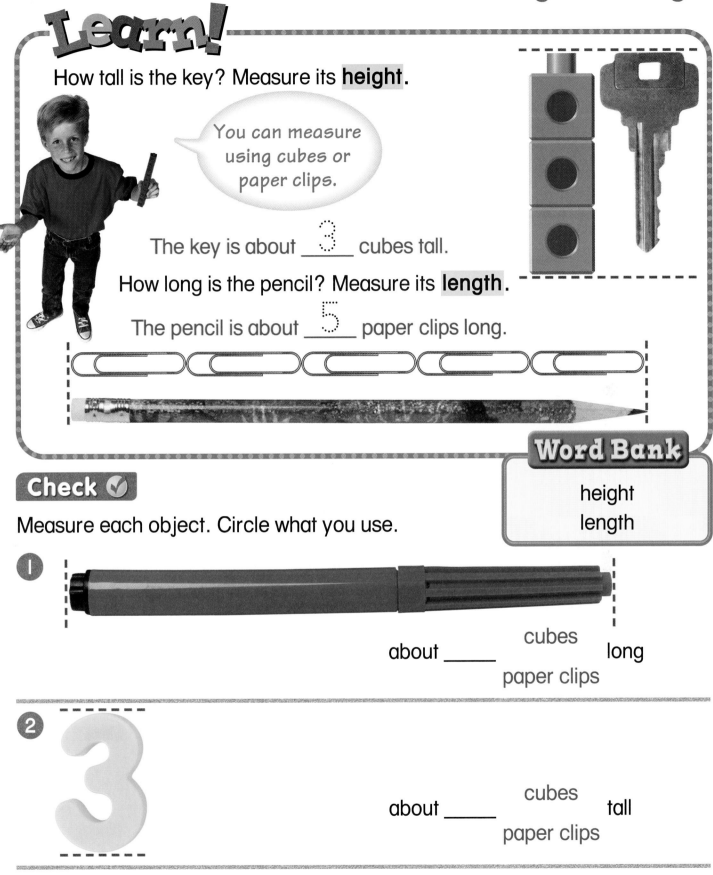

Word Bank

height

length

Check ✓

Measure each object. Circle what you use.

1.

about _____ cubes / paper clips long

2.

about _____ cubes / paper clips tall

Think About It   Reasoning

Why do you get different answers when you measure the same object using cubes and paper clips?

Measure each classroom object using cubes or paper clips.
Circle the word or words that make sense.

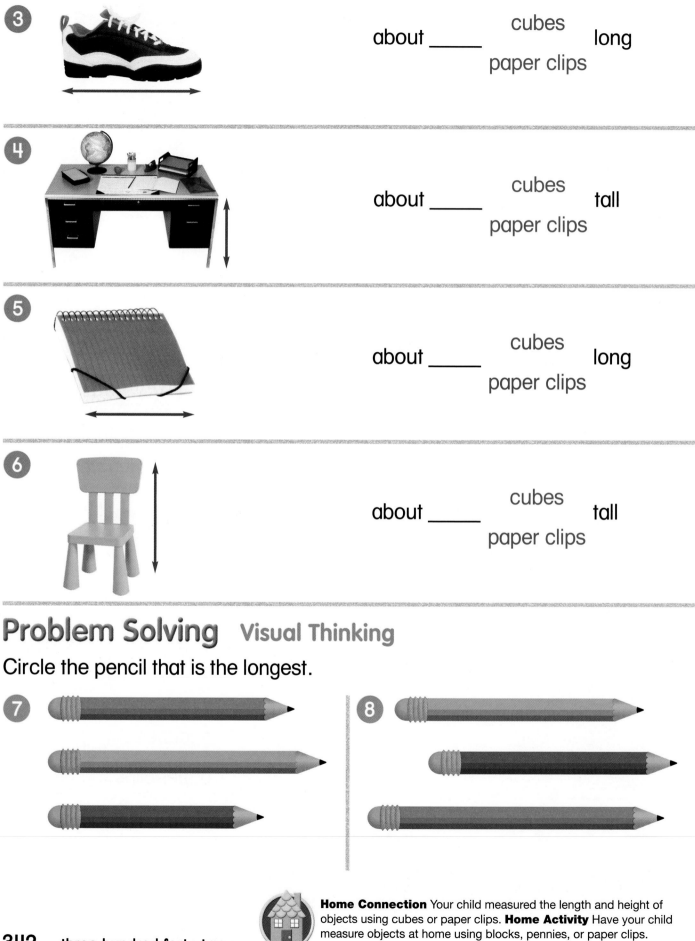

③ about _____ cubes
paper clips long

④ about _____ cubes
paper clips tall

⑤ about _____ cubes
paper clips long

⑥ about _____ cubes
paper clips tall

Problem Solving Visual Thinking

Circle the pencil that is the longest.

⑦

⑧

Home Connection Your child measured the length and height of objects using cubes or paper clips. **Home Activity** Have your child measure objects at home using blocks, pennies, or paper clips.

Name _____

Learn!

The paper clip is about 1 **inch** long.
Look at the **ruler**.
How long is the notebook?
There are 12 inches in one **foot** .

The notebook is about __12__ inches long.

The notebook is about __1__ **foot** long.

Check ✓

Estimate the length or height of each object.
Then use a ruler to measure.

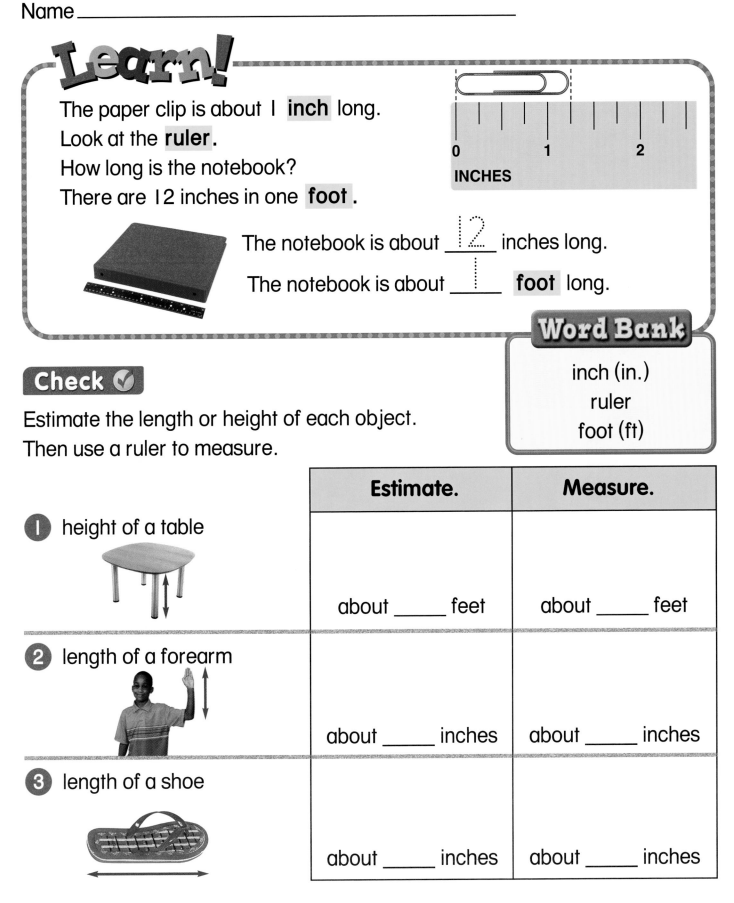

	Estimate.	Measure.
1 height of a table	about _____ feet	about _____ feet
2 length of a forearm	about _____ inches	about _____ inches
3 length of a shoe	about _____ inches	about _____ inches

Think About It   Number Sense

If there are 12 inches in 1 foot, how many inches
are in 2 feet? How do you know?

Practice

Estimate the length or height of each object.
Then use a ruler to measure.

	Estimate.	Measure.
4 length of a bookshelf	about _____ feet	about _____ feet
5 length of an eraser	about _____ inches	about _____ inches
6 height of a chair	about _____ feet	about _____ feet

Problem Solving   Reasonableness

Circle the better estimate for the length or height of each object.

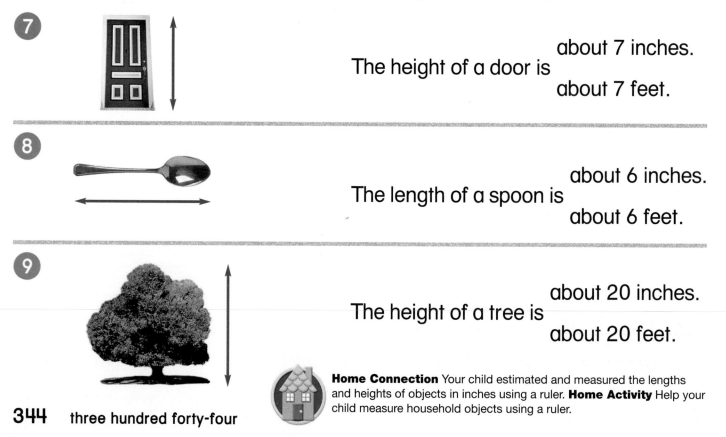

7 The height of a door is
about 7 inches.
about 7 feet.

8 The length of a spoon is
about 6 inches.
about 6 feet.

9 The height of a tree is
about 20 inches.
about 20 feet.

Home Connection Your child estimated and measured the lengths and heights of objects in inches using a ruler. **Home Activity** Help your child measure household objects using a ruler.

Learn!

What is the **width** of the door?

There are 3 feet in 1 **yard**.

There are 36 inches in 1 yard.

The door is about _____ yard wide.

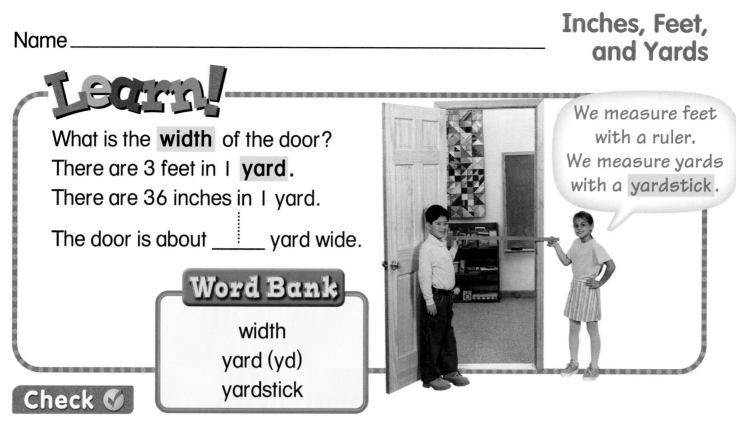

We measure feet with a ruler. We measure yards with a **yardstick**.

Word Bank

width

yard (yd)

yardstick

Check ✓

Estimate the width, height, or length of each object.

Then use a ruler or yardstick to measure.

		Estimate.	Measure.
1	width of a chalkboard	about _____ yards	about _____ yards
2	height of a table	about _____ feet	about _____ feet
3	length of a crayon	about _____ inches	about _____ inches

Think About It   Reasoning

Would you measure the length of the playground using yards or inches? Explain.

Estimate the width, height, or length of each object.
Then use a ruler or yardstick to measure.

		Estimate.	Measure.
4	width of a desktop	about _____ feet	about _____ feet
5	length of a rug	about _____ yards	about _____ yards
6	height of a wastebasket	about _____ inches	about _____ inches

Problem Solving Reasonableness

Circle inches, feet, or yards.

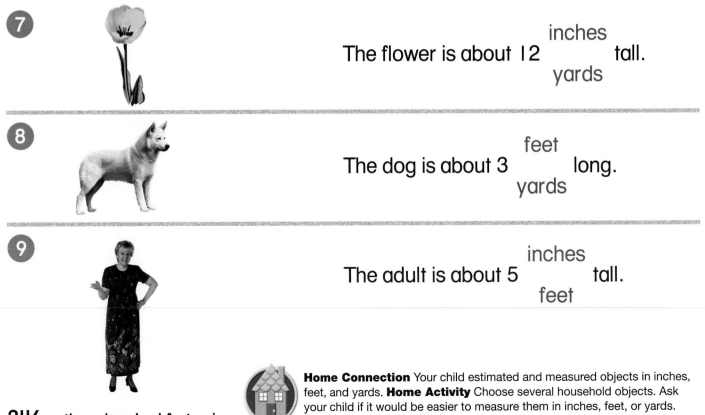

7 The flower is about 12 inches / yards tall.

8 The dog is about 3 feet / yards long.

9 The adult is about 5 inches / feet tall.

Home Connection Your child estimated and measured objects in inches, feet, and yards. **Home Activity** Choose several household objects. Ask your child if it would be easier to measure them in inches, feet, or yards.

Centimeters and Meters

Learn!

How wide is the large paper clip?
Look at the **centimeter ruler**.

CENTIMETERS
1 2 3 4 5 6

It is about _____ **centimeter** wide.

How tall is the easel?
Look at the **meterstick**.

1

METER

It is about _____ **meter** tall.
There are 100 centimeters in 1 meter.

Check ✓

Estimate the length or height of each object.
Then use a ruler to measure.

Word Bank

centimeter (cm)
centimeter ruler
meter (m)
meterstick

	Estimate.	Measure.
① a classroom shelf	about _____ meters	about _____ meters
② connecting cubes	about _____ centimeters	about _____ centimeters

Think About It Reasoning

Find an object that is about 5 centimeters long.
Find an object that is about 1 meter tall.

Estimate the length or height of each object.
Then use a ruler to measure it.

	Estimate.	Measure.
3 length of a book	about _____ cm	about _____ cm
4 height of a room	about _____ m	about _____ m
5 width of a lunchbox	about _____ cm	about _____ cm

Problem Solving Writing in Math

6 Andie says that her dollhouse is about 8 meters tall. Do you think this is a good estimate? Why or why not?

_____

_____

_____

Home Connection Your child measured objects using centimeters and meters. **Home Activity** Have your child measure several household objects using a centimeter ruler. Ask your child, "Which is a smaller unit of measurement, a centimeter or a meter?"

Visualize

1 Look at these groups of stars. A group of stars is called a **constellation.** Long, long ago, people looked up into the night sky and imagined pictures in the stars. Some of these star-pictures were of animals. Match each constellation to the animal it looks like.

2 Today scientists try to visualize how big the universe is.

How many stars do you think there are?

Ⓐ About 1 hundred   Ⓒ About 1 million

Ⓑ About 3 thousand   Ⓓ More than 1 million

Think About It   Number Sense

Write these numbers.

1 hundred _____   1 million _____

3 thousand _____

3 The sun is a star. It is the star nearest to Earth.
How far away do you think the sun is?

Ⓐ About 12 miles   Ⓒ About 15 thousand miles

Ⓑ About 6 hundred miles   Ⓓ About 93 million miles

4 First, make 154 **X**'s.

Now think about this: If you took off in a rocket,
it would take you **154 days** to reach the sun.
That's more than **5 months.** (No one can
really go to the sun, because it's too hot.)

5 Pretend you are standing next to a
skyscraper with a dog beside you. If
you were the planet **Earth,** the dog
would be the size of the **moon.** And
the skyscraper would be the size of
the **sun.** The sun is big!

Home Connection Your child visualized distance and size, and talked about
the relative magnitude or "size" of numbers. **Home Activity** Talk with your
child about what each of you visualizes doing tomorrow. Write down your plans.
Then check back to see if things went according to plans.

Name _____

Learn!

Read and Understand

The distance around a shape is called its **perimeter**. The space inside a shape is called its **area**. What is the perimeter of this rectangle? What is its area?

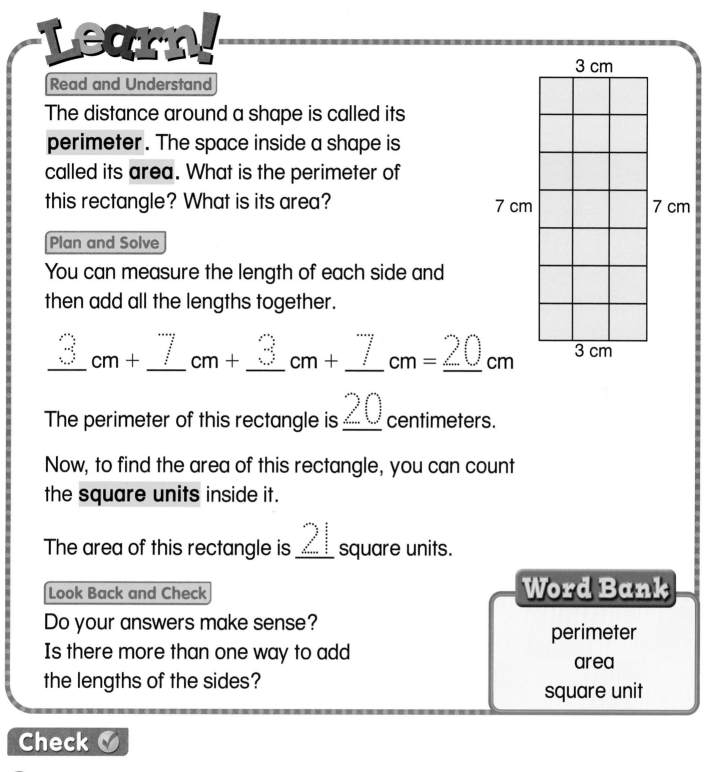

3 cm

7 cm

7 cm

3 cm

Plan and Solve

You can measure the length of each side and then add all the lengths together.

__3__ cm + __7__ cm + __3__ cm + __7__ cm = __20__ cm

The perimeter of this rectangle is __20__ centimeters.

Now, to find the area of this rectangle, you can count the **square units** inside it.

The area of this rectangle is __21__ square units.

Look Back and Check

Do your answers make sense?
Is there more than one way to add the lengths of the sides?

Word Bank

perimeter
area
square unit

Check ✓

1 Find the **perimeter** and the **area** of each shape.

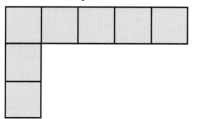

perimeter: _____ cm

area: _____ square units

Find the **perimeter** and the **area** of each shape.

2

perimeter: 14 cm

area: 12 square units

3

perimeter: _____ cm

area: _____ square units

4

perimeter: _____ cm

area: _____ square units

5

perimeter: _____ cm

area: _____ square units

Writing in Math

6 How can you find the number of square units inside of this trapezoid?

_____

_____

_____

_____

Home Connection Your child found the perimeters and the areas of various shapes. **Home Activity** Ask your child to tell how many square units are NOT inside the trapezoid in Exercise 6. *(2: 1 whole square unit and two half square units, which combine to make another whole)*

Learn!

Which holds more, the cup or the bowl?

I think the bowl will hold more rice than the cup.

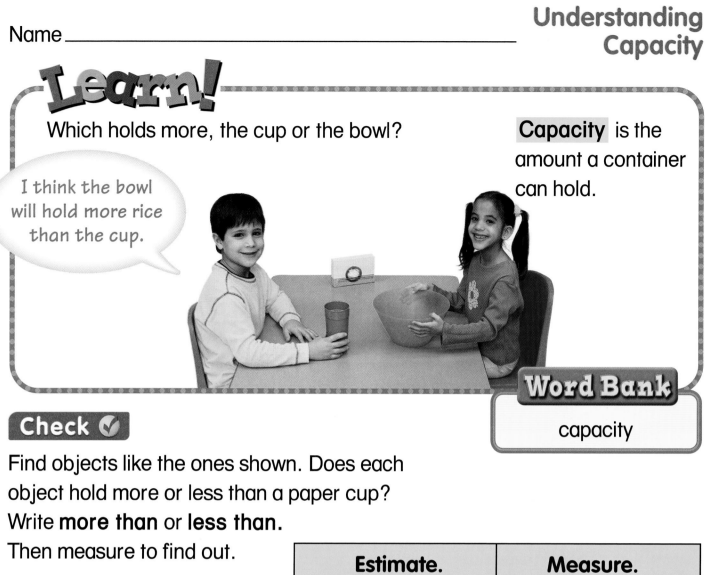

Capacity is the amount a container can hold.

Check ✓

Find objects like the ones shown. Does each object hold more or less than a paper cup?
Write **more than** or **less than.**
Then measure to find out.

	Estimate.	Measure.
❶ 🥄	less than	less than
❷		
❸		

Think About It   Number Sense

If 2 cups of rice fill 1 bowl,
how many cups of rice will fill 3 bowls?

Circle the object that holds the most.

4

5

6

Circle the object that holds the least.

7

8

9

Problem Solving   Writing in Math

10 Tell why it makes more sense to drink water
from a glass rather than from a teaspoon.

_____

_____

_____

_____

Home Connection Your child estimated, measured, and ordered
objects by capacity. **Home Activity** Show your child several containers
and have him or her tell you which container holds the most.

Learn! Algebra

We use these units to measure capacity.

2 **cups** = 1 **pint**   4 **cups** = 2 **pints** = 1 **quart**

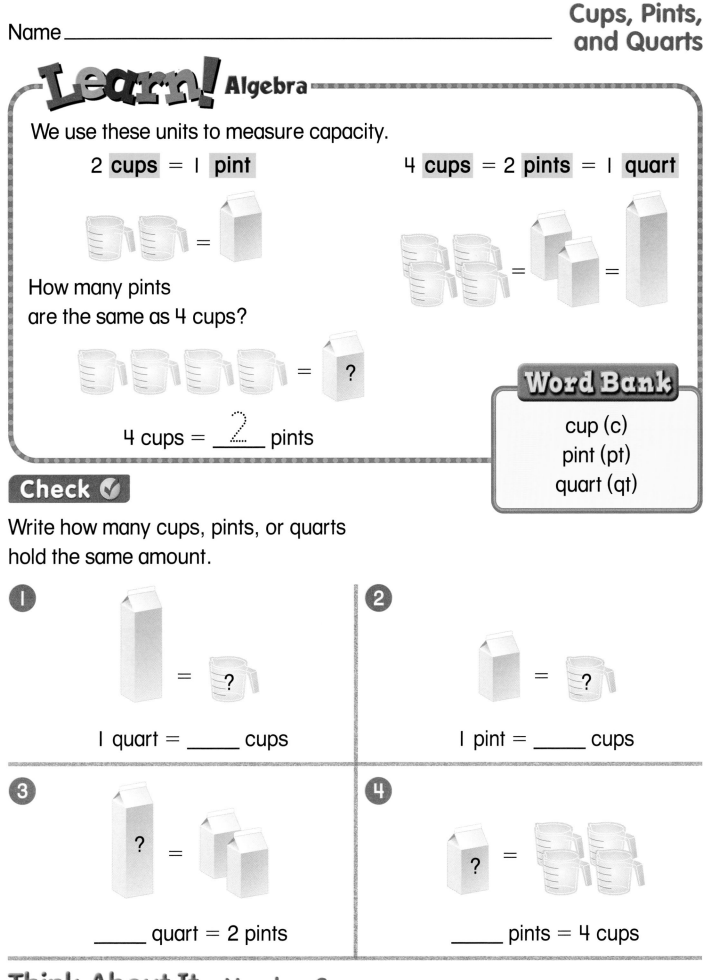

How many pints
are the same as 4 cups?

4 cups = __2__ pints

Word Bank

cup (c)
pint (pt)
quart (qt)

Check ✓

Write how many cups, pints, or quarts
hold the same amount.

1

1 quart = _____ cups

2

1 pint = _____ cups

3

_____ quart = 2 pints

4

_____ pints = 4 cups

Think About It   Number Sense

How many pints are the same as 2 quarts?

Circle the number of containers that hold the same amount.

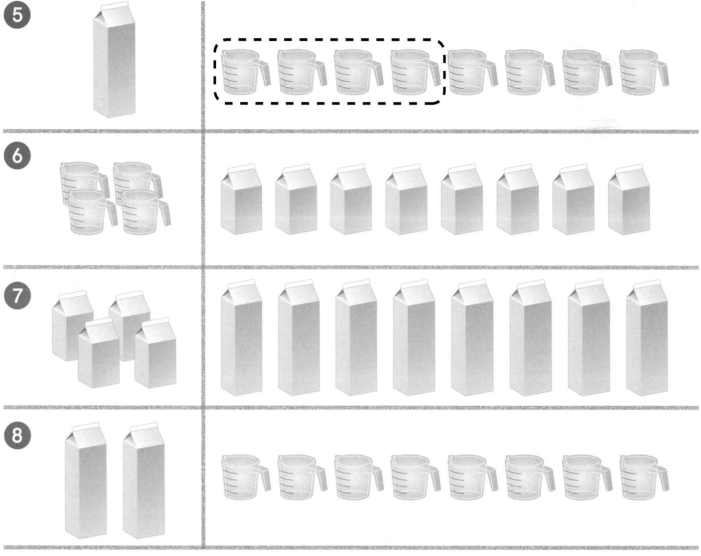

Problem Solving   Visual Thinking

Use the pictures to answer the questions.
Write **more than** or **less than.**

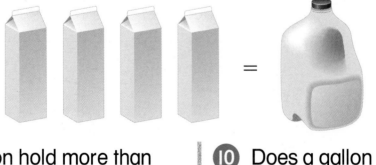

9 Does a gallon hold more than
or less than 5 quarts?

_____

10 Does a gallon hold more than
or less than 1 pint?

_____

Home Connection Your child compared the capacities of cups, pints,
and quarts. **Home Activity** Have your child identify cup, pint, and quart
containers at home. Have him or her tell which containers hold the most
and which hold the least.

Name _____

Learn!

Does the glass hold more than or less than I **liter**?

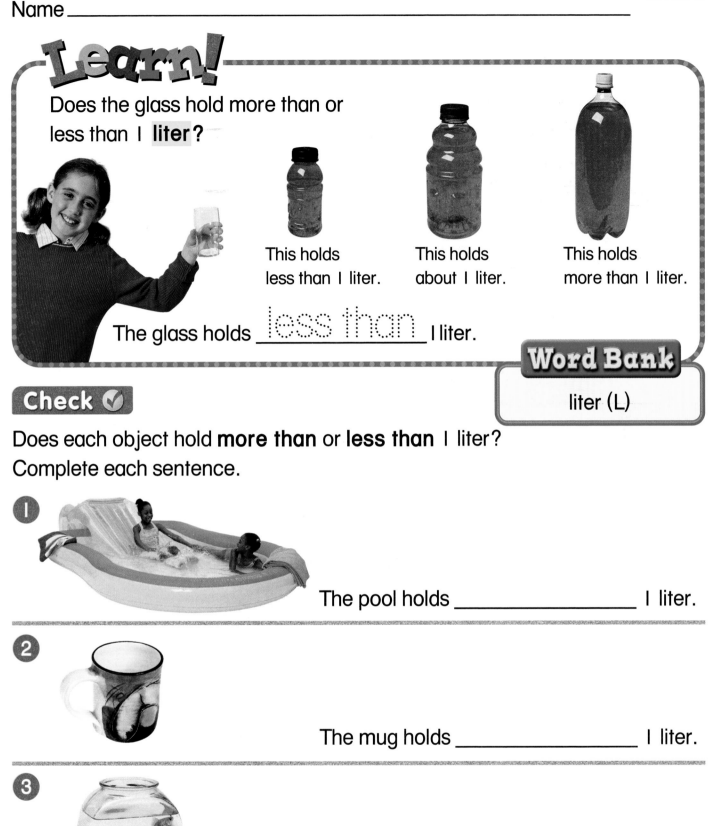

This holds less than I liter.

This holds about I liter.

This holds more than I liter.

The glass holds ___less than___ I liter.

Check ✓

Does each object hold **more than** or **less than** I liter?
Complete each sentence.

1 The pool holds _____ I liter.

2 The mug holds _____ I liter.

3 The fish bowl holds _____ I liter.

Think About It Reasoning

Name some things that hold more than a liter.
Name some things that hold less than a liter.

About how many liters does the object hold?
Circle the better estimate.

4

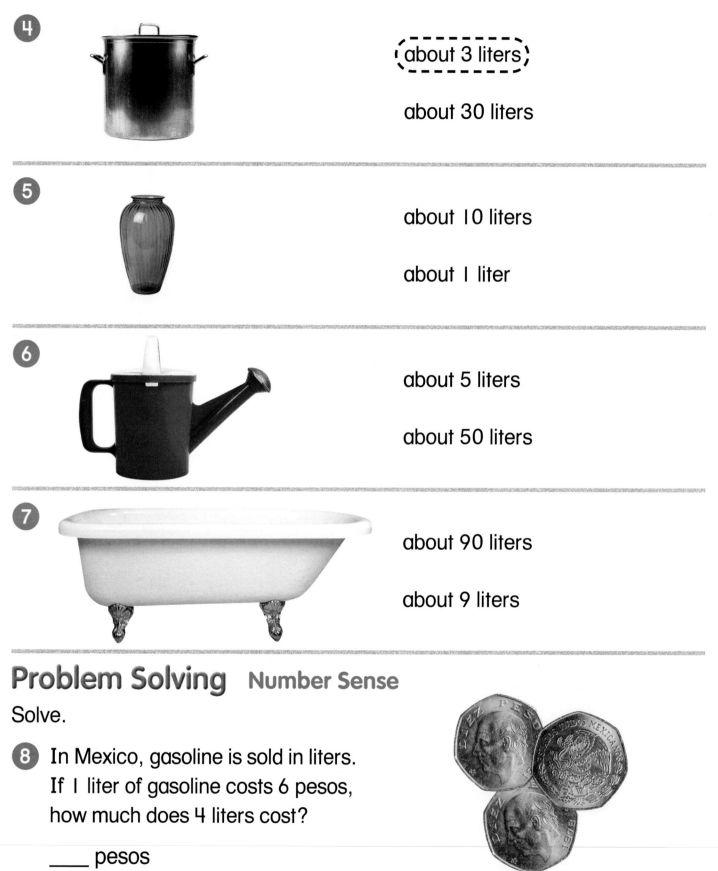

about 3 liters

about 30 liters

5

about 10 liters

about 1 liter

6

about 5 liters

about 50 liters

7

about 90 liters

about 9 liters

Problem Solving   Number Sense

Solve.

8 In Mexico, gasoline is sold in liters.
If 1 liter of gasoline costs 6 pesos,
how much does 4 liters cost?

_____ pesos

Home Connection Your child compared the capacities of objects
to a liter and then estimated how many liters an object holds.
Home Activity Help your child find objects that hold about a liter,
less than a liter, and more than a liter.

© Pearson Education, Inc.

Learn!

How many cubes does it take to fill this box? Make the shape to find out.

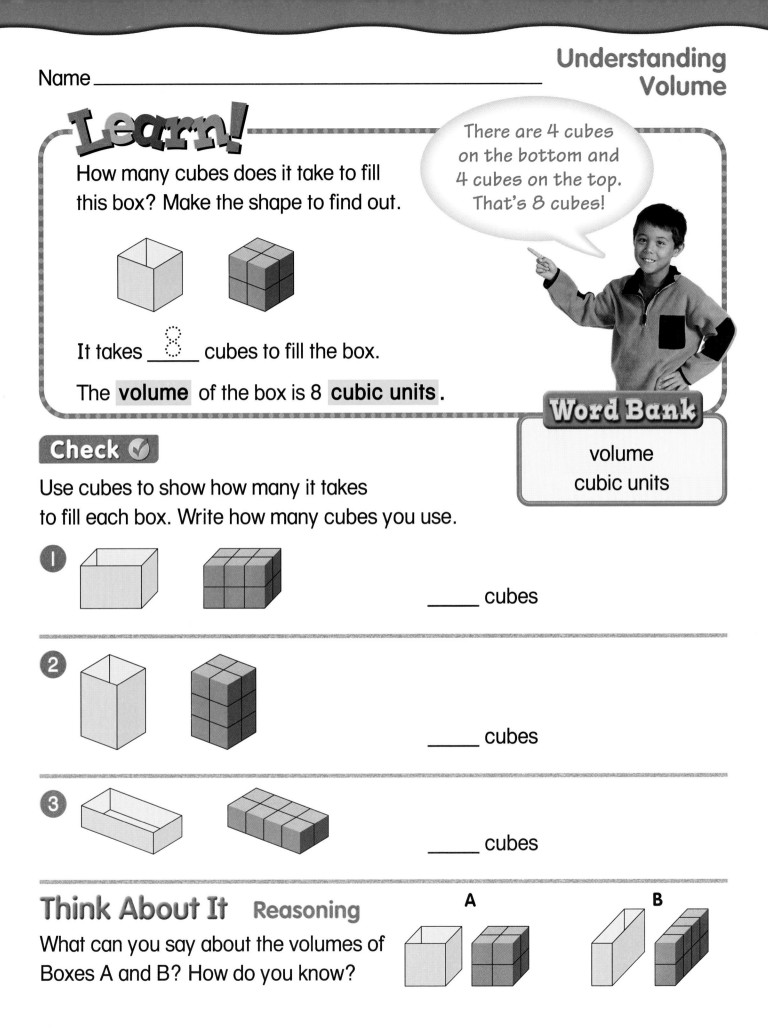

There are 4 cubes on the bottom and 4 cubes on the top. That's 8 cubes!

It takes ____8____ cubes to fill the box.

The **volume** of the box is 8 **cubic units**.

Word Bank

volume
cubic units

Check ✓

Use cubes to show how many it takes to fill each box. Write how many cubes you use.

1. _____ cubes

2. _____ cubes

3. _____ cubes

Think About It   Reasoning

What can you say about the volumes of Boxes A and B? How do you know?

A

B

Circle the number of cubes that will fit in each box.

4 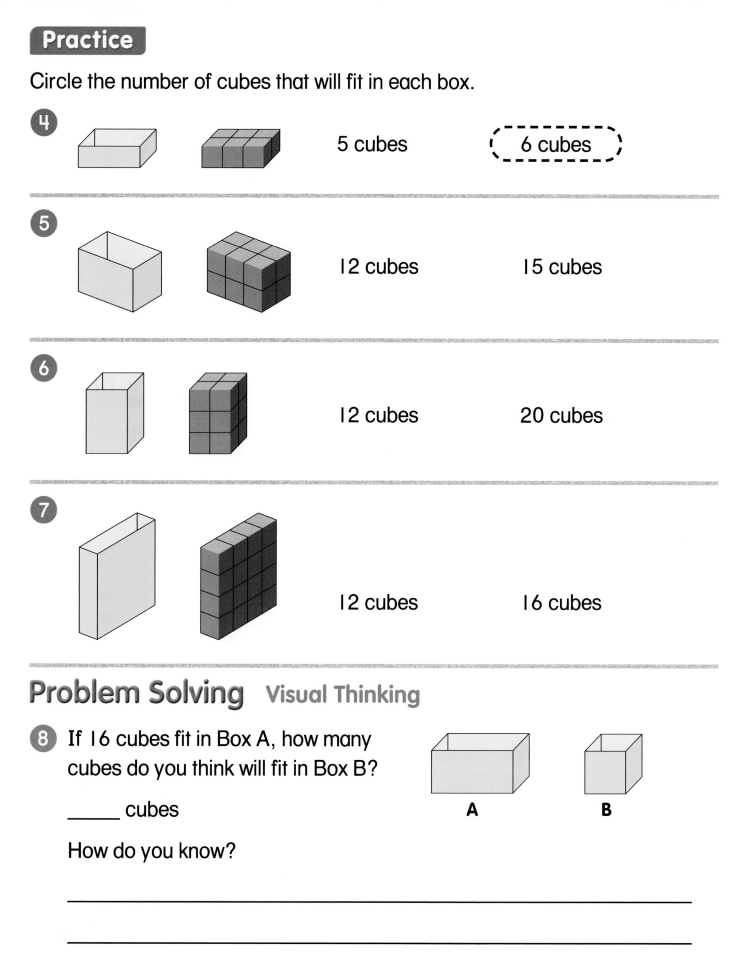 5 cubes (6 cubes)

5 12 cubes 15 cubes

6 12 cubes 20 cubes

7 12 cubes 16 cubes

Problem Solving Visual Thinking

8 If 16 cubes fit in Box A, how many cubes do you think will fit in Box B?

_____ cubes

How do you know?

_____

_____

A   B

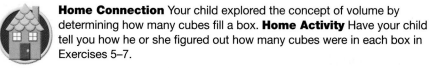

Home Connection Your child explored the concept of volume by determining how many cubes fill a box. **Home Activity** Have your child tell you how he or she figured out how many cubes were in each box in Exercises 5–7.

Name_____

Circle the better estimate.

1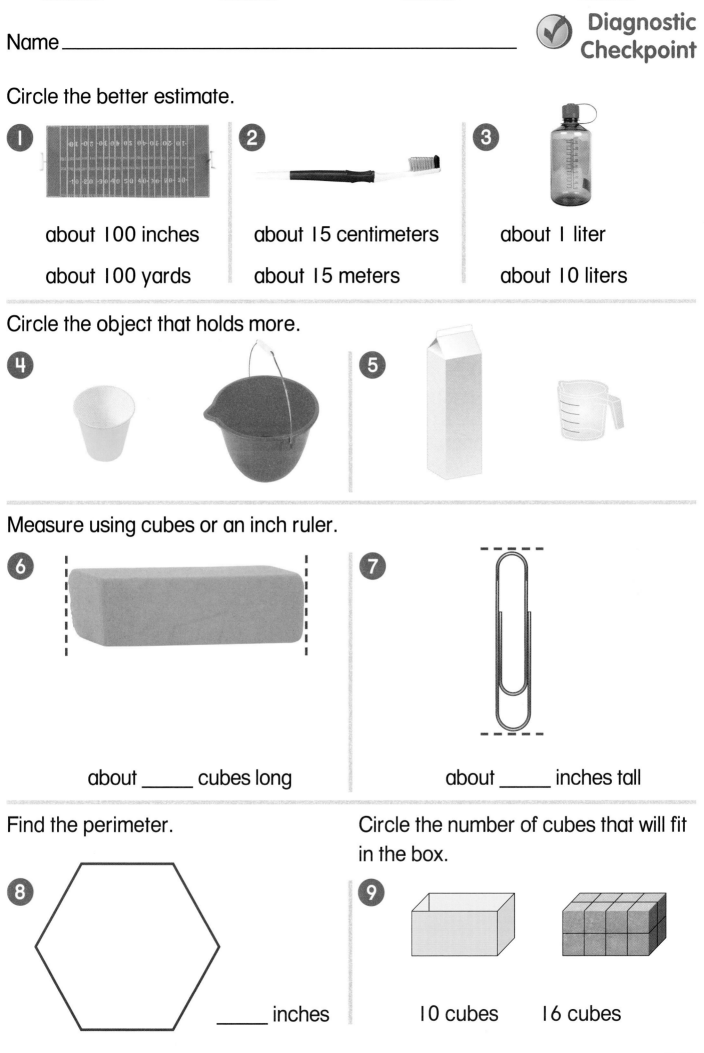

about 100 inches

about 100 yards

2

about 15 centimeters

about 15 meters

3

about 1 liter

about 10 liters

Circle the object that holds more.

4

5

Measure using cubes or an inch ruler.

6

about _____ cubes long

7

about _____ inches tall

Find the perimeter.

8

_____ inches

Circle the number of cubes that will fit in the box.

9

10 cubes   16 cubes

Mark the time.

1.
Ⓐ 2:35
Ⓑ 7:05
Ⓒ 7:10
Ⓓ 2:10

2.
Ⓐ 4:10
Ⓑ 4:50
Ⓒ 5:10
Ⓓ 5:50

Add on to find the other part of 100. Mark the answer.

3. **50 and ____ is 100.**

50	60	40	30
Ⓐ	Ⓑ	Ⓒ	Ⓓ

4. **35 and ____ is 100.**

55	75	65	15
Ⓐ	Ⓑ	Ⓒ	Ⓓ

Mark the shape that is congruent to the first shape.

5.
Ⓐ   Ⓑ   Ⓒ   Ⓓ

6.
Ⓐ   Ⓑ   Ⓒ   Ⓓ

Mark the addition problem that shows an estimate.

7. **22 + 59**

20 + 60	20 + 50	30 + 50	30 + 60
Ⓐ	Ⓑ	Ⓒ	Ⓓ

Writing in Math

8. Find the difference. Tell why you need to regroup.

_____

_____

$$\begin{array}{r} 61 \\ -\ 28 \\ \hline \end{array}$$

Name _____

Learn!

Which **weighs** more? Which weighs less?

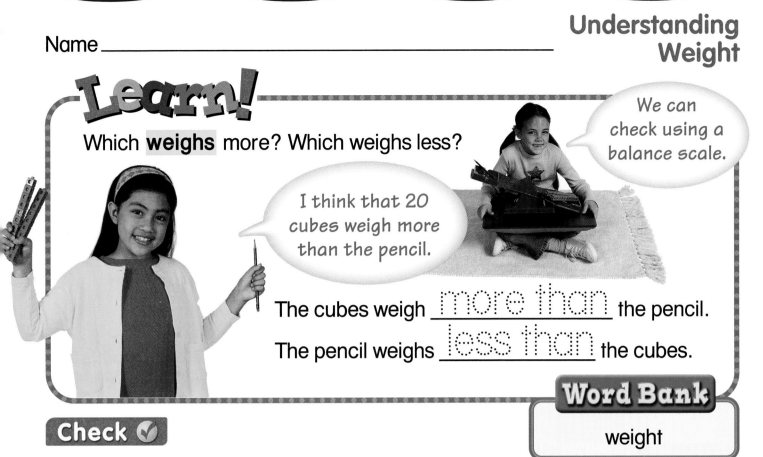

I think that 20 cubes weigh more than the pencil.

We can check using a balance scale.

The cubes weigh ___more than___ the pencil.

The pencil weighs ___less than___ the cubes.

Word Bank

weight

Check ✓

Find objects like the ones shown. Estimate if the object weighs more than or less than 20 cubes. Then weigh the object using a balance.

	Estimate.	Measure.
❶	more than 20 cubes	more than 20 cubes
❷	_____ 20 cubes	_____ 20 cubes
❸	_____ 20 cubes	_____ 20 cubes

Think About It   Reasoning

Find an object that you think weighs about the same as 20 cubes. How can you tell how much the object weighs?

Circle the object that weighs more.

4

5

6

Circle the object that weighs less.

7

8

Problem Solving   Reasoning

9 Name 3 objects that you think weigh
   less than a watermelon.

_____   _____   _____

© Pearson Education, Inc.

Home Connection Your child estimated and measured the weight
of objects, and identified which of two objects weighs more or less.
Home Activity Take 5 objects from the kitchen shelf. Have your child
line up the objects from heaviest to lightest.

Name_____

Learn!

This is 1 **pound** of butter.
There are 16 **ounces** in 1 pound.

About how much does each object or group of objects weigh?

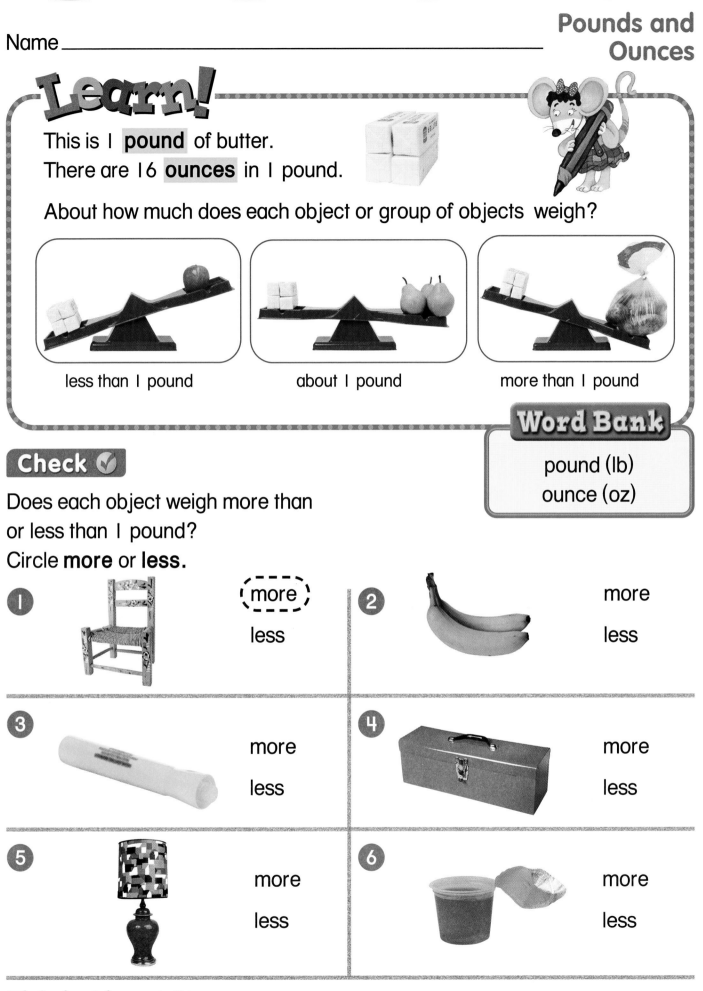

less than 1 pound   about 1 pound   more than 1 pound

Word Bank

pound (lb)
ounce (oz)

Check ✓

Does each object weigh more than
or less than 1 pound?
Circle **more** or **less**.

1   ~~more~~
    less

2   more
    less

3   more
    less

4   more
    less

5   more
    less

6   more
    less

Think About It   Number Sense

How many ounces are in 2 pounds?

About how much does each object weigh?
Circle the better estimate.

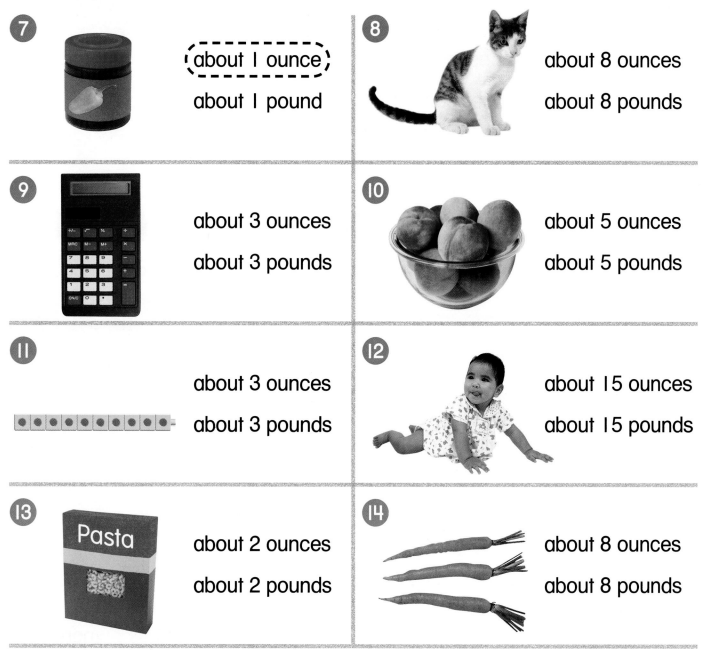

7

about 1 ounce

about 1 pound

8

about 8 ounces

about 8 pounds

9

about 3 ounces

about 3 pounds

10

about 5 ounces

about 5 pounds

11

about 3 ounces

about 3 pounds

12

about 15 ounces

about 15 pounds

13

Pasta

about 2 ounces

about 2 pounds

14

about 8 ounces

about 8 pounds

Problem Solving **Algebra**

Solve.

15 I pound is 16 ounces.
How many ounces are in
a half pound?

1 pound = 16 ounces
$\frac{1}{2}$ pound = ? ounces

Home Connection Your child estimated and compared the weights of
objects using ounces and pounds. **Home Activity** Have your child find
items in your home that are measured in ounces and/or pounds.

Name _____

Learn!

This large jar of peanut butter measures about 1 **kilogram**.
There are 1,000 **grams** in 1 kilogram.
A marker cap measures about 1 gram.

About how much does each object or group of objects measure?

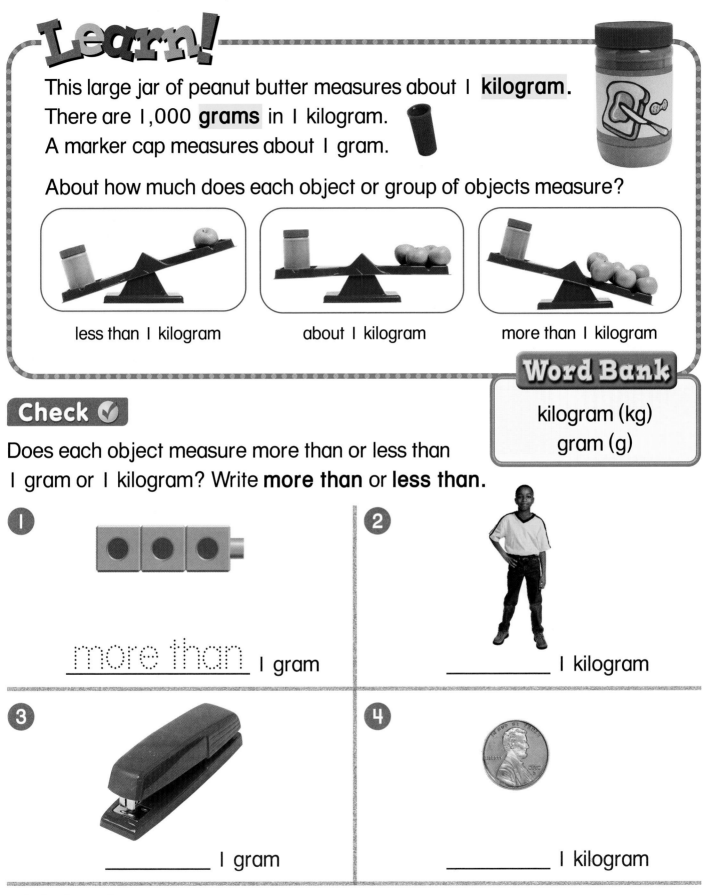

less than 1 kilogram   about 1 kilogram   more than 1 kilogram

Check ✓

Does each object measure more than or less than
1 gram or 1 kilogram? Write **more than** or **less than**.

1 _more than_ 1 gram

2 _____ 1 kilogram

3 _____ 1 gram

4 _____ 1 kilogram

Think About It   Reasoning

Would you use grams or kilograms to find out how
much 2 paper clips measure? Explain.

Practice

About how much does each object measure?
Circle the better estimate.

5

(about 30 grams)

about 30 kilograms

6

Rice

about 500 grams

about 500 kilograms

7

about 5 grams

about 5 kilograms

8

about 4 grams

about 4 kilograms

9

about 2 grams

about 2 kilograms

10

about 65 grams

about 65 kilograms

Problem Solving   Number Sense

Solve.

1,000 g = 1 kg

11 If 1 large paper clip measures
about 1 gram, how many paper clips
measure about 1 kilogram?

about _____ paper clips

Home Connection Your child estimated and compared the
measurements of objects using grams and kilograms.
Home Activity Help your child find food packages that show
grams and kilograms. Order them from lightest to heaviest.

Learn!

What is the **temperature**? You can measure temperature in **degrees** Fahrenheit or in degrees Celsius.

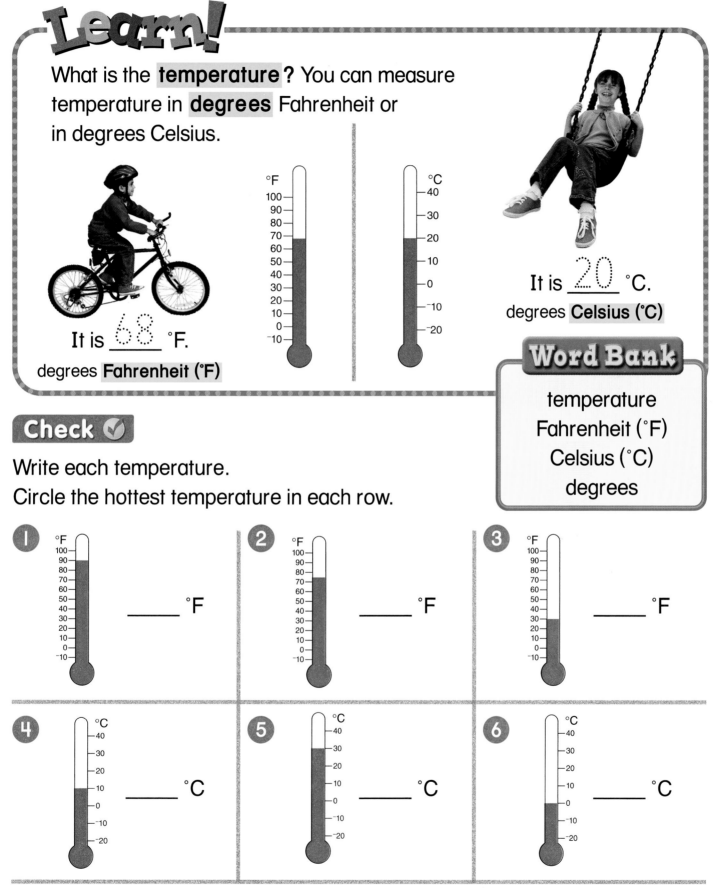

It is 68 °F.

degrees **Fahrenheit (°F)**

It is 20 °C.

degrees **Celsius (°C)**

Word Bank

temperature
Fahrenheit (°F)
Celsius (°C)
degrees

Check ✓

Write each temperature.
Circle the hottest temperature in each row.

1. _____ °F

2. _____ °F

3. _____ °F

4. _____ °C

5. _____ °C

6. _____ °C

Think About It   Reasoning

It is 82°F. Would you go swimming or sledding outdoors? Why?

Color to show the temperature.
Circle hot or cold to tell about the temperature.

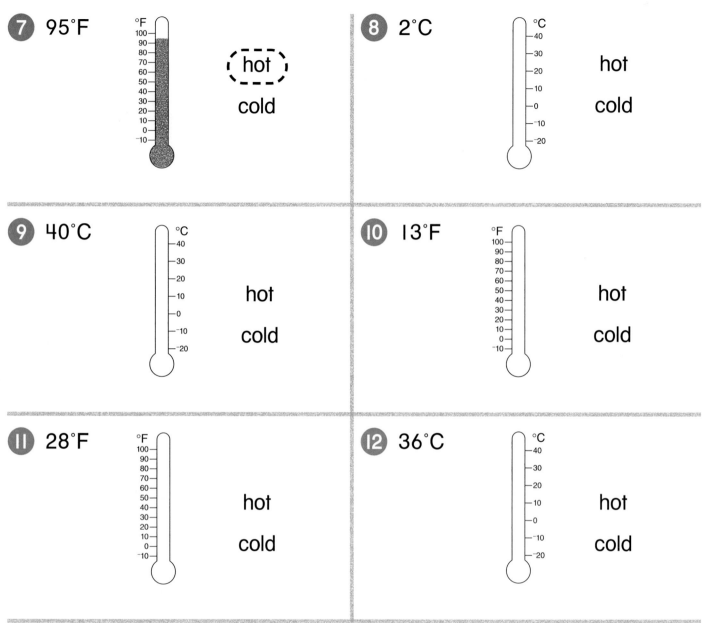

7 95°F

°F
100
90
80
70
60
50
40
30
20
10
0
-10

(hot)

cold

8 2°C

°C
40
30
20
10
0
-10
-20

hot

cold

9 40°C

°C
40
30
20
10
0
-10
-20

hot

cold

10 13°F

°F
100
90
80
70
60
50
40
30
20
10
0
-10

hot

cold

11 28°F

°F
100
90
80
70
60
50
40
30
20
10
0
-10

hot

cold

12 36°C

°C
40
30
20
10
0
-10
-20

hot

cold

Problem Solving Writing in Math

13 Tell about the things you would do if it were 65°F outside.

_____

_____

_____

Home Connection Your child read temperatures and learned how to show temperatures on a thermometer. **Home Activity** Help your child read the temperature on a home thermometer or find the temperature of your state in the newspaper.

Circle the object that weighs more.

1

2

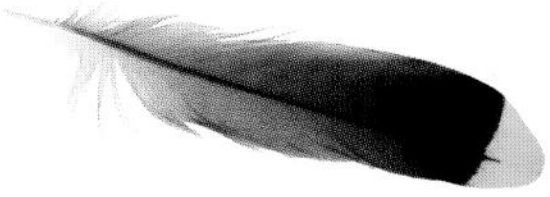

Circle the better estimate.

3

about 2 ounces

about 2 pounds

4

about 2 ounces

about 2 pounds

5

about 9 grams

about 9 kilograms

6

about 1 gram

about 1 kilogram

Color to show the temperature.
Circle **hot** or **cold** to tell about the temperature.

7 3°F

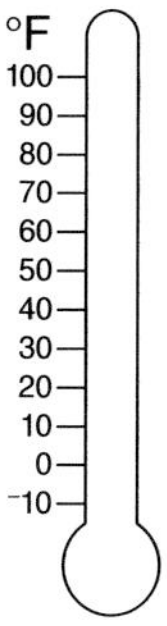

°F
100
90
80
70
60
50
40
30
20
10
0
-10

hot

cold

8 34°C

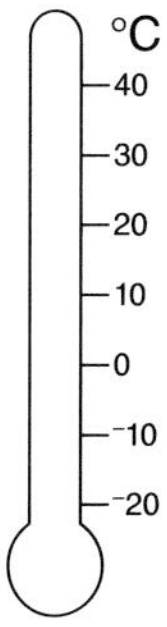

°C
40
30
20
10
0
-10
-20

hot

cold

Name _____

Mark the fraction that tells how much is shaded.

1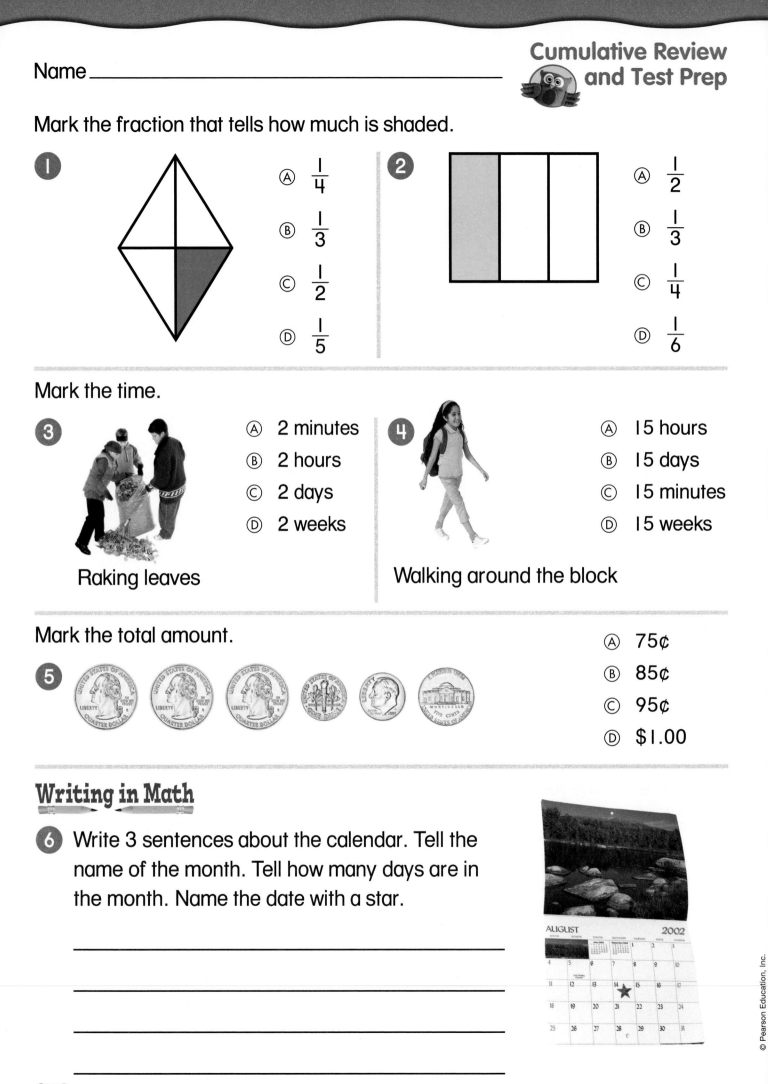
    Ⓐ $\frac{1}{4}$

    Ⓑ $\frac{1}{3}$

    Ⓒ $\frac{1}{2}$

    Ⓓ $\frac{1}{5}$

2   Ⓐ $\frac{1}{2}$

    Ⓑ $\frac{1}{3}$

    Ⓒ $\frac{1}{4}$

    Ⓓ $\frac{1}{6}$

Mark the time.

3   Ⓐ 2 minutes

    Ⓑ 2 hours

    Ⓒ 2 days

    Ⓓ 2 weeks

    Raking leaves

4   Ⓐ 15 hours

    Ⓑ 15 days

    Ⓒ 15 minutes

    Ⓓ 15 weeks

    Walking around the block

Mark the total amount.

5   Ⓐ 75¢

    Ⓑ 85¢

    Ⓒ 95¢

    Ⓓ $1.00

Writing in Math

6   Write 3 sentences about the calendar. Tell the name of the month. Tell how many days are in the month. Name the date with a star.

_____

_____

_____

_____

AUGUST   2002

© Pearson Education, Inc.

Name _____

Learn!

Let's **predict** what might happen! Write the color.

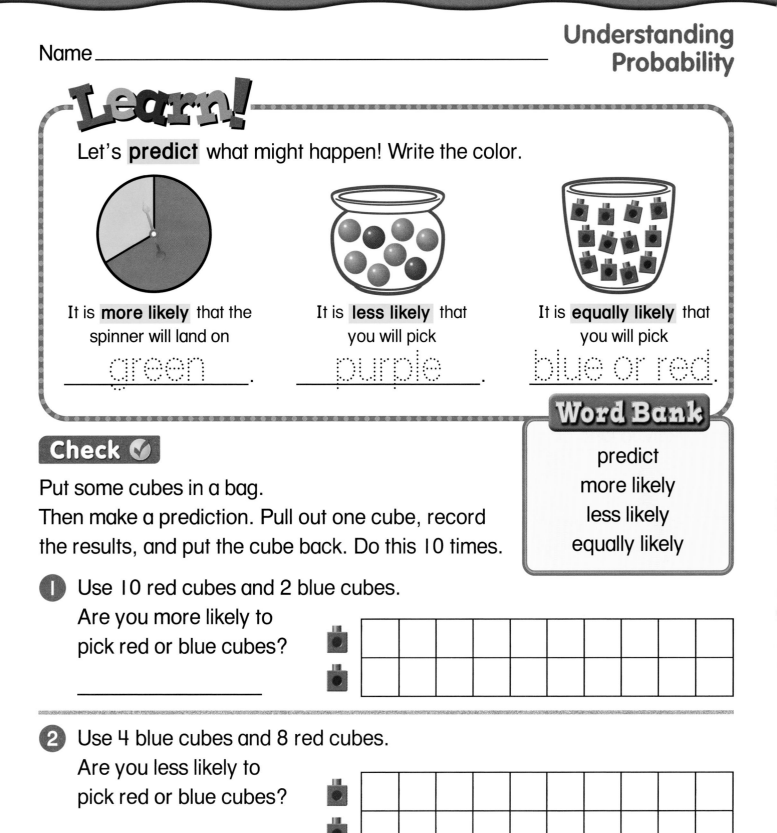

It is **more likely** that the spinner will land on

___green___.

It is **less likely** that you will pick

___purple___.

It is **equally likely** that you will pick

___blue or red___.

Word Bank

predict
more likely
less likely
equally likely

Check ✓

Put some cubes in a bag.
Then make a prediction. Pull out one cube, record
the results, and put the cube back. Do this 10 times.

1 Use 10 red cubes and 2 blue cubes.
Are you more likely to
pick red or blue cubes?

_____

2 Use 4 blue cubes and 8 red cubes.
Are you less likely to
pick red or blue cubes?

_____

Think About It   Reasoning

You have 12 cubes. It is equally likely that you will pick a red cube or
a blue cube. How many cubes do you have of each color? Explain.

If you were to spin once, which color is the spinner
most likely to land on?

3 red

(yellow)

4 red

yellow

5 red

yellow

blue

6 red

yellow

blue

If you were to spin once, which color is the spinner
least likely to land on?

7 green

yellow

8 green

yellow

9 green

purple

red

10 green

purple

red

Problem Solving   Reasoning

Write **more likely, less likely,** or **equally likely**
to answer the question.

11 How likely is it that the spinner will land on red?

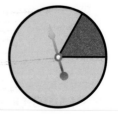   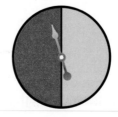   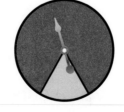

_____   _____   _____

 Home Connection Your child predicted the outcome of
activities using the terms *more likely, less likely,* and *equally likely.*
Home Activity Draw several spinners with equal and unequal
sections colored. Have your child tell you which color the spinner
is more likely to land on.

Name_____

Learn!

Put 10 purple cubes and 10 orange cubes in a bag. If you pick 10 cubes, predict the outcome.

Compare your predictions with your results.

> It is **certain** that you will pick purple or orange cubes.

> It is **probable** that you will pick an orange cube.

> It is **impossible** that you will pick a red cube.

Number of: purple cubes _____ orange cubes _____

Check ✓

Put 20 green cubes and 5 yellow cubes in a bag.
If you pull out 10 cubes, predict the outcome.
Circle the missing word to complete the sentence.

Word Bank

certain
probable
impossible

1 It is _____ that you will pick a yellow cube.

probable

impossible

2 It is _____ that you will pick a red cube.

impossible

probable

Pick 10 cubes and record the results.

3
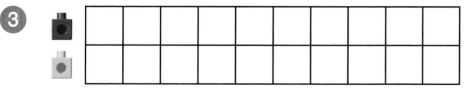

Number of: green cubes _____ yellow cubes _____

Think About It   Reasoning

There are 5 blue cubes and 20 red cubes in a bag.
Is it more probable to pick a blue cube or a red cube?
Why?

Use the tally chart to help you answer the questions.
Circle the missing word to complete the sentence.

Marbles	
Purple	⊞⊞ ⊞⊞ ⊞⊞ ll
Red	⊞⊞ lll

4 There are more _____ marbles in the jar.

purple

red

5 You can pick one marble. It is _____ that you will pick a purple marble.

probable

certain

6 It is _____ that you will pick a yellow marble.

probable

impossible

7 It is _____ that you will pick a purple or a red marble.

probable

certain

Problem Solving Reasoning

8 There are red, yellow, and green marbles in each jar.
Color the marbles to match the description below each jar.

It is most probable
to pick a green marble.

It is least probable
to pick a green marble.

Home Connection Your child predicted, recorded, and analyzed results of probability experiments. **Home Activity** Have your child put 12 coins in a bag, predict the results from picking 10 coins, and record the results.

Name _____

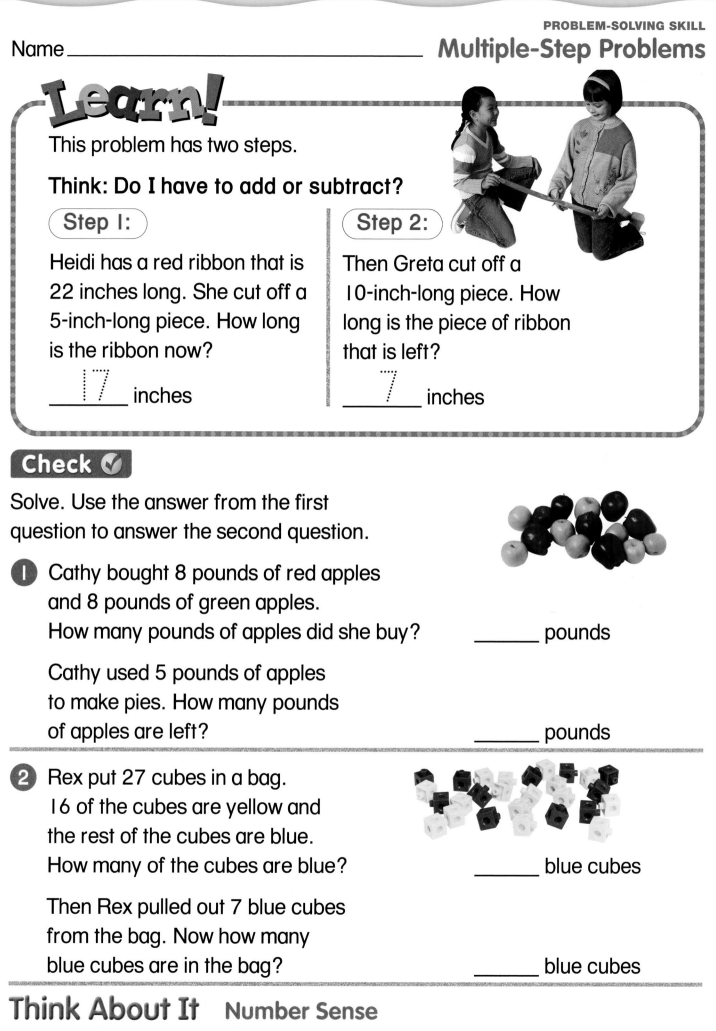

Learn!

This problem has two steps.

Think: Do I have to add or subtract?

Step 1:

Heidi has a red ribbon that is 22 inches long. She cut off a 5-inch-long piece. How long is the ribbon now?

____17____ inches

Step 2:

Then Greta cut off a 10-inch-long piece. How long is the piece of ribbon that is left?

____7____ inches

Check ✓

Solve. Use the answer from the first question to answer the second question.

1. Cathy bought 8 pounds of red apples and 8 pounds of green apples. How many pounds of apples did she buy?

_____ pounds

Cathy used 5 pounds of apples to make pies. How many pounds of apples are left?

_____ pounds

2. Rex put 27 cubes in a bag. 16 of the cubes are yellow and the rest of the cubes are blue. How many of the cubes are blue?

_____ blue cubes

Then Rex pulled out 7 blue cubes from the bag. Now how many blue cubes are in the bag?

_____ blue cubes

Think About It Number Sense

Tell a two-step story problem with addition and subtraction.

Chapter 9 ★ Lesson 16   three hundred seventy-seven **377**

Solve. Use the answer from the first question to answer the second question.

3 Tom bought 2 quarts of apple juice
and 6 quarts of orange juice. How many
quarts of juice did he buy? _____ quarts

Tom's family drank 4 quarts of the juice.
How many quarts of juice are left? _____ quarts

4 On Monday, the temperature was
78 degrees F. On Tuesday it was
11 degrees cooler than it was on Monday.
What was the temperature on Tuesday? _____ degrees F

On Wednesday it was 15 degrees warmer
than it was on Tuesday. What was the
temperature on Wednesday? _____ degrees F

5 There are 20 blue marbles and 10 yellow
marbles in a jar. How many marbles
are in the jar? _____ marbles

Henry added 18 red marbles to the jar.
Now how many marbles are in the jar? _____ marbles

Mental Math

Solve using mental math.

6 Marty brought 60 liters and Tina
brought 20 liters of water to the
school picnic. Later Paco
brought 10 liters. How many
liters of water are there?

_____ liters

Home Connection Your child solved two-step problems involving
addition and subtraction. **Home Activity** Have your child explain
how he or she solved Exercise 4.

378 three hundred seventy-eight

Name _____

Dorling Kindersley

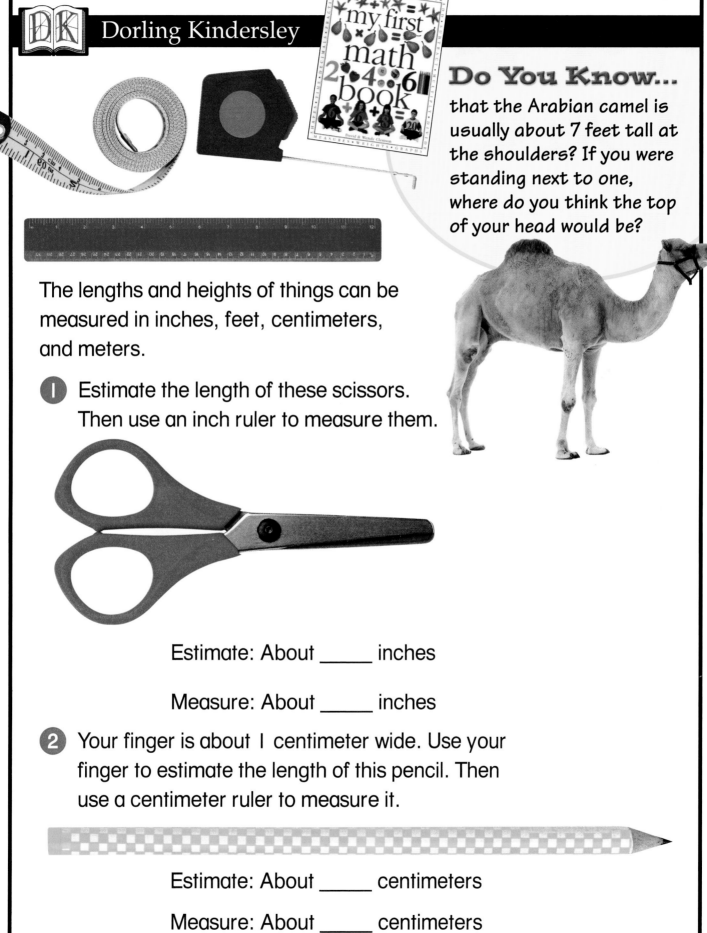

Do You Know...

that the Arabian camel is usually about 7 feet tall at the shoulders? If you were standing next to one, where do you think the top of your head would be?

The lengths and heights of things can be measured in inches, feet, centimeters, and meters.

1 Estimate the length of these scissors. Then use an inch ruler to measure them.

Estimate: About _____ inches

Measure: About _____ inches

2 Your finger is about 1 centimeter wide. Use your finger to estimate the length of this pencil. Then use a centimeter ruler to measure it.

Estimate: About _____ centimeters

Measure: About _____ centimeters

Circle the answer that makes more sense.

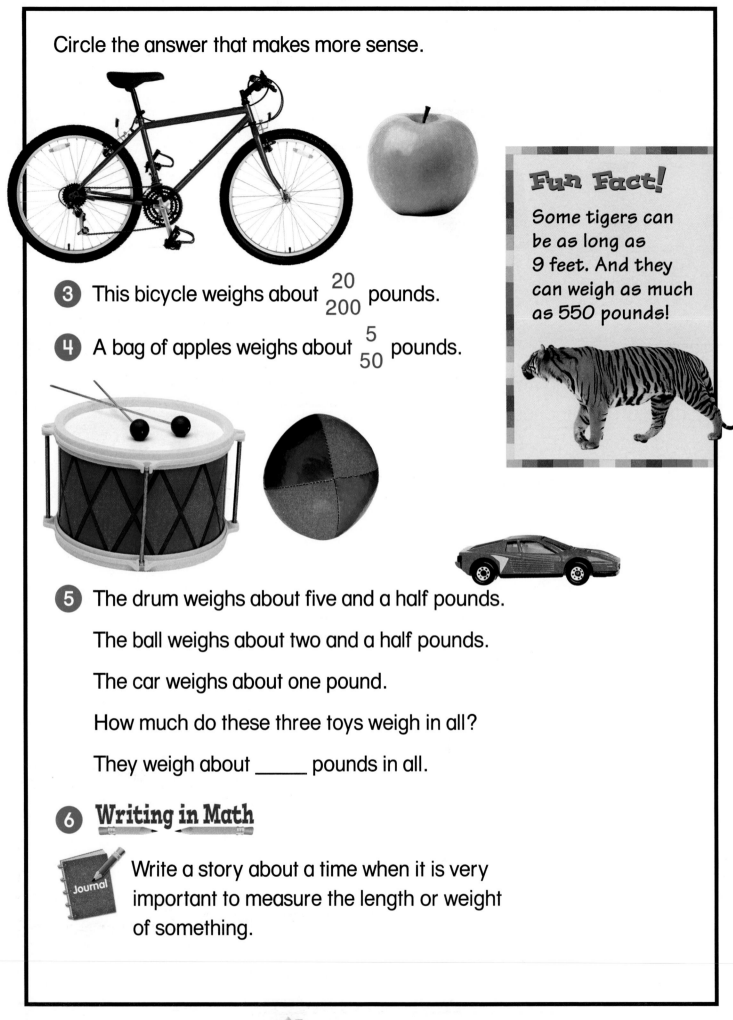

Fun Fact!

Some tigers can be as long as 9 feet. And they can weigh as much as 550 pounds!

③ This bicycle weighs about $\frac{20}{200}$ pounds.

④ A bag of apples weighs about $\frac{5}{50}$ pounds.

⑤ The drum weighs about five and a half pounds.

The ball weighs about two and a half pounds.

The car weighs about one pound.

How much do these three toys weigh in all?

They weigh about _____ pounds in all.

⑥ **Writing in Math**

Write a story about a time when it is very important to measure the length or weight of something.

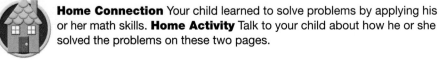

Home Connection Your child learned to solve problems by applying his or her math skills. **Home Activity** Talk to your child about how he or she solved the problems on these two pages.

If you spin once, which color is the spinner most likely to land on?

1

blue

red

2

blue

red

green

Which color is the spinner least likely to land on?

3

blue

purple

yellow

4

blue

red

yellow

Use the tally chart to help you answer.
Circle the missing word to complete the sentence.

Cubes	
Yellow	ЖІ
Red	ЖІ ЖІ І

5 If you pick one cube, it is _____ that you will choose a red or a yellow cube.

impossible

certain

6 It is _____ that you will pick a red cube.

certain

probable

Write a number sentence for each part of the problem.

7 There are 76 beads in the bag.
38 of the beads are orange and the
rest are green. How many beads
are green?

_____ beads

Jamie pulled out 30 of the green beads.
How many green beads were left?

_____ beads

Name_____

How much is left? Mark the best estimate.

1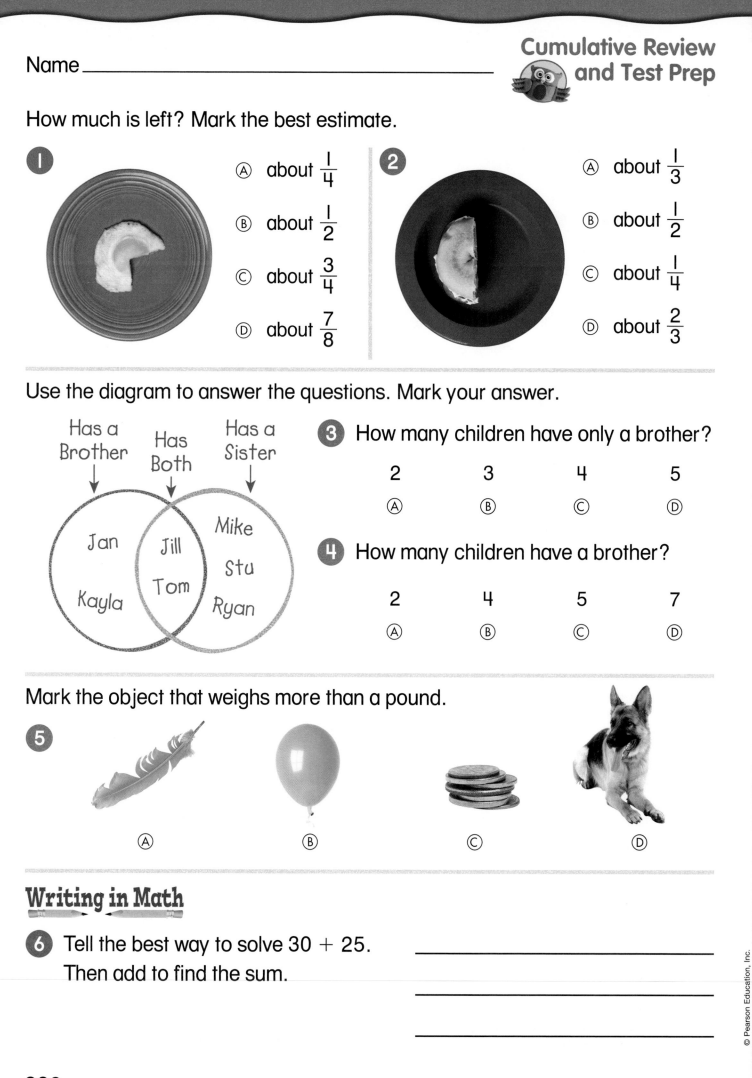

Ⓐ about $\frac{1}{4}$

Ⓑ about $\frac{1}{2}$

Ⓒ about $\frac{3}{4}$

Ⓓ about $\frac{7}{8}$

2

Ⓐ about $\frac{1}{3}$

Ⓑ about $\frac{1}{2}$

Ⓒ about $\frac{1}{4}$

Ⓓ about $\frac{2}{3}$

Use the diagram to answer the questions. Mark your answer.

Has a Brother   Has Both   Has a Sister

Jan   Jill   Mike
Kayla   Tom   Stu   Ryan

3 How many children have only a brother?

2   3   4   5
Ⓐ   Ⓑ   Ⓒ   Ⓓ

4 How many children have a brother?

2   4   5   7
Ⓐ   Ⓑ   Ⓒ   Ⓓ

Mark the object that weighs more than a pound.

5

Ⓐ   Ⓑ   Ⓒ   Ⓓ

Writing in Math

6 Tell the best way to solve 30 + 25.
Then add to find the sum.

_____

_____

_____

Choosing a Measuring Tool

Circle the measuring tool you would use.

1 How long is the clown's shoe?

2 How cold is it outside?

3 Which dog is heavier?

4 How much water does the dish hold?

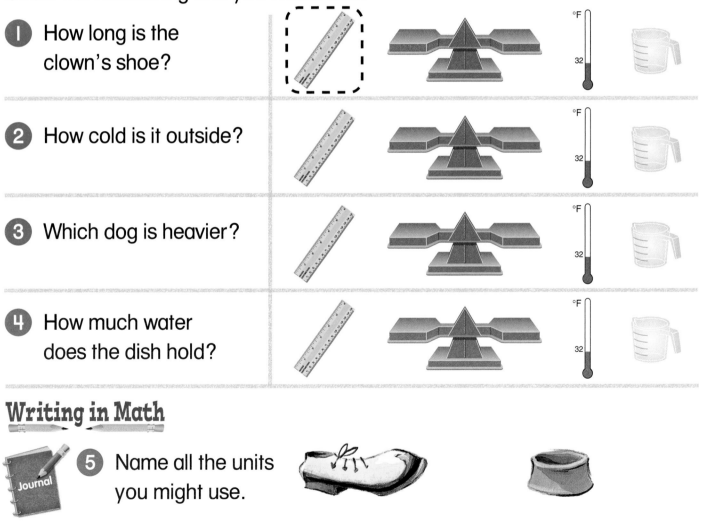

Writing in Math

5 Name all the units you might use.

Home Connection Your child chose the right tool to measure an object.
Home Activity Ask your child to explain two of his or her answers above.

Name _____

Use a Computer to Find Perimeter

You can use a computer to find the perimeters of different shapes.

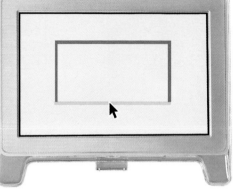

1 Go to the Geometry Drawing eTool on a computer.

2 Draw a rectangle in the Geoboard workspace.

3 Find the length of each side of your rectangle. Record these lengths on a separate sheet of paper.

4 Use the tool to find the perimeter. Write the perimeter on your paper.

5 Repeat Exercises 1–4 for a **pentagon** and a **hexagon.**

Think About It   Reasoning

How did your computer find the perimeter of each shape? Use the lengths on your sheet of paper to help you explain your thinking.

Home Connection Your child used a computer to find the perimeters of different shapes.
Home Activity Ask your child to draw a shape with 4 or 5 sides, measure each side to the nearest inch, and then find the perimeter of the shape to the nearest inch.

384 three hundred eighty-four

Chapter 9

© Pearson Education, Inc.

Name_____

Make Smart Choices

Removing wrong answer choices can help you find the correct answer choice.

Understand the Question

Get Information for the Answer

Plan How to Find the Answer

Make Smart Choices

Use Writing in Math

① Matt has 78¢. He spends 15¢ for a pencil. How much money does he have left?

Ⓐ 78¢ + 15¢ = 93¢

Ⓑ 78¢ − 15¢ = 63¢

Ⓒ 78¢ + 5¢ = 83¢

Ⓓ 78¢ − 25¢ = 53¢

Do you need to add or subtract to solve this problem? Since Matt spent money, you need to subtract. Which two answer choices are **not** subtraction sentences?

Now look at the two subtraction sentences. Which one answers the question?

Fill in the answer bubble.

Do I need to add or subtract?

Your Turn

Solve another problem about Matt.
Fill in the answer bubble.

② After Matt bought the pencil, he earned 35¢.
How much money does he have now?

Ⓐ 63¢ − 45¢ = 18¢   Ⓒ 63¢ + 35¢ = 98¢

Ⓑ 63¢ − 35¢ = 28¢   Ⓓ 53¢ + 35¢ = 88¢

Home Connection Your child prepared for standardized tests by eliminating wrong answer choices to help find the correct answer choice. **Home Activity** Ask your child to explain why three of the answer choices are wrong in Exercise 2.

three hundred eighty-five **385**

Name _____

Discover Math in Your World

When Is a Foot Not a Foot?

How many inches long do you think your foot is?
Is your foot 1 foot long? Work with a partner to
find out.

Measuring Up

1 Take off your shoes. Stand on a large piece
of paper. Have your partner trace your foot.
Then trace your partner's foot.

2 Use a ruler. Find the length of your foot and
then your partner's foot to the nearest inch.
Write your names and the measurements
in the table.

Name	Foot Length (in inches)

3 Make a tally chart like the one below to show the lengths of the feet
for the children in your class.

Length	Number of Children
_____ inches	
_____ inches	
_____ inches	

Take It to the NET
Video and Activities
www.scottforesman.com

Home Connection Your child measured the length of his or her foot
and made a chart showing the lengths of classmates' feet.
Home Activity With your child, trace the foot of a member of your
family and measure its length to the nearest inch.

© Pearson Education, Inc.

386   three hundred eighty-six   **Chapter 9**

Name _____

Measure with cubes. Then measure with a centimeter ruler.

1

about _____ cubes   about _____ centimeters

Find the perimeter and the area of this shape.

2

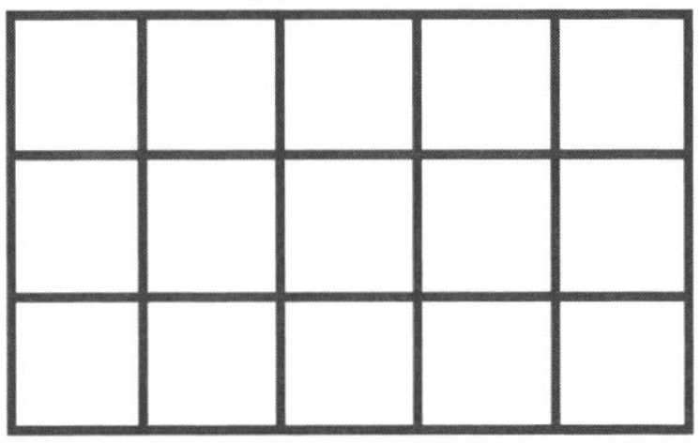

perimeter: _____ cm

area: _____ square units

Circle the object that holds less.

3     **4**

Does it hold more than or less than 1 liter? Circle **more** or **less.**

5    more   **6**   more

less   less

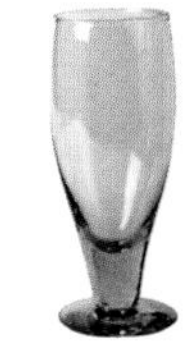

Circle the object that weighs less.

7 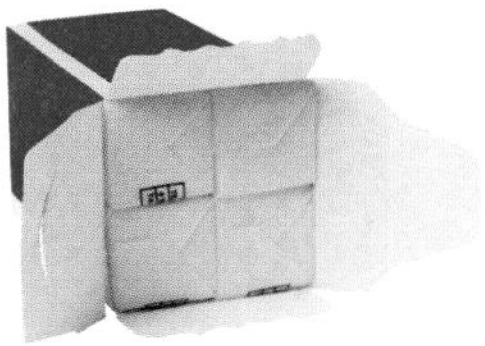 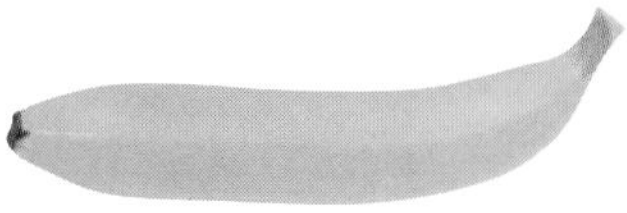   **8**

Circle the best estimate.

9    about 5 inches   **10**    about 3 grams

about 5 feet   about 3 kilograms

about 5 yards

⑪ Write the temperature.

°F
100
90
80
70
60
50
40
30
20
10
0
-10

_____ °F

⑫ Circle the number of cubes that will fit in the box.

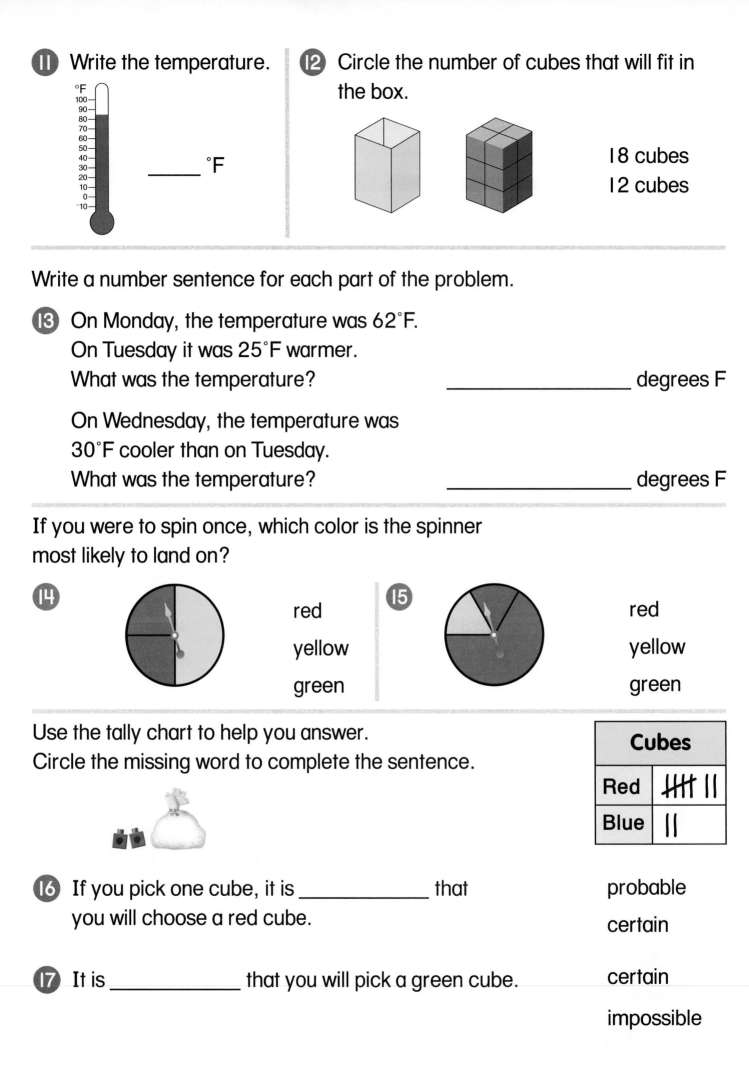

18 cubes

12 cubes

Write a number sentence for each part of the problem.

⑬ On Monday, the temperature was 62°F.
On Tuesday it was 25°F warmer.
What was the temperature? _____ degrees F

On Wednesday, the temperature was
30°F cooler than on Tuesday.
What was the temperature? _____ degrees F

If you were to spin once, which color is the spinner most likely to land on?

⑭

red

yellow

green

⑮

red

yellow

green

Use the tally chart to help you answer.
Circle the missing word to complete the sentence.

Cubes	
Red	⦀⦀ II
Blue	II

⑯ If you pick one cube, it is _____ that you will choose a red cube.

probable

certain

⑰ It is _____ that you will pick a green cube.

certain

impossible

388 three hundred eighty-eight

© Pearson Education, Inc.

"Let's See," Said Betty Bee

Written by John Carlisle
Illustrated by K. Michael Crawford

Mail

Mail

This Math Storybook belongs to

_____

"Let's see," said Betty Bee.

Betty was planning a Big Family Picnic.
And she didn't want to forget anyone.

"Aunt Rose has **122** bees in her family.
Aunt Tulip has **144** bees in her family.
Aunt Bluebell has **231** bees in her family.
That's **497** bees, plus my **3** aunts," Betty said to herself.
"And then there are those **500** cousins!"

"That's **1,000** bees! There will be **1,000** bees
at our picnic!"

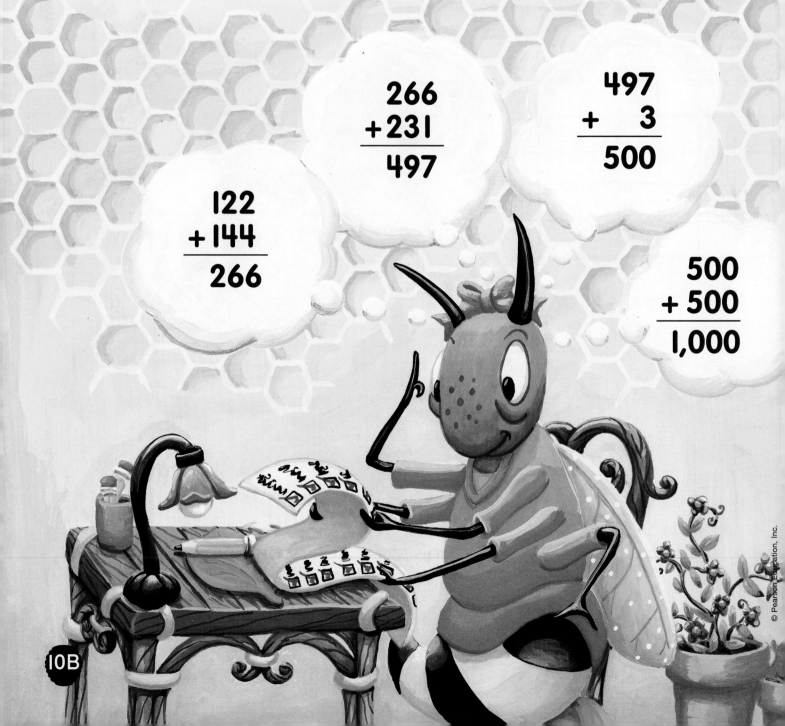

$$\begin{array}{r} 266 \\ +231 \\ \hline 497 \end{array} \qquad \begin{array}{r} 497 \\ +\quad 3 \\ \hline 500 \end{array}$$

$$\begin{array}{r} 122 \\ +144 \\ \hline 266 \end{array} \qquad \begin{array}{r} 500 \\ +500 \\ \hline 1,000 \end{array}$$

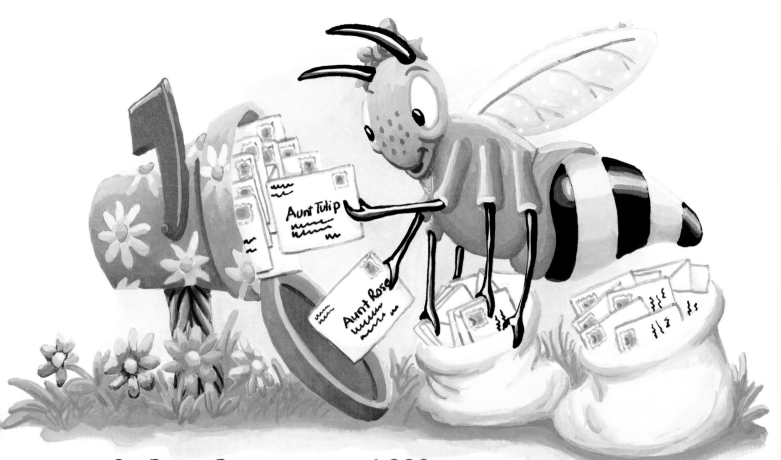

So Betty Bee sent out **1,000** invitations.

And she got back **1,000** letters saying Yes.

Everyone was coming!

Betty had a LOT of work to do.

Seating

☑ 10 Tables

ood

500
nectar treats

500
Pollen treats

Recipes
Seating
Setup
Food

Picnic
Invites
List
Tables
planning

Aunt Rose
Aunt Tulip
Aunt Bluebell
Fran

"Let's see," said Betty Bee.

"If I seat **100** bees at each table,
I'll need **10** tables."

"Now, what should we eat? Hmmm.
I think I will plan for **500** pollen treats
and **500** nectar treats."

"Yes, this sounds like a good plan
to me," said Betty Bee.

"**10** tables. **1,000** seats. **1,000** treats. Perfect!"

Cat
Karen
Jacquie
Denny

1,000 + 1 = 1,001

The Big Day arrived at last.

Betty's whole family came.

Everyone sat down at a table.
Everyone, that is, except Betty.

Everyone had something to eat.
Everyone, that is, except Betty.

"Let's see," said Betty Bee,
scratching her head.

Wait a minute!

There were 1,001 bees at the Big Family Picnic.

Betty had forgotten to count herself!

But Betty didn't care.

Even though she felt a little silly
for making such a simple mistake,
she decided just to have a great time
with her family. Good idea, right?

Home-School Connection

Dear Family,

Today my class started Chapter 10, **Numbers to 1,000.** I will learn how to build, read, write, compare, and order numbers to 1,000. I will also learn more about the value of each digit in a 3-digit number. Here are some of the math words I will be learning and some things we can do to help me with my math.

Love,

_____

Math Activity to Do at Home

Collect 1,000 of something! (Pennies work particularly well, but paper clips, craft sticks, reinforcement labels, and stickers work well too.) Organize your collection by tens and hundreds and talk about it as 1,000 ones, as 100 tens, and as 10 hundreds. Have fun!

Books to Read Together

Reading math stories reinforces concepts. Look for these titles in your local library:

Millions of Cats
By Wanda Ga'g (Penguin Putnam, 1996)

Math Curse
By Jon Scieszka and Lane Smith (Penguin Putnam, 1995)

Take It to the NET
More Activities
www.scottforesman.com

My New Math Words

Our place-value number system is based on groups of ten. It takes 10 ones to make 1 ten. It takes 10 tens to make 1 hundred. And it takes 10 **hundreds** to make 1 **thousand.**

1,000 one thousand	100 one hundred	10 ten	1 one

Here is a number written in **standard form:**

456

Here is the same number written in **expanded form:**

400 + 50 + 6

Name _____

Don't Get Stung!

How to Play

1. Place your markers on START.
2. Take turns moving from hive to hive. Whenever you land on a new hive, your partner says, "I challenge you!"
3. Then your partner tells you what you have to do:

> • Name the numbers that are **1 more** and **1 less**.
> OR
> • Name the numbers that are **2 more** and **2 less**.
> OR
> • Name the numbers that are **10 more** and **10 less**.

4. If your partner thinks you have answered incorrectly, you have to work together to find the answers.
5. Keep playing until both of you make it to FINISH without getting stung!

What You Need

1 game marker for each player

START

100

200

300

400

500

600

700

800

900

1,000

FINISH

Name_____

Learn!

How many tens make 100?

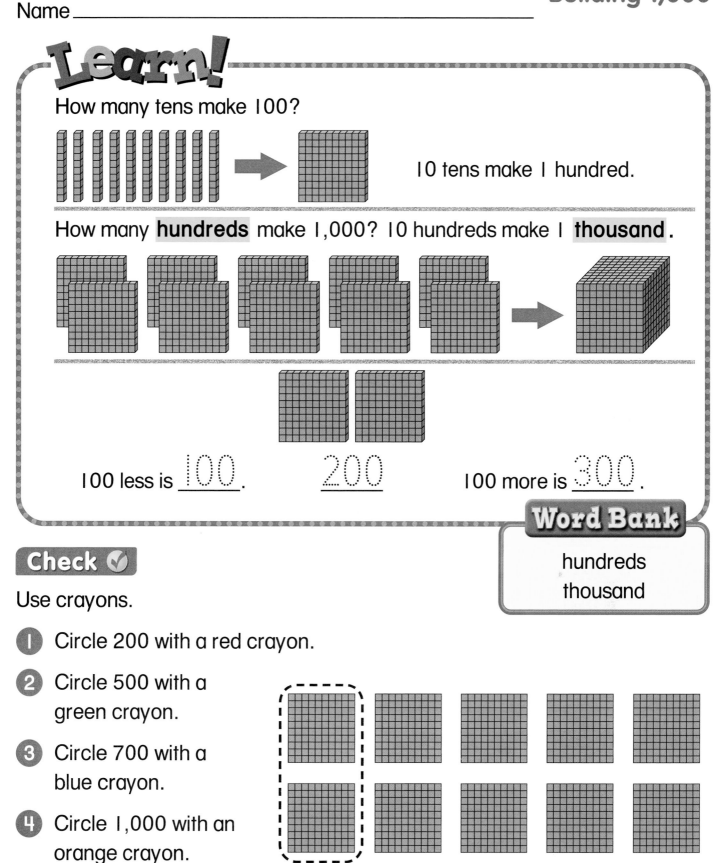

10 tens make 1 hundred.

How many **hundreds** make 1,000? 10 hundreds make 1 **thousand**.

100 less is 100.   200   100 more is 300.

Check ✓

Use crayons.

1. Circle 200 with a red crayon.

2. Circle 500 with a green crayon.

3. Circle 700 with a blue crayon.

4. Circle 1,000 with an orange crayon.

Think About It   Number Sense

Count by 100s to 1,000. How do you know how many ones you are counting?

Write how many. Use models if you need to.

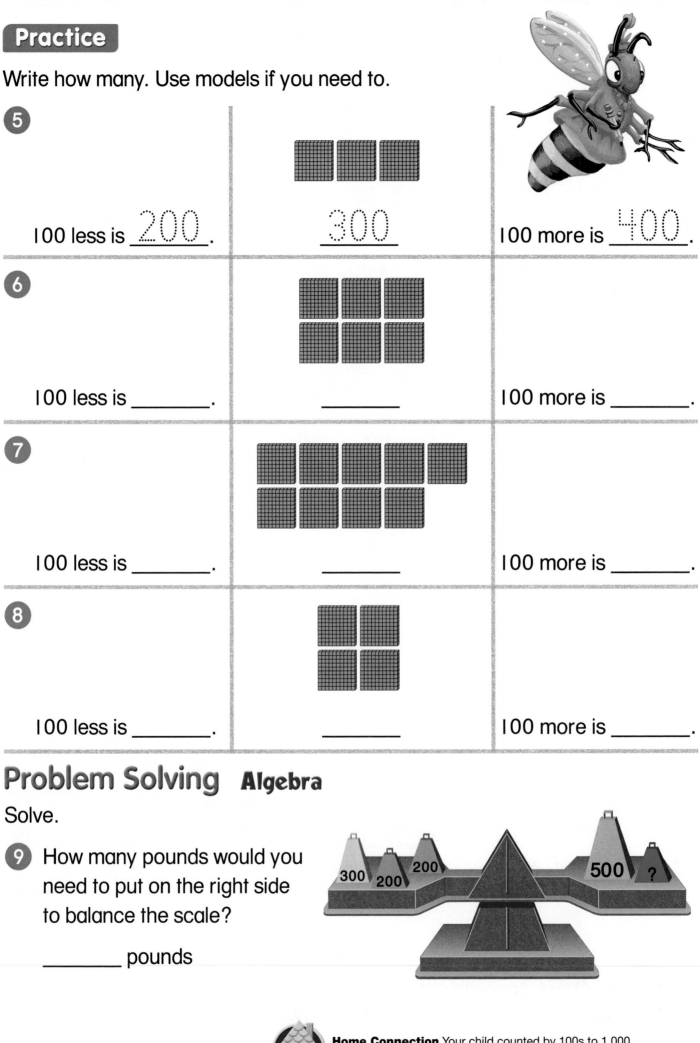

5

100 less is ___200___.

___300___

100 more is ___400___.

6

100 less is _____.

_____

100 more is _____.

7

100 less is _____.

_____

100 more is _____.

8

100 less is _____.

_____

100 more is _____.

Problem Solving **Algebra**

Solve.

9 How many pounds would you need to put on the right side to balance the scale?

300 200 200   500 ?

_____ pounds

© Pearson Education, Inc.

Name_____

Learn!

What number do the models show?

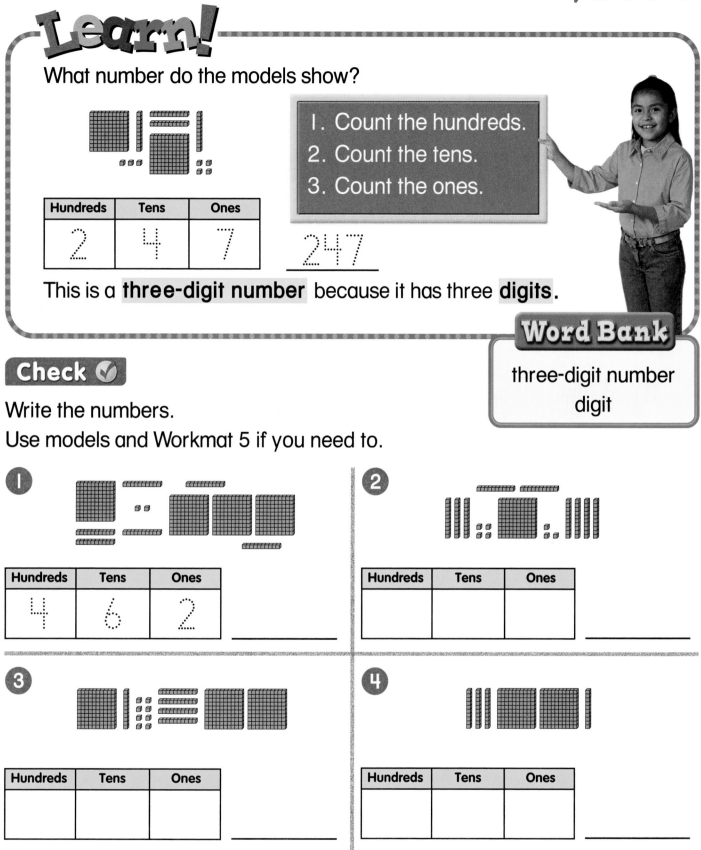

1. Count the hundreds.
2. Count the tens.
3. Count the ones.

Hundreds	Tens	Ones
2	4	7

247

This is a **three-digit number** because it has three **digits**.

Word Bank

three-digit number
digit

Check ✓

Write the numbers.
Use models and Workmat 5 if you need to.

1

Hundreds	Tens	Ones
4	6	2

_____

2

Hundreds	Tens	Ones

_____

3

Hundreds	Tens	Ones

_____

4

Hundreds	Tens	Ones

_____

Think About It   Number Sense

What does the zero mean in each number:
30, 506, 680?

Write the numbers.
Use models and Workmat 5 if you need to.

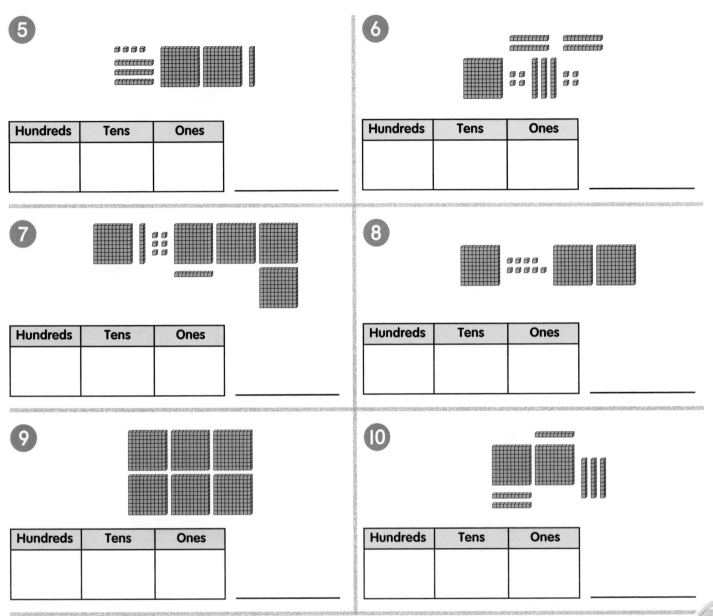

5

Hundreds	Tens	Ones

_____

6

Hundreds	Tens	Ones

_____

7

Hundreds	Tens	Ones

_____

8

Hundreds	Tens	Ones

_____

9

Hundreds	Tens	Ones

_____

10

Hundreds	Tens	Ones

_____

Problem Solving   Reasoning

Use the clues to find the number.

11 What is the number?
- The hundreds digit is 4.
- The ones digit is 8.
- The tens digit is 5.

_____

12 What is the number?
- The tens digit is 6.
- The ones digit is 3.
- The hundreds digit is 9.

_____

Home Connection Your child counted hundreds, tens, and ones to make three-digit numbers. **Home Activity** Have your child make the greatest and least possible numbers with the digits 7, 3, and 9. *(973 and 379)*

Learn!

What are some ways to write numbers?

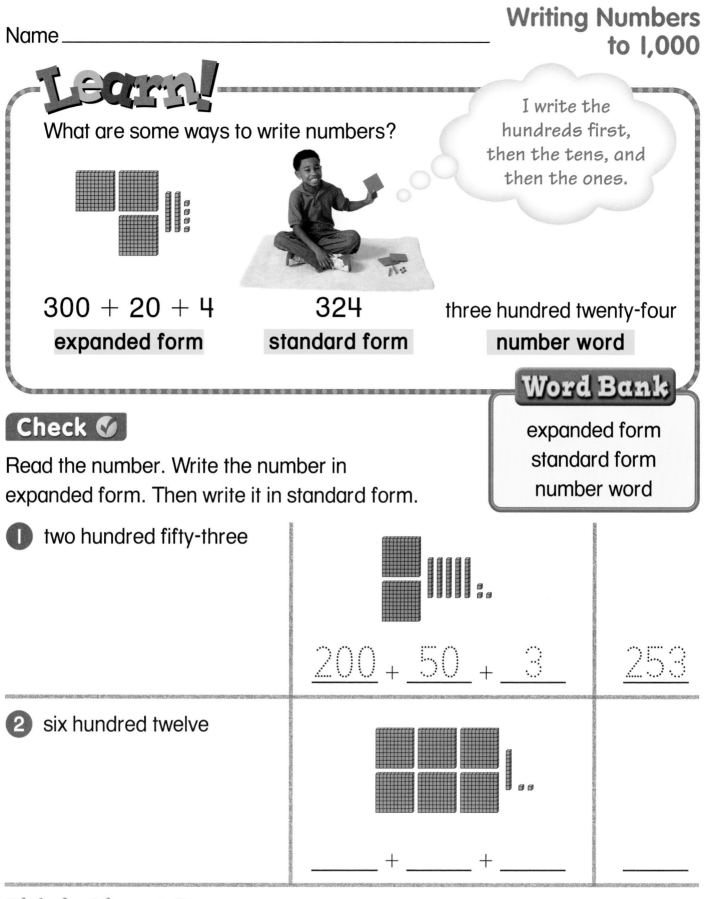

> I write the hundreds first, then the tens, and then the ones.

300 + 20 + 4
expanded form

324
standard form

three hundred twenty-four
number word

Word Bank

expanded form
standard form
number word

Check ✓

Read the number. Write the number in expanded form. Then write it in standard form.

1 two hundred fifty-three

200 + 50 + 3   253

2 six hundred twelve

_____ + _____ + _____   _____

Think About It   Number Sense

How do you know when to write a zero in these numbers?

one hundred ninety-two   one hundred ninety   one hundred nine

Circle the models to match the expanded form.
Write the number in standard form.

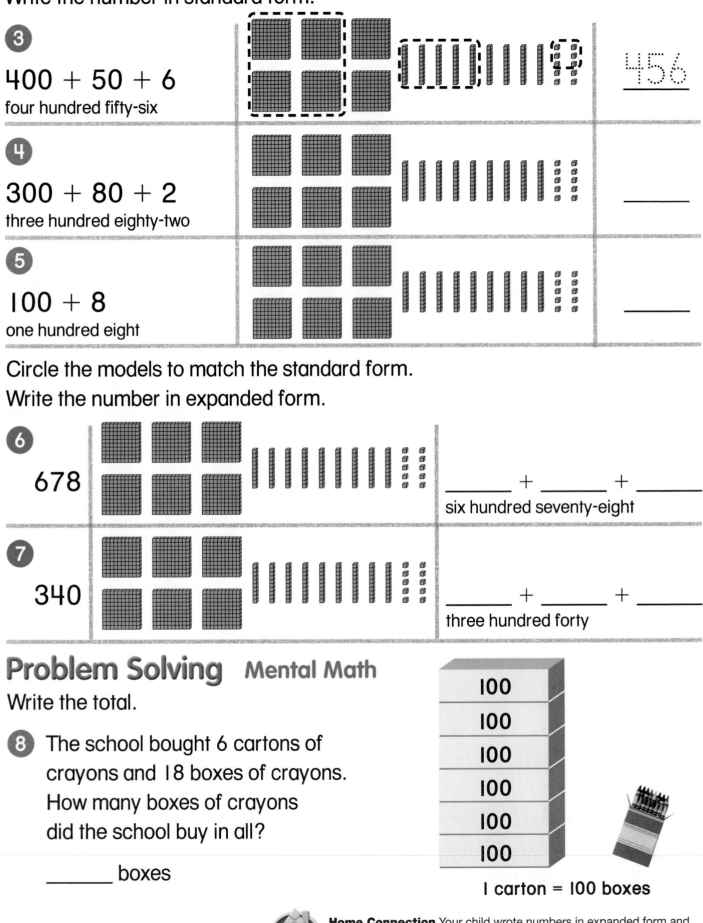

3

$400 + 50 + 6$
four hundred fifty-six

456

4

$300 + 80 + 2$
three hundred eighty-two

_____

5

$100 + 8$
one hundred eight

_____

Circle the models to match the standard form.
Write the number in expanded form.

6

678

_____ + _____ + _____
six hundred seventy-eight

7

340

_____ + _____ + _____
three hundred forty

Problem Solving   Mental Math

Write the total.

8 The school bought 6 cartons of
crayons and 18 boxes of crayons.
How many boxes of crayons
did the school buy in all?

_____ boxes

| 100 |
| 100 |
| 100 |
| 100 |
| 100 |
| 100 |

1 carton = 100 boxes

© Pearson Education, Inc.

Home Connection Your child wrote numbers in expanded form and
standard form. **Home Activity** Ask your child to explain what those
terms mean.

Learn! Algebra

You can use models, drawings, or **mental math** to add or subtract hundreds and tens.

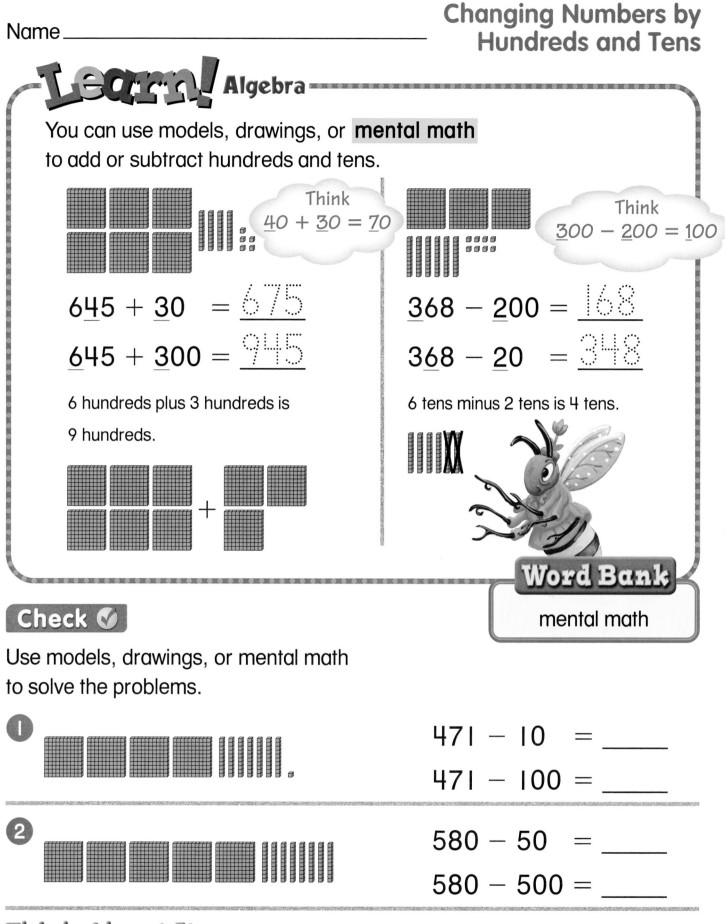

Think
$40 + 30 = 70$

$645 + 30 = 675$

$645 + 300 = 945$

6 hundreds plus 3 hundreds is 9 hundreds.

Think
$300 - 200 = 100$

$368 - 200 = 168$

$368 - 20 = 348$

6 tens minus 2 tens is 4 tens.

Word Bank

mental math

Check ✓

Use models, drawings, or mental math to solve the problems.

1

$471 - 10 = \underline{}$

$471 - 100 = \underline{}$

2

$580 - 50 = \underline{}$

$580 - 500 = \underline{}$

Think About It   Number Sense

How does a number change when you add 30? 300?

Use models, drawings, or mental math to solve the problems.

3
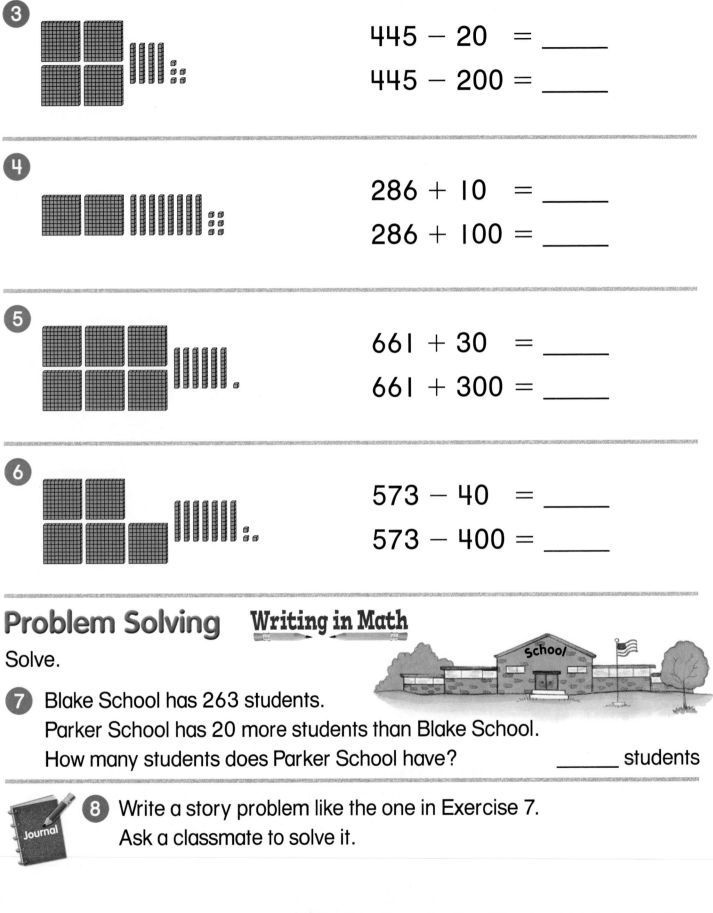

$445 - 20 \ =$ _____

$445 - 200 =$ _____

4

$286 + 10 \ =$ _____

$286 + 100 =$ _____

5

$661 + 30 \ =$ _____

$661 + 300 =$ _____

6

$573 - 40 \ =$ _____

$573 - 400 =$ _____

Problem Solving   Writing in Math

Solve.

7 Blake School has 263 students.
Parker School has 20 more students than Blake School.
How many students does Parker School have? _____ students

8 Write a story problem like the one in Exercise 7.
Ask a classmate to solve it.

Home Connection Your child used mental math, drawings, or models to add and subtract multiples of 10 and 100.
Home Activity Ask your child to explain how he or she solved Exercise 6.

© Pearson Education, Inc.

Name_____

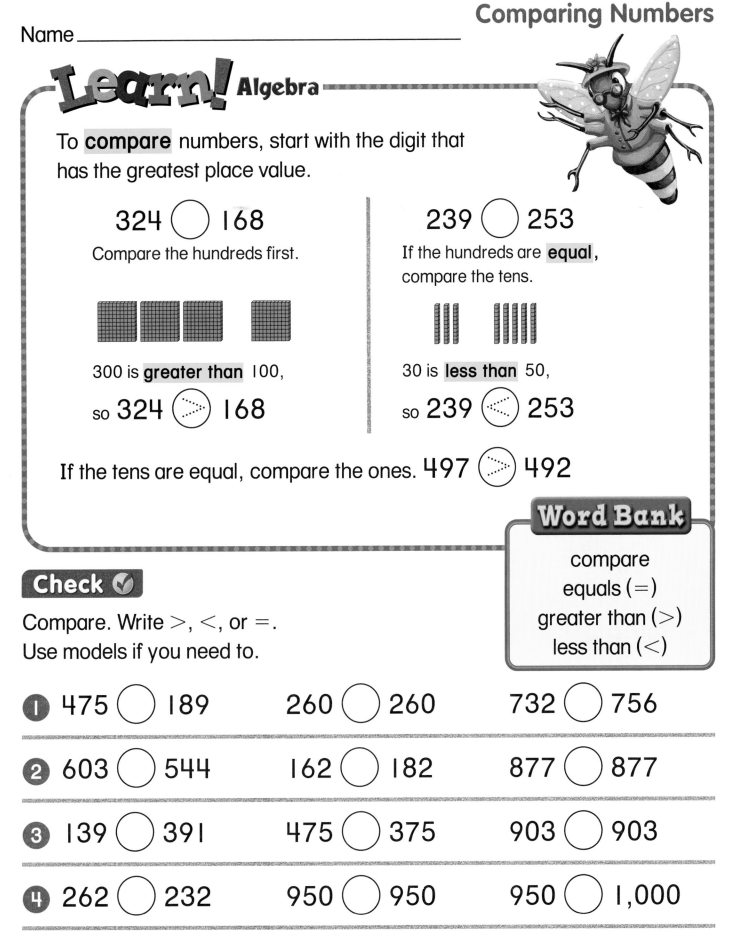

Learn! Algebra

To **compare** numbers, start with the digit that has the greatest place value.

324 ◯ 168
Compare the hundreds first.

300 is **greater than** 100,

so 324 ⊜> 168

239 ◯ 253
If the hundreds are **equal**, compare the tens.

30 is **less than** 50,

so 239 ⊜< 253

If the tens are equal, compare the ones. 497 ⊜> 492

Word Bank
compare
equals (=)
greater than (>)
less than (<)

Check ✔

Compare. Write >, <, or =.
Use models if you need to.

❶ 475 ◯ 189   260 ◯ 260   732 ◯ 756

❷ 603 ◯ 544   162 ◯ 182   877 ◯ 877

❸ 139 ◯ 391   475 ◯ 375   903 ◯ 903

❹ 262 ◯ 232   950 ◯ 950   950 ◯ 1,000

Think About It   Number Sense

How would you compare 235 and 78?

Practice

Compare. Write >, <, or =.
Use models if you need to.

5 148 ◯ 172   502 ◯ 502   246 ◯ 231

6 800 ◯ 399   653 ◯ 660   413 ◯ 305

7 728 ◯ 728   450 ◯ 440   926 ◯ 854

8 1,000 ◯ 999   286 ◯ 189   408 ◯ 413

Problem Solving   Visual Thinking

9 Draw lines to show which pony each child raised.

Kirk said:

My pony weighs less than Jenny's pony.

Natalie said:

My pony weighs more than Kirk's pony.

Jenny said:

My pony weighs less than 240 pounds.

241 pounds

188 pounds

237 pounds

Home Connection Your child compared three-digit numbers.
Home Activity Ask your child whether 106 is less than or is greater than 601 and to explain how he or she knows.

Name _____

Learn! Algebra

There are many ways to make 1,000.

> I have 750 points.
> I need 1,000 points to win.
> How many more points
> do I need?

Count on to make 1,000.
First, count on by 100s. Then count on by 10s.

750 850 950   950 960 970 980 990 1,000
   100   200   10   20   30   40   50

$750 + 250 = 1,000$ 250 points

Check ✓

Count on to solve each problem.

1 Paul has 550 points.
He needs 1,000 points to win.
How many more points does
he need?

$550 + \underline{} = 1,000$

_____ points

---

2 Grace has 600 points.
She needs 1,000 points to win.
How many more points does
she need?

$600 + \underline{} = 1,000$

_____ points

Think About It   Reasoning

How many 50s are in 100?
How many 500s are in 1,000?

Count on to solve each problem.

3 Michelle has 950 points.
How many more points does
she need to get to 1,000?

$950 + \underline{\quad\quad} = 1{,}000$

$\underline{\quad\quad}$ points

4 Pat has 450 points.
If he needs 1,000 points to win,
how many more points does
he need?

$450 + \underline{\quad\quad} = 1{,}000$

$\underline{\quad\quad}$ points

5 Brian has 300 points.
How many more points does
he need to get to 1,000?

$300 + \underline{\quad\quad} = 1{,}000$

$\underline{\quad\quad}$ points

6 Elena has 250 points.
She needs 1,000 points to win.
How many more points does
she need?

$250 + \underline{\quad\quad} = 1{,}000$

$\underline{\quad\quad}$ points

7 Mutaz has 900 points.
How many more points does
she need to get to 1,000?

$900 + \underline{\quad\quad} = 1{,}000$

$\underline{\quad\quad}$ points

Problem Solving Number Sense

Skip count by 50s.

8 50, 100, 150, 200, $\underline{\quad\quad}$,

300, 350, $\underline{\quad\quad}$, 450, $\underline{\quad\quad}$,

550, $\underline{\quad\quad}$, 650, 700, $\underline{\quad\quad}$,

$\underline{\quad\quad}$, $\underline{\quad\quad}$, 900, $\underline{\quad\quad}$, 1,000

Home Connection Your child found two numbers that together make 1,000.
Home Activity Ask your child to solve and explain: $850 + \underline{\quad\quad} = 1{,}000$. *(150)*

Name _____

Write how many. Use models if you need to.

1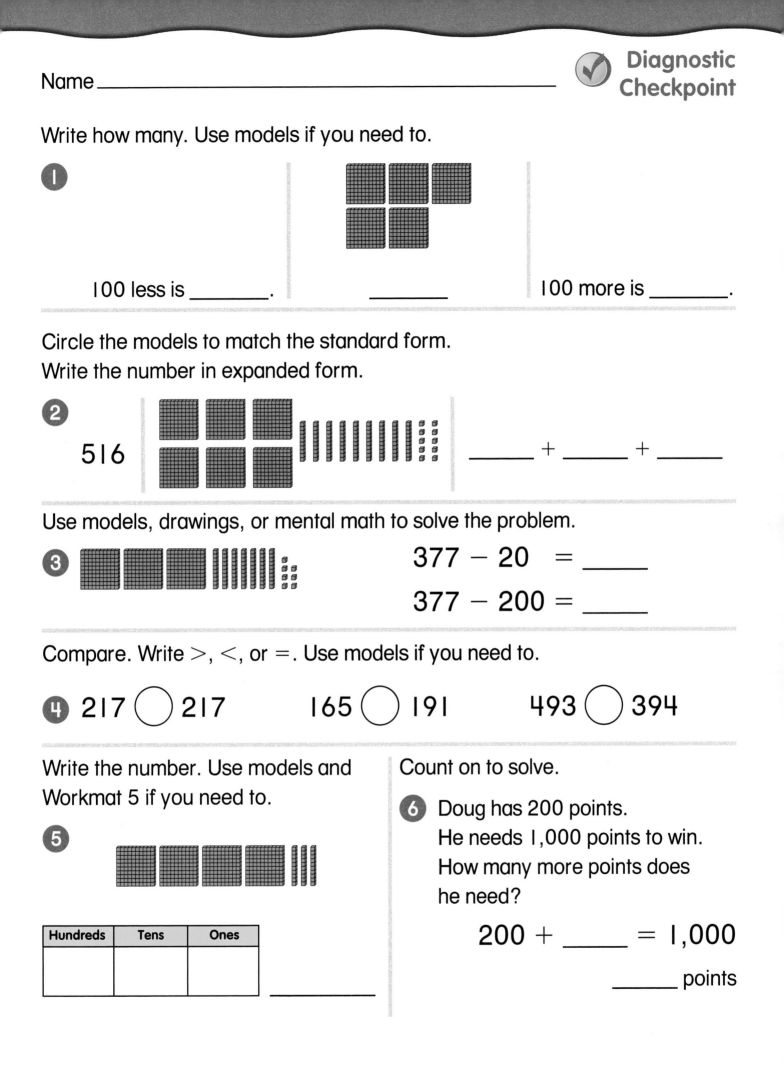

100 less is _____.   _____   100 more is _____.

Circle the models to match the standard form.
Write the number in expanded form.

2 516   _____ + _____ + _____

Use models, drawings, or mental math to solve the problem.

3 $377 - 20 = $ _____

$377 - 200 = $ _____

Compare. Write $>$, $<$, or $=$. Use models if you need to.

4 217 ◯ 217   165 ◯ 191   493 ◯ 394

Write the number. Use models and Workmat 5 if you need to.

5

Hundreds	Tens	Ones

_____

Count on to solve.

6 Doug has 200 points.
He needs 1,000 points to win.
How many more points does
he need?

$200 + $ _____ $ = 1,000$

_____ points

Mark the fraction that names the shaded part.

1

Ⓐ $\frac{1}{5}$

Ⓑ $\frac{1}{4}$

Ⓒ $\frac{1}{3}$

Ⓓ $\frac{1}{2}$

2

Ⓐ $\frac{1}{2}$

Ⓑ $\frac{1}{3}$

Ⓒ $\frac{1}{4}$

Ⓓ $\frac{1}{6}$

Mark the number sentence that will help solve the problem.

3 Sylvia bought a brush for 35¢ and a comb for 20¢.
How much did she spend in all?

$35¢ + 20¢ = \underline{\hspace{1cm}}$ $35¢ - 20¢ = \underline{\hspace{1cm}}$ $25¢ + 20¢ = \underline{\hspace{1cm}}$ $35¢ + 35¢ = \underline{\hspace{1cm}}$
Ⓐ   Ⓑ   Ⓒ   Ⓓ

Mark the time shown on the clocks.

4

11:20

Ⓐ 20 minutes before 11
Ⓑ 20 minutes after 11
Ⓒ 40 minutes after 11
Ⓓ 40 minutes before 11

Mark the answer.

5 How many cups are in 2 pints?

2   4   6   8
Ⓐ   Ⓑ   Ⓒ   Ⓓ

Writing in Math

6 There are 3 digits in a number.
What is the digit with the
greatest value?

_____

_____

_____

Use Data from a Chart

Name_____

Learn!

The **data chart** tells how many children play each sport in the Woodland School District.

Sports Children Play	
Sport	Number of Children
Soccer	710
Football	435
Basketball	286
Track	509
Baseball	628

Word Bank

data

chart

Check ✓

Use data from the chart to answer the questions.

1 How many children play football?   435 children

2 How many children are on the track team?   _____ children

3 Which sport do 600 + 20 + 8 children play?   _____

4 Seven hundred ten children play which sport?   _____

5 Do more children play basketball or football?   _____

Think About It   Reasoning

Why would you record data in a chart?

Use data from the chart to answer the questions.

Baseball Infield

90 feet

Lengths of Playing Spaces	
Sport	Length of Field/Court
Football	360 feet
Soccer	390 feet
Baseball	90 feet
Basketball	94 feet

6 Which field is longer,
a football field or a soccer field?

_____

7 A basketball court is how many
feet long, in tens and ones?

_____ tens _____ ones

8 Which game space is
300 + 60 feet long?

_____

Reasonableness

Circle the number or word that makes more sense.

9 Together two football fields are

about $\begin{matrix}80\\800\end{matrix}$ feet long.

11 Two baseball infields are $\begin{matrix}\text{shorter}\\\text{longer}\end{matrix}$
than one soccer field.

10 Together a soccer field

and a baseball infield are

about $\begin{matrix}100\\500\end{matrix}$ feet long.

12 Together, a football field and a

baseball infield are $\begin{matrix}\text{shorter}\\\text{longer}\end{matrix}$ than

a soccer field and a basketball

court.

Home Connection Your child used data from a chart to answer questions.
Home Activity Have your child ask you a question that can be answered
using data from one of the charts on Pages 405–406.

Learn! Algebra

What are the missing numbers?

___131___, 132, 133, ___134___, 135, 136, ___137___, 138

131 is **before** 132.   134 is **after** 133.   137 is **between** 136 and 138.

Word Bank

before
after
between

Check ✓

Write the missing numbers.

1

201	202	203	204	205	206	207	208	209	210
211	212		214	215		217	218	219	220
221	222	223		225	226	227		229	230
231		233	234		236	237	238	239	240
241	242	243		245	246		248		250
	252		254	255		257	258	259	
261		263	264		266	267		269	270
271	272	273		275	276		278		280
281	282	283	284			287	288	289	
	292		294	295	296	297		299	300

Think About It   Number Sense

What numbers would be in the row that comes after 300?

What numbers would be in the row that comes before 201?

Write the number that comes after.

② 123, 124   539, _____   168, _____

③ 699, _____   407, _____   999, _____

Write the number that comes before.

④ _____, 156   _____, 482   _____, 299

⑤ _____, 260   _____, 803   _____, 400

Write the number that comes between.

⑥ 153, _____, 155   118, _____, 120   810, _____, 812

⑦ 799, _____, 801   628, _____, 630   209, _____, 211

Write the number.

⑧ What number is one before 357? _____

⑨ What number is one after 682? _____

⑩ What number is between 499 and 501? _____

Problem Solving Reasoning

Find the pattern. Write the next three numbers.

⑪ 250, 252, 254, _____, _____, _____

⑫ 760, 750, 740, _____, _____, _____

⑬ 115, 110, 105, _____, _____, _____

⑭ 899, 896, 893, _____, _____, _____

What's the pattern?

Home Connection Your child identified the positions of numbers as before, after, or between other numbers. **Home Activity** Ask your child what number is between 150 and 152. *(151)*

Name_____

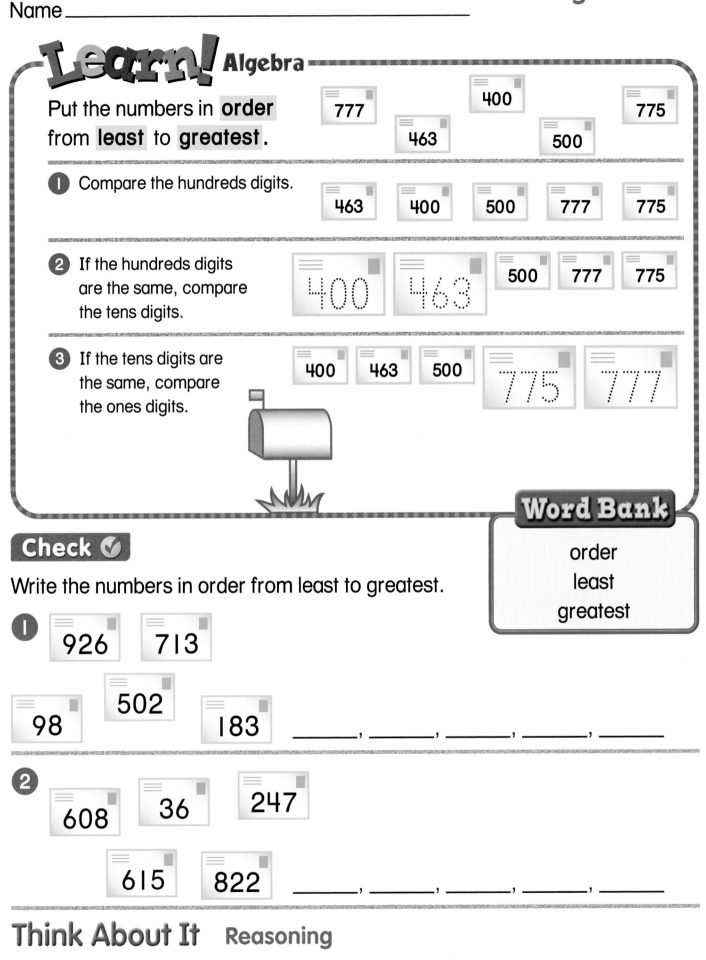

Learn! Algebra

Put the numbers in **order** from **least** to **greatest**.

777   463   400   500   775

1 Compare the hundreds digits.

463   400   500   777   775

2 If the hundreds digits are the same, compare the tens digits.

400   463   500   777   775

3 If the tens digits are the same, compare the ones digits.

400   463   500   775   777

Word Bank

order
least
greatest

Check ✓

Write the numbers in order from least to greatest.

1 926   713   98   502   183

_____, _____, _____, _____, _____

2 608   36   247   615   822

_____, _____, _____, _____, _____

Think About It Reasoning

When you order numbers, how can the number of digits be a clue?

Practice

Write the numbers in order from least to greatest.

3 (756, 812, 321, 765, 365) _____, _____, _____, _____, _____

4 (171, 143, 170, 209, 109) _____, _____, _____, _____, _____

5 (538, 382, 627, 566, 340) _____, _____, _____, _____, _____

Write the numbers in order from greatest to least.

6 (904, 940, 611, 573, 601) _____, _____, _____, _____, _____

7 (264, 320, 227, 302, 229) _____, _____, _____, _____, _____

8 (461, 783, 720, 451, 490) _____, _____, _____, _____, _____

Problem Solving Writing in Math

Use the space on the right to solve the problems.

9 In the numbers 411 to 430, are there more even or odd numbers? How do you know?

_____

_____

10 In the numbers 411 to 431, are there more even or odd numbers? How do you know?

_____

_____

Home Connection Your child ordered two- and three-digit numbers.
Home Activity Have your child write the following numbers in order from least to greatest: 401, 395, 410, 399, 411. *(395, 399, 401, 410, 411)*

Name_____

Predict and Verify

1 Read this knock-knock joke:

Knock knock.
> Who's there?

Tennis.
> Tennis who?

Tennis five plus five!

2 Now read this knock-knock joke:

Knock knock.
> Who's there?

Banana.
> Banana who?

Knock knock.
> Who's there?

Banana.
> Banana who?

Knock knock.
> Who's there?

Orange.
> Orange who?

Orange you glad I didn't say banana?

3 How is the second knock-knock joke different?

_____

_____

Think About It   Reasoning

Predict which number will come next in this pattern: 10, 8, 6, 4, _____
How do you know?

4 Look at the rows of dots below.
What pattern do you see?

_____

_____

_____

● ● ●

● ● ● ● ●

● ● ● ● ● ● ●

5 Now use the dots to play a game with a partner.

Each partner takes a turn crossing out either **one dot** or **two dots**
on a single line. One partner can use the letter **X.**
The other partner can use a checkmark (✔).

The winner is the one who does NOT have to cross off the last dot!

© Pearson Education, Inc.

Home Connection Your child is learning to look for patterns in both
reading and math. **Home Activity** Help your child look for patterns around
the house in wallpaper, tiles, carpeting, and so on.

Name _____

Learn! Algebra

What number **pattern** will help you find the number that comes next in this skip-counting sequence?

247   257   267   277   287   297   307   ___

Read and Understand

Find the number pattern that will help you think of the next skip-counting number.

Plan and Solve

Look for the digits that change.
Do they **increase** or **decrease**?

What is the next number? 317

Look Back and Check

How does knowing a number pattern help you find the next skip-counting number?

The tens digits increase by 1. Each number increases by 1 ten.

Word Bank

pattern
increase
decrease

Check ✓

Write the missing numbers. Describe the pattern.

1 600, 620, 640, 660, 680, _____, _____, _____

_____

2 200, 225, 250, 275, _____, _____, _____

_____

Think About It Reasoning

Show a pattern in which the numbers decrease by 10.

Write the missing numbers. Describe the pattern.

3 200, 190, 180, 170, _____, _____, _____

_____

4 600, 550, 500, 450, _____, _____, _____

_____

Write the number that is 20 less.

5   560   361   837   494

_____   _____   _____   _____

What pattern do you see? _____

Write the number that is 200 more.

6   172   607   583   381

_____   _____   _____   _____

What pattern do you see? _____

Write the number that is 200 less.

7   640   905   728   462

_____   _____   _____   _____

What pattern do you see? _____

Reasoning

Find the pattern. Write the missing numbers.

8   25,   50,   75,   100,   _____,   150,

175,   _____,   225,   250,   _____,   300,

325,   _____,   _____,   _____,   425,   _____

Home Connection Your child looked for skip-counting patterns to solve problems. **Home Activity** Have your child continue and then describe this pattern: 525, 530, 535, 540, ____, ____, ____. *(545, 550, 555)*

Dorling Kindersley

DK BIG BOOK OF RESCUE VEHICLES
THE STRONGEST, MOST POWERFUL RESCUE MACHINES

Do You Know...
that fire engines often respond when someone calls for an ambulance? Firefighters are trained to handle medical emergencies until an ambulance arrives.

1 One fire engine carries 700 gallons of water.

How much is 100 gallons less than that?

_____ gallons

How much is 100 gallons more than that?   _____ gallons

2 The aerial platform on this fire engine can be raised 100 feet.

How much is 10 feet less than that?   _____ feet

How much is 10 feet more than that?   _____ feet

3 A fire engine responded to 100 alarms in April.
It responded to 145 alarms in May.
How many times did it respond
in those two months?

_____ times

4 A fireboat pumped about 125 gallons of water in 1 second. Record the number of hundreds, tens, and ones in 125.

_____ hundred

_____ tens

_____ ones

Fun Fact!

Special lights on an ambulance send a signal that can change traffic lights to green.

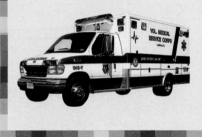

5 One fireboat is 134 feet long. Another fireboat is 107 feet long. Compare these two lengths. Write >, <, or =.

134 ◯ 107

6 An all-weather lifeboat responded to an alarm at 10 minutes to 6. What is another way to write this time?

_____ : _____

7 **Writing in Math**

Write a number story about a fire engine. Use four numbers between 400 and 600. At the end of your story, list the numbers in order from least to greatest.

Home Connection Your child learned how to solve problems by applying his or her math skills. **Home Activity** Talk to your child about how he or she solved the problems on these two pages.

© Pearson Education, Inc.

Name_____

Use data from the chart to answer the two questions.

1 Are there more children at Camp A or Camp B?

_____

2 At which camp are there 200 + 20 + 3 children?

_____

Children at Camp	
Camp	Number of Children
A	220
B	223
C	105
D	33

Write the number that comes after.

3 438, _____   116, _____   795, _____

Write the number that comes between.

4 564, _____, 566   206, _____, 208   353, _____, 355

Write the numbers in order from greatest to least.

5 (815, 336, 306, 845, 363) _____, _____, _____, _____, _____

Write the missing numbers. Describe the pattern.

6 910, 810, 710, 610, _____, _____, _____

_____

7 135, 145, 155, 165, _____, _____, _____

_____

Mark the fraction that is green.

1

$\frac{2}{6}$ $\frac{1}{6}$ $\frac{4}{6}$ $\frac{1}{2}$

Ⓐ   Ⓑ   Ⓒ   Ⓓ

---

2 About how long would this take?

Ⓐ   about 3 minutes

Ⓑ   about 3 hours

Ⓒ   about 3 days

Ⓓ   about 3 months

---

3 Mark the number of children who like only spaghetti.

    0   1   2   4
    Ⓐ   Ⓑ   Ⓒ   Ⓓ

Likes Spaghetti   Likes Pizza

Pam
Ralph   Amy   Nora
Liz   Mike
Tim

Likes Both

---

4 What is the crayon's length?

INCHES

about 2 inches   about 3 feet   about 3 inches   about 3 meters

Ⓐ   Ⓑ   Ⓒ   Ⓓ

Writing in Math

5 Color the spinner so that you are more likely to land on red than blue.

Name_____

Order on the Number Line

You can write numbers in order
if you locate them on the number line.

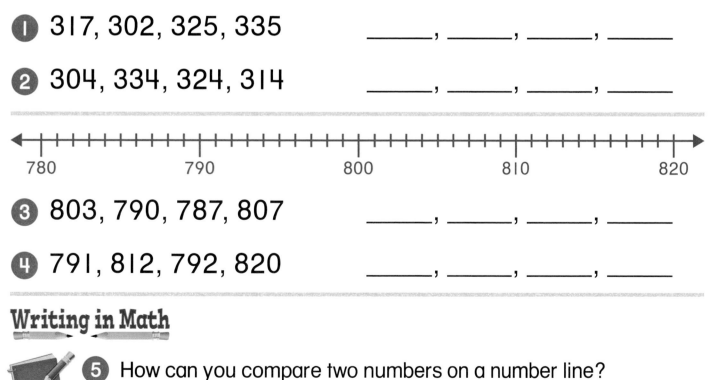

325 is greater than 320.

338 is greater than 330.

325   320   318   338

300   310   320   330   340

| Least number at the left | 318, 320, 325, 338 | Greatest number at the right |

Find these numbers on the number line.
Write them in order.

1 317, 302, 325, 335   _____, _____, _____, _____

2 304, 334, 324, 314   _____, _____, _____, _____

780   790   800   810   820

3 803, 790, 787, 807   _____, _____, _____, _____

4 791, 812, 792, 820   _____, _____, _____, _____

Writing in Math

5 How can you compare two numbers on a number line?

Home Connection Your child located numbers on a number line and wrote them in order. **Home Activity** Ask your child to explain how he or she did Exercise 3.

Name_____

Find Patterns Using a Calculator

You can use a calculator to find patterns.
Press ON/C . Press the keys that you see below.
Write what the display shows each time you press = .

1 | 2 | 5 | + | 2 | 5 | = | = | = |

Display: __50__ _____ _____

The pattern is count by __25s__.

2 | 3 | 2 | + | 5 | 0 | = | = | = |

Display: _____ _____ _____

The pattern is count by _____.

3 | 6 | 4 | + | 1 | 0 | 0 | = | = | = |

Display: _____ _____ _____

The pattern is count by _____.

4 | 7 | 5 | + | 5 | 0 | 0 | = | = | = |

Display: _____ _____ _____

The pattern is count by _____.

> I like to look for patterns!

Think About It   Number Sense

In Exercise 4, what calculator key would you press to find the next number in the pattern?

Home Connection Your child used a calculator to find patterns and to count by 25s, 50s, 100s, and 500s. **Home Activity** Ask your child to explain how he or she found the pattern in Exercise 3.

Name _____

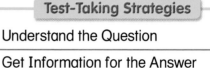

Use Writing in Math

Some math tests ask you to write your answer and explain your thinking. You can use words from the problem to help you do this.

1 What number is 10 more than 370? How do you know?

380 is 10 more than 370. I know this because 370 + 10 = 380.

Test-Taking Strategies

Understand the Question

Get Information for the Answer

Plan How to Find the Answer

Make Smart Choices

Use Writing in Math

The girl who solved this problem thought, "370 has 7 tens. So the answer has 8 tens. The answer is 380." Then she used words from the problem to help her write her answer.

Which words from the problem did she use? If you can find some of them, raise your hand.

Your Turn

Read and solve the problem. Then use words from the problem to help you write your answer.

2 What number is 100 more than 589? How do you know?

_____

_____

_____

_____

I see some words I can use!

Home Connection Your child prepared for standardized tests by learning how to use words from a math problem to completely answer the question. **Home Activity** Have your child explain which words in Exercise 2 helped him or her solve the problem.

Name _____

Discover Math in Your World

Your Money at Work!

Why is it a good idea to put money in a bank? The bank pays you a small amount of money called **interest**.

When this happens, your money makes more money for you!

You Can Bank on It!

Miguel, Sara, and Philip are saving money for college.

1. Miguel had $375 in his savings account.
   He **withdrew** $100. How much is in his account now? _____

2. Sara has $1,000 in her savings account.
   Tom has $450 in his savings account.
   Who has more money in the bank, Sara or Tom? _____

   How much more? _____ more

3. Philip is **depositing** money in his account.
   He gives the bank teller two $100 bills and
   nine $10 bills. How much money is Phil depositing? _____

Take It to the NET
Video and Activities
www.scottforesman.com

Home Connection Your child solved problems about saving money in a bank. **Home Activity** Ask your child to explain how he or she solved one of the problems on this page.

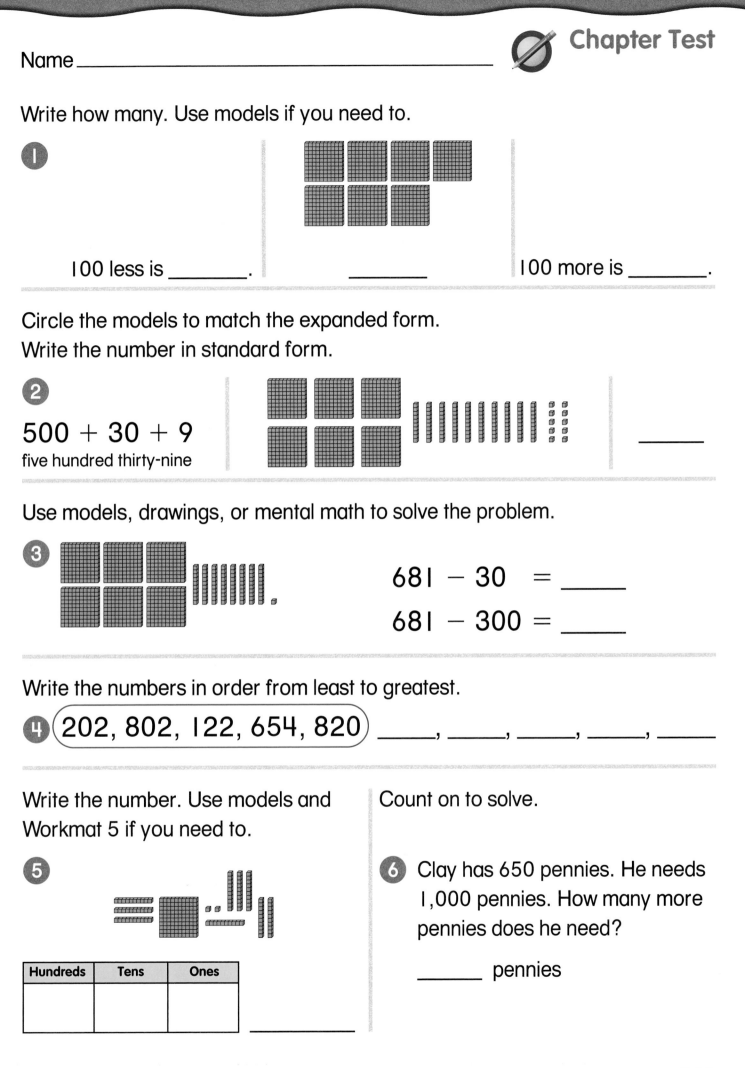

Write how many. Use models if you need to.

1

100 less is _____.   _____   100 more is _____.

Circle the models to match the expanded form.
Write the number in standard form.

2

$500 + 30 + 9$
five hundred thirty-nine

_____

Use models, drawings, or mental math to solve the problem.

3

$681 - 30 \ = $ _____

$681 - 300 = $ _____

Write the numbers in order from least to greatest.

4 (202, 802, 122, 654, 820) _____, _____, _____, _____, _____

Write the number. Use models and Workmat 5 if you need to.

5

Hundreds	Tens	Ones

_____

Count on to solve.

6 Clay has 650 pennies. He needs 1,000 pennies. How many more pennies does he need?

_____ pennies

Compare. Write >, <, or =.

7 350 ◯ 340   811 ◯ 811   672 ◯ 762

Write the number that comes before.

8 _____, 390   _____, 741   _____, 582

Write the number that comes after.

9 619, _____   400, _____   299, _____

Write the number that comes between.

10 100, _____, 102   509, _____, 511   998, _____, 1,000

Write the number that is 30 more.

11   407   813   956   260

          _____   _____   _____   _____

What pattern do you see? _____

Use data from the chart to answer the questions.

12 Write the number of fish in order
from least to greatest.

_____, _____, _____, _____

13 Are there more goldfish or more guppies?

_____

School Fish	
Fish	**Number**
Goldfish	177
Guppies	259
Neon tetras	128
Angelfish	163

Writing in Math

14 Write a story using data from the chart.
In your story, compare the number of goldfish
to the number of angelfish.

_____

_____

Mark the related addition fact.

1 $3 + 6 = 9$

$3 + 3 = 6$	$6 + 3 = 9$	$9 - 3 = 6$	$4 + 5 = 9$
Ⓐ	Ⓑ	Ⓒ	Ⓓ

Mark the statement that is true.

2

$21 = 12$	$68 < 67$	$50 > 49$	$73 < 70$
Ⓐ	Ⓑ	Ⓒ	Ⓓ

3

$329 > 328$	$151 = 150$	$486 < 475$	$516 > 561$
Ⓐ	Ⓑ	Ⓒ	Ⓓ

Mark the total.

4

57¢	62¢	87¢	92¢
Ⓐ	Ⓑ	Ⓒ	Ⓓ

Mark the other part of 100.

5   **20 and _____ is 100.**

Ⓐ 20

Ⓑ 45

Ⓒ 60

Ⓓ 80

6   **65 and _____ is 100.**

Ⓐ 25

Ⓑ 35

Ⓒ 40

Ⓓ 45

7 Which pair shows a **flip**?

Ⓐ   Ⓑ   Ⓒ   Ⓓ

Add in any order.

8

24	45	62	21	3
15	35	17	43	27
+ 36	+ 10	+ 8	+ 29	+ 50

Subtract to find the difference.

9

52¢	68¢	79¢	81¢	37¢
− 41¢	− 39¢	− 25¢	− 53¢	− 16¢

Write the fraction for the shaded part.

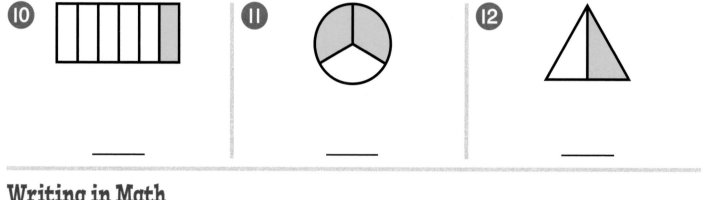

10 _____

11 _____

12 _____

Writing in Math

13 Circle the congruent shapes.
Tell why they are congruent.

_____

_____

14 Write the time on the digital clock.
Then write a story that tells about
what you might do at this time.

_____

_____

_____

424B

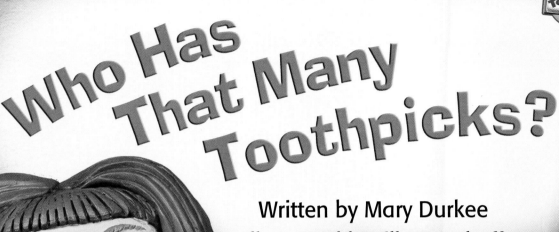

Who Has That Many Toothpicks?

Written by Mary Durkee

Illustrated by Jill Meyerhoff

This Math Storybook belongs to

_____

IIA

Becky opened her new castle-building kit.

The directions began like this:

You will need about 1,000 toothpicks.

"1,000 toothpicks!" thought Becky.
"Who has that many toothpicks?"

Becky looked on the kitchen shelf.
She found a box of toothpicks, but it wasn't full.

She counted them very carefully.
There were only **225**.

So Becky put them in an empty shoebox
and wrote **225** on the lid.

Then Becky asked her brother, the model airplane king,
if she could have some of his toothpicks.

Fortunately, her brother was feeling very generous that day.
He gave her two brand-new boxes.
Each box had **250** toothpicks in it.
Then he gave her **5** bundles of **25** each.

250

250

225
500
+125

225   500   125

Becky put all the toothpicks in her shoebox.
Then she wrote the numbers on the lid.

"Hmmm, let's see," she said as she added
the numbers in her head.

"I started with **225** toothpicks.

"Then Bobby gave me **500** more when he
gave me those two brand-new boxes.
That makes **725**.

"Then he gave me **125** more when he gave
me those **5** bundles of **25** each.
That makes **850** toothpicks in all.

But the directions said I need **1,000**!"

"1,000 what?" asked her grandpa.

"Toothpicks!" said Becky. "I have 850, but I need 150 more!"

"Let's see," said Grandpa. "It says here that you need only 750 toothpicks to make the tower. But you should get 1,000 just to be on the safe side."

"Hooray!" said Becky. "That means that I already have 100 more than I need!"

"Then let's build that castle!" said Grandpa.

$$1000 - 850 = 150$$

$$850 - 750 = 100$$

Dear Family,

Today my class started Chapter 11, **Addition and Subtraction of Three-Digit Numbers**. I will learn how to add and subtract numbers of this size mentally and on paper. I will also learn to estimate sums and differences. Here are some of the math words I will be learning and some things we can do to help me with my math.

Love,

_____

Math Activity to Do at Home

Number nine index cards from 100 to 900. Pick up a 300 card and say, "Help! My full name is 1,000. Part of me is missing! Where is my other part?" Your child then finds your missing part (in this case, 700) to put you back together.

Books to Read Together

Reading math stories reinforces concepts. Look for these titles in your local library:

The 500 Hats of Bartholomew Cubbins
By Dr. Seuss
(Random House, 1989)

So Many Cats!
By Beatrice Schenk de Regniers
(Houghton Mifflin, 1988)

Take It to the NET
More Activities
www.scottforesman.com

My New Math Words

estimate When it's a verb, you say something like this: "I estimate that the answer is about 400." When it's a noun, you say something like this: "My estimate is 400."

mental math It's often a good idea to use this problem-solving strategy when you're estimating and when you're working with numbers that end in one or more zeros or in 5.

regroup If you're adding 469 and 291, you need to regroup the 10 ones as 1 ten 0 ones. And then you need to regroup the 16 tens as 1 hundred 6 tens.

Sum Game!

 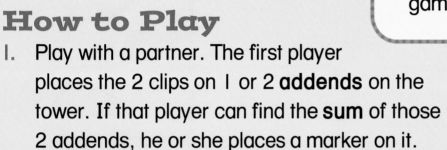
How to Play

1. Play with a partner. The first player places the 2 clips on 1 or 2 **addends** on the tower. If that player can find the **sum** of those 2 addends, he or she places a marker on it.

2. The second player moves **only** 1 of the clips to a **new** addend. If that player can find the **sum** of those 2 addends, he or she places a marker on it.

3. Partners keep taking turns until one of them has 5 markers in a row, in a column, or on a diagonal.

ADDENDS

125	
200	
243	
260	
335	
370	
442	

SUMS

503	884	460	777	460
325	250	705	685	595
520	400	495	578	812
670	486	443	630	385
368	740	613	567	702

Name _____

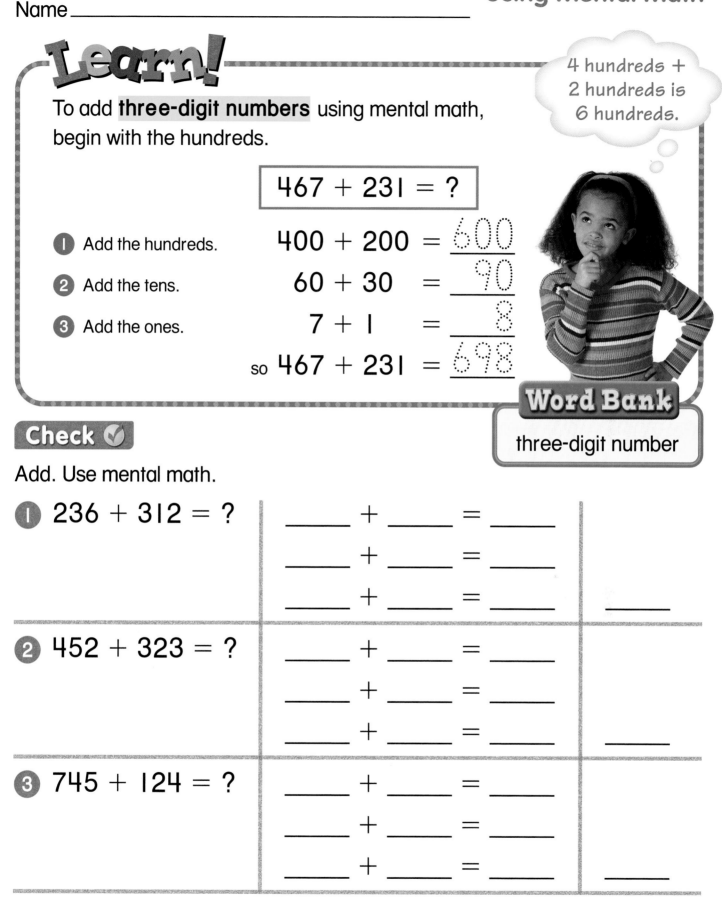

Learn!

To add **three-digit numbers** using mental math, begin with the hundreds.

> 4 hundreds + 2 hundreds is 6 hundreds.

$$467 + 231 = ?$$

1. Add the hundreds. $400 + 200 = 600$

2. Add the tens. $60 + 30 = 90$

3. Add the ones. $7 + 1 = 8$

so $467 + 231 = 698$

Word Bank

three-digit number

Check ✓

Add. Use mental math.

1. $236 + 312 = ?$

   ___ + ___ = ___
   ___ + ___ = ___
   ___ + ___ = ___   ___

2. $452 + 323 = ?$

   ___ + ___ = ___
   ___ + ___ = ___
   ___ + ___ = ___   ___

3. $745 + 124 = ?$

   ___ + ___ = ___
   ___ + ___ = ___
   ___ + ___ = ___   ___

Think About It   Number Sense

Find the sum of 324 and 415. Then find two different three-digit numbers with the same sum.

Practice

Solve.

$$620 + 159 = \underline{\hspace{2cm}}$$

4 $402 + 167 = \underline{\hspace{1.5cm}}$

5 $517 + 201 = \underline{\hspace{1.5cm}}$ $\qquad 263 + 415 = \underline{\hspace{1.5cm}}$

6 $\underline{\hspace{1.5cm}} = 714 + 180$ $\qquad 305 + 602 = \underline{\hspace{1.5cm}}$

7 $\underline{\hspace{1.5cm}} = 816 + 111$ $\qquad 428 + 350 = \underline{\hspace{1.5cm}}$

8 $602 + 184 = \underline{\hspace{1.5cm}}$ $\qquad 522 + 362 = \underline{\hspace{1.5cm}}$

9 $703 + 23 = \underline{\hspace{1.5cm}}$ $\qquad \underline{\hspace{1.5cm}} = 425 + 262$

10 $504 + 205 = \underline{\hspace{1.5cm}}$ $\qquad 421 + 475 = \underline{\hspace{1.5cm}}$

11 $222 + 555 = \underline{\hspace{1.5cm}}$ $\qquad \underline{\hspace{1.5cm}} = 331 + 520$

Problem Solving Algebra

Write the missing number that makes
the number sentence true.

12 $300 + 300 = 400 + \underline{200}$

13 $500 + \underline{\hspace{1.5cm}} = 400 + 400$

14 $\underline{\hspace{1.5cm}} + 300 = 200 + 700$

15 $700 + 100 = 300 + \underline{\hspace{1.5cm}}$

16 $200 + 600 = \underline{\hspace{1.5cm}} + 800$

 Home Connection Your child added three-digit numbers using
mental math. **Home Activity** Ask your child to explain how to
add 307 and 451, using mental math.

428 four hundred twenty-eight

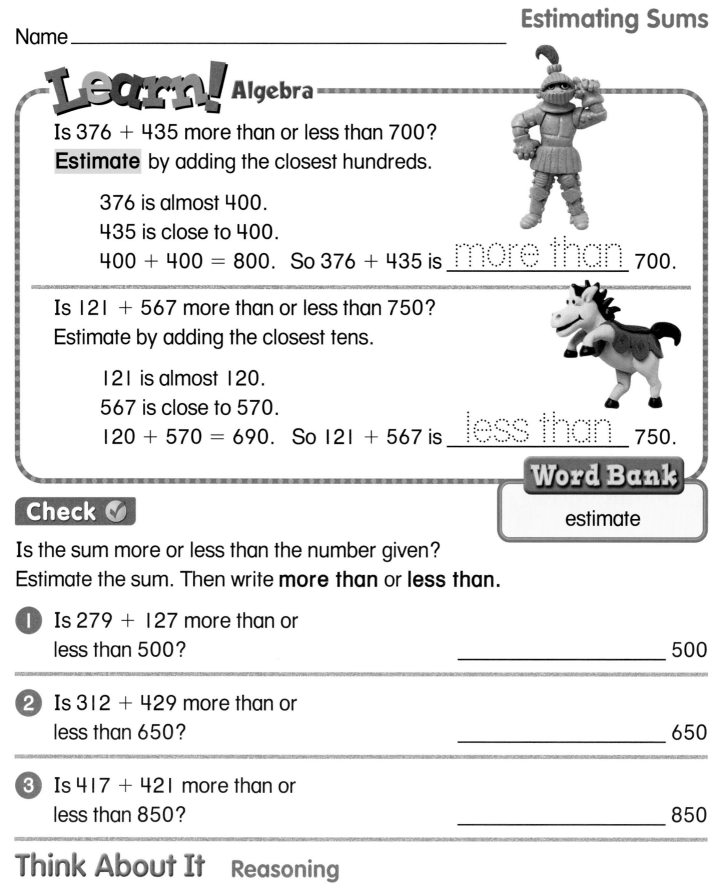

Learn! Algebra

Is 376 + 435 more than or less than 700?
Estimate by adding the closest hundreds.

376 is almost 400.
435 is close to 400.
400 + 400 = 800. So 376 + 435 is _more than_ 700.

Is 121 + 567 more than or less than 750?
Estimate by adding the closest tens.

121 is almost 120.
567 is close to 570.
120 + 570 = 690. So 121 + 567 is _less than_ 750.

Word Bank

estimate

Check ✓

Is the sum more or less than the number given?
Estimate the sum. Then write **more than** or **less than.**

1 Is 279 + 127 more than or
less than 500?   _____ 500

2 Is 312 + 429 more than or
less than 650?   _____ 650

3 Is 417 + 421 more than or
less than 850?   _____ 850

Think About It   Reasoning

How do you decide which ten or hundred a number
is closest to?

Is the sum more or less than the number?
Estimate the sum. Write **more than** or **less than.**

4) Is 531 + 284 more than or
less than 700?   _____ 700

5) Is 378 + 109 more than or
less than 550?   _____ 550

6) Is 427 + 214 more than or
less than 600?   _____ 600

7) Is 629 + 309 more than or
less than 950?   _____ 950

8) Is 430 + 299 more than or
less than 800?   _____ 800

9) Is 341 + 349 more than or
less than 700?   _____ 700

Problem Solving   Number Sense

Choose a pair of numbers to give the sum.
Use each number one time.

10) Sum of about 500   _____ and _____

11) Sum of more than 700   _____ and _____

12) Sum of less than 700   _____ and _____

275   153

431   318

422   351

Home Connection Your child estimated whether the sum of
two three-digit numbers was more or less than a given number.
Home Activity Have your child estimate whether the sum of
218 and 395 is more or less than 700.

Learn!

Second graders in the library book club read 463 books. Third graders read 275 books. How many books did they read altogether?

You can **regroup** 10 tens to make another hundred.

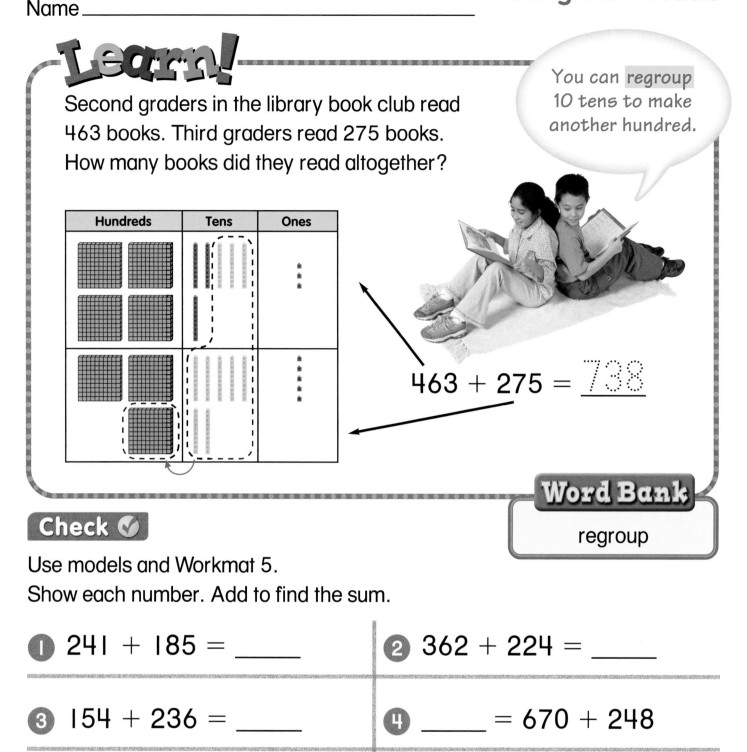

Hundreds	Tens	Ones

$463 + 275 = \underline{738}$

Check ✓

Use models and Workmat 5.
Show each number. Add to find the sum.

Word Bank

regroup

1 $241 + 185 = \underline{}$ **2** $362 + 224 = \underline{}$

3 $154 + 236 = \underline{}$ **4** $\underline{} = 670 + 248$

5 $452 + 520 = \underline{}$ **6** $\underline{} = 350 + 350$

Think About It   Number Sense

What do you do when you have 10 or more ones?
What do you do when you have 10 or more tens?

Use models and Workmat 5.
Show each number. Add to find the sum.

7 $209 + 715 = $ _____

8 $421 + 333 = $ _____

9 $125 + 250 = $ _____

10 _____ $= 362 + 298$

11 $600 + 245 = $ _____

12 _____ $= 407 + 392$

13 $591 + 309 = $ _____

14 _____ $= 777 + 222$

Problem Solving   Estimation

Circle the best estimate.

15

Class	Pages Read This Week
Ms. Collins	428
Ms. Stallings	346

About how many pages were read this week?

750   900   600

16

Class	Pages Read This Week
Mr. Grant	204
Ms. Eve	197

About how many pages were read this week?

300   400   500

17 Susie read 2 chapter books last month.
They were both 124 pages.
About how many pages did she read?

150   250   400

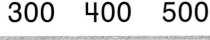

Home Connection Your child added three-digit numbers using models. **Home Activity** Ask your child to tell you how he or she solved Exercise 12, using hundreds, tens, and ones place-value models.

© Pearson Education, Inc.

Learn!

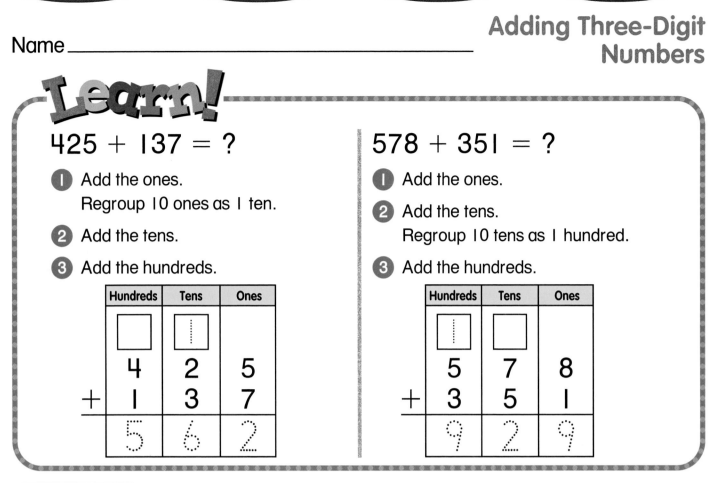

$425 + 137 = ?$

1 Add the ones.
  Regroup 10 ones as 1 ten.

2 Add the tens.

3 Add the hundreds.

Hundreds	Tens	Ones
☐	⌐	
4	2	5
+ 1	3	7
5	6	2

$578 + 351 = ?$

1 Add the ones.

2 Add the tens.
  Regroup 10 tens as 1 hundred.

3 Add the hundreds.

Hundreds	Tens	Ones
⌐	☐	
5	7	8
+ 3	5	1
9	2	9

Check ✔

Add. Use models and Workmat 5 if you need to.

1

Hundreds	Tens	Ones
☐	☐	
4	5	1
+ 2	9	6

Hundreds	Tens	Ones
☐	☐	
1	0	2
+ 3	5	1

Hundreds	Tens	Ones
☐	☐	
3	1	4
+ 5	4	8

2

Hundreds	Tens	Ones
☐	☐	
3	0	3
+ 4	5	7

Hundreds	Tens	Ones
☐	☐	
2	3	8
+ 1	1	9

Hundreds	Tens	Ones
☐	☐	
2	4	7
+ 1	6	1

Think About It   Reasoning

How do you know when to regroup?

Add. Use models and Workmat 5 if you need to.

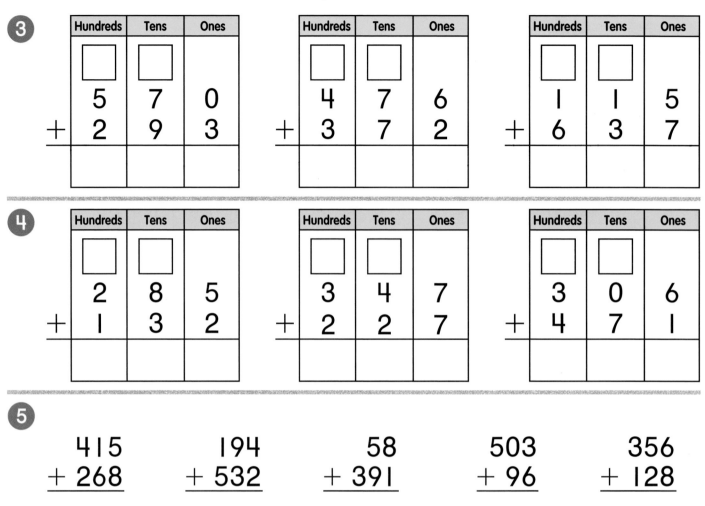

③

Hundreds	Tens	Ones
☐	☐	
5	7	0
+ 2	9	3

Hundreds	Tens	Ones
☐	☐	
4	7	6
+ 3	7	2

Hundreds	Tens	Ones
☐	☐	
1	1	5
+ 6	3	7

④

Hundreds	Tens	Ones
☐	☐	
2	8	5
+ 1	3	2

Hundreds	Tens	Ones
☐	☐	
3	4	7
+ 2	2	7

Hundreds	Tens	Ones
☐	☐	
3	0	6
+ 4	7	1

⑤

```
  415        194         58        503        356
+ 268      + 532      + 391      +  96      + 128
```

Problem Solving   Number Sense

For each problem, use each number in only one place.

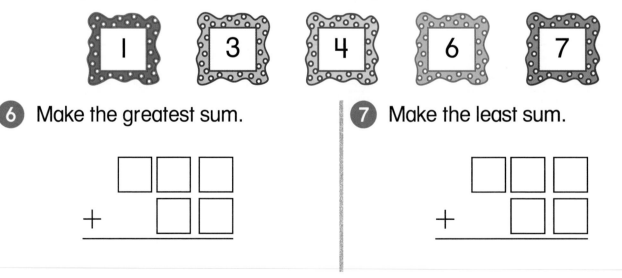

1   3   4   6   7

⑥ Make the greatest sum.

```
  ☐ ☐ ☐
+   ☐ ☐
```

⑦ Make the least sum.

```
  ☐ ☐ ☐
+   ☐ ☐
```

Home Connection Your child added three-digit numbers.
Home Activity Ask your child to show you how to add 218 and 356.

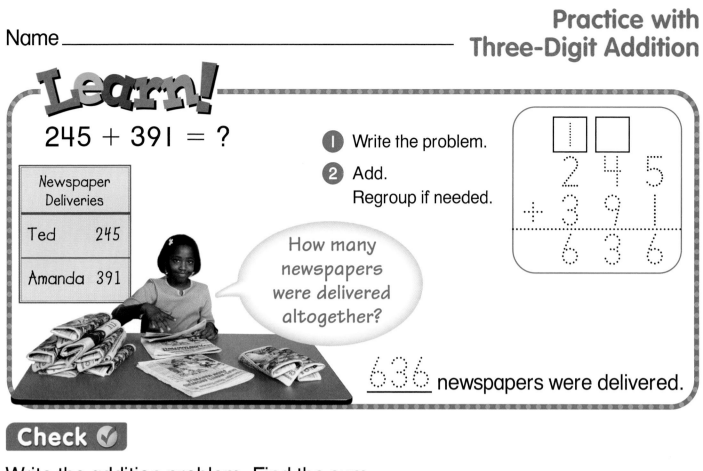

Learn!

245 + 391 = ?

Newspaper Deliveries	
Ted	245
Amanda	391

How many newspapers were delivered altogether?

1. Write the problem.
2. Add. Regroup if needed.

```
  1 1
  2 4 5
+ 3 9 1
-------
  6 3 6
```

636 newspapers were delivered.

Check ✓

Write the addition problem. Find the sum.

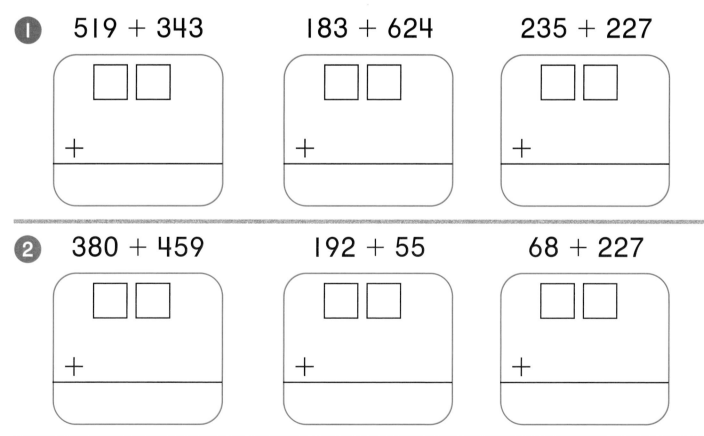

1 519 + 343

183 + 624

235 + 227

2 380 + 459

192 + 55

68 + 227

Think About It   Number Sense

How do you find the sum of 251, 102, and 345?

Write the addition problem. Find the sum.

3 620 + 289

$$
\begin{array}{r}
\overset{1}{6}20 \\
+\ 289 \\
\hline
909
\end{array}
$$

491 + 243

738 + 55

4 269 + 400

175 + 53

97 + 342

5 205 + 715

263 + 91

556 + 362

Problem Solving   Number Sense

Solve the number riddle.

6 When I am added to 249, the sum is 659. What number am I? _____

7 When I am added to 382, the sum is 597. What number am I? _____

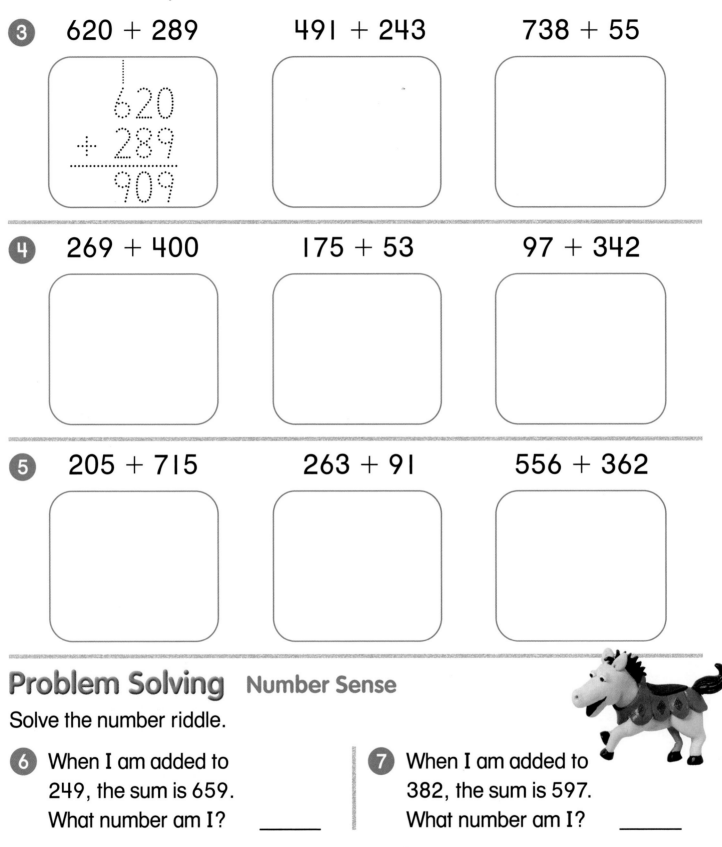

Home Connection Your child wrote and practiced adding three-digit numbers. **Home Activity** Have your child show you how he or she can add 413 and 369.

Name _____

Understand Graphic Sources: Graphs

1 Look at the chalkboard and check the math.
Circle the problems that have mistakes.

Red Riding Hood

100	212	540
+ 600	+ 102	+ 23
800	314	593

Big Bad Wolf

622	732	569
+ 345	+ 111	+ 430
967	843	999

Grandma

267	623	400
+ 120	+ 105	+ 100
387	739	500

2 Look at the graph. Color a square
for each problem the character got **right**.

Problems Answered Correctly			
Little Red Riding Hood			
The Big Bad Wolf			
Grandma			

3 Who got the most right? _____

4 Who got the fewest right? _____

Think About It Reasoning

Why is a graph helpful?

Little Red Riding Hood, the Big Bad Wolf, and Grandma
are characters in a storybook.

5 Make a graph about books.
Ask 6 classmates which one of the following
books they would most like to read.
Write the person's name in a box above that book.
Start with your own name!

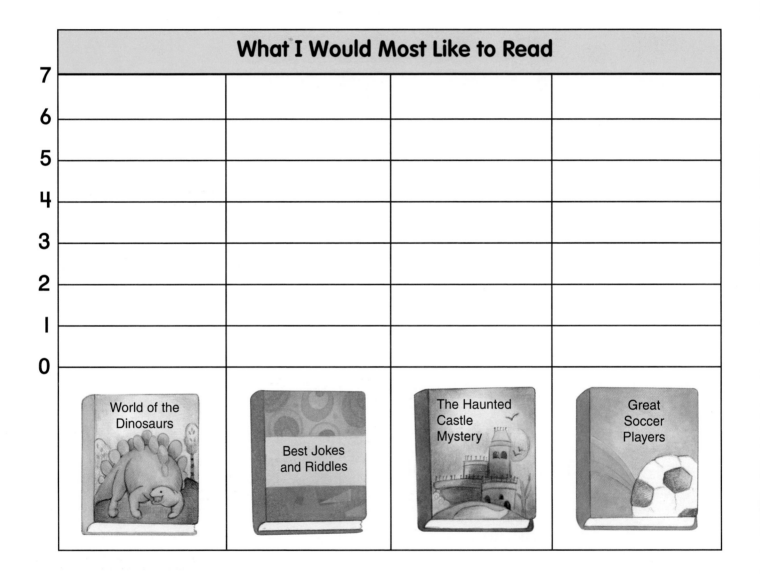

What I Would Most Like to Read

7
6
5
4
3
2
1
0

World of the Dinosaurs

Best Jokes and Riddles

The Haunted Castle Mystery

Great Soccer Players

6 Which book did the most children want to read?

_____

Home Connection Your child used graphs to organize information.
Home Activity Create a graph showing each family member's favorite
meal (out of a choice of 3 or 4). If your family is small, you might help
your child call or e-mail a few relatives to solicit their choices.

Did the second grade sell more tickets to the school carnival than the first grade sold?

Classroom 2A sold 150 tickets.
Classroom 2B sold 250 tickets.

Read and Understand

You need to find out how many tickets the second grade sold.

Plan and Solve

First, add the number of tickets Classrooms 2A and 2B sold.

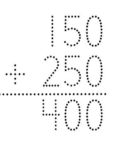

$$150 + 250 = 400$$

400 ____ tickets

Then, add this information to the graph.

The second grade sold more tickets than the first grade.

Look Back and Check

How do you know just by looking at the graph that the second grade sold more tickets?

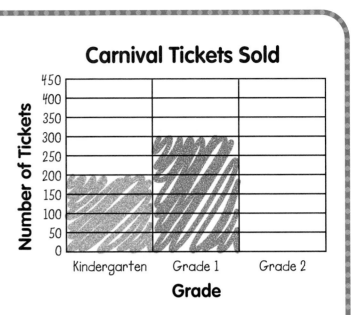

Carnival Tickets Sold

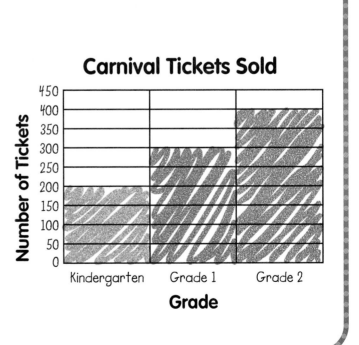

Carnival Tickets Sold

Think About It Number Sense

Write the number of tickets sold in order from greatest to least.

Practice

Use the chart to answer the questions.

People at the Carnival			
	Friday	Saturday	Sunday
Morning	100	350	250
Afternoon	150	450	400

1 How many people came to the carnival on Friday?

_____ people

2 How many came on Saturday?

_____ people

3 How many attended on Sunday?

_____ people

4 Use your answers from Exercises 1–3 to complete the graph. Show how many people came to the carnival each day.

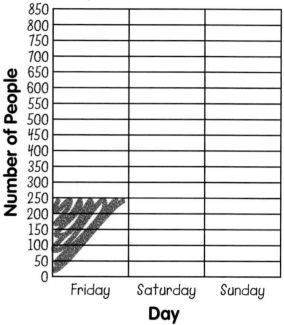

People at the Carnival

Problem Solving   Writing in Math

5 Look at the graph. Tell which day the greatest number of people came to the carnival and which day the least number of people came.

_____

_____

6 Look at the graph and compare Saturday with Sunday. How many more people needed to come to the carnival on Sunday to equal the number of people who came on Saturday?

_____ more people

Home Connection Your child made graphs to solve problems.
Home Activity Ask your child to use the graph to determine how many people in all came to the carnival on Friday and Sunday.

440   four hundred forty

Name _____

Add. Use mental math.

1 $651 + 238 =$ ____ $402 + 457 =$ ____

2 $115 + 563 =$ ____   ____ $= 710 + 264$

Is the sum more than or less than the number given?
Write **more than** or **less than.**

3 Is $382 + 107$ more than
or less than 600?   _____ 600

Use models and Workmat 5.
Show each number. Add to find the sum.

4 $183 + 725 =$ ____   **5** $216 + 357 =$ ____

Add. Use models and Workmat 5
if you need to.

6

Hundreds	Tens	Ones
□	□	
1	4	4
+ 2	9	0

Write the addition problem.
Find the sum.

7 $538 + 426$

Complete the graph.

8 Color the graph to show
that there are 150 books
about animals.

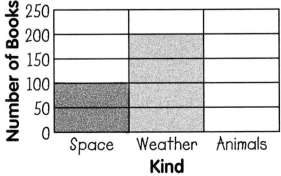

Kinds of Books

Name _____

Add. Use mental math or cubes.

1

49 and

49 + 17 = ____

Ⓐ 56
Ⓑ 67
Ⓒ 87
Ⓓ 66

2

31 and

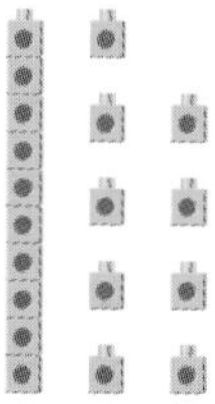

31 + 19 = ____

Ⓐ 50
Ⓑ 40
Ⓒ 49
Ⓓ 79

Count on to find the total amount.

3

Ⓐ 62¢
Ⓑ 72¢
Ⓒ 47¢
Ⓓ 80¢

Use the graph to answer the question.

4 How many children wear mittens?

8   7   22   14
Ⓐ   Ⓑ   Ⓒ   Ⓓ

Favorite Hand Warmers

Each 𝟃 = 2 children.

Mark the one that weighs the most.

5

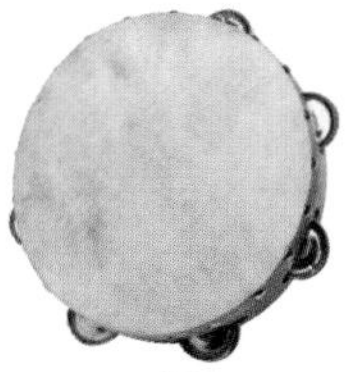

Ⓐ   Ⓑ   Ⓒ   Ⓓ

Writing in Math

6 Count on to solve the problem.   200 + ____ = 1,000
Write a story using the number sentence.

_____

_____

_____

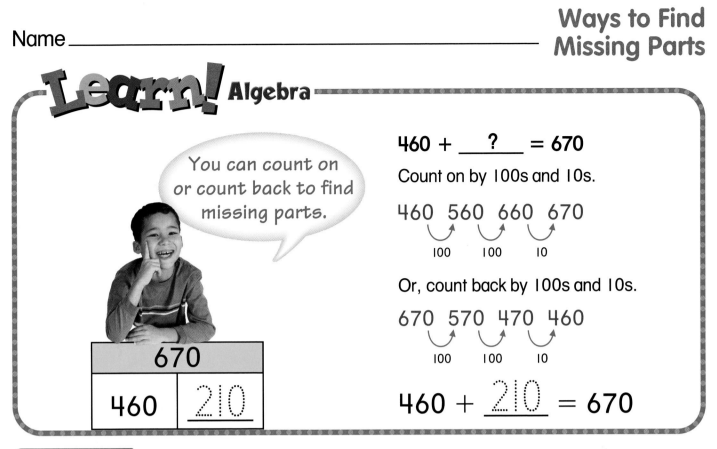

You can count on or count back to find missing parts.

$460 + \underline{\quad ? \quad} = 670$

Count on by 100s and 10s.

460 560 660 670
     100 100   10

Or, count back by 100s and 10s.

670 570 470 460
     100 100   10

$460 + \underline{210} = 670$

670	
460	210

Check ✓

Count on or count back to find the missing part.
Write the number.

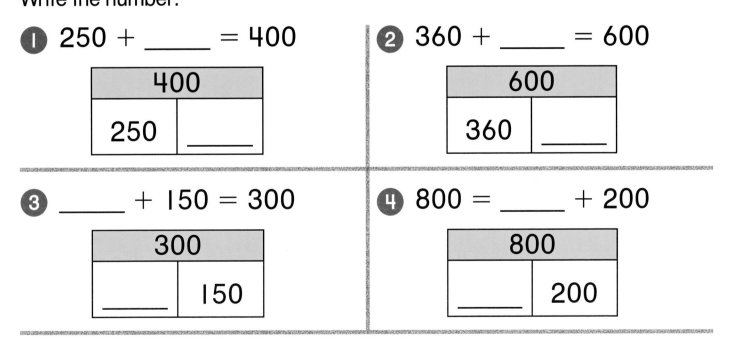

1 $250 + \underline{\quad\quad} = 400$

400	
250	_____

2 $360 + \underline{\quad\quad} = 600$

600	
360	_____

3 $\underline{\quad\quad} + 150 = 300$

300	
_____	150

4 $800 = \underline{\quad\quad} + 200$

800	
_____	200

Think About It   Number Sense

How are $4 + 3 = 7$, $40 + 30 = 70$, and $400 + 300 = 700$
the same and how are they different?

Count on or count back to find the missing part.

⑤ $120 + \underline{\hspace{1cm}} = 500$

⑥ $340 + \underline{\hspace{1cm}} = 400$

⑦ $410 + \underline{\hspace{1cm}} = 600$

⑧ $200 = 80 + \underline{\hspace{1cm}}$

⑨ $430 + \underline{\hspace{1cm}} = 800$

⑩ $300 = \underline{\hspace{1cm}} + 160$

⑪ $700 = \underline{\hspace{1cm}} + 250$

⑫ $\underline{\hspace{1cm}} + 450 = 900$

⑬ $500 = 150 + \underline{\hspace{1cm}}$

⑭ $290 + \underline{\hspace{1cm}} = 800$

Problem Solving Algebra

⑮ Which side of the scale is lighter, the left side or the right side?

_____

⑯ How many pounds should you add to the lighter side to balance the scale?

_____

⑰ Explain how $160 + \underline{\hspace{0.5cm}?\hspace{0.5cm}} = 400$ is like the picture.

_____

_____

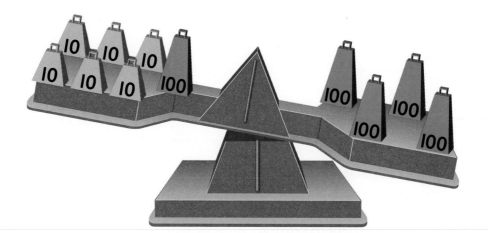

Home Connection Your child counted on or counted back to find the missing part. **Home Activity** Have your child count on or count back to find the missing part: $250 + \underline{\hspace{1cm}} = 700$. The blank line stands for the amount needed to balance both sides.

Name_____

Learn! Algebra

Which two numbers have a difference of about 400? $705 - 193$ or $582 - 217$

Estimate by subtracting the closest hundreds.

$700 - 200 = 500$ $600 - 200 = 400$

$582 - 217$ is about 400.

582 is close to 600.
217 is about 200.

705 is close to 700.
193 is about 200.

Check ✓

Circle the problem that matches the estimate.

1 about 100 $(319 - 187)$ or $875 - 221$

2 about 500 $710 - 218$ or $602 - 369$

3 about 300 $494 - 302$ or $842 - 531$

Think About It   Number Sense

How would you decide which two numbers have a difference of about 150? $457 - 301$ or $792 - 689$

Circle the problem that matches the estimate.

4 about 200 | $487 - 230$ or $472 - 310$

5 about 600 | $938 - 289$ or $694 - 480$

6 about 300 | $923 - 640$ or $870 - 307$

7 about 200 | $546 - 210$ or $583 - 370$

8 about 100 | $385 - 270$ or $672 - 301$

9 about 500 | $831 - 170$ or $879 - 360$

Problem Solving   Number Sense

Choose a pair of numbers to give the sum or difference.
Use each number one time.

10 Sum of about 500 _____ and _____

11 Difference of about 200 _____ and _____

12 Difference of less than 100 _____ and _____

351   728

490   350

320   148

Home Connection Your child estimated to decide which 2 three-digit numbers had a given difference. **Home Activity** Ask your child to estimate $689 - 207$.

Learn!

$427 - 183 =$ ___?___

Show 427 with models.

Take away 183 from 427.
First, take away 3 ones.

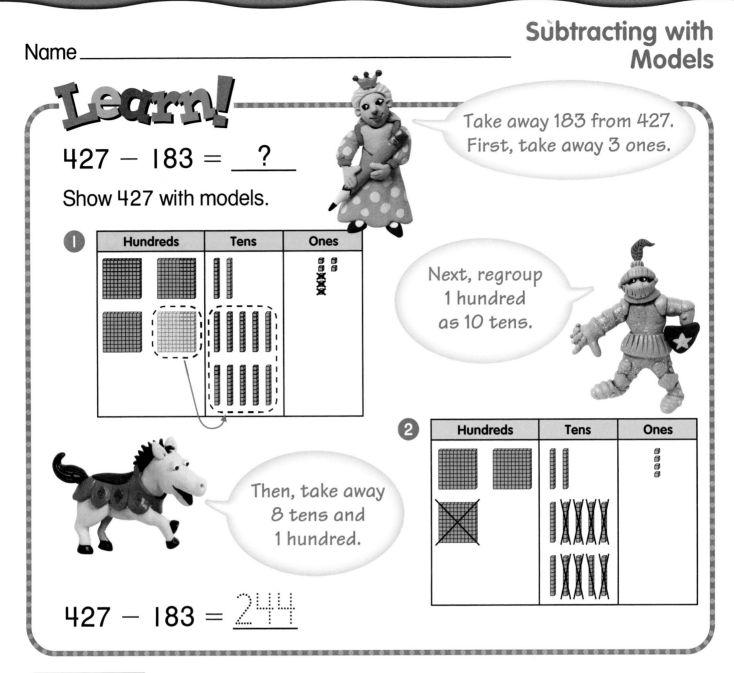

Next, regroup
1 hundred
as 10 tens.

Then, take away
8 tens and
1 hundred.

$427 - 183 = \underline{244}$

Check ✓

Use models and Workmat 5.
Subtract to find the difference.

1 $536 - 174 = \underline{362}$

2 $825 - 433 = $ _____

3 $642 - 472 = $ _____

4 _____ $= 486 - 275$

5 _____ $= 780 - 536$

6 $632 - 317 = $ _____

Think About It   Number Sense

When you are subtracting and you need more tens,
what do you do?

Subtract. Use models and Workmat 5.

7 $508 - 201 =$ _____

8 $729 - 165 =$ _____

9 $413 - 320 =$ _____

10 _____ $= 914 - 652$

11 $520 - 304 =$ _____

12 _____ $= 693 - 537$

13 _____ $= 954 - 245$

14 $881 - 510 =$ _____

15 $391 - 241 =$ _____

16 _____ $= 632 - 321$

Problem Solving   Reasoning

17 Write the name of each person with his or her total votes.

Vote for Mayor

Mrs. Jones   Mr. Hare   Ms. Taylor   Mr. Niles

• Mr. Niles had about 200 more votes than Mrs. Jones.

• Ms. Taylor had the most votes.

• Mr. Hare had 100 fewer votes than Mrs. Jones.

_____   _____   _____   _____
610 votes   500 votes   305 votes   205 votes

Home Connection Your child used models to subtract three-digit numbers. **Home Activity** Have your child explain how to subtract 358 from 675.

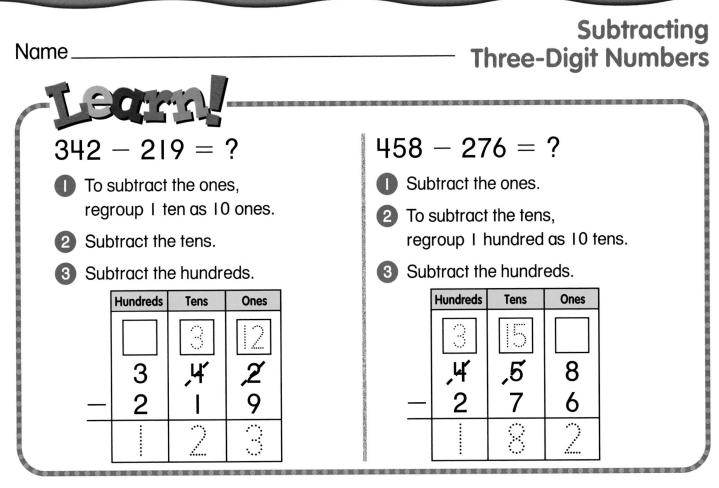

Learn!

342 − 219 = ?

1. To subtract the ones, regroup 1 ten as 10 ones.
2. Subtract the tens.
3. Subtract the hundreds.

Hundreds	Tens	Ones
	3	12
3	4	2
− 2	1	9
1	2	3

458 − 276 = ?

1. Subtract the ones.
2. To subtract the tens, regroup 1 hundred as 10 tens.
3. Subtract the hundreds.

Hundreds	Tens	Ones
3	15	
4	5	8
− 2	7	6
1	8	2

Check ✓

Subtract. Use models and Workmat 5 if you need to.

1

Hundreds	Tens	Ones
7	3	6
− 3	7	2

Hundreds	Tens	Ones
5	6	0
− 1	2	7

Hundreds	Tens	Ones
2	5	7
− 1	0	4

2

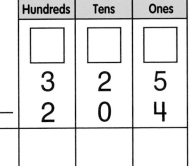

Hundreds	Tens	Ones
4	1	8
− 1	5	2

Hundreds	Tens	Ones
3	2	5
− 2	0	4

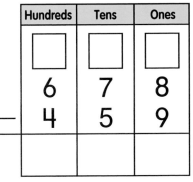

Hundreds	Tens	Ones
6	7	8
− 4	5	9

Think About It   Reasoning

Will you regroup to solve 597 − 452? Why or why not?

Subtract. Use models and Workmat 5 if you need to.

3

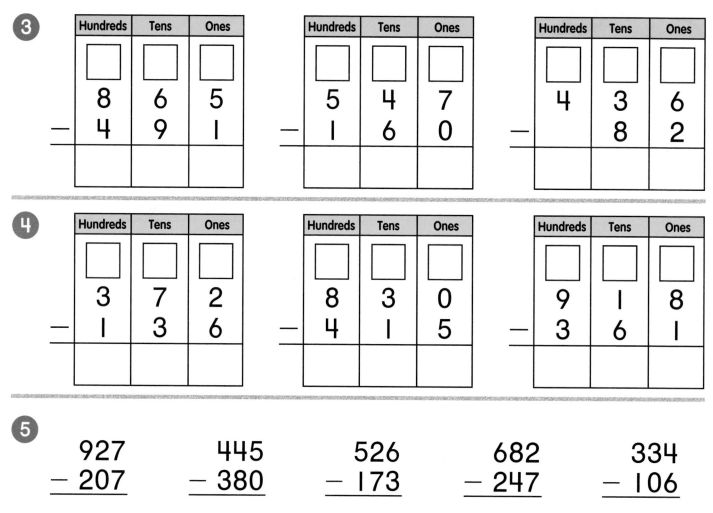

Hundreds	Tens	Ones
☐	☐	☐
8	6	5
− 4	9	1

Hundreds	Tens	Ones
☐	☐	☐
5	4	7
− 1	6	0

Hundreds	Tens	Ones
☐	☐	☐
4	3	6
−	8	2

4

Hundreds	Tens	Ones
☐	☐	☐
3	7	2
− 1	3	6

Hundreds	Tens	Ones
☐	☐	☐
8	3	0
− 4	1	5

Hundreds	Tens	Ones
☐	☐	☐
9	1	8
− 3	6	1

5

$$927 - 207$$ $$445 - 380$$ $$526 - 173$$ $$682 - 247$$ $$334 - 106$$

Problem Solving   Visual Thinking

- The sum of each row is at the end of that row.
- The sum of each column is at the bottom of that column.
- Each square stands for the same number.
- Each circle stands for the same number.

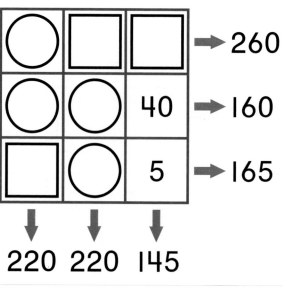

○	☐	☐	→ 260
○	○	40	→ 160
☐	○	5	→ 165

220 220 145

6 What number is ☐ ? _____

7 What number is ○ ? _____

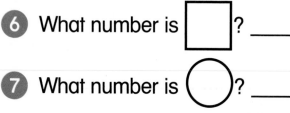

Home Connection Your child subtracted three-digit numbers.
Home Activity Have your child explain how to solve 758 − 319.

Learn!

Lucy counted 716 footsteps around the playground.
Marcus counted 583 footsteps.
How many more footsteps did Lucy count?

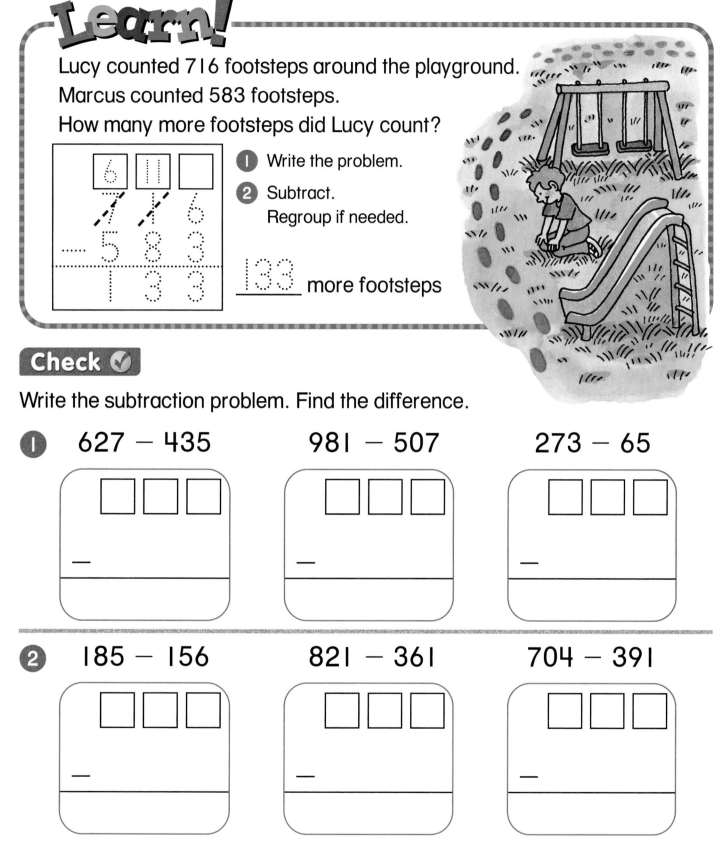

$$
\begin{array}{r}
\overset{6}{\cancel{7}}\ \overset{11}{\cancel{1}}\ 6 \\
-\ 5\ 8\ 3 \\
\hline
1\ 3\ 3
\end{array}
$$

1 Write the problem.

2 Subtract.
Regroup if needed.

__133__ more footsteps

Check ✓

Write the subtraction problem. Find the difference.

1   627 − 435   981 − 507   273 − 65

2   185 − 156   821 − 361   704 − 391

Think About It   Reasoning

How do you think knowing that 125 + 150 = 275
can help you solve 275 − 150 = ?

Write the subtraction problem. Find the difference.

3 749 − 182

```
    6 14
  7̸ 4̸ 9
−   1 8 2
─────────
    5 6 7
```

463 − 250

382 − 57

4 529 − 109

235 − 140

327 − 309

5 872 − 757

999 − 888

136 − 73

Problem Solving Estimation

Estimate each sum or difference.
Draw a line to match.

Estimate

6 391 − 205

120 + 675

593 − 88

417 + 498

500

900

200

800

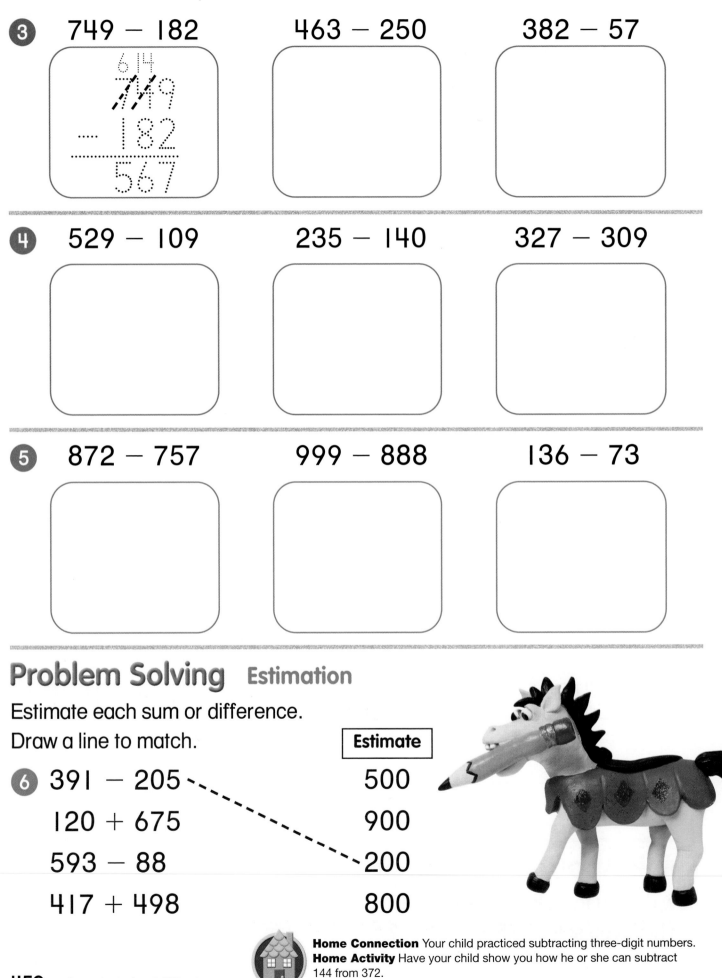

Home Connection Your child practiced subtracting three-digit numbers.
Home Activity Have your child show you how he or she can subtract
144 from 372.

Exact Answer or Estimate?

Learn!

Alma saw this sign in the gym:

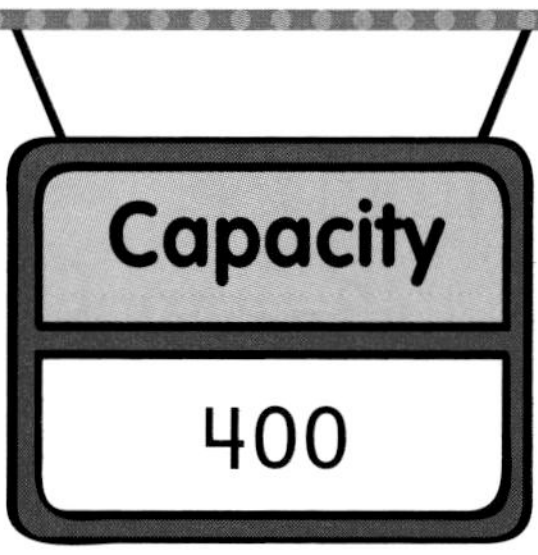

Capacity

400

She wondered if all of the first grade and second grade children could fit.

Does she need an exact answer?
Can she estimate?

Since she is only wondering, she can estimate.

Each number is less than 200. So 180 + 171 is less than 400.

Grade	Number of Children
1	180
2	171

Check ✓

Circle **estimate** or **exact answer.** Answer the question.

1. The second grade children collected 152 food labels in January. They collected 194 food labels in February. They need 350 labels. Do they have enough?

   estimate   exact answer

   _____

Think About It   Reasoning

How do you know when to solve for an exact answer, and when to estimate?

Circle **estimate** or **exact answer.**
Answer the questions.

2️⃣ Cory has 112 stamps from the
United States. He has 139 stamps
from other countries. He can fit
275 stamps in a book. Will all of
the stamps fit?

estimate   exact answer

©1990 USPS

_____

3️⃣ There are 624 children at Smith
School. About 400 eat school
lunch. About how many children
do not eat the school lunch?

estimate   exact answer

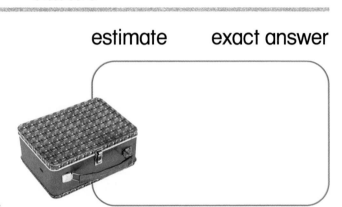

_____

4️⃣ Jon's uncle drove his truck
498 miles one day and
375 miles the next day.
About how many miles did he
drive in two days?

estimate   exact answer

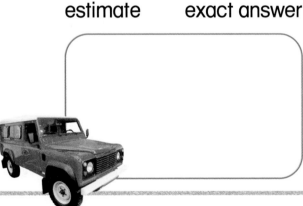

_____

Problem Solving Writing in Math

5️⃣ Write a math problem in which only an estimate
is needed for the answer.

_____

_____

_____

Home Connection Your child distinguished between problems
needing an exact answer and problems needing only an estimate.
Home Activity Ask your child to explain what an estimate is.

Dorling Kindersley

JUNGLE
Discover life in the tropical rain forest — from the exotic birds in the treetops to the millions of insects on the forest floor

Do You Know...
that a tarantula has 8 legs? And if a leg is lost, it will grow back in about 7 years!

1 This tree frog climbed 120 feet down to the forest floor. Later, it climbed 140 feet back up into a tree. How many feet did it climb altogether?

_____ feet

2 This Blue-and-yellow Macaw flew to a branch that was 102 feet high. Then it flew 100 feet higher than that. How high did it fly in all?

_____ feet

3 Leaf cutter ants live in underground nests. They travel high into the trees to gather leaves. A group of leaf cutter ants left their nest at 8:00 A.M. The ants started crawling up a tall tree 2 hours later. What time was it when the ants started crawling?

_____ : _____ A.M.

4 A toucan perched on a branch that was 95 feet high.
It flew 20 feet higher to another branch.
Then it flew 30 feet higher to a third branch.
How high was the third branch?

_____ feet

5 A male gorilla can weigh up to 600 pounds.
A female gorilla can weigh up to 300 pounds.
How many more pounds can a male weigh?

_____ more pounds

Fun Fact!

The flying tree snake can flatten its body and glide through the air. It can travel distances up to 165 feet!

6 **Writing in Math**

Journal

Write an addition story about flying tree snakes. Use three-digit numbers.

Home Connection Your child learned to solve problems by applying his or her math skills. **Home Activity** Talk to your child about how he or she solved the problems on these two pages.

Add on to find the missing part.
Write the number.

1 170 + _____ = 440

440	
170	_____

Count on or count back to find the
missing part. Write the number.

2 90 + _____ = 400

3 500 = _____ + 130

Subtract. Use models and
Workmat 5 if you need to.

4

Hundreds	Tens	Ones
☐	☐	☐
8	1	7
− 2	5	2

Write the subtraction problem.
Find the difference.

5   964 − 73

Circle the problem that matches the estimate.

6

about 250   564 − 320   or   714 − 193

Circle **estimate** or **exact answer.**
Answer the question.

7 For the school bake sale, the third grade
baked 289 cookies. The first grade baked
112 cookies. 500 cookies are needed
for the sale. Are there enough?

_____

estimate   exact answer

Name_____

Add to find the total amount.

1   71¢
      + 19¢

Ⓐ 90
Ⓑ 80¢
Ⓒ 89
Ⓓ 90¢

2   36¢
      + 25¢

Ⓐ 51¢
Ⓑ 61¢
Ⓒ 62¢
Ⓓ 61

Subtract. Regroup if you need to.

3

Tens	Ones
8	4
−	7

Ⓐ 91
Ⓑ 77
Ⓒ 89
Ⓓ 87

4

Tens	Ones
6	9
−	5

Ⓐ 64
Ⓑ 74
Ⓒ 63
Ⓓ 614

Mark the time that matches the clock face.

5

Ⓐ 1:20
Ⓑ 4:05
Ⓒ 4:20
Ⓓ 9:00

6

Ⓐ 9:30
Ⓑ 9:00
Ⓒ 8:00
Ⓓ 8:30

Mark the length of the marker.

7

1 2 3 4 5 6 7 8 9 10 11 12 13

CENTIMETERS

Ⓐ 13 cm
Ⓑ 12 cm
Ⓒ 14 cm
Ⓓ 11 cm

8 **Writing in Math**

Write a subtraction story for this problem: **57 − 24**

_____

_____

Adding and Subtracting Dollars and Cents

Tad's sister Sara earned $5.75 and
$2.40 babysitting. She spent $3.30.

How much did Sara earn?   How much does she have now?

$5.75   575¢   815¢ $8.15
+ $2.40   + 240¢   − 330¢   − $3.30
$8.15 $4.85

Add or subtract.

1 $1.45 $1.45 $7.86 $2.70 $5.67
       + $2.00   + $2.19   − $2.00   + $4.30   − $1.62

2 $3.64 $2.94 $4.65 $6.09 $0.38
       + $3.18   − $2.37   + $0.93   − $4.89   + $1.91

3 $5.87 $5.87 $5.87 $5.87 $5.87
       − $1.07   − $2.39   − $2.90   − $3.48   − $4.91

Writing in Math

4 Before you subtract in Exercise 3, what do you
know about your answers? Why?

Home Connection Your child added and subtracted
amounts of money. **Home Activity** Ask your child to
add $2.89 to $4.50 and then subtract $1.07 from $4.50.

Chapter 11   four hundred fifty-nine   **459**

Name_____

Add and Subtract Three-Digit Numbers Using a Calculator

You can use a calculator to add and subtract three-digit numbers.

Solve each problem. Use your calculator and the numbers in the box.
Press ON/C each time you begin.

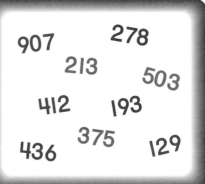

907   278
  213   503
412   193
436   375   129

1 Find the sum of all of the numbers with a 4 in the hundreds place.

848

2 Subtract the least number from the greatest number.

_____

3 Find the sum of all of the numbers with a 7 in the tens place.

_____

Solve each problem. Do **not** use your calculator for Exercise 4. Use your calculator for Exercise 5.

4 **Estimate** the sum of all of the numbers with a 3 in the ones place.

_____

5 Find the exact sum of all the numbers with a 3 in the ones place.

_____

Think About It   Number Sense

In Exercises 4 and 5, how would you use a calculator to find the difference between your estimated sum and the actual sum?

Home Connection Your child used a calculator to add and subtract three-digit numbers. **Home Activity** Ask your child to explain how he or she used a calculator to find the sum in Exercise 3.

Name _____

 Understand the Question

If you turn a question into a statement, it can help you solve a math problem.

Test-Taking Strategies

Understand the Question

Get Information for the Answer

Plan How to Find the Answer

Make Smart Choices

Use Writing in Math

1 On Friday, 243 people attended the school play. On Saturday, 318 people attended the school play. How many people in all attended the school play?

Ⓐ 561 people   Ⓒ 574 people

Ⓑ 575 people   Ⓓ 675 people

First, change the question into a statement:

I need to find how many people in all attended the school play.

Then add to find the answer.

Finally, fill in the answer bubble.

Your Turn

Change the question into a statement. Solve the problem. Fill in the answer bubble.

2 How many more people attended the play on Saturday than on Friday?

Ⓐ 65 more people   Ⓒ 75 more people

Ⓑ 165 more people   Ⓓ 175 more people

Let me see...

 Home Connection Your child prepared for standardized tests by turning a question into a statement to help solve a problem.
Home Activity Ask your child to tell you the statement he or she used to help solve Exercise 2.

Name _____

Discover Math in Your World

Big, Bigger, Biggest!

The pyramids in Egypt have been standing for nearly 5,000 years. The biggest one is the **Great Pyramid.** Two smaller ones are named **Menkaure** and **Khafre.** Use addition and subtraction to learn more about these world-famous pyramids.

Powerful Pyramids

1 Menkaure is 216 feet tall.
Khafre is 230 feet taller than that.
How tall is Khafre?

_____ feet tall

2 A long time ago, The Great Pyramid was 481 feet tall. Today it is about 452 feet tall.
How many feet shorter is the Great Pyramid now?

About _____ feet shorter

3 The base of each pyramid is a square. One side of Menkaure is 346 feet long. One side of the Great Pyramid is 756 feet long. Find the difference between these two lengths.

_____ feet

Take It to the NET
Video and Activities
www.scottforesman.com

Home Connection Your child solved problems about the pyramids in Egypt by adding and subtracting. **Home Activity** Ask your child to estimate whether the perimeter of Menkaure is more than or less than 1,000 feet. *(More than 1,000 feet)*

Goldilocks and the Three Bears Part 2: The Untold Story

Written by Gene Howard   Illustrated by Maryn Roos

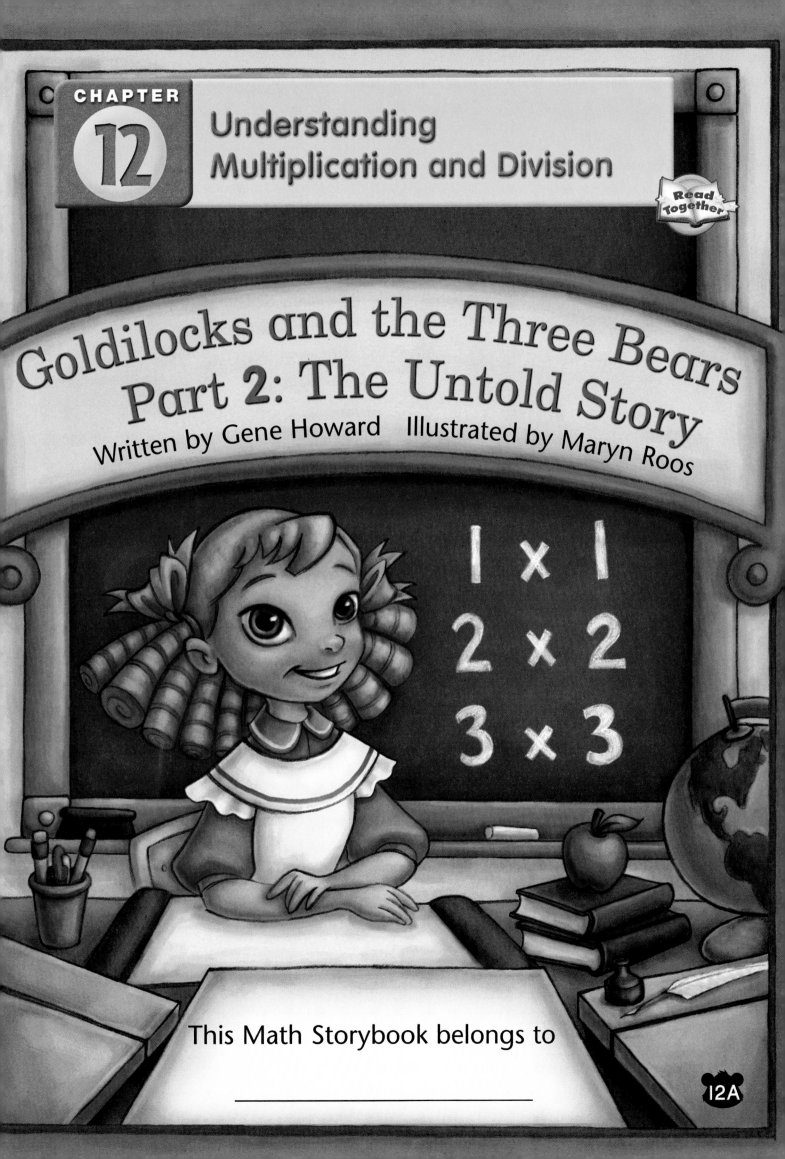

$$1 \times 1$$
$$2 \times 2$$
$$3 \times 3$$

This Math Storybook belongs to

_____

Most people know **Part I** of the Goldilocks story.

How she ate all of Baby Bear's porridge.
How she broke his chair.
How she fell asleep on his bed.

And how when Baby Bear and his mom and dad found her there, she had to run all the way back home.

Well, that was not the end of the story.

When Goldilocks got home,
her mom found out what she had done.
And her mom said that she had to do
something nice for the Bear family
to make up for all the trouble she had caused them.

So Goldilocks, who was very good at math, said,
"I know! I will teach Baby Bear and his cousins,
Rodney and Alexis, how to do multiplication!"

"I am a good little girl, and I will be an
excellent teacher," she said.

2 times 2 is always 4. Always that and never more.
2 2×2=4
×2
4
This is so COOL!
I get it! I get it! If you say "2 times 2," it's like saying "2 twos."
And 2 twos is … 4. 2 plus 2 is 4. And 2 times 2 is 4.

In her own house,
and in her own bed,
this time.

Goldilocks decided that
she needed to take a nap.

In her own house,
and in her own bed,
this time.

Home-School Connection

Dear Family,

Today my class started Chapter 12, **Understanding Multiplication and Division.** I will learn how to understand these operations and how to write multiplication and division sentences. Here are some of the math words I will be learning and some things we can do to help me with my math.

Love,

_____

Math Activity to Do at Home

Use bottle caps or other small objects to build equal groups—for example, 3 groups of 3 bottle caps each. Add them: 3 + 3 + 3 = 9. Skip count them: 3, 6, 9. Combine the equal groups into one larger group. Then separate the larger group into smaller, equal groups again.

Books to Read Together

Reading math stories reinforces concepts. Look for these titles in your local library:

What Comes in 2's, 3's, & 4's?
By Suzanne Aker
(Simon & Schuster, 1992)

Where the Sidewalk Ends: 25th Anniversary Edition
By Shel Silverstein
(HarperCollins, 2000)

Take It to the NET
More Activities
www.scottforesman.com

My New Math Words

multiply When two numbers are multiplied, the answer is called the product.

$3 \times 3 = 9$ ⟵ **product**

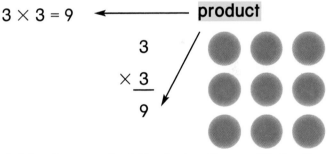

$$\begin{array}{r} 3 \\ \times\ 3 \\ \hline 9 \end{array}$$

A 3-by-3 array that illustrates the multiplication fact $3 \times 3 = 9$

divide When one number is divided into another number, the answer is called the quotient.

$9 \div 3 = 3$

quotient

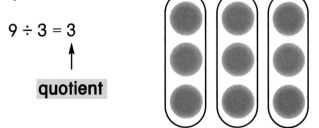

9 divided into 3 equal groups

Name _____

Multiplication Pathways

What You Need

I dot cube 🎲
5 small game markers for
each player ⚪ ⚫

How to Play

1. Play with a partner. Place your markers on START.

2. Toss the cube. Place a marker on the cottage that shows **that number being multiplied by itself.**

3. Read the problem on the cottage. Count the dots to find the answer.

4. Take turns. The first player to cover all five cottages gets to take a nap in the last one!

5. BONUS ACTIVITY: On a separate sheet of paper, draw pictures that show 6×6, 7×7, 8×8, 9×9, and 10×10.

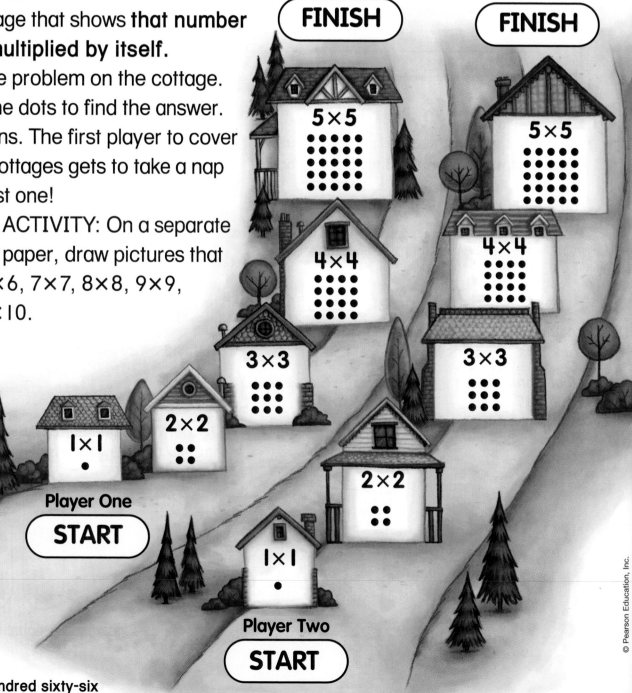

Name _____

Learn! Algebra

You can skip count to find how many basketballs there are in all.

Count by 2s to find how many in all.
2, 4, 6, 8.

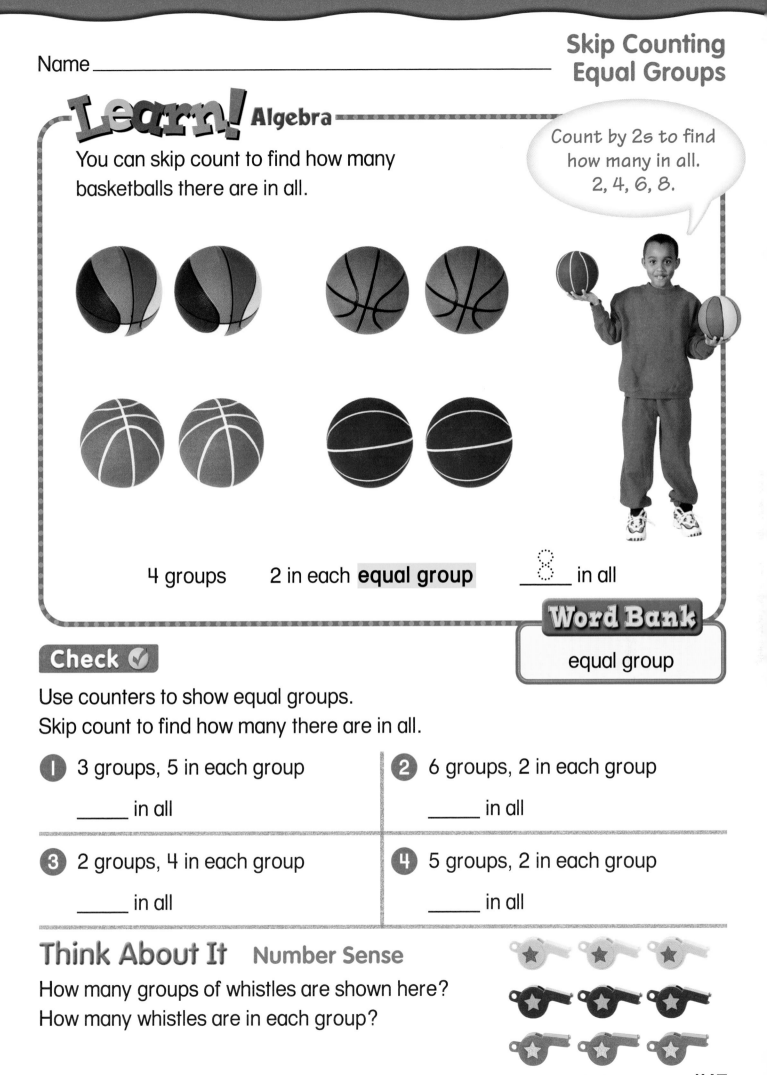

4 groups   2 in each **equal group**   ____ in all

Word Bank

equal group

Check ✓

Use counters to show equal groups.
Skip count to find how many there are in all.

1 3 groups, 5 in each group

_____ in all

2 6 groups, 2 in each group

_____ in all

3 2 groups, 4 in each group

_____ in all

4 5 groups, 2 in each group

_____ in all

Think About It   Number Sense

How many groups of whistles are shown here?
How many whistles are in each group?

Draw to show equal groups. Skip count to find
how many there are in all. Use counters if you need to.

5 3 groups, 3 in each group

_____ in all

6 4 groups, 1 in each group

_____ in all

7 5 groups, 2 in each group

_____ in all

8 3 groups, 5 in each group

_____ in all

Problem Solving Writing in Math

Make up your own equal groups.
Skip count to find how many in all.

9 _____ groups,

_____ in each group

_____ in all

10 _____ groups,

_____ in each group

_____ in all

Learn! Algebra

When you have equal groups, you can add or **multiply** to find how many objects there are in all.

There are 3 groups of 4.

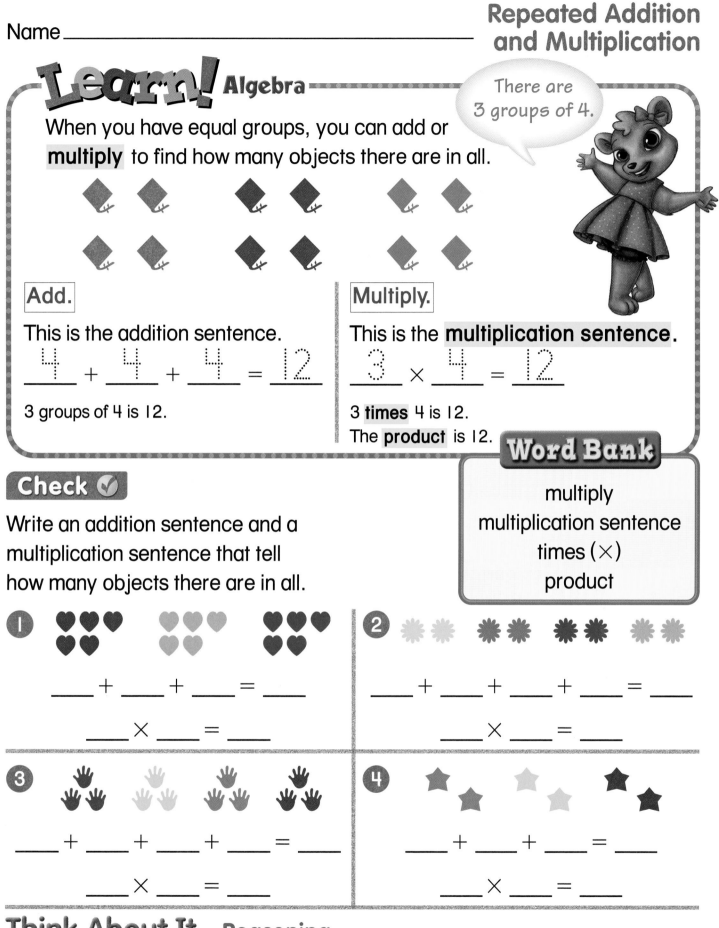

Add.

This is the addition sentence.

___4___ + ___4___ + ___4___ = ___12___

3 groups of 4 is 12.

Multiply.

This is the **multiplication sentence**.

___3___ × ___4___ = ___12___

3 **times** 4 is 12.
The **product** is 12.

Word Bank

multiply
multiplication sentence
times (×)
product

Check ✓

Write an addition sentence and a multiplication sentence that tell how many objects there are in all.

❶
___ + ___ + ___ = ___

___ × ___ = ___

❷
___ + ___ + ___ + ___ = ___

___ × ___ = ___

❸
___ + ___ + ___ + ___ = ___

___ × ___ = ___

❹
___ + ___ + ___ = ___

___ × ___ = ___

Think About It   Reasoning

Can you write a multiplication sentence for all three of these groups? Why or why not?

Write an addition sentence and a multiplication sentence
that tell how many there are in all.

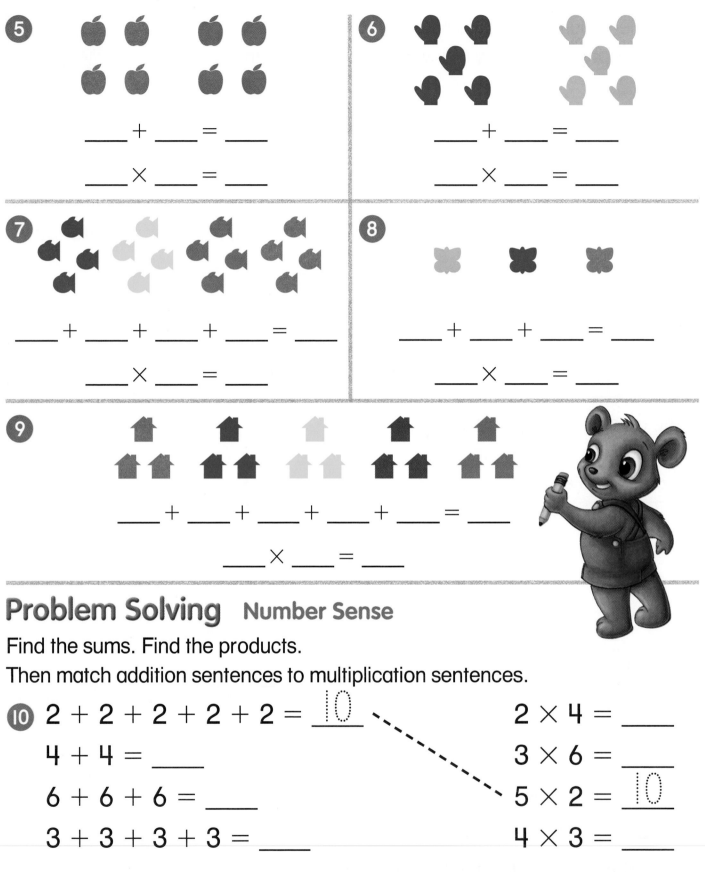

5

___ + ___ = ___

___ × ___ = ___

6

___ + ___ = ___

___ × ___ = ___

7

___ + ___ + ___ + ___ = ___

___ × ___ = ___

8

___ + ___ + ___ = ___

___ × ___ = ___

9

___ + ___ + ___ + ___ + ___ = ___

___ × ___ = ___

Problem Solving Number Sense

Find the sums. Find the products.
Then match addition sentences to multiplication sentences.

10 $2 + 2 + 2 + 2 + 2 =$ __10__

$4 + 4 =$ ___

$6 + 6 + 6 =$ ___

$3 + 3 + 3 + 3 =$ ___

$2 × 4 =$ ___

$3 × 6 =$ ___

$5 × 2 =$ __10__

$4 × 3 =$ ___

Home Connection Your child wrote an addition sentence
and a multiplication sentence to tell how many there are in all.
Home Activity Ask your child to explain how $2 + 2 + 2 = 6$
and $3 × 2 = 6$ are related.

Name _____

Learn!

A collection of equal groups arranged in rows and columns is called an **array**.

5 and 3 are called **factors**.

5 rows

3 in each row

$5 \times 3 = \underline{15}$

5 rows of 3 is 15.

Word Bank

array

factor

Check ✓

Use cubes to make the arrays.
Color to show your rows.
Write the multiplication sentence.

1 4 rows
4 in each row

$\underline{4} \times \underline{4} = \underline{16}$

2 2 rows
5 in each row

$\underline{} \times \underline{} = \underline{}$

3 5 rows
4 in each row

$\underline{} \times \underline{} = \underline{}$

4 1 row
4 in that row

$\underline{} \times \underline{} = \underline{}$

Think About It   Reasoning

How are these groups alike?

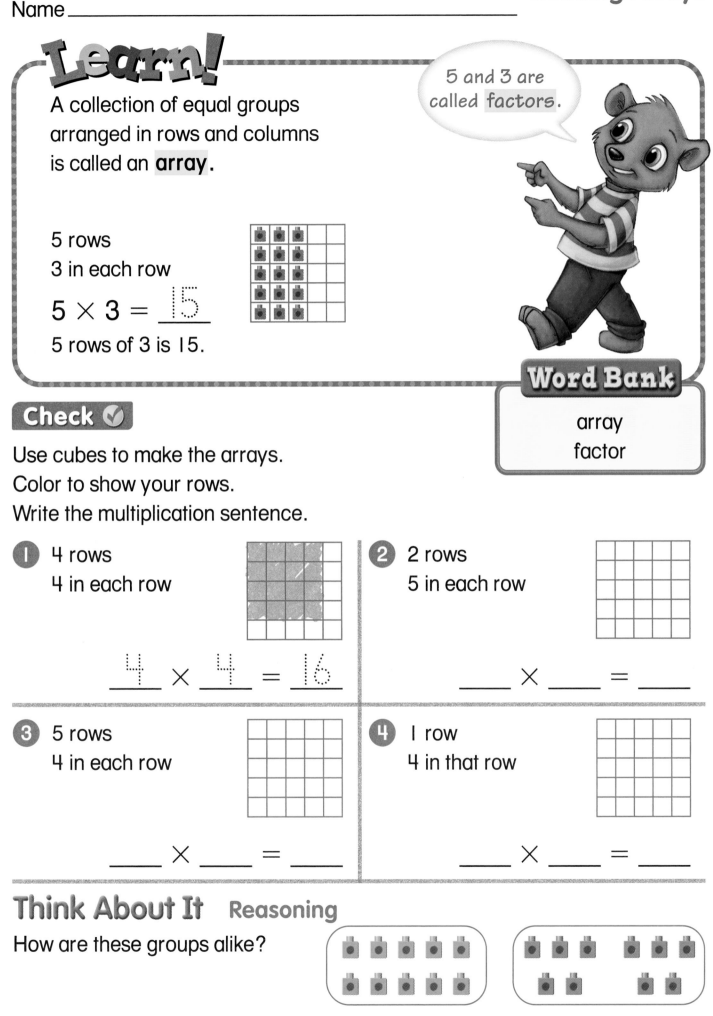

Write a multiplication sentence to describe the array.

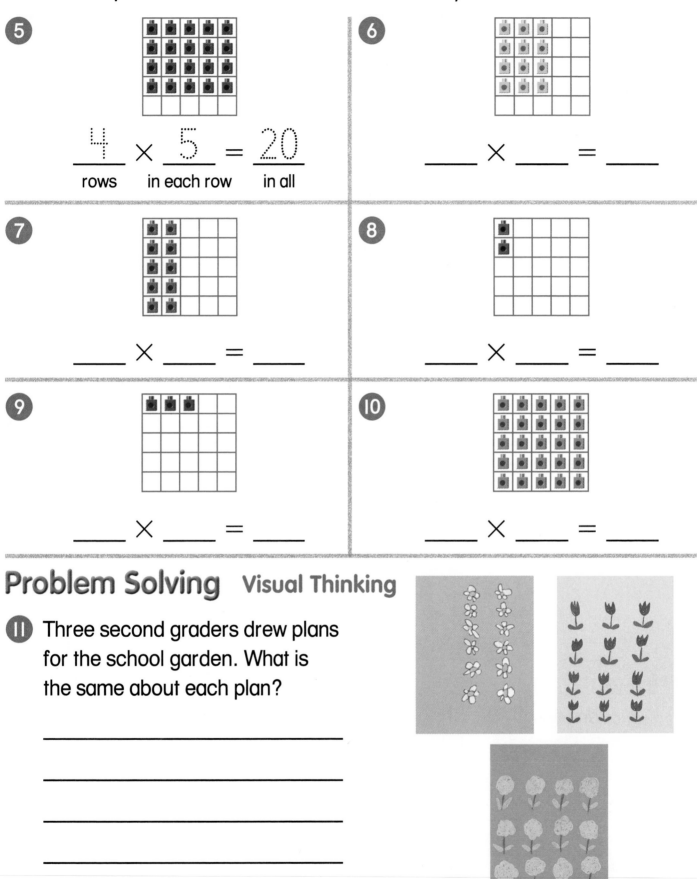

5

$$\underline{4} \times \underline{5} = \underline{20}$$
rows   in each row   in all

6

___ × ___ = ___

7

___ × ___ = ___

8

___ × ___ = ___

9

___ × ___ = ___

10

___ × ___ = ___

Problem Solving   Visual Thinking

11 Three second graders drew plans for the school garden. What is the same about each plan?

_____

_____

_____

_____

Home Connection Your child made arrays to model multiplication sentences. **Home Activity** Have your child show you an array of 2 rows with 6 objects in each row.

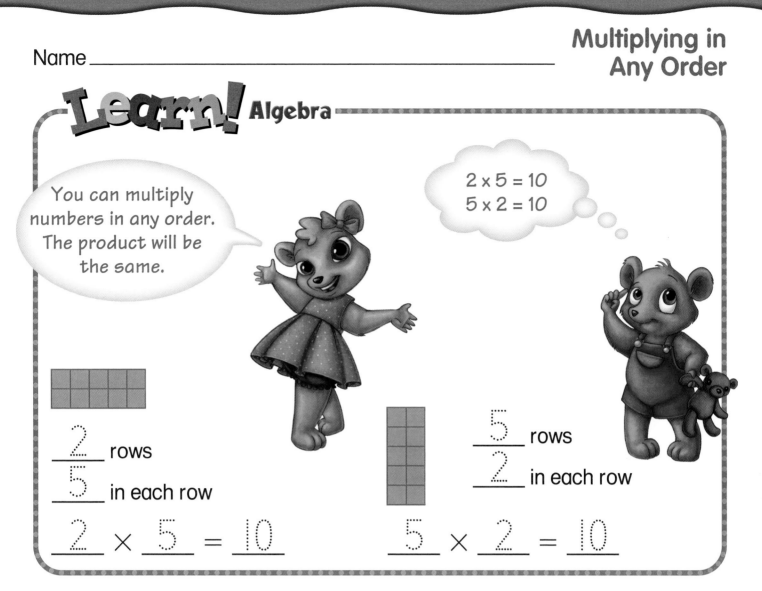

Learn! Algebra

You can multiply numbers in any order. The product will be the same.

$2 \times 5 = 10$
$5 \times 2 = 10$

__2__ rows
__5__ in each row

__2__ × __5__ = __10__

__5__ rows
__2__ in each row

__5__ × __2__ = __10__

Check ✓

Write the numbers. Multiply to find the product.

1

_____ rows

_____ in each row

____ × ____ = ____

_____ rows

_____ in each row

____ × ____ = ____

Think About It Number Sense

Change the order of the numbers being multiplied in the multiplication sentence. What is the new multiplication sentence? How will the array change?

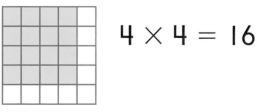

$4 \times 4 = 16$

Write the numbers. Multiply to find the product.

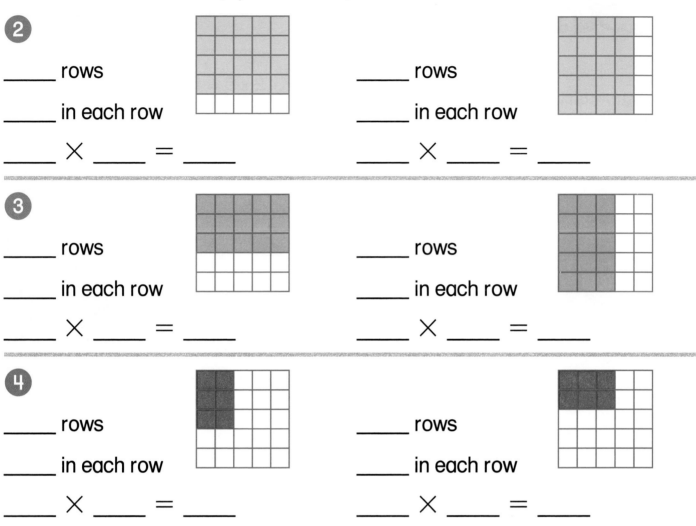

2

_____ rows

_____ in each row

_____ × _____ = _____

_____ rows

_____ in each row

_____ × _____ = _____

3

_____ rows

_____ in each row

_____ × _____ = _____

_____ rows

_____ in each row

_____ × _____ = _____

4

_____ rows

_____ in each row

_____ × _____ = _____

_____ rows

_____ in each row

_____ × _____ = _____

Problem Solving   Algebra

Complete the number sentences.

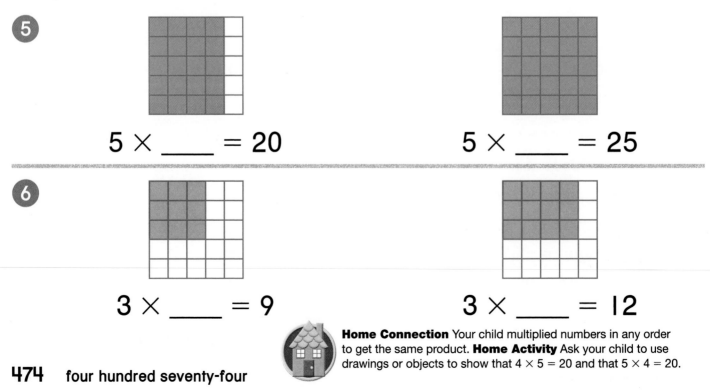

5

5 × _____ = 20

5 × _____ = 25

6

3 × _____ = 9

3 × _____ = 12

Home Connection Your child multiplied numbers in any order to get the same product. **Home Activity** Ask your child to use drawings or objects to show that 4 × 5 = 20 and that 5 × 4 = 20.

Name _____

Learn!

You can multiply across or down.
A **vertical** problem is down.

There are 2 rows of 3 bananas.

how many in each group

$2 \times 3 = 6$

how many groups

$$\begin{array}{r} 3 \\ \times\, 2 \\ \hline 6 \end{array}$$

Word Bank

vertical

Check ✓

Multiply across and down.

1 2 rows of 4

$$\begin{array}{r} 4 \\ \times\, 2 \\ \hline \end{array}$$

$2 \times 4 =$ ___

2 3 groups of 5

$$\begin{array}{r} 5 \\ \times\, 3 \\ \hline \end{array}$$

$3 \times 5 =$ ___

3 4 groups of 4

$$\begin{array}{r} 4 \\ \times\, 4 \\ \hline \end{array}$$

$4 \times 4 =$ ___

4 4 rows of 5

$$\begin{array}{r} 5 \\ \times\, 4 \\ \hline \end{array}$$

$4 \times 5 =$ ___

Think About It   Number Sense

Look at these multiplication problems.
Why are the products the same?

$$\begin{array}{r} 3 \\ \times\, 4 \\ \hline 12 \end{array} \qquad \begin{array}{r} 4 \\ \times\, 3 \\ \hline 12 \end{array}$$

Multiply across and down.

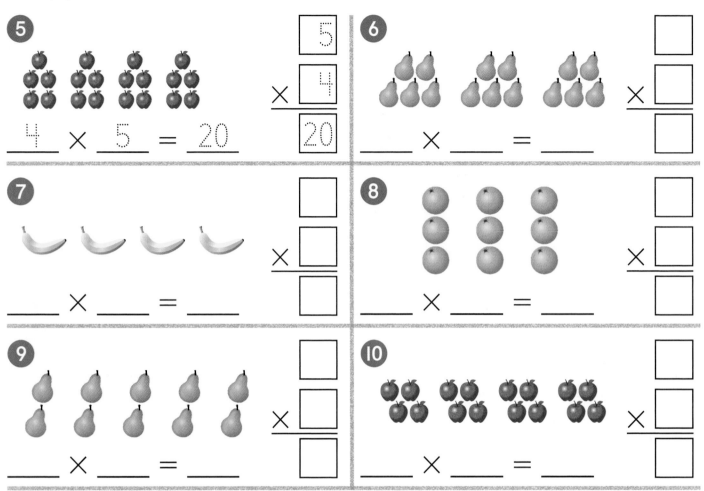

5

___4___ × ___5___ = ___20___

× | 5 |
  | 4 |
  | 20 |

6

_____ × _____ = _____

× | |
  | |
  | |

7

_____ × _____ = _____

× | |
  | |
  | |

8

_____ × _____ = _____

× | |
  | |
  | |

9

_____ × _____ = _____

× | |
  | |
  | |

10

_____ × _____ = _____

× | |
  | |
  | |

Problem Solving Reasoning

11 Draw what comes next. Write the multiplication sentence.
Describe the pattern.

2 × 2 = 4   3 × 3 = 9   4 × 4 = 16   _____

_____

_____

_____

© Pearson Education, Inc.

Home Connection Your child solved multiplication problems across
and down. **Home Activity** Have your child show you another way to
multiply 2 × 3.

Understand Graphic Sources: Pictures

1 Mrs. Murphy's class is going on a picture hunt.
Each team must find a picture that has at least 10 things with wheels. Can you find 10 things with wheels in this picture?

_____ cars

_____ taxis

_____ buses

_____ bicycle

_____ trucks

_____ cart

_____ **things with wheels**

2 Can you find the one-way street?

Think About It   Number Sense

How much is 5 + 5 + 5 + 5 + 5 + 5? _____
How do you know?

3 What a mess! Help the vendor put the apples back into the crate. Put an **X** on one of the apples on the ground. Then draw an apple in one of the spaces in the crate. Keep doing this until you have put all of the apples back where they belong.

4 How many rows of apples are there? _____ rows

5 How many apples are in each row? _____ apples

6 How many apples are there altogether? _____ apples

7 Write a number sentence that shows this.

_____

Home Connection Your child looked at details in a picture and drew a picture to represent a multiplication number sentence (equation). **Home Activity** To further help your child notice picture details, look through family photographs and talk about them, perhaps creating number sentences about different numbers of uncles, aunts, cousins, and so on.

Name_____

Learn! Algebra

3 × 5 = 15 windows

Read and Understand

There are 3 houses on Lake Street.
Each house has 5 windows.
How many windows are there in all?

Plan and Solve

Draw a picture. Then write a
number sentence and solve.

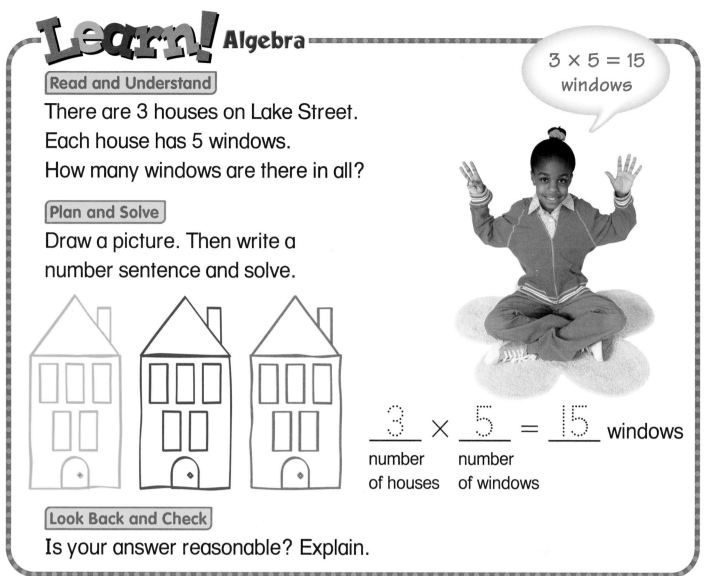

$$\underline{}3 \times \underline{}5 = \underline{}15 \text{ windows}$$

number   number
of houses   of windows

Look Back and Check

Is your answer reasonable? Explain.

Check ✓

Draw a picture to solve each problem.
Then write the multiplication sentence.

1 There are 4 tables. Each table has
5 plates. How many plates are
there in all?

_____ × _____ = _____ plates

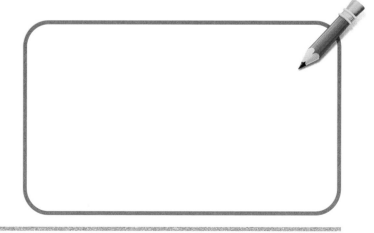

Think About It Reasoning

Sammy drew 5 tables. Each table had
4 plates. Was he correct?

Draw a picture to solve each problem.
Then write a multiplication sentence.

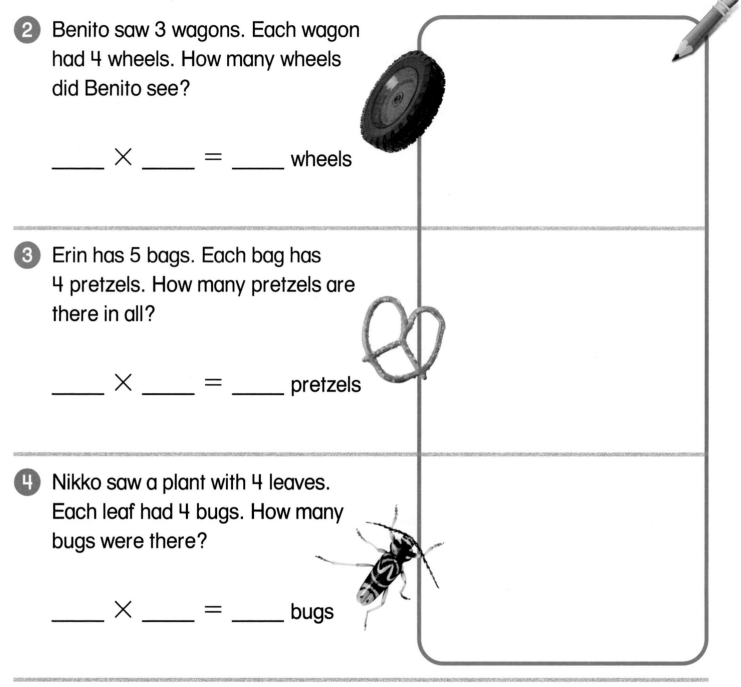

2 Benito saw 3 wagons. Each wagon had 4 wheels. How many wheels did Benito see?

_____ × _____ = _____ wheels

3 Erin has 5 bags. Each bag has 4 pretzels. How many pretzels are there in all?

_____ × _____ = _____ pretzels

4 Nikko saw a plant with 4 leaves. Each leaf had 4 bugs. How many bugs were there?

_____ × _____ = _____ bugs

Estimation

5 The art table has 6 cups on it. There are 5 paintbrushes in each cup. Are there more or fewer than 20 brushes? Explain.

_____

_____

_____

_____

Home Connection Your child drew a picture to solve a problem.
Home Activity Ask your child to draw a picture to help solve this problem:
*There are 3 plants with 3 leaves each. How many leaves are
there in all?* Then have your child write a multiplication sentence.

Name_____

Draw to show equal groups. Skip count to find how many in all.

1 2 groups, 3 in each group

_____ in all

2 4 groups, 4 in each group

_____ in all

Write an addition sentence and a multiplication sentence
that tell how many objects there are in all.

3

___ + ___ + ___ + ___ = ___

___ × ___ = ___

4

___ + ___ = ___

___ × ___ = ___

Write the number of rows and the number in each row.
Write a multiplication sentence to describe each array.

5

_____ rows

_____ in each row

_____ × _____ = _____

6

_____ row

_____ in that row

_____ × _____ = _____

Multiply across and down.

7 4 rows of 2

_____ × _____ = _____

8 3 rows of 5

_____ × _____ = _____

What is the end time?

1 Practice the flute.

Starts	Lasts

4:00

30 minutes

Ⓐ 4:00

Ⓑ 3:30

Ⓒ 5:00

Ⓓ 4:30

Mark the object that weighs the most.

2

Ⓐ   Ⓑ   Ⓒ   Ⓓ

Mark the number that comes right before.

3 _____, 500

399	501	499	490
Ⓐ	Ⓑ	Ⓒ	Ⓓ

Mark the number that comes right after.

4 860, _____

861	859	870	960
Ⓐ	Ⓑ	Ⓒ	Ⓓ

Mark the sum.

5
$$127 + 348$$

375	475	465	4,715
Ⓐ	Ⓑ	Ⓒ	Ⓓ

Writing in Math

6 Tell something that you do in the A.M. and something that you do in the P.M.

_____

_____

_____

Name _____

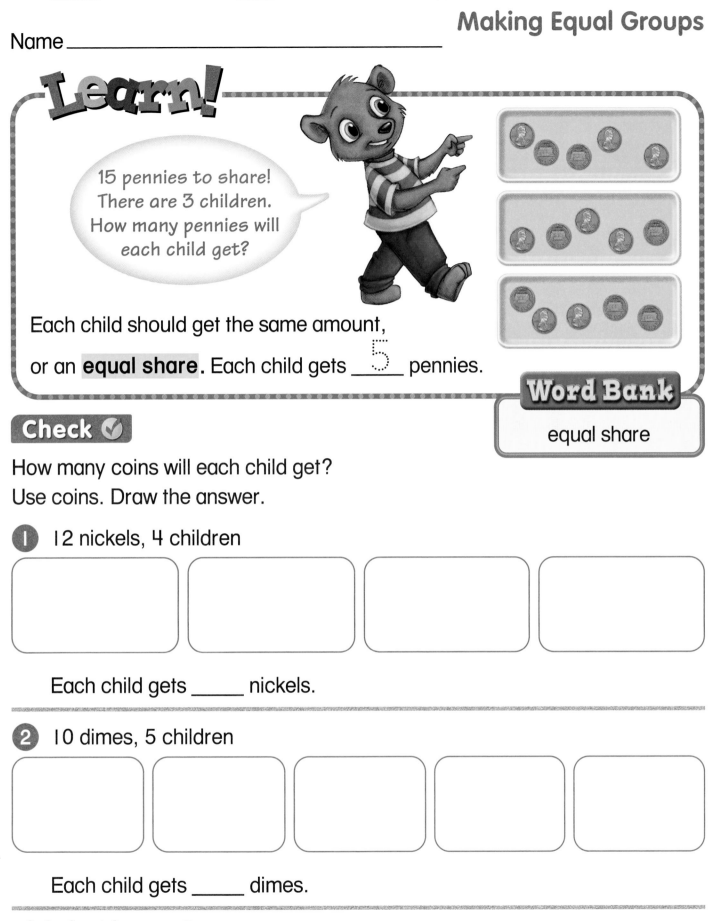

Learn!

15 pennies to share! There are 3 children. How many pennies will each child get?

Each child should get the same amount,

or an **equal share**. Each child gets __5__ pennies.

Word Bank

equal share

Check ✓

How many coins will each child get?
Use coins. Draw the answer.

1 12 nickels, 4 children

Each child gets _____ nickels.

2 10 dimes, 5 children

Each child gets _____ dimes.

Think About It   Reasoning

There were 6 coins. Each child got the same amount. If each child got 2 coins, how many children were there?

How many coins will each child get?
Write the answer. Use coins if you need to.

③ 16 pennies, 4 children Each child gets __4__ pennies.

④ 12 pennies, 6 children Each child gets _____ pennies.

⑤ 4 pennies, 4 children Each child gets _____ penny.

Complete the table.

	Number of pennies:	Number of children:	How many pennies does each child get?
⑥	12	3	_____
⑦	25	5	_____
⑧	10	2	_____
⑨	8	1	_____
⑩	6	2	_____

Problem Solving Number Sense

⑪ You have 12 pennies. Can you find
6 different ways to show equal groups?

_____ group of _____   _____ groups of _____

_____ groups of _____   _____ groups of _____

_____ groups of _____   _____ groups of _____

© Pearson Education, Inc.

Home Connection Your child divided a set of objects into a given number of equal groups. **Home Activity** Have your child show you equal groups of objects.

Writing Division Sentences

Learn!

To share things equally, you can **divide**.

12 rings are divided among 4 children.

How many rings does each child get?

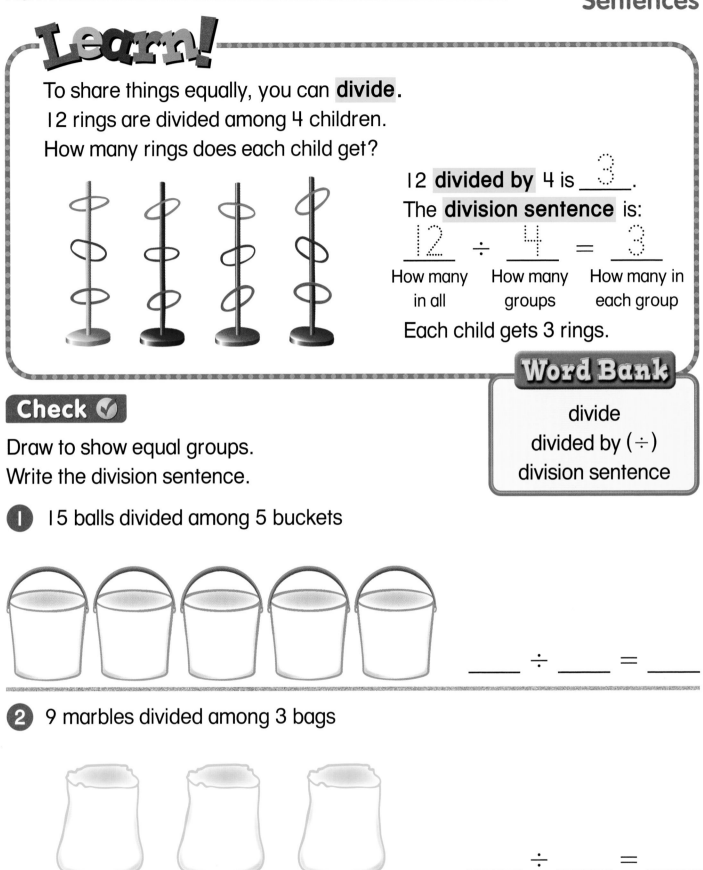

12 **divided by** 4 is ___3___.

The **division sentence** is:

__12__ ÷ __4__ = __3__

How many in all   How many groups   How many in each group

Each child gets 3 rings.

Word Bank

divide

divided by (÷)

division sentence

Check ✓

Draw to show equal groups.

Write the division sentence.

1 15 balls divided among 5 buckets

_____ ÷ _____ = _____

2 9 marbles divided among 3 bags

_____ ÷ _____ = _____

Think About It   Number Sense

Mr. Carter gave his 2 children 5 tickets to share equally. How many tickets did each child get?

Draw to show equal groups. Write the division sentence.

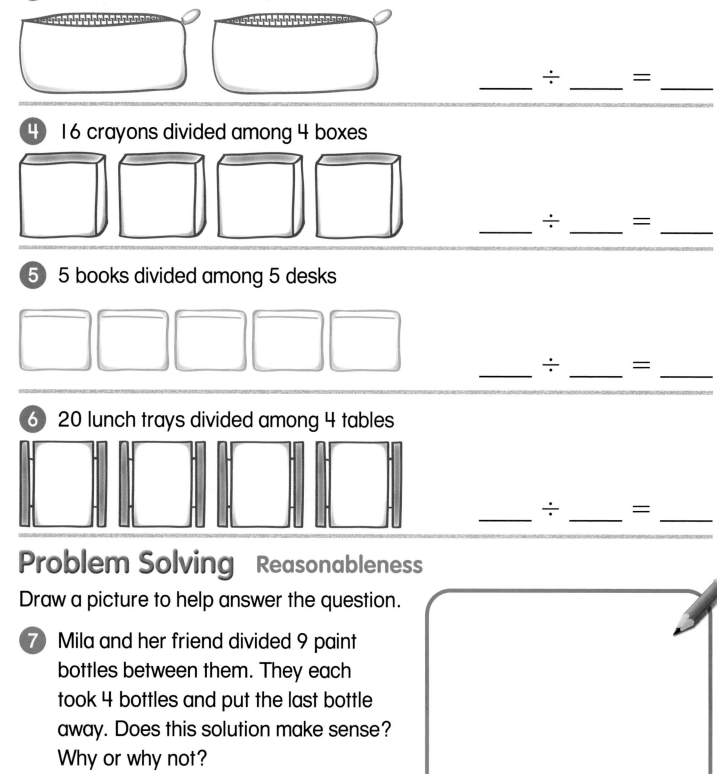

3 6 pencils divided among 2 pencil cases

_____ ÷ _____ = _____

4 16 crayons divided among 4 boxes

_____ ÷ _____ = _____

5 5 books divided among 5 desks

_____ ÷ _____ = _____

6 20 lunch trays divided among 4 tables

_____ ÷ _____ = _____

Problem Solving   Reasonableness

Draw a picture to help answer the question.

7 Mila and her friend divided 9 paint bottles between them. They each took 4 bottles and put the last bottle away. Does this solution make sense? Why or why not?

_____

_____

Home Connection Your child wrote division sentences to represent equal groups. **Home Activity** Have your child divide 10 spoons into 5 groups. Then have him or her write a division sentence to tell how many are in each group.

© Pearson Education, Inc.

Learn! Algebra

3 children collected 5 leaves each.
How many leaves are there in all?

> 3 groups with 5 in each group.

Marissa Annette George

Circle the number sentence that solves the problem.

$3 + 5 = 8$ $(3 \times 5 = 15)$ $5 - 3 = 2$

There are __15__ leaves in all.

Check ✓

Circle the number sentence that solves the problem.

1 There are 20 balloons. 5 children will share them.
How many balloons will each child get?

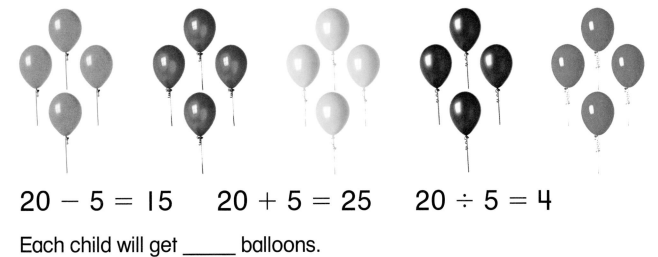

$20 - 5 = 15$ $20 + 5 = 25$ $20 \div 5 = 4$

Each child will get _____ balloons.

Think About It Reasoning

Explain why you chose the number sentence that
you did.

Circle the number sentence that solves the problem.

2 Kara has 2 winter hats and 3 straw hats. How many hats does she have in all?

$$3 + 2 = 5 \qquad 3 - 2 = 1 \qquad 3 \times 2 = 6$$

Kara has _____ hats.

3 4 friends have some bead dolls. Each has 3 bead dolls. How many bead dolls are there in all?

$$4 - 3 = 1 \qquad 4 + 3 = 7 \qquad 4 \times 3 = 12$$

There are _____ bead dolls in all.

4 Sam needs 9 buttons for a puppet. He has 3. How many more buttons does he need?

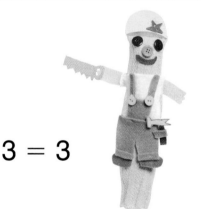

$$9 - 3 = 6 \qquad 9 + 3 = 12 \qquad 9 \div 3 = 3$$

He needs _____ more buttons.

5 There are 16 pine cones to go in 4 baskets. How many pine cones will be in each basket?

$$16 \div 4 = 4 \qquad 16 + 4 = 20 \qquad 16 - 4 = 12$$

Each basket gets _____ pine cones.

Home Connection Your child chose a number sentence to solve each problem. **Home Activity** Have your child explain to you the meaning of the four operations: $+, -, \times, \div$.

Name _____

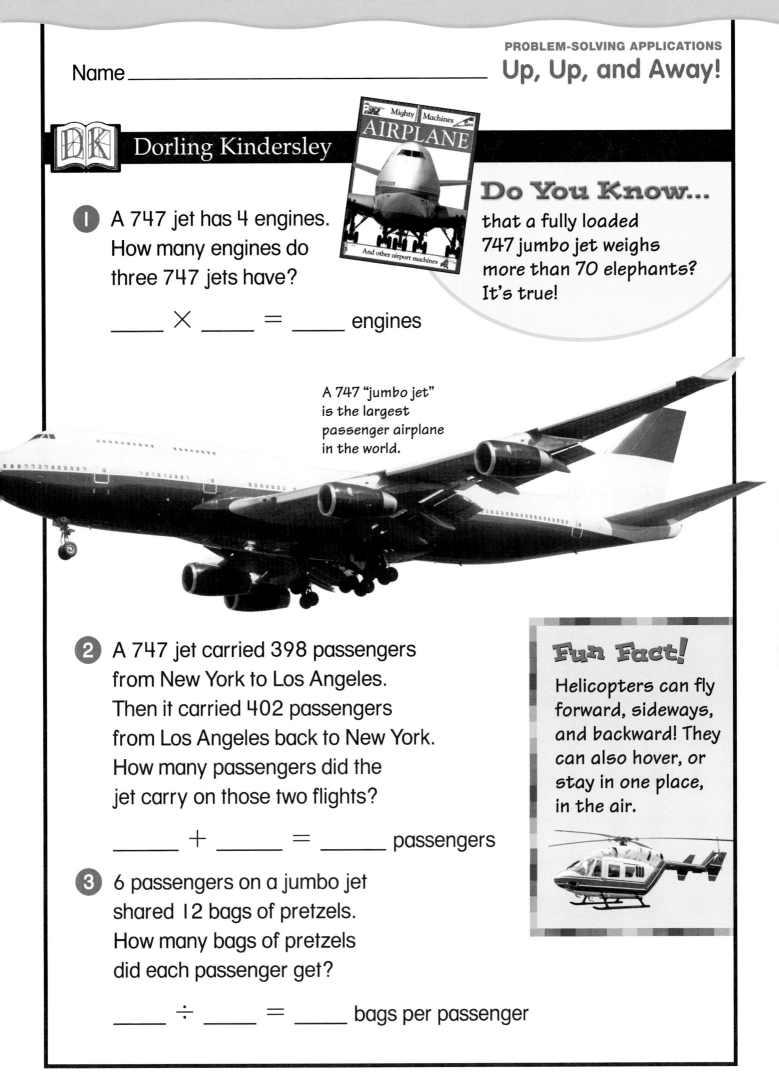

Dorling Kindersley

Mighty Machines
AIRPLANE
And other airport machines

1 A 747 jet has 4 engines. How many engines do three 747 jets have?

_____ × _____ = _____ engines

Do You Know...
that a fully loaded 747 jumbo jet weighs more than 70 elephants? It's true!

A 747 "jumbo jet" is the largest passenger airplane in the world.

2 A 747 jet carried 398 passengers from New York to Los Angeles. Then it carried 402 passengers from Los Angeles back to New York. How many passengers did the jet carry on those two flights?

_____ + _____ = _____ passengers

Fun Fact!
Helicopters can fly forward, sideways, and backward! They can also hover, or stay in one place, in the air.

3 6 passengers on a jumbo jet shared 12 bags of pretzels. How many bags of pretzels did each passenger get?

_____ ÷ _____ = _____ bags per passenger

4 The Concorde flies 1 mile in about 3 seconds.
About how many seconds does it take
the Concorde to fly 4 miles?

_____ miles $\times$ _____ seconds per mile $=$ _____ seconds in all

5 The Concorde carried 98 passengers on one trip,
89 passengers on another trip, and 96 passengers
on a third trip. How many passengers in all did
the Concorde carry on those 3 trips?

_____ $+$ _____ $+$ _____ $=$ _____ passengers in all

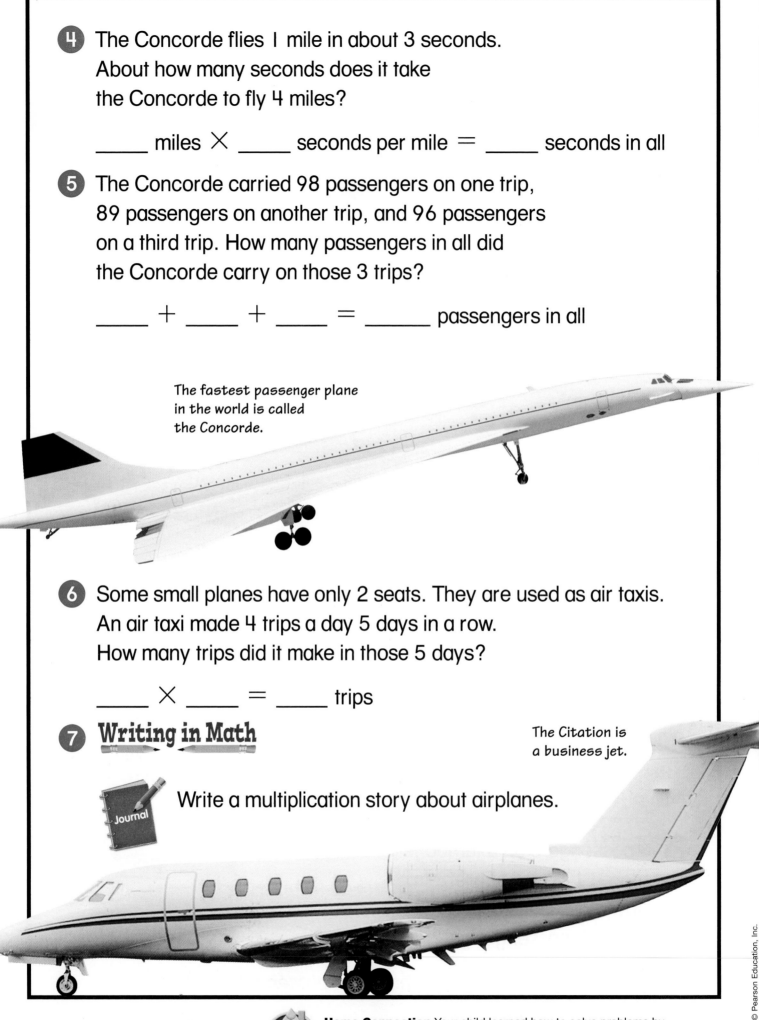

The fastest passenger plane
in the world is called
the Concorde.

6 Some small planes have only 2 seats. They are used as air taxis.
An air taxi made 4 trips a day 5 days in a row.
How many trips did it make in those 5 days?

_____ $\times$ _____ $=$ _____ trips

7 **Writing in Math**

The Citation is
a business jet.

Write a multiplication story about airplanes.

Home Connection Your child learned how to solve problems by
applying his or her math skills. **Home Activity** Talk to your child
about how he or she solved the problems on these two pages.

Name_____

How many coins will each child get?
Use coins. Draw the answer.

1 12 pennies, 3 children

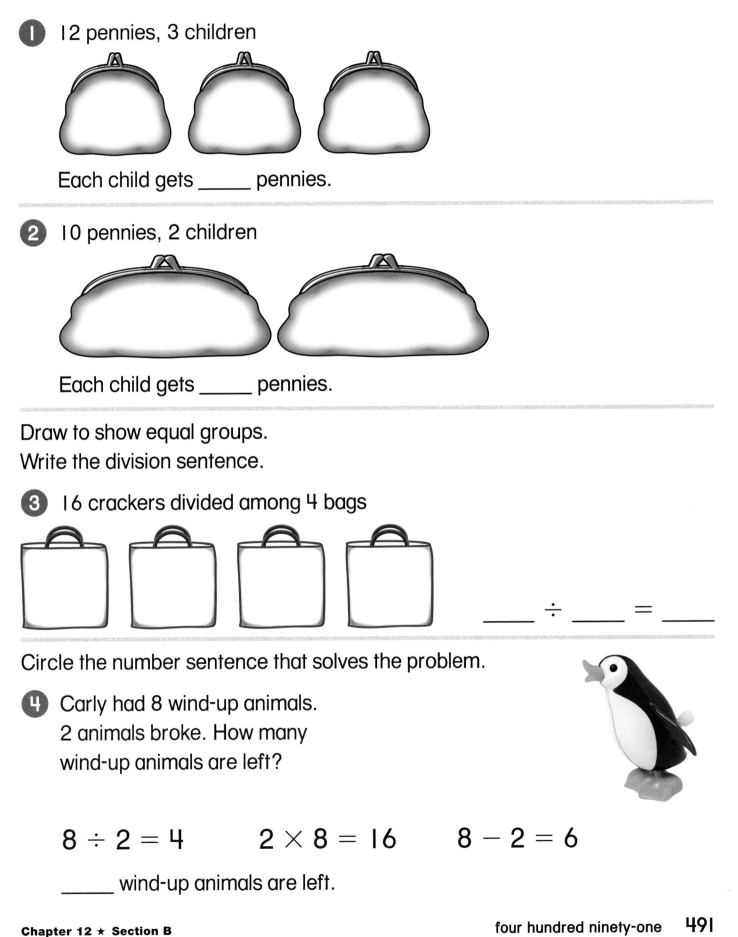

Each child gets _____ pennies.

2 10 pennies, 2 children

Each child gets _____ pennies.

Draw to show equal groups.
Write the division sentence.

3 16 crackers divided among 4 bags

_____ ÷ _____ = _____

Circle the number sentence that solves the problem.

4 Carly had 8 wind-up animals.
2 animals broke. How many
wind-up animals are left?

$8 \div 2 = 4$ $2 \times 8 = 16$ $8 - 2 = 6$

_____ wind-up animals are left.

1 You have 50¢. Mark the pair of toys you can buy.

60¢   15¢   25¢   30¢   Ⓐ

60¢   15¢   30¢   Ⓑ

15¢   30¢   Ⓒ

60¢   25¢   Ⓓ

Find the sum or difference.

2
$$\begin{array}{r} 71 \\ +\ 19 \\ \hline \end{array}$$

Ⓐ 89
Ⓑ 910
Ⓒ 90
Ⓓ 80

3
$$\begin{array}{r} 64 \\ -\ 37 \\ \hline \end{array}$$

Ⓐ 27
Ⓑ 37
Ⓒ 33
Ⓓ 91

Use the graph to answer each question.

Favorite Colors

Number of Children

10
8
6
4
2
0

Red   Yellow   Blue   Green

Color

4 How many children's favorite color is blue?

2   4   6   8
Ⓐ   Ⓑ   Ⓒ   Ⓓ

5 Which is the favorite color of most children?

red   yellow   blue   green
Ⓐ   Ⓑ   Ⓒ   Ⓓ

Writing in Math

6 Draw the triangle to show a flip.

Dividing by Subtracting **Algebra**

If you start at 0 and add 3s,
in 4 jumps you will get to 12.

$$4 \times 3 = 12$$

$$0 + 3 = 3$$
$$3 + 3 = 6$$
$$6 + 3 = 9$$
$$9 + 3 = 12$$

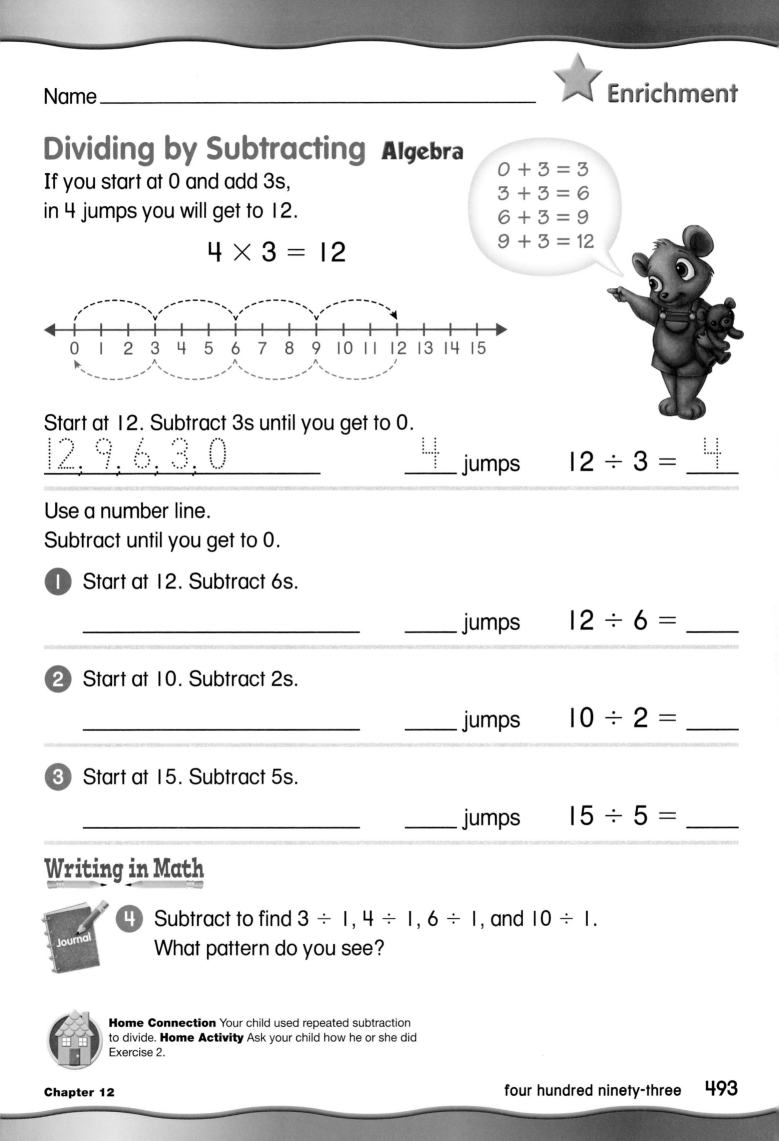

Start at 12. Subtract 3s until you get to 0.

12, 9, 6, 3, 0 _____   __4__ jumps $12 \div 3 =$ __4__

Use a number line.
Subtract until you get to 0.

1 Start at 12. Subtract 6s.

_____   _____ jumps $12 \div 6 =$ _____

2 Start at 10. Subtract 2s.

_____   _____ jumps $10 \div 2 =$ _____

3 Start at 15. Subtract 5s.

_____   _____ jumps $15 \div 5 =$ _____

Writing in Math

4 Subtract to find $3 \div 1$, $4 \div 1$, $6 \div 1$, and $10 \div 1$.
What pattern do you see?

Home Connection Your child used repeated subtraction
to divide. **Home Activity** Ask your child how he or she did
Exercise 2.

Multiply Using a Calculator

You can use a calculator to multiply.
Press ON/C each time you begin.
Follow the directions. Use each number once.

1. Cross out two numbers with a product of 9.

2. Circle two numbers with a product of 15.

3. Underline two numbers with a product of 20.

4. Draw squares around two numbers with a product of 28.

5. Put check marks next to two numbers with a product of 100.

6. Draw a star next to the number that is left over.

Think About It   Reasoning

How could you use a calculator to find two numbers with a product of 18?

Home Connection Your child used a calculator to multiply two numbers.
Home Activity Ask your child to explain two ways to find the product of 3 and 2 using a calculator.

Name _____

Use Writing in Math

Some math tests ask you to explain how you found your answer.
Use math words to help you do this.

Test-Taking Strategies

Understand the Question

Get Information for the Answer

Plan How to Find the Answer

Make Smart Choices

Use Writing in Math

1 For a party, Jay's mom bought 24 balloons for 8 children to share equally. How many balloons will each child get? Use counters. Then explain how you found your answer.

Each child will get 3 balloons. I divided 24 counters

into 8 equal groups. Then I counted the counters in

each group. There were 3 counters in each group.

A boy named Terry used these math words to help him explain how he found his answer: **divided, equal groups,** and **counted.**

Your Turn

Solve. Then explain how you found your answer.

2 Jay gave each of the 8 children at his party 2 toy cars. How many toy cars did Jay give away? Use counters. Explain how you found your answer.

_____

_____

_____

 Home Connection Your child prepared for standardized tests by using math terms correctly to explain how he or she solved a problem. **Home Activity** Have your child point out math words that he or she used to explain the answer to Exercise 2. *(Possible response: I used counters to make 8 equal groups of 2. Then I counted by 2s to find how many counters in all.)*

Name _____

Discover Math in Your World

 Read Together

Frog or Toad?

Both frogs and toads spend time on land and in the water. But frogs have longer back legs than most toads have. Frogs also have wet and smooth skin, while toads have bumpy and dry skin.

Toad

Frog Facts

Write an addition sentence and a multiplication sentence to solve each problem.

Frog

1 A frog has 2 front legs. Each front leg has 4 toes. How many toes are on the frog's 2 front legs?

 ____ + ____ = ____ toes   ____ × ____ = ____ toes

2 A frog has 2 hind legs. Each hind leg has 5 toes. How many toes are on the frog's 2 hind legs?

 ____ + ____ = ____ toes   ____ × ____ = ____ toes

3 The largest frog in the world is the Goliath frog of Africa. It can weigh as much as 7 pounds. How much would 4 Goliath frogs weigh?

 ___ + ___ + ___ + ___ = ___ lb   ____ × ____ = ____ lb

Take It to the NET
Video and Activities
www.scottforesman.com

Home Connection Your child solved problems about frogs and toads by writing addition sentences and multiplication sentences. **Home Activity** Ask your child to explain how he or she solved one of the problems on this page.

Chapter Test

Use counters to show equal groups.
Skip count to find how many there are in all.

1 4 groups, 1 in each group

_____ in all

2 5 groups, 5 in each group

_____ in all

Write an addition sentence and a multiplication sentence
that tell how many objects there are in all.

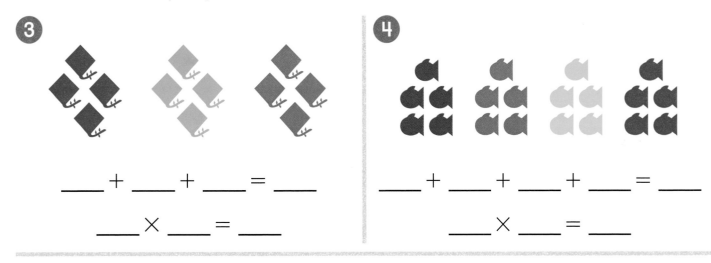

3

___ + ___ + ___ = ___

___ × ___ = ___

4

___ + ___ + ___ + ___ = ___

___ × ___ = ___

Write a multiplication sentence
to describe the array.

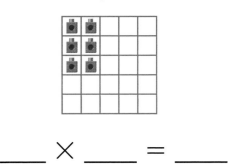

5

____ × ____ = ____

Write the number of rows and the
number in each row. Find the product.

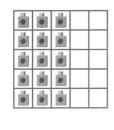

6

____ × ____ = ____

How many are there in all?

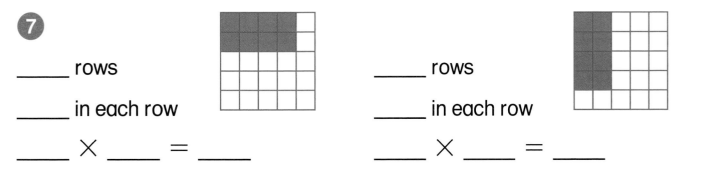

7

_____ rows

_____ in each row

____ × ____ = ____

_____ rows

_____ in each row

____ × ____ = ____

Multiply across and down.

8

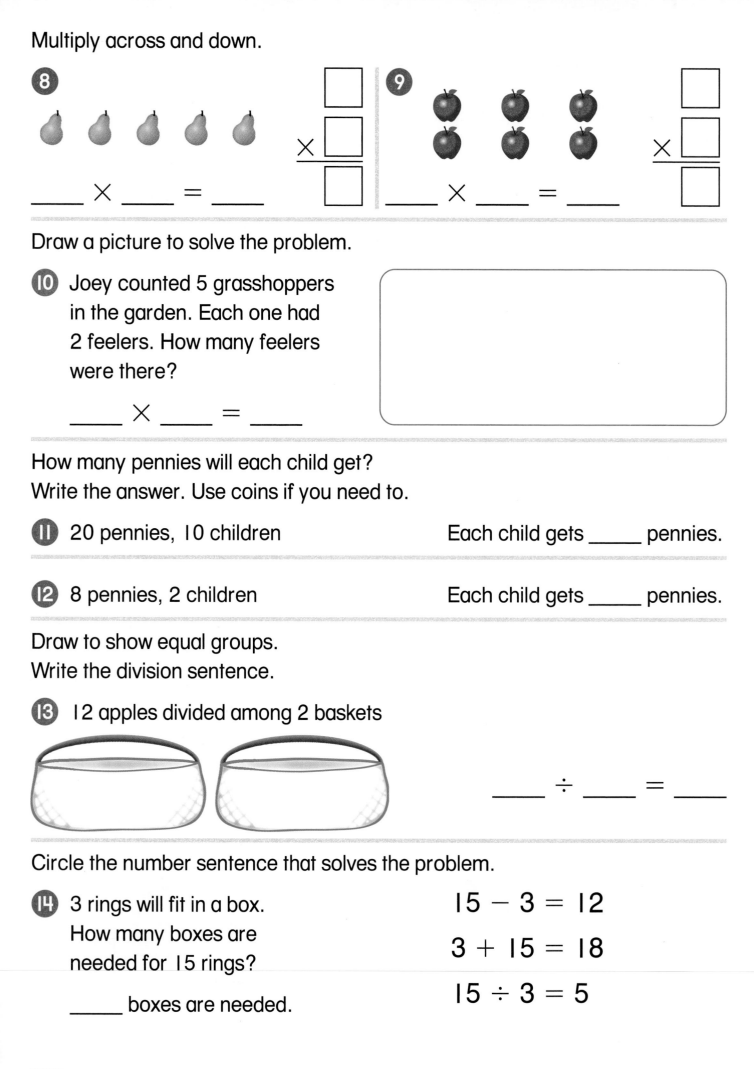

___ × ___ = ___

9

___ × ___ = ___

Draw a picture to solve the problem.

10 Joey counted 5 grasshoppers in the garden. Each one had 2 feelers. How many feelers were there?

___ × ___ = ___

How many pennies will each child get?
Write the answer. Use coins if you need to.

11 20 pennies, 10 children

Each child gets _____ pennies.

12 8 pennies, 2 children

Each child gets _____ pennies.

Draw to show equal groups.
Write the division sentence.

13 12 apples divided among 2 baskets

____ ÷ ____ = ____

Circle the number sentence that solves the problem.

14 3 rings will fit in a box.
How many boxes are needed for 15 rings?

_____ boxes are needed.

$$15 - 3 = 12$$

$$3 + 15 = 18$$

$$15 \div 3 = 5$$

Mark the number that makes the statement true.

1 ___ < 27

30	25	44	29
Ⓐ	Ⓑ	Ⓒ	Ⓓ

2 63 > ___

65	78	63	61
Ⓐ	Ⓑ	Ⓒ	Ⓓ

Mark the doubles fact that helps you solve the problem.

3
$$\begin{array}{r} 20 \\ -\ 10 \\ \hline \end{array}$$

$$\begin{array}{r} 6 \\ +\ 5 \\ \hline 11 \end{array}$$
Ⓐ

$$\begin{array}{r} 9 \\ +\ 9 \\ \hline 18 \end{array}$$
Ⓑ

$$\begin{array}{r} 10 \\ +\ 10 \\ \hline 20 \end{array}$$
Ⓒ

$$\begin{array}{r} 5 \\ +\ 5 \\ \hline 10 \end{array}$$
Ⓓ

Mark the plane shape you could show by tracing the solid figure.

4

Ⓐ   Ⓑ   Ⓒ   Ⓓ

Mark how many. Use models if you need to.

5

100 more is _____.

Ⓐ 500
Ⓑ 600
Ⓒ 700
Ⓓ 800

Mark the object that holds the least.

6

Ⓐ   Ⓑ   Ⓒ   Ⓓ

Estimate. Circle **more** or **less** to answer the question.

You have:	You buy:	Answer:
7 70¢	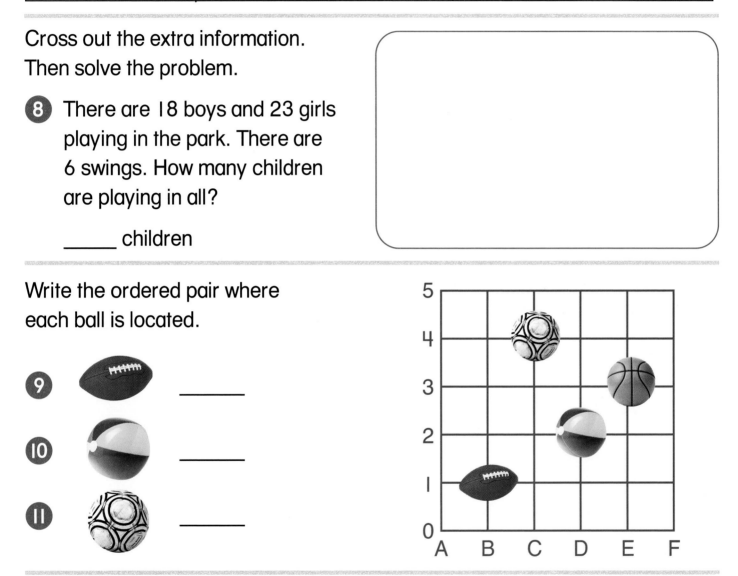 51¢	Will you have more or less than 30¢ left? more less

Cross out the extra information.
Then solve the problem.

8 There are 18 boys and 23 girls
playing in the park. There are
6 swings. How many children
are playing in all?

_____ children

Write the ordered pair where
each ball is located.

9 _____

10 _____

11 _____

Writing in Math

12 Write a math story in which the numbers
34 and 65 are added together. Then solve.

_____

_____

_____

Picture Glossary

addition sentence

$$3 + 2 = 5$$

addends

---

area

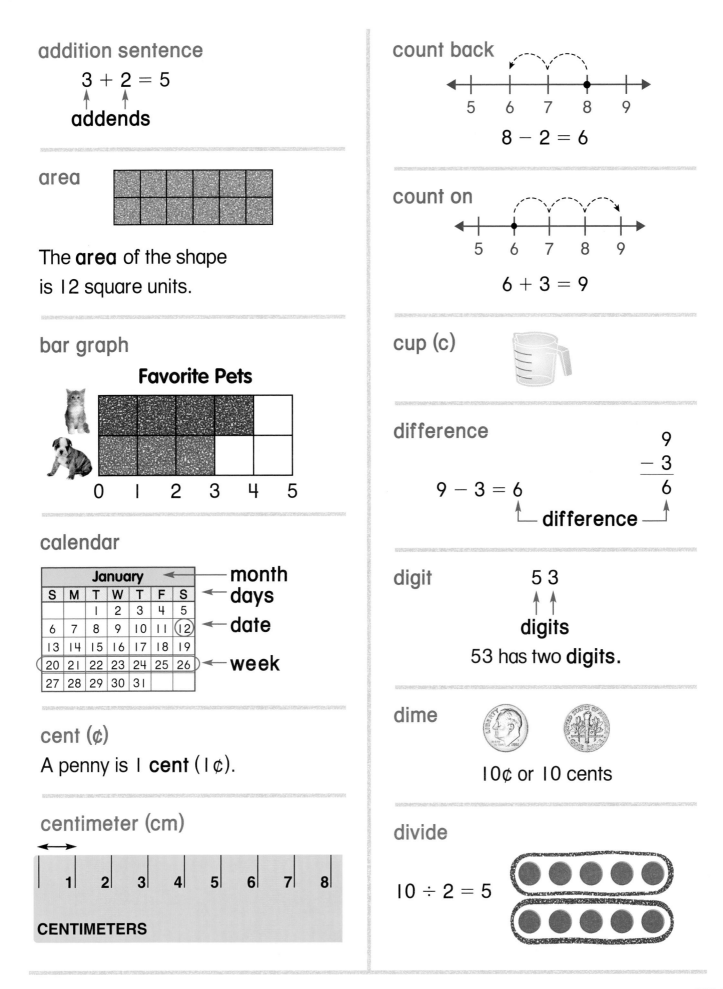

The **area** of the shape is 12 square units.

---

bar graph

Favorite Pets

| | | | | | |
|0|1|2|3|4|5|

---

calendar

	January					
S	M	T	W	T	F	S
		1	2	3	4	5
6	7	8	9	10	11	12
13	14	15	16	17	18	19
20	21	22	23	24	25	26
27	28	29	30	31		

← month
← days
← date
← week

---

cent (¢)

A penny is 1 **cent** (1¢).

---

centimeter (cm)

CENTIMETERS

---

count back

$$8 - 2 = 6$$

---

count on

$$6 + 3 = 9$$

---

cup (c)

---

difference

$$9 - 3 = 6$$

$$\begin{array}{r} 9 \\ - 3 \\ \hline 6 \end{array}$$

difference

---

digit

5 3

digits

53 has two **digits.**

---

dime

10¢ or 10 cents

---

divide

$$10 \div 2 = 5$$

division sentence

$18 \div 3 = 6$

dollar ($)

$1.00 or 100¢

estimate

$38 + 19$ is about 60.

even numbers

2, 4, 6, 8, 10, ...

fact family

$9 + 3 = 12$ $12 - 9 = 3$

$3 + 9 = 12$ $12 - 3 = 9$

foot (ft)

A **foot** is 12 inches.

fraction

$\dfrac{1}{2}$ $\dfrac{1}{3}$ $\dfrac{1}{4}$

greater than (>)

68 is **greater than** 49.

$68 > 49$

half-dollar

50¢, $0.50, or 50 cents

half hour

A **half hour** is 30 minutes.

hour

An **hour** is 60 minutes.   **hour hand**

It is 7 o'clock.

inch (in.)

kilogram (kg)

This book measures about
1 **kilogram**.

less than (<)

32 is **less than** 48.

$32 < 48$

line of symmetry

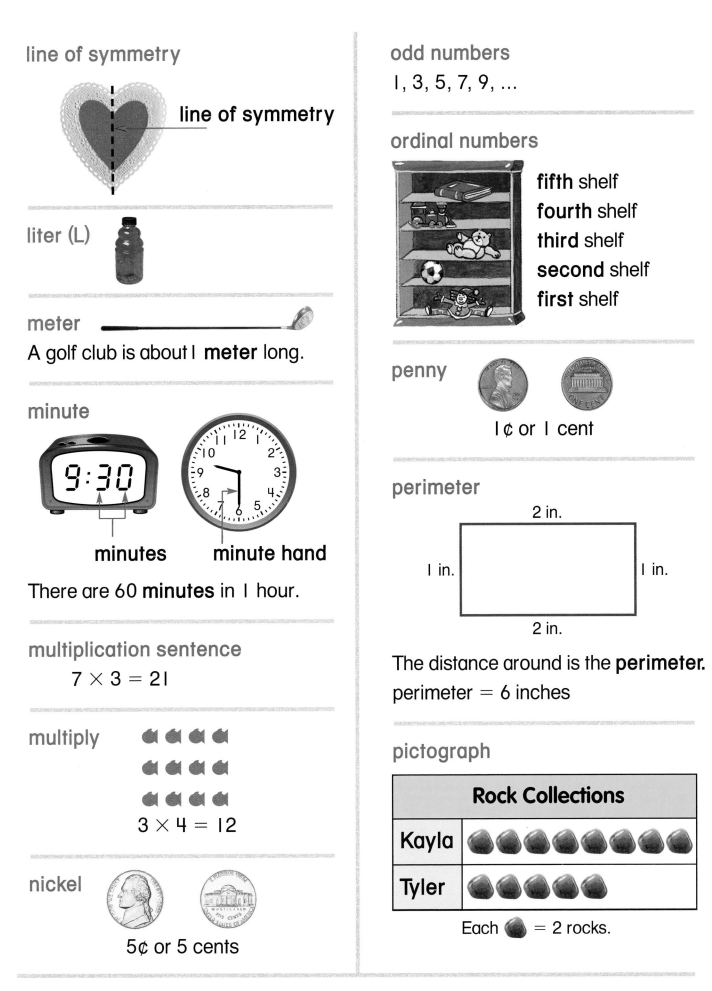

line of symmetry

liter (L)

meter

A golf club is about 1 **meter** long.

minute

minutes   minute hand

There are 60 **minutes** in 1 hour.

multiplication sentence

$7 \times 3 = 21$

multiply

$3 \times 4 = 12$

nickel

5¢ or 5 cents

odd numbers

1, 3, 5, 7, 9, ...

ordinal numbers

fifth shelf
fourth shelf
third shelf
second shelf
first shelf

penny

1¢ or 1 cent

perimeter

2 in.

1 in.   1 in.

2 in.

The distance around is the **perimeter.**
perimeter = 6 inches

pictograph

Rock Collections	
Kayla	🪨🪨🪨🪨🪨🪨🪨🪨
Tyler	🪨🪨🪨🪨🪨

Each 🪨 = 2 rocks.

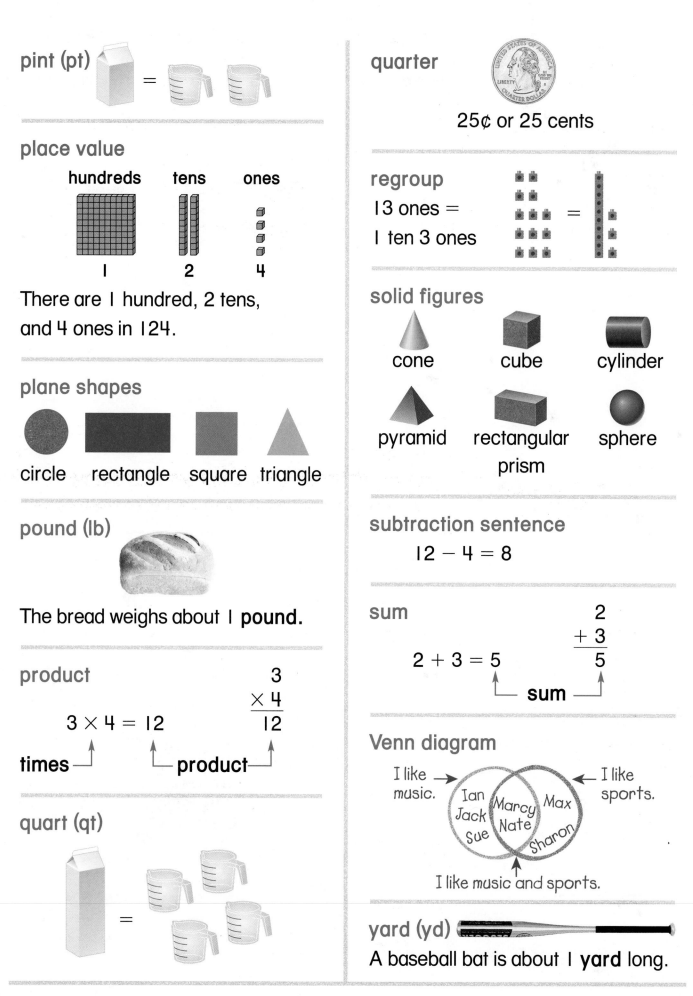

pint (pt)

place value

hundreds   tens   ones

1   2   4

There are 1 hundred, 2 tens, and 4 ones in 124.

plane shapes

circle   rectangle   square   triangle

pound (lb)

The bread weighs about 1 **pound.**

product

$$3 \times 4 = 12 \qquad \begin{array}{r} 3 \\ \times\, 4 \\ \hline 12 \end{array}$$

times ⌐   ⌐ **product** ⌐

quart (qt)

=

quarter

25¢ or 25 cents

regroup

13 ones =
1 ten 3 ones

=

solid figures

cone   cube   cylinder

pyramid   rectangular   sphere
         prism

subtraction sentence

$$12 - 4 = 8$$

sum

$$2 + 3 = 5 \qquad \begin{array}{r} 2 \\ +\, 3 \\ \hline 5 \end{array}$$

⌐ **sum** ⌐

Venn diagram

I like music. →   ← I like sports.

Ian   Marcy   Max
Jack   Nate
Sue   Sharon

I like music and sports.

yard (yd)
A baseball bat is about 1 **yard** long.